D1082862

The cult of the Virgin Mary is associated by most medievalists with the twelfth and succeeding centuries. This book, however, provides a wide-ranging exploration of the cult in England from *c.* 700 to the Conquest. Interest in and devotion to Mary flourished in the late seventh and eighth centuries and, especially, in the period of the Benedictine reform from the mid tenth century onwards. In this latter period Mary, as patron saint of almost all of the reformed houses, was the most important saint of the monastic movement.

Dr Clayton describes and illustrates the development of Marian devotion and doctrine from the early church to the Carolingians discussing Anglo-Saxon feasts of the Virgin, liturgical texts, prayers, monastic dedications, art and vernacular poetry and prose.

CAMBRIDGE STUDIES IN
ANGLO-SAXON ENGLAND

2

THE CULT OF THE VIRGIN MARY IN
ANGLO-SAXON ENGLAND

CAMBRIDGE STUDIES IN ANGLO-SAXON ENGLAND

EDITORS

SIMON KEYNES

MICHAEL LAPIDGE

Editors' preface

Cambridge Studies in Anglo-Saxon England is a series of scholarly texts and monographs intended to advance our knowledge of all aspects of the field of Anglo-Saxon studies. The scope of the series, like that of *Anglo-Saxon England*, its periodical counterpart, embraces original scholarship in various disciplines: literary, historical, archaeological, philological, art-historical, palaeographical, architectural, liturgical and numismatic. It is the intention of the editors to encourage the publication of original scholarship which advances our understanding of the field through interdisciplinary approaches.

Volumes published

THE CULT OF THE VIRGIN MARY IN ANGLO-SAXON ENGLAND

MARY CLAYTON

Lecturer in English Literature,
University College, Dublin

CAMBRIDGE
UNIVERSITY PRESS

Published by the Press Syndicate of the University of Cambridge
The Pitt Building, Trumpington Street, Cambridge CB2 1RP
40 West 20th Street, New York, NY 10011–4211, USA
10 Stamford Road, Oakleigh, Victoria 3166, Australia

First published 1990
Reprinted 1993

Printed in Great Britain at
Antony Rowe Ltd, Chippenham, Wiltshire

British Library cataloguing in publication data
Clayton, Mary
The cult of the Virgin Mary in Anglo-Saxon England.
1. England. Mary, Mother of Jesus Christ. Worship,
history
I. Title
232.91'0942

Library of Congress cataloguing in publication data
Clayton, Mary.
The cult of the Virgin Mary in Anglo-Saxon England / Mary Clayton.
p.   cm. – (Cambridge studies in Anglo-Saxon England)
Bibliography.
Includes index.
ISBN 0 521 34101 9
1. Mary, Blessed Virgin, Saint – Cult – England – History.
2. England – Church history – Anglo-Saxon period, 449–1066.
I. Title. II. Series.
B1652.E54C57 1990
232.91'0942'09021 – dc20   89-31508   CIP

ISBN 0 521 34101 9

CE

For my mother and father, Helen and Patrick Clayton

Contents

Plates

Acknowledgements

This book began as a doctoral thesis for Oxford University under the supervision of Malcolm Godden, who has always been most generous with his scholarship, encouragement and friendship; Michael Lapidge oversaw its metamorphosis from thesis to book with patience, meticulous learning and stimulating suggestions. I thank them both. My first debt, however, is to Éamonn Ó Carragáin, who introduced me to Old English and has fostered my love for it ever since. Celia Sisam and Jimmy Cross, my D.Phil. examiners, corrected many details and have given freely of their time and advice. Robert Deshman, Malcolm Parkes and Barbara Raw have generously discussed numerous points and Mary Brennan has patiently improved upon the Latin translations. I should also like to thank the following friends and scholars for their help and support: Valerie Allen, Terry Dolan, Alan Fletcher, Jan Gijsel, Helmut Gneuss, Joyce Hill, Doreen Innes, Marybeth Joyce, Peter Lucas, Niall MacMonagle, Maria Madigan, Jennifer Morrish, Jennifer O'Reilly, Peter Orton, Patti-Anne Palmer, Don Scragg, Patrick Sims-Williams, Eric Stanley and Janet Wilson.

St Hilda's College, Oxford, offered most congenial surroundings for work and the librarians of the Bodleian Library, the British Library and University College, Dublin have been extremely helpful.

Permission to reproduce photographs has been granted by the Ashmolean Museum, Oxford (pl. XV); the Bibliothèque municipale, Rouen (pls. VII and XI); the British Library, London (pls. IV, V, VI, VIII, IX and XIII); the Dean and Chapter of Durham Cathedral (pl. I); the Museum of Archaeology and Ethnology, Cambridge (pl. XVI); the National Monuments Record (pls. II and III); the Master and Fellows of Pembroke College, Cambridge (pl. XII); the Pierpont Morgan Library, New York (pls. X and XIV).

Acknowledgements

Work on my D.Phil. thesis was made possible by a Travelling Studentship from the National University of Ireland and the publication of this book has been aided by a grant from University College, Dublin. Cambridge University Press has kindly given permission to reprint chapter 2 in an altered form.

Abbreviations

AB	*Analecta Bollandiana*
ASE	*Anglo-Saxon England*
ASPR	The Anglo-Saxon Poetic Records, ed. Krapp and Dobbie
BCS	*Cartularium Saxonicum*, ed. Birch
BH	*The Blickling Homilies*, ed. Morris
BL	British Library
CCSL	Corpus Christianorum, Series Latina (Turnhout)
CH I	*The Homilies of the Anglo-Saxon Church* I, ed. Thorpe
CH II	*Ælfric's Catholic Homilies*, ed. Godden.
CSEL	Corpus Scriptorum Ecclesiasticorum Latinorum (Vienna)
EEMF	Early English Manuscripts in Facsimile (Copenhagen)
EETS	Early English Text Society
	os Original Series
	ss Supplementary Series
EL	*Ephemerides Liturgicae*
HBS	Henry Bradshaw Society
MÆ	*Medium Ævum*
MGH	*Monumenta Germaniae Historica*
MLN	*Modern Language Notes*
MLQ	*Modern Language Quarterly*
MS	Mediaeval Studies
N&Q	*Notes and Queries*
PBA	*Proceedings of the British Academy*
PL	*Patrologia Latina*
PO	*Patrologia Orientalis*
RB	*Revue Bénédictine*
RES	*Review of English Studies*
S	*Anglo-Saxon Charters*, ed. Sawyer

I

Introduction

It is widely recognized that there was an exceptionally developed cult of the Virgin Mary in pre-Conquest England. Edmund Bishop commented on the spread of devotion to Mary from the end of the tenth century to the Conquest,[1] while Rosemary Woolf went so far as to say that England 'had been one of the chief originators in western Europe' of many forms of Marian piety;[2] and Frank Barlow, too, remarked on the 'wave of devotion' to the Virgin in England in the tenth century.[3] There has, however, been no detailed examination of the cult and the present study is an attempt to fill this lacuna.

By the tenth century, Anglo-Saxon devotion to the Virgin had resulted in the dedication of large numbers of churches and monasteries to her, in the composition of private and of public liturgical prayers, in the celebration of the yearly round of Marian feasts, in the acquisition of relics of Mary and in the composition and dissemination of vernacular texts describing the life and death of the Virgin. Few of these practices were invented in England and the Anglo-Saxon cult of the Virgin cannot be understood without some knowledge of how devotion to Mary had developed throughout the church in the preceding centuries. In this introductory chapter, I should like to survey briefly the growth of Marian doctrines and legends, concentrating particularly on those aspects most relevant to an understanding of the English evidence.[4]

We know almost nothing about the historical mother of Christ. The

---

[1] 'On the Origin of the Prymer', in his *Liturgica Historica*, p. 227.
[2] *The English Religious Lyric in the Middle Ages* (Oxford, 1968), p. 114.
[3] *The English Church 1000–1066*, p. 18.
[4] General introductions to the cult of the Virgin can be found in Graef, *Mary*; du Manoir, ed., *Maria*; G. Söll, *Mariologie*.

earliest references to her are in the gospels, but here the Virgin's place is a comparatively minor one.[5] In Mark she is mentioned only twice: in Mark III. 31–5, in a context which appears to be derogatory, Jesus rejects his earthly mother and brothers in favour of those who do the will of God, and in Mark VI. 3 the Jews refuse to believe in Christ's divinity, asking 'Is this not the carpenter, the son of Mary and brother of James and Joses and Judas and Simon, and are not his sisters here with us?' Matthew begins his gospel with the genealogy of Joseph, not Mary, and continues with a description of the events surrounding Christ's birth. He affirms the conception through the Holy Ghost and the fulfilment of the prophecy in Isaiah VII. 14: 'Behold a virgin shall conceive and shall bring forth a son . . .' Matthew then relates the story of the Adoration of the Magi, the flight into Egypt and the eventual return to Nazareth, again in fulfilment of Old Testament prophecies. Christ's explicit presentation in Matthew as Emmanuel (in Hebrew 'God is with us'), from the moment of his birth, was of great importance for the beginnings of Marian doctrine, leading to an affirmation of Mary's divine maternity. Mary is not mentioned by name in the rest of Matthew, being introduced only in the repetition of the scene in Mark where Christ asks 'Who is my mother . . . ?' (Matt. XII. 46–50). Luke offers an even more extended infancy gospel, describing the Annunciation, the Presentation in the Temple after forty days and the losing of the twelve-year-old Jesus in Jerusalem. In his account of the public ministry, Luke, like Mark and Matthew, shows Christ's deliberate distancing from his mother (Luke VIII. 21 and XI. 28). He shares Matthew's affirmation of the conception by the Holy Ghost, and his infancy gospel is composed of a web of Old Testament quotations and reminiscences. Mary's behaviour at the Annunciation is schematically contrasted with that of Zachariah at the annunciation of the birth of John the Baptist and was, therefore, of importance in the later ethical portraits of the Virgin. The greetings of Gabriel and Elizabeth and Mary's hymn, the *Magnificat*, were also of primary importance in the development of devotion to the Virgin. In John, Mary is mentioned in only two scenes: the marriage at Cana, in which she asks her son to perform a miracle (John II. 1–11); and at the Passion, where Christ commends Mary and John to each other's care (XIX. 26–7). The last reference to Mary in the New Testament is in the Acts, where she prays with the apostles (I. 14), and her death is not mentioned.

[5] For Mary in the New Testament see A. Feuillet, 'La Vierge Marie dans le Nouveau Testament'.

From the whole of the New Testament, therefore, the early Christian community would have derived the impression of a betrothed virgin, who conceived through the Holy Ghost without loss of her virginity and was prominent in the story of her son's infancy, but who had little to do with his public ministry. The New Testament contains no explicit statement about Mary's virginity after the birth of Christ, but the natural inference from the reference to brothers and sisters is that she did not remain a virgin.

The bible tells us nothing about Mary's life before the Annunciation, but already by the second half of the second century there were attempts to fill in the missing background. A combination of natural curiosity about biblical characters and the necessity to counter anti-Christian calumnies lies behind the earliest Greek apocryphon describing the birth and conception of Mary. This narrative, the *Proteuangelium Iacobi*, was extremely influential in the West and gave rise, directly or indirectly, to all other legendary treatments of the topic.[6] It is named after its supposed author, James, the brother of Christ and first bishop of Jerusalem, but appears to have been written by a non-Jew, possibly in Egypt.[7] The oldest incontestable reference to the *Proteuangelium* is by Origen (*ob.c.* 253),[8] but the text may lie behind Clement of Alexandria's (*ob.* 215) allusion to the midwife who proclaimed Mary's virginity *post partum*.[9] The oldest manuscript dates from the fourth century.

The *Proteuangelium* deals with Mary's parents, Joachim and Anna, and their long period of childlessness, her miraculous conception and birth, her upbringing in the temple until the age of puberty, when she was committed into the care of Joseph, the Annunciation, the birth of Christ, the visit of the Magi and the Massacre of the Innocents. The need to combat Jewish and pagan charges naturally led the author to exalt Mary, and he followed biblical models for the story of her conception and birth: Anna and Samuel, Sarah and Isaac, Elizabeth and John the Baptist and Mary herself and Christ all influenced his portrayal of Anna and Mary. The whole apocryphal gospel has even been described as a midrashic exegesis of the

---

[6] *Evangelia Apocrypha*, ed. C. Tischendorf, pp. 1–48; *Le protévangile de Jacques*, ed. E. Amann, pp. 178–281.

[7] For the view that the author was an Egyptian, see E. de Strycker, *La forme la plus ancienne*, pp. 419–23; H. R. Smid, *Proteuangelium Iacobi*, pp. 20–4, presents a cautious argument for a Syrian provenance.

[8] See Amann, *Le protévangile de Jacques*, p. 82.   [9] *Ibid.*, p. 81.

3

first two chapters of Matthew and Luke.[10] The *Proteuangelium*'s interest does not lie only in its narrative: it also testifies to the development of nonbiblical Marian beliefs even at this early date. In some early manuscripts it has a reading which implies that Mary was conceived without sexual intercourse: the angel announces to Joachim (who, ashamed of his barrenness, has fled to the desert) that his wife has already conceived and the time-scale of the work suggests that the conception took place while Joachim was in the desert.[11] Other manuscripts have a future tense here instead, reflecting a widespread unease at the implications of the past. Mary's virginity *post partum* is explicitly affirmed in an episode obviously modelled on the disbelieving Thomas and Christ's wounds: the disbelieving midwife, Salome, tests Mary's virginity after the birth and is punished for her lack of faith. The brothers of the Lord, including the eponymous James, are presented here as children of Joseph by a former marriage, an explanation which continued to find favour in the East. In this and other early apocrypha (the *Ascension of Isaiah*[12] and the *Odes of Solomon*,[13] for example), Mary gives birth without pain and, although it is nowhere asserted that the act of childbirth took place without violation of her virginity, this lack of pain, coupled with the insistence on her virginity *post partum*, opened the way for a belief in her virginity *in partu*. There is no complete surviving text of the Latin translation of the *Proteuangelium*, but different fragments have been transmitted in various ways.[14]

References to the Virgin in the works of the Christian Fathers also begin

[10] Smid, *Proteuangelium Iacobi*, p. 8

[11] See the discussion by Amann, *Le protévangile de Jacques*, pp. 17–21; J. Galot, 'L'Immaculée Conception', in *Maria*, ed. du Manoir (1964) VII, 9–116; J. Gijsel, 'Zu welcher Textfamilie des Pseudo-Matthäus gehört die Quelle von Hrotsvits Maria?', p. 286.

[12] This text dates from the second century. It is translated and discussed in *Neutestamentliche Apokryphen*, ed. Hennecke and Schneemelcher, II, 454–68. See also E. Cothenet, 'Marie dans les apocryphes', p. 78, who interprets the text as a witness to Mary's virginity *in partu*.

[13] W. Bauer, 'Die Oden Salomos', *Neutestamentliche Apokryphen*, ed. Hennecke and Schneemelcher, II, 576–625. The text dates from the second century.

[14] In, for example, *Latin Infancy Gospels: A New Text with a Parallel Version from Irish*, ed. M. R. James (Cambridge, 1927); in a version ed. F. Vattioni, 'Frammento latino del Vangelo di Giacomo', *Augustinianum* 17 (1977), 505–9, from Vatican City, Reg. lat. 537, but also found in the English manuscripts Cambridge, Pembroke College 25 (s. xi) and Cambridge, St John's College B. 20 (s. xiii); and in many fragments, on which see E. de Strycker, 'Une ancienne version latine du protévangile de Jacques avec les extraits de la Vulgate de Matthieu 1–2 et Luc 1–2', *AB* 83 (1965), 365–90.

in the second century. The first to mention Mary is Ignatius of Antioch (*ob. c.* 110).[15] For him and for the other Fathers of the second and third centuries Mary is of importance chiefly for what the manner of her childbirth revealed about the nature of Christ. Defence of Christ's full humanity, on the one hand, and his divinity, on the other, in opposition to both Gnosticism and Judaism, led to a stress on the reality of his birth from Mary and on her virginity *ante partum*. Justin the Martyr (*ob. c.* 165) was the first to discern a parallel between Mary and Eve, suggested probably by Paul's parallel between Christ and Adam.[16] This underlined Mary's importance in the plan of redemption and was to be much developed by later writers. The idea of Mary's powers of intercession was introduced by Irenaus of Lyons (*ob.* 202), who emphasized her active participation in the redemption of mankind, and he also seems to have been the first to propose Mary's purification by the Holy Ghost at the Incarnation.[17] There was, however, some controversy over Mary's virginity *in partu* and *post partum*. Tertullian (*ob. c.* 220) denied Mary's virginity both in and after the birth and also asserted, on the evidence of the gospels, that Mary had refused to believe in Christ.[18] It seems probable that his pupil Origen (*ob.* 253), too, denied the virginity *in partu*.[19] Origen also believed, as did Irenaus, that Mary had faults, but despite this he regarded her as a model worthy of imitation. Growing devotion to Mary is attested by the title *Theotokos*, which came into use about this time (the earliest incontestable reference is in the works of Alexander of Alexandria, who died in 382, but it may have been already used by Origen)[20] and by the beginnings of prayer to the Virgin. A fourth-century fragment of the prayer *Sub tuum praesidium* is extant.[21]

The following period saw a gradual change in the comparative freedom of views evinced by the early Fathers in Mariological questions, especially

---

[15] Söll, *Mariologie*, pp. 31–3.

[16] *Ibid.*, pp. 33–4; but see also G. Joussard, 'La nouvelle Eve', pp. 35–6.

[17] See J. Garcon, *La Mariologie de S. Irenée* (Lyons, 1932); G. Joussard, 'Marie à travers la patristique', pp. 73–5.

[18] *Ibid.*, pp. 77–80.

[19] Origen seems to have held that Mary's womb was opened in childbirth and closed immediately afterwards, but his writings are unclear and contradictory on this point. See Söll, *Mariologie*, p. 46 and Graef, *Mary*, I, 44.

[20] Söll, *Mariologie*, p. 48.

[21] O. Stegmüller, 'Sub tuum praesidium: Bemerkungen zur ältesten Uberlieferung', *Zeitschrift für katholische Theologie* 74 (1952), 76–82.

in the West. Affirmations of Mary's virginity *in partu* and *post partum* became more frequent, and the title ever-virgin came into use (for the first time in Peter of Alexandria (*ob.* 311)).[22] The flourishing of asceticism contributed to the growth of a depiction of Mary as the ideal virgin, for example, in Athanasius (*ob.* 373), and the idea that Mary herself had voluntarily taken a vow of virginity, soon to be brought into prominence by Augustine, was broached by Gregory of Nyssa. The concept of what was considered fitting for the mother of God, of what seemed appropriate to the *sensus fidelium*, also became evident, as in its use by Basil of Caesarea (*ob.* 379) as a proof of Mary's virginity *post partum*, and this was to be of great importance in the working out of Mariological doctrine. Ephraem (*ob.* 373) was the first in the East to suggest that Mary had conceived through the ear (an image of the faith she manifested at the Annunciation), an idea taken up by Zeno of Verona in the West (*ob.* 372).

The subject of Mary's death was first discussed at length by Epiphanius (*ob.* 403). The only New Testament reference to Mary after Christ's death is in the Acts of the Apostles 1. 14, in which it is reported that the apostles 'with one accord devoted themselves to prayer, together with the women and Mary the mother of Jesus, and with his brethren'. Epiphanius raised the question of Mary's end in the course of combating opponents of her perpetual virginity:

let them search the traces of Mary in the scriptures, and they will find there no mention of her death, neither whether she died or did not die, nor whether she was buried or was not buried . . . Still, though we are unable to certify her death, we may perchance find some traces of that holy and blessed one that bear upon it. For there is, on the one hand, what Simeon says to her: 'Thine own soul also shall a sword pierce, that the thoughts of many hearts may be revealed' and, on the other hand, St John tells us in the Apocalypse that the dragon hastened against the woman, who had brought forth the man-child, and there were given to her the wings of an eagle, and she was taken into the desert that the dragon might not seize her. This then may have been fulfilled in Mary. However, I do not decide, nor say that she remained immortal; nor either will I vouch that she died.[23]

This passage is generally regarded as crucial evidence on whether or not there was an early Christian tradition concerning Mary's death. It is usually interpreted negatively, although the theory has been propounded that Epiphanius was deliberately ignoring anterior traditions and restricting

---

[22] Graef, *Mary*, I, 46.

[23] Translated in T. Livius, *The Blessed Virgin in the Fathers*, p. 343.

himself to the bible.[24] Whether or not such traditions existed before him, Epiphanius's formulation of the question was of paramount importance to later writers. In particular, his attitude to the subject – a confession of ignorance and an unwillingness to state categorically his own views on the matter – was imitated by many.

Epiphanius, then, may or may not have known about the apocryphal assumption narratives, but there is no doubt about his knowledge of the *Proteuangelium*. In the course of a condemnation of a Marian sect called the Collyridians, Epiphanius contended that the past tense in the angel's speech to Joachim, which seemed to imply Mary's conception in the absence of her father, referred only to God's foreknowledge of the event, and he insisted that Mary was born of Joachim and Anna, in accordance with the normal laws of nature.[25]

Despite his reservations about Mary's birth and death, however, Epiphanius also declared that he was willing to ascribe to Mary whatever was most excellent in any other saint. This sentiment was a leading one in the development of Mariology and had important repercussions for the development of the belief that the assumption of the Virgin occurred in the same fashion as that described in the apocryphal *Acta Ioannis* concerning John the Evangelist, who had been assumed into heaven, body and soul. Those saints whose resurrection at Christ's Passion is described in Matthew XXVII.52 were also commonly judged to have been assumed into heaven with him – a view held, for example, by Ambrose and Augustine.[26]

One long-lasting result of the Eastern theological crisis of 429–31, which culminated in the Council of Ephesus, was a major advance in Marian devotion. The controversy was in essence Christological, with Nestorius claiming that there were two separate persons in Christ, human and divine, but it had been sparked off by his objections to the use of the term *Theotokos*, 'God-bearer', to describe Mary. At the height of the Council in 431, a torch-lit procession progressed through the streets of Ephesus chanting *Theotokos*, and a side-effect of the dispute was a greater emphasis on the importance of the Virgin.

---

[24] See Cothenet, 'Marie dans les apocryphes', p. 144; J. Galot, 'Le mystère de l'assomption', in *Maria*, ed. du Manoir VII, 153–237, at 166.

[25] Amann, *Le protévangile de Jacques*, p. 20.

[26] See PL 33, 712 for Augustine's views and M. Jugie, *Le mort et l'assomption de la Sainte Vierge*, p. 69, for a discussion of Ambrose's rather contradictory statements on this question.

Just as the *Proteuangelium* emanated from a desire amongst the faithful for information about Mary's life before the Annunciation, so, too, there was a desire to be informed about her life after Christ's ascension and about her final fate. By the fifth century, at the latest, apocryphal accounts of Mary's death and assumption were circulating.[27] These numerous accounts existed in many different languages and offered widely differing descriptions of the circumstances surrounding Mary's departure from the world. The earliest apocryphal narratives probably took the mention of Mary in the Acts of the Apostles as their starting-point and they seem to have been modelled to some extent on the apocryphal *Acta* of the saints.[28] The apostles probably featured even more prominently in the first accounts than they do in the surviving ones. Evidence of this can be seen, for example, in the discussion between John and Peter on who is to precede the coffin bearing the palm-branch given to Mary by the angel and, in particular, in the final part of *Transitus* B, where the apostles are asked by Christ to decide on the fate of Mary's body.[29] The main theological reason offered by the apocrypha for Mary's corporal assumption is her virginal maternity: that the body which had given birth without corruption should not suffer corruption in death is the reasoning behind the scene in which Christ and the apostles decide the fate of Mary in *Transitus* B2, for example.

In order to be able to classify the Anglo-Saxon texts dependent on the apocrypha, it is necessary to describe the Western branches of this tradition in some detail. There are two main textual families. The first family, which is represented in Syriac and Coptic, in a Greek text which is ascribed to John the Evangelist and in a Latin version known as *Transitus* D, recounts how the Virgin's incorruptible body was brought to paradise, where, surrounded by light and fragrantly scented, it was worshipped by the

---

[27] Some critics, e.g. Cothenet, 'Marie dans les apocryphes', p. 145 and O. Faller, *De priorum saeculorum silentio circa assumptionem B. Mariae Virginis*, Analecta Gregoriana 36 (1946), place these apocrypha much earlier, as far back as the beginning of the third century. In view of the already very widespread diffusion by the end of the fifth century, an early dating does not seem unlikely.

[28] See B. Capelle, 'La tradition orientale de l'assomption d'après un ouvrage récent', *RB* 40 (1958), 173–86, reprinted in his *Travaux liturgiques*, III, 376.

[29] There are two versions of this text: *Transitus* B1 is ed. C. Tischendorf, *Evangelia Apocrypha*, pp. 124–36; *Transitus* B2 is ed. M. Haibach-Reinisch, *Ein neuer 'Transitus Mariae'*.

saints, while her soul was assumed into heaven.[30] The second family, the R-texts, originally described the corporal assumption of Mary and the reuniting of her body and soul, although some of the surviving versions have an altered ending which does not have this reunification.[31] The texts which survive from Anglo-Saxon England all belong to the R-family.

In the R-texts Mary dies and her soul is taken to heaven immediately, while her body is laid in the sepulchre for three days. Christ then comes and either takes the body with him to paradise, where it is reunited with the soul, or, bearing with him Mary's soul, he joins it with the body at the tomb, before bringing Mary back with him to paradise. A lost fifth-century Greek text appears to be the source of most of this group of texts and it must have been very similar to the Syriac fragments in manuscripts of the fifth century which were published by Wright.[32] This Greek text was the direct source of another Greek version R,[33] shortened for liturgical use, and of the two accounts of John of Thessalonica (610–49), T and TI.[34] It was also the direct source of a lost Latin translation which can be partly reconstructed from the variants entered in the M manuscript of *Transitus* C.[35] In turn this Latin text was the source of a shortened version A, written some time between the seventh and ninth centuries.[36] Its awkward Latin shows that is is still very close to the original Greek source. The same lost translation was the source of the account which Gregory of Tours (*c.* 540–94) summarizes in his *Miraculorum libri*[37] and of another lost rendering. This lost text in turn gave rise to *Transitus* C, the Colbert narrative[38] and the two versions of the *Gospel of Pseudo-Melito*, *Transitus* B1 and *Transitus* B2. *Transitus* B2, the older, probably dates from the fifth century and shows how quickly the apocryphal texts were disseminated and revised. The only other well-known apocryphon, *Transitus* A (not to be confused with the A of the diagram),

---

[30] For a translation of the Greek text, see *The Apocryphal New Testament*, ed. James, pp. 201–9. The Latin *Transitus* D is ed. A. Wilmart, *Analecta Reginensia*, pp. 357–62.

[31] For this textual family, see especially A. Wenger, *L'assomption de la très Sainte Vierge*.

[32] *Contributions to the Apocryphal Literature of the New Testament*, ed. W. Wright (London, 1865).

[33] Summarized by Wenger, *L'assomption de la très Sainte Vierge*, pp. 31–58.

[34] *Iohannis Archiepiscopus Thessalonicensis sermo de dormitione B. Mariae Virginis*, ed. M. Jugie, PO 19 (1926), 375–431.

[35] Collated by Wilmart in his edition of *Transitus* C, *Analecta Reginensia*, pp. 323–57.

[36] Ed. Wenger, *L'assomption de la très Sainte Vierge*, pp. 245–56.   [37] PL 71, 708.

[38] See Capelle, 'Vestiges grecs et latins'.

was thought by Tischendorf to be the oldest text but it is now recognized as a late composite account.[39]

In unravelling the complexities of this textual family, Wenger's diagram is helpful:[40]

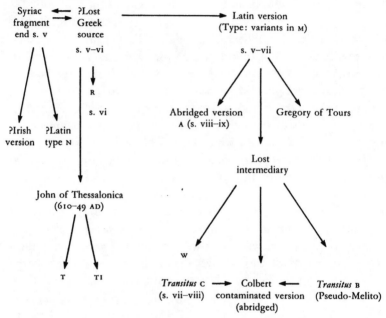

FIG. I The relationship of apocryphal accounts of Mary's death and assumption in the R-family of texts

Wenger has shown that the ultimate source of the R-family undoubtedly asserted the Virgin's corporal assumption.[41] But the many objections voiced by the Fathers of the church were not without effect and in the extant texts there is a wide variety of endings. Some preserve the full corporal assumption, others prevaricate and avoid an explicit statement on the issue: John of Thessalonica, for example, omitted the resurrection of Mary's body. Similarly, the manuscripts of *Transitus* C differ widely in their conclusions: the version in Cambridge, Pembroke College 25 (a late eleventh-century English manuscript not collated by Wilmart), for example, ends:

[39] *Evangelia Apocrypha*, ed. Tischendorf, pp. 113–23.
[40] *L'assomption de la très Sainte Vierge*, p. 66
[41] *Ibid.*, pp. 62–6.

Verumptamen apostoli, portantes corpus Mariae, peruenerunt ad monumentum ubi praedixerat eis Iesus, et sepelierunt eam in ualle Iosaphat, et sedentibus iuxta monumentum, subito aduenit Iesus cum multitudine angelorum, et ait eis: Pax uobis, fratres, et sic iussit angelis tolli corpus Mariae, nescientibus apostolis ubi transtulerunt illud. Ipsi autem in nubibus translati sunt per aera ad loca unde uenerant, praedicantes uerbum Dei. Hodie quidem exaltata est sancta Maria Dei genitrix super choros angelorum ad caelestia regna. Hodie uirgo uirginum caelos ascendit, quae regem gloriae in aluo gestare meruit. Gaudete, quia cum Christo regnat in aeternum. Et ipsa intercedat pro nobis ad Dominum Iesum Christum, ut mereamur uitam possidere aeternam per omnia saecula saeculorum.[42]

This redactor, then, was unwilling to commit himself on Mary's corporal assumption and has instead taken refuge in liturgical quotations. Such liberties were common among scribes copying the apocrypha, who expanded, shortened and combined at will. Different versions could also be combined: the Colbert manuscript, for example, combines its text (an abbreviated version of the source it has in common with *Transitus* B and *Transitus* C) with the beginning and end of *Transitus* B.

While these apocryphal texts were proliferating, more orthodox works dealing with Mary were also multiplying. Ambrose, Jerome and Augustine determined the course of western Mariology for centuries.[43] All three saw Mary as having been free of all taint of actual sin and encouraged

---

[42] Quoted by H. Barré, *Les homéliaires carolingiens*, p. 22: 'But the apostles, carrying the body of Mary, arrived at the sepulchre, at the place Jesus had determined beforehand, and they buried her in the valley of Josaphat, and, as they were sitting next to the sepulchre, suddenly Jesus came with a multitude of angels and said to them: "Peace be with you, brothers", and so he ordered the angels that the body of Mary be raised up, without the apostles knowing where they conveyed it. But they were conveyed on clouds through the air to the place whence they had come preaching the word of God. Today in truth holy Mary the mother of God is raised up above the choirs of angels into the kingdom of heaven. Today the virgin of virgins, who deserved to bear in her womb the king of glory, ascended into heaven. Rejoice, for she reigns with Christ for ever. And let her intercede for us to the Lord Jesus Christ, so that we may deserve to possess eternal life forever and ever.'

[43] See J. Niessen, *Die Mariologie des heiligen Hieronymus* (Münster in Westfalen, 1913); J. Huhn, *Das Geheimnis der Jungfrau-Mutter nach dem Kirchenvater Ambrosius* (Würzburg, 1954); C. W. Neumann, *The Virgin Mary in the Works of St Ambrose*, Paradosis 17 (Fribourg, 1962); P. Friedrich, *Die Mariologie des heiligen Augustinus* (Cologne, 1907); H. Coathelm, *Le parallélisme entre la Sainte Vierge et l'eglise dans la tradition latine jusqu'à la fin du xiie siècle*, Analecta Gregoriana, 74 (1954); A. Müller, *Ecclesia-Maria: Die Einheit Marias und der Kirche*, 2nd ed., Paradosis 5 (Fribourg, 1955); and H. Barré, 'L'apport Marial'.

imitation of her, particularly by those vowed to virginity. Mary's virginity *ante, in* and *post partum* (although Jerome avoids the question of the virginity *in partu*) is affirmed strongly, with arguments drawn chiefly from Old Testament prophecies. Ambrose and Augustine develop the Eve–Mary parallel and the Mary–church parallel, and Ambrose first applied verses from the Song of Songs, hitherto applied only to the church, to Mary. The earliest use of the title *Sancta Maria* was by Ambrose.[44] Augustine was the first in the West to deduce from Mary's answer to Gabriel at the Annunciation that she had already taken a vow of virginity, and he explained her marriage to Joseph as being a means of affording her protection and of providing a witness to her continued virginity. The famous passage in which Augustine introduced the picture of Mary suckling her child was enormously influential: 'Lacta, mater, cibum nostrum; lacta panem de coelo uenientem et in praesepi positum uelut piorum cibaria iumentorum . . .'[45] Both Ambrose and Augustine discuss Mary's death in connection with Simeon's prophecy that a sword should pierce her heart. Both reject the possibility of a bodily martyrdom which had been implicit in Epiphanius's discussion of the subject and interpret the words as a prophecy of Mary's grief under the cross; Ambrose, for example, says:

Nec littera, nec historia docet ex hac uita Mariam corporalis necis passione migrasse; non enim anima, sed corpus materiali gladio transuerberatur. Et ideo prudentiam Mariae haud ignarem mysterii coelestis ostendit. 'Viuum' enim 'uerbum Dei et ualidum et acutum omni gladio acutissimo . . .'[46]

Nothing essentially new was added to Mariological doctrine for several centuries after this, although a certain change in sentiment and mood is apparent in the works of Venantius Fortunatus (*ob. c.* 610) and, especially, in Ildefonsus of Toledo (*ob.* 667) – a mood of enthusiasm and fervour, with

---

[44] H. Barré, *Prières anciennes*, p. 30.

[45] PL 39, 1655: 'Suckle, mother, our food; suckle the bread coming from heaven and placed in a manger as the provisions of devout beasts of burden.' On the attribution of this sermon to Augustine, see C. Lambot, 'L'authenticité du sermon 369 de S. Augustin pour la fête de Noël', *Colligere fragmenta: Festschrift Alban Dold zum 70. Geburtstag am 7. 7. 1952*, ed. B. Fischer and V. Fiala (Beuron, 1952), pp. 103–112.

[46] PL 15, 1574: 'Neither writing nor history teaches us that Mary passed away from this life with the suffering of a bodily death; for not the soul but the body is pierced by a material sword. And it therefore shows the wisdom of Mary who was not at all ignorant of the heavenly mystery. Truly, the word of God is living and powerful and sharp, the sharpest of all swords . . .'

much emphasis on Mary's powers of intercession. The Pseudo-Augustinian African homilies also are notable for the ardour of their direct addresses to Mary. On the subject of the death of Mary, Isidore of Seville (*ob.* 636) combined the sentiments of Epiphanius and Ambrose:

Hanc quidam crudeli necis passione asserunt ab hac uita migrasse, pro eo quod iustus Simeon, complectens brachiis suis Christum, prophetauerit, matri dicens: Et tuam ipsius animam pertransibit gladius. Quod quidem incertum est, utrum pro materiali gladio dixerit an pro uerbo Dei ualido et acutiori omni gladio ancipiti. Specialiter tamen nulla docet historia, Mariam gladii animaduersione peremptam, quia nec obitus eius uspiam legitur, dum tamen reperiatur eius sepulcrum, ut aliqui dicunt, in ualle Iosaphat.[47]

However, the last words of this quotation show a new development in the centuries between Ambrose and Isidore – the legend of Mary's tomb in the valley of Josaphat, to which Isidore cautiously bears witness. This seems to have arisen in the mid-fifth century and was the result of locating in this valley the house in which Mary was said to have lived with Joseph. The house was gradually transformed into her sepulchre, or the two were regarded as being in close proximity to each other.

Between 550 and 700 the *Gospel of Pseudo-Matthew*, or the *Liber de ortu beatae Mariae*, was composed in Latin.[48] This is in origin a free rehandling of the *Proteuangelium*, which was later combined with stories of the flight into Egypt and the *Infancy Gospel of Thomas*. There are at present approximately 130 known manuscripts of this text, the earliest of which was written before 825, and the gospel seems to have achieved an immediate, though contested, popularity.[49] Although it met with opposition, it appears to have even been used for reading in church at an early date. Between 845 and 849, for example, Hincmar of Reims had a copy of a *Libellus de ortu sanctae Mariae* transcribed in a *de luxe* manuscript to be read

[47] PL 83, 148–9: 'Some say that she passed away from this life by the cruel suffering of death because the pious Simeon, holding Christ in his arms, prophesied, saying to the mother: "And a sword shall pierce your own soul." For it is uncertain whether he spoke of a material sword or of the word of God, powerful and sharper than any two-edged sword. In particular, however, no text teaches that Mary was killed by the punishment of the sword, because her death is not read of anywhere; while, as some say, her sepulchre may be found, however, in the valley of Josaphat.'

[48] *Evangelia Apocrypha*, ed. Tischendorf, pp. 49–112; *Le protévangile de Jacques*, ed. Amann, pp. 272–339. The date is Amann's, now confirmed by J. Gijsel, *Die unmittelbare Textüberlieferung*, pp. 12–3. A new edition by Gijsel is forthcoming.

[49] See Gijsel, *Die unmittelbare Textüberlieferung*, on the manuscripts.

in church.[50] A more orthodox revision of *Pseudo-Matthew* was made in the Carolingian period or, more probably, later, entitled *De natiuitate Mariae*.[51] Until the recent new edition of the text it was normally ascribed to Paschasius Radbertus, but Rita Beyers has now shown that this attribution is improbable. The first proof of its existence is in a sermon for the Nativity of Mary by Fulbert of Chartres (952–1028).

Insular writers of the late seventh and early eighth centuries made the next significant contribution to western Mariology. The earliest such discussion of Mary's fate after death is in Adamnan's (*ob.* 704) *De locis sanctis*. In recounting Arculf's visit to Josaphat he describes the church dedicated to Mary there:

in cuius orientali parte altarium habetur, ad dexteram uero eius partem Mariae saxeum inest uacuum sepulchrum, in quo aliquando sepulta pausauit. Sed de eodem sepulchro quo modo uel quo tempore aut a quibus personis sanctum corpusculum eius sit sublatum uel in quo loco resurrectionem exspectat nullus, ut refert, pro certo scire potest.[52]

In this passage Adamnan implies that Mary had died and had been buried in Josaphat, but he excludes the resurrection of her body. That he alludes to the fate of Mary's body as an open question intimates that he knew of discussion on the topic, presumably from apocryphal sources. Otherwise his attitude, one of discreet agnosticism, is typical of the orthodox position, although the implied certainty that Mary's body had not already been resurrected goes further than most statements on the topic.

Aldhelm (*ob.* 709) treats of Mary in his *De uirginitate*, describing her as a worthy mother of Christ because of her virginal purity. A dizzy accumulation of epithets, drawing on Isaiah, the Song of Songs, the liturgy and perhaps Isidore of Seville, is used to depict her:

beata Maria, uirgo perpetua, *hortus conclusus, fons signatus, uirgula radicis, gerula floris*, aurora solis, nurus patris, genetrix et germana filii simulque sponsa ac felix bernacula, sanctarum socrus animarum, supernorum regina ciuium, *columba inter .LX. reginas et bis quadragenas pelices*, propter perenne puritatis priuilegium

[50] See C. Lambot, 'L'homélie du Pseudo-Jérôme sur l'assomption'.

[51] See *De natiuitate Mariae*, ed. R. Beyers.

[52] *Adamnan's de locis sanctis*, ed. D Meehan, Scriptores Latini Hiberniae 3 (Dublin, 1958), 58: 'In the eastern portion of it is an altar, and at the right-hand side of the altar is the empty stone sepulchre of the holy Mary, where she was once laid to rest. But how, or when, or by what persons her holy remains were removed from this sepulchre, no one, it is said, can know for certain' (trans. Meehan, p. 59).

obsidem saeculi, monarchum mundi, rectorem poli, redemptorem soli archangelo pronuntiante, paracleto obumbrante praecordiis trepudiantibus feliciter suscipere meruit.[53]

Aldhelm's Mariological views are firmly orthodox and traditional: Mary is always seen in her role of *Dei genitrix* and as the fulfilment of Old Testament prophecies. He also subscribed to the view that Mary received even greater grace at the Annunciation.

Bede dealt extensively with the Virgin in his biblical commentaries and in his homilies, which include the first homily specifically composed for the feast of the Purification. His views on Mary are mainly derived from Ambrose, Jerome and Augustine and are firmly grounded in an orthodox Christology, with Mary's divine maternity being used as a touchstone to refute the heresies of both Nestorius and Eutyches.[54] Bede affirms Mary's descent from the royal line of David, sees in her the fulfilment of many Old Testament prophecies, develops the parallel between Mary and Eve and Mary and the church and regards her as a model for virgins, especially in the humility she manifested at the Annunciation. He also reproduces Augustine's view that Mary had taken a vow of virginity and he believed that she had been purified from sin by the Holy Ghost at the Incarnation.

The view that the Virgin had been purified at the Incarnation necessarily entails the belief that she had, until then, been subject to sin. As her perfection and freedom from actual sin were generally accepted from about the fourth century onwards, her purification at the Incarnation could only be from original sin. The question of Mary's subjection to original sin had been explicitly raised by Augustine in the Pelagian controversy. For Augustine, original sin was indissolubly bound up with the *concupiscentia carnalis* accompanying all human generation and it is clear that he believed Mary to have been born in it, although protected by grace against its

---

[53] *Aldhelmi opera*, ed. R. Ehwald, p. 292: 'the blessed Mary, the perpetual virgin, "a garden enclosed, a fountain sealed up", "the rod out of the root of Jesse bearing a flower", the dawn of the sun, the daughter-in-law of her father, the mother and sister of the Son and at the same time his bride and blessed handmaid, the mother-in-law of holy souls, the queen of heavenly citizens, "a dove among threescore queens and fourscore concubines": because of the privilege of her perpetual purity, was blessedly found worthy to beget, with joyful heart, the ransom of the world, the monarch of the earth, with the archangel announcing [this to her] and the Holy Ghost enveloping [her]' (*Aldhelm: The Prose Works*, trans. M. Lapidge and M. Herren (Cambridge, 1979), pp. 106–7).

[54] See, for example, Bede's *In Lucae Euangelium expositio*, ed. D. Hurst, p. 34 and pp. 236–7. See also M. T. A. Carroll, *The Venerable Bede*.

consequences.[55] Augustine's doctrine of original sin is linked with his belief in Traducianism, which he held to involve the spiritual generation of the human soul by its parents. He was, however, one of the last orthodox theologians to adhere to this doctrine, condemned by Pope Anastasius in 498. Most medieval theologians subscribed to a Creationist doctrine, holding that God creates a soul for each individual, a teaching which facilitated the adoption of the view that God could intervene especially in the creation of an individual soul. Although Bede clearly believed that Mary had been born in original sin, he made a significant advance towards the view that she could have been preserved from it in his teaching on John the Baptist.[56] Augustine had taught that John's sanctification in the womb was 'a simple, transitory communication of the spirit of God, designed to enable the Precursor to recognize from then on the Messiah whom he was later to announce'.[57] Bede, however, regarded this sanctification as a purification from sin before birth, arguing: 'Neque enim dubitandum est quod spiritus sanctus qui eum repleuit etiam a peccatis omnibus absoluit. Constat quippe ueredica patrum sententia quia lege non stringitur sancti spiritus donum.'[58] This break with the Augustinian conviction of the generic necessity of birth in sin was of great importance in later treatments of Mary's birth, as it was argued that whatever pertained to John the Baptist must apply to her to an even greater degree.

Bede's views on Mary's death were also of considerable importance, influencing the Carolingians in particular. In his *Liber de locis sanctis*, he abridged Adamnan's account of the empty tomb: 'ad eius dexteram monumentum uacuum, in quo sancta Maria aliquando pausasse dicitur, sed a quo uel quando sit ablata, nescitur'.[59] Bede omits Adamnan's implied denial that the resurrection of Mary could already have taken place and

---

[55] See, for example, Augustine's *Opus imperfectum aduersus Iulianum*, PL 45, 1418: 'Non transcribimus diabolo Mariam conditione nascendi; sed ideo, quia ipsa conditio soluitur gratia renascendi.'

[56] See G. Joussard, 'The Fathers of the Church', p. 78   [57] *Ibid.*, p. 78

[58] 'In uigilia natiuitatis S. Iohannis Baptistae', *Bedae Venerabilis opera homiletica*, ed. D. Hurst, p. 325: 'Truly there is no doubt that the Holy Spirit which filled him also absolved him of all sins. Certainly the true judgement of the fathers, that the gift of the Holy Spirit is is not bound by law, is well known.'

[59] *Bedae liber de locis sanctis, Itinera Hierosolymitana saeculi iiii-viii*, ed. P. Geyer, CSEL 39 (Vienna, 1898), 301–24, at 309: 'at its right an empty sepulchre in which the holy Mary was once said to have rested but it is not known by whom or when it was taken'.

follows his declaration of nescience in all other respects. Adamnan probably knew of apocryphal stories on the death of Mary; Bede certainly did and this renders his terse 'nescitur' all the more interesting. In his second commentary on the Acts of the Apostles, Bede, to whom chronology was the foundation of all orthodoxy, joins issue with Pseudo-Melito on the question of Mary's death.[60] The passages on which he is commenting come at the beginning of ch. VIII: 'And on that day a great persecution arose against the church in Jerusalem; and they were all scattered throughout the region of Judea and Samaria, except the apostles', and ch. XIII: 'the Holy Spirit said "Set apart for me Barnabas and Saul for the work to which I have called them."' Bede points to the discrepancy between Pseudo-Melito, which places the death of Mary in the second year after the Ascension, and the Acts, and he argues:

Si dispersa ecclesia apostoli *remanserunt in Hierusalem*, ut Lucas ait, constat quia mendacium scripsit ille qui ex persona Militonis episcopi Asiae, librum exponens de obitu beatae genetricis dei, dicit quod secundo post ascensionem domini anno apostoli fuerint omnes toto orbe ad praedicandum in suam quisque prouinciam diuisi. Qui uniuersi adpropinquante obitu sanctae Mariae *de locis in quibus praedicabant uerbum dei eleuati in nubibus rapti sunt Hierusolymam ac depositi ante ostium domus eius*, inter quos etiam Paulus nuper ex persecutore ad fidem Christi conuersus, qui adsumptus fuerat cum Barnaba in ministerium gentium. Quae scriptura etiam specialiter de Iohanne apostolo refert quod eo tempore Ephesi praedicauerit. Quae cuncta uerbis beati Lucae aperte contradicunt, quibus narrat apostolos ceteris fidelibus ab Hierosolyma propulsis remanisse ibidem et praedicasse per omnia, donec ecclesia per totam Iudaeam et Galilaeam et Samariam pacem haberet, quod in uno anno perfici non potuisse nulli dubium est; qui etiam manifeste insinuat Paulum non secundo post ascensionem domini anno, sed longo post tempore in ministerium gentium cum Barnaba ordinatum. Absit autem ut credamus beatum Iohannem apostolum, cui dominus in cruce matrem suam uirginem uirgini commendauit, post unum annum recessisse et eam reliquisse solam ac tanto tempore deiectam, ut etiam corpus suum defunctae timeret ab hostibus esse comburendum eumque, postquam raptus in nubibus ad se redisset, uelut oblìtum siue incuriosum sui sollicita precaretur, dicens: *Rogo te, fili Iohannes, ut memor sis uerbi magistri tui, domini mei, Iesu Christi, qui me commendauit tibi. Ecce enim uocata ingrediar uiam uniuersae terrae. Audiui autem consilia Iudaeorum dicentium, expectemus diem quando moriatur quae portauit Iesum Nazarenum et corpus eius igne comburamus. Nunc ergo curam habeto obsequiarum mearum.* Haec ideo commemorare

---

[60] See Haibach-Reinisch, *Ein neuer 'Transitus Mariae'*, p. 177.

curaui quia noui nonnullos praefato uolumini contra auctoritatem beati Lucae
incauta temeritate adsensum praebere.[61]

Bede's second comment makes the same point and ends with a stern
warning: 'ac per hoc praefatum de obitu beatae Mariae libellum, cum
manifeste erret in tempore, in ceteris quoque suspectae fidei esse comper-
it'.[62] I have quoted Bede's comments at length as they demonstrate his
extensive knowledge of this suspect text, from which he quotes verbatim.
These citations are so literal that the recension of Pseudo-Melito used by
Bede can be determined: B2, the version which later seems to have been the
one most widely known in England. Given that Bede is commenting on

---

[61] *Retractatio in Actus Apostolorum*, ed. Laistner, pp. 134–5: 'If, when the church was
scattered, the apostles remained in Jerusalem, as Luke says, it is evident that he wrote a
lie who said, under the guise of Bishop Melito of Asia, in a book describing the death of
the blessed mother of God, that in the second year after the Ascension of the Lord all the
apostles were divided throughout the world, each one preaching in his province. They
were all, as the death of the blessed Mary was approaching, raised up in clouds and
carried off to Jerusalem from the places in which they were preaching the word of God
and were set down in front of the door of her house, amongst them also Paul, recently
converted from being a persecutor to the faith of Christ, who had been received into the
ministry of the Gentiles with Barnabas. That composition specifically reports about the
apostle John that he preached at that time in Ephesus. All this clearly contradicts the
words of blessed Luke, in which he tells that, when the rest of the faithful were driven
away from Jerusalem, the apostles remained there and preached everywhere, until the
church had peace throughout Judea and Galilee and Samaria which, there is no doubt,
could not have been achieved in one year; he also clearly makes known that Paul,
together with Barnabas, was appointed to the ministry of the Gentiles, not in the second
year after the Ascension of Christ, but after a long time. Far be it from us, however, to
believe that the blessed apostle John, to whom, being a virgin, the Lord on the cross
commended his virgin mother, departed after one year and left her alone and so
dispirited by the passage of time that she feared that her body, when she was dead, was
to be burned by her enemies and, after he had returned to her, having been caught up by
clouds, she begged him anxiously, as if he were forgetful or unconcerned about her,
saying: "I beseech you, my son John, to remember the word of your master, my lord
Jesus Christ, who commended me to you. For behold, when I have been called I shall
enter upon the way of all the earth. I have heard the councils of the Jews, who are saying:
'Let us await the day when she dies who bore Jesus of Nazareth and let us burn her body
in fire.' And so now attend to my funeral rites." This, therefore, I have taken care to
mention because I know that some, by heedless thoughtlessness, grant approval to the
aforesaid volumes against the authority of blessed Luke.'

[62] *Ibid.*, p. 145: 'and so as far as this aforementioned short book on the death of holy Mary
is concerned, since it clearly errs on the question of time, in other respects also its
credibility is suspect'.

the Acts, and given that Pseudo-Melito is a tangential topic, it is somewhat peculiar that he introduces the apocryphon at all, and that, having
done so, he evades the central theme of the book. Bede's silence on the
corporal assumption could be interpreted as condemnation or belief, but
either view would probably misrepresent his attitude; he was equally unwilling to condemn or accept the belief and did not wish to assent to
anything that had not been revealed in scripture.

The next English account of a pilgrimage to Jerusalem is not as
circumspect as those of Adamnan and Bede. This is included in the *Vita SS
Willibaldi et Wynnebaldi* by Hygeburg, an Anglo-Saxon nun who wrote in
Heidenheim, a monastery founded by Willibald, *c.* 780. Her account of
the Jews' attempt to capture the body of Mary is obviously apocryphal, but
differs from any published apocryphon:

ubi Iudei uolebant tollere corpus sanctae Mariae. Cumque illi .xi. apostoli tollentes
corpus sanctae Mariae portauerunt illum de Hierusalem, et statim cumque ad
portam uenerunt ciuitatis, Iudaei uoluerunt conprehendere illum. Statimque illi
homines qui porrigebant ad feretra et eam tollere conabant, retentis brachiis quasi
glutinati inherebant in feretro et non poterant se mouere, antequam Dei gratia et
apostolorum petitione iterum resoluti fuerant, et tunc eos reliquerunt. Sancta
Maria in illo loco in medio Hierusalem exiuit de seculo, qui nominatur Sancta
Sion: et tunc apostoli .xi. portauerunt illum, sicut prius dixi, et tunc angeli
uenientes tulerunt illum de manibus apostolorum et portauerunt in paradiso.[63]

In this version not one but all of the Jews seem to have become attached to
Mary's coffin and Mary is not buried and then resurrected, but carried
straight to heaven from the hands of the apostles. This account is probably
not based on any written text, but on hearsay, as Hygeburg is not
conversant with the details of the story. In describing the same church as
that which Adamnan and Bede described, she also mentions 'sepulcrum

---

[63] *Vita Willibaldi*, ed. Holder-Egger, pp. 97–8: 'where the Jews attempted to take away
the body of our Lady. For when the eleven Apostles were bearing the body of Holy Mary
away from Jerusalem the Jews tried to snatch it away as soon as they reached the gate of
the city. But as soon as they stretched out their hands towards the bier and endeavoured
to take her their arms became fixed, stuck as it were to the bier, and they were unable to
move until, by the grace of God and the prayers of the Apostles, they were released and
then they let them go. Our Lady passed from this world in that very spot in the centre of
Jerusalem which is called Holy Sion. And then the eleven Apostles bore her, as I have
already said, and finally the angels came and took her away from the hands of the
Apostles and carried her to paradise' (*The Anglo-Saxon Missionaries in Germany*, trans.
C. H. Talbot, p. 166).

eius, non de eo quod corpus eius ibi requiescat, sed ad memoriam eius'.[64] Hygeburg, and possibly Willibald, can therefore be reckoned among the advocates of the corporal assumption because of this uncritical acceptance of the apocrypha, and they provide further evidence for the polarization apparent at the beginning of western discussion of Mary's death. The belief was either accepted from the apocrypha or the apocrypha were rejected, accompanied by silence on the belief.

The opposition between the two currents of thought on the death of Mary, already to be seen in the writings of Bede, is summed up by Barré for the Carolingians: 'La grande peur des uns est de majorer inconsidérément les données de la révélation, celle des autres est de ne pas reconnaître en Marie toute la gloire qui lui est due.'[65] The pronouncements of Adamnan and Bede exercised a profound influence over the Carolingians and, although homilies for the feast of the Assumption were composed, none treats of the corporal assumption as an established belief and many avoid the question altogether. Pseudo-Augustine *Sermo* ccviii, the work of Ambrosius Autpertus, abbot of Benevento (*ob.* 784), for example, defends the feast as one which merits acceptance and goes on to discuss its object:

Sed quo ordine hinc ad superna transierit regna, nulla catholica narrat historia. Non solum autem respuere apocrypha, uerum etiam ignorare dicitur haec eadem Dei Ecclesia. Et quidem sunt nonnulla sine auctoris nomine de eius assumptione conscripta; quae, ut dixi, ita cauentur, ut ad confirmandam rei ueritatem legi minime permittantur. Hinc sane pulsantur nonnulli, quia nec corpus eius in terra inuenitur, nec assumptio eius cum carne, ut in apocrypha legitur, in catholica historia reperitur.[66]

This homily is inspired by the three homilies for the feast in the homiliary

---

[64] *Ibid.*, p. 98: 'her tomb (not that her body lies at rest there, but as a memorial to her)' (*The Anglo-Saxon Missionaries in Germany*, trans. Talbot, p. 167).

[65] H. Barré, 'La croyance à l'assomption corporelle', p. 112: 'The great fear of some is rashly to increase the facts of revelation, that of others is not to acknowledge to Mary all the glory due to her.'

[66] PL 39, 2129–34, at 2130: 'But no catholic history tells by what means she passed hence to the celestial realms. For the church of God is said not only to reject the apocrypha but even to be unaware of these same events. And indeed there are many anonymous writings on her assumption against which, as I have said, one is so warned, that even for the confirmation of the truth one is barely allowed to read them. Hence many people are indeed disturbed because her body was not found in the earth, nor is her corporal assumption found in catholic history, as it is read in the apocrypha.'

of Alan of Farfa, none of which mentions the assumption,[67] and Ambrosius Autpertus's explicit discussion of the subject is an innovation which was promptly imitated by his successors. Although rejecting the apocrypha, Ambrosius Autpertus goes on to praise Mary in the highest of terms, stressing that 'assumptam super Angelos credamus'[68] and also emphasizing that she is above all praise, thus regarding the question of her corporal assumption, as almost redundant. The extravagance of his tribute is new in the West and must derive in some way from the Greeks.

In the two homilies he composed for the feast of the Assumption, Paul the Deacon is similarly reticent, although rather more positive than Ambrosius Autpertus on the possibility of the corporal assumption, declaring of Mary's body: 'restat ergo ut cum non inuenitur in terris, non incongrue fortasse credatur, non tamen sine anima, delatum in coelis'.[69] He raises the question of those resurrected at Christ's death and concludes that if we believe them to be in heaven, then 'intemerata scilicet Domini semper Virgine matre similia uel etiam potiora suspicantur'.[70] This benevolent neutrality, as Scheffczyk terms it,[71] is similar to the attitudes expressed in *Cogitis me*, an epistolary tract which is most probably to be attributed to Paschasius Radbertus (*ob. c.* 860), but which professes to be a letter of Jerome's.[72]

Although Paschasius Radbertus begins by warning against 'illud apocryphum de transitu eiusdem uirginis' and the dangers of receiving 'dubium pro certis',[73] his description of Mary's passage into heaven does not stress the purely spiritual aspect of the event, which is described in very physical terms. It is depicted in detail, in terms mainly taken from the Song of Songs, deliberately, as Radbertus says, to fill the lack of such accounts. Raising the subject of the corporal assumption, Radbertus

---

[67] See H. Barré, 'Deux sermons du xiiᵉ siècle pour la fête de la Conception', *Sciences ecclésiastiques* 10 (1958), 341–59, at 349.

[68] PL 39, 2130: 'we believe her to be assumed above the angels'.

[69] Paul the Deacon's homilies for the Assumption are printed in PL 95, 1565–74. This passage comes, however, from a page missing in Migne's source and supplied by L. Scheffczyk, *Das Mariengeheimnis*, pp. 451–2: 'It remains to be added, therefore, as she is not found on earth she may perhaps not unsuitably be believed to have been brought to heaven, not, however, without her soul.'

[70] *Ibid.*, p. 451: 'then the pure and ever virgin mother of God is, of course, esteemed similarly or to an even greater degree'.

[71] *Ibid.*, p. 451.   [72] *Der Pseudo-Hieronymus-Brief* ıx, ed. A. Ripberger.

[73] *Ibid.*, pp. 59–60.

compares the case of Mary to that of John the Evangelist, of those resurrected with Christ and of David, but concludes: 'Quod, quia Deo nihil est impossibile, nec nos de beata Maria factum abnuimus, quamquam propter cautelam, salua fide, pio magis desiderio opinari oporteat quam inconsulte definire, quod sine periculo nescitur.'[74] As if to compensate for his caution with regard to Mary's assumption, Radbertus stresses, in support of her spiritual assumption and its superiority to that of all other saints, the Virgin's overwhelming love and desire for Christ, her unpolluted virginity, her spiritual martyrdom at the Crucifixion and the plenitude of grace which raises her above the angels. All of these arguments in favour of Mary's uniquely privileged spiritual assumption were to be of great importance in the development of belief in her corporal assumption.

Radbertus also addressed himself to the problem of Mary's freedom or purification from sin, and his attitude to this is somewhat ambiguous. Arguing from the church's celebration of the Nativity of Christ, John the Baptist and Mary only, Radbertus asserts that this proves her to be 'ab omni originali peccato immunem'[75] (Radbertus, of course, accepts Bede's teaching on John the Baptist's birth without sin). This seemingly unequivocal declaration, however, clashes with other passages of the *De partu uirginis*, at least apparently: for example, with the words 'neque contraxit in utero sanctificata originale peccatum',[76] a seemingly self-contradictory statement, or the explanation that she was purified by the Holy Ghost at the Annunciation. Scheffczyk argues convincingly that this purification is not from any sin, but merely from the potential consequences of giving birth.[77] The seeming discrepancy between a sanctification in the womb and a freedom from contracting original sin is probably to be explained as a result of the fact that, for Radbertus, precision in this matter was not important – all that he wished to convey was his firm belief in Mary's complete purity. The question of whether this purity was a result of a purification at a very early stage of existence or of a preservation from any stain of original sin (i.e. an immaculate conception) did not present

---

[74] *Ibid.*, p. 63: 'Nothing is impossible for God and we do not deny that this has happened concerning the blessed Mary, although for caution's sake and in order to preserve our faith, it is more appropriate to imagine it with pious desire than ill-advisedly to define that which is safely unknown.'

[75] PL 120, 1372.

[76] *Ibid.*, 1371: 'nor, sanctified in the womb, did she contract original sin'.

[77] Scheffczyk, *Das Mariengeheimnis*, p. 329.

itself in this way. Radbertus also asserts that Christ's sinlessness was directly dependent on Mary's sinlessness at the moment of his conception[78] and, in thus making Mary's purity a necessary precondition of Christ's, Radbertus was both advancing significantly beyond previous statements and also preparing the way for the future use of such principles of metaphysical necessity.

The main contribution of the Carolingians to Mariological thinking was probably the greater emphasis they placed upon the person of Mary. Whereas patristic writers concentrated on Mary's role as mother of God and its consequences for Christological doctrine, the Carolingians sought rather to explore the consequences for Mary herself. The Marian issues treated in the early Anglo-Latin texts were also substantially developed by the Carolingian writers. From being little more than a necessary factor in the life of Christ, Mary had, by the Carolingian period, become a figure of importance in her own right. Apocryphal narratives, designed to supply the details of her life missing from the bible, had proliferated. As well as this accumulation of narrative detail, doctrinal theorizing and theological debate had also progressed. Alongside these developments, her relative importance in Christian ritual and devotion was increasing too, as subsequent chapters will show.

Of the texts discussed here, some remained unknown and unread in Anglo-Saxon England, while others exerted an important influence. There is plenty of evidence to show that the apocryphal texts dealing with Mary's birth and death were popular: Bede knew *Transitus* B2 well; the ninth-century *Old English Martyrology*[79] draws on the *Gospel of Pseudo-Matthew*, which was also translated into Old English (probably in the eleventh century);[80] *Transitus* B2[81] (twice) and *Transitus* C[82] were translated; and many eleventh-century homiliaries copied in England include apocryphal texts among their entries for the feasts of the Nativity and the Assumption of the Virgin. A Latin translation of part of the Greek *Protevangelium* is contained in the Bury St Edmunds collection, Cambridge, Pembroke College, 25; the *Gospel of Pseudo-Matthew* forms part of the collection of

---

[78] PL 120, 1371.   [79] *Das altenglische Martyrologium*, ed. Kotzor, pp. 201–3.

[80] *Angelsächsische Homilien und Heiligenleben*, ed. Assmann, pp. 117–37.

[81] As part of Blickling XIII, *The Blickling Homilies*, ed. Morris, pp. 155–9 (see below, pp. 232–4) and in Cambridge, Corpus Christi College 41, *Three Homilies*, ed. Grant, pp. 13–31.

[82] In Blickling XIII, pp. 136–55.

saints' lives in London, British Library, Cotton Nero E. i, a Worcester manuscript; and the *De natiuitate Mariae* is included in the versions of the homiliary of Paul the Deacon in Durham, Cathedral Library, A. III. 29 and in Salisbury, Cathedral Library, 179. *Transitus* C is contained in Pembroke 25. Many of the patristic texts, too, were known, at least in excerpts, and sermons by Augustine and Ambrose were included in most homilaries. Bede's homilies on the Annunciation, the Visitation and the Purification, together with excerpts on Mary from his gospel commentaries, were all included in versions of Paul the Deacon's homiliary in manuscripts from Anglo-Saxon England. Paschasius Radbertus's *Cogitis me* is found in Cambridge, University Library, Kk. 4. 13, a Norwich homiliary, in Durham A. III. 29 and in Cotton Nero E. i, but there is no evidence of knowledge of his *De partu uirginis*. Ambrosius Autpertus's homily on the Purification is included in Cambridge, University Library, Kk. 4.13, Lincoln, Cathedral Library, 158 and in London, BL, Royal 2. C. III, but his homily on the Assumption (= Pseudo-Augustine, *Sermo* ccviii) does not seem to have been known in England (parts of it, however, were mediated through the liturgy). Although little can be deduced about the ninth and tenth centuries, for which evidence is lacking, it would seem that in England in the early period, to judge from the work of Bede and his contemporaries, both patristic and apocryphal works on Mary were readily available, while many of the same texts, augmented now by the works of Bede himself and some later writers, circulated in the eleventh century.

2

Feasts of the Virgin: origin and development

By the end of the Anglo-Saxon period six feasts of the Virgin were celebrated in England; this large number represents an honour granted to no other saint. These feasts – the Purification, Annunciation, Assumption, Nativity, Presentation in the Temple and Conception – did not originate in England however, and, before turning to the English evidence, it is therefore necessary to consider first the background of Marian feasts at Rome and elsewhere in the context of the development of ritual from the seventh century to the eleventh.

MARIAN FEASTS: THE HISTORICAL BACKGROUND

The feasts of Mary were a relatively late development in the Christian church. The early church first celebrated the date of Christ's Passion and the descent of the Holy Ghost on the apostles, then subsequently the death-days of the martyrs. Even the day of Christ's birth was not celebrated, but the fact that Christian tradition had not preserved the date was recognized as a problem from the beginning of the third century, at the latest.[1] By 336, however, this event was being celebrated in Rome on 25 December, as it is mentioned in the Roman *Depositio martyrum*; in the East it was celebrated on 6 January, the winter solstice in the Egyptian calendar. The earliest extant sermon for the feast of Christmas was preached *c.* 383 by Optatus of Milevis.[2] The subject-matter of the early sermons for the feast of Christmas includes the story of the Annunciation, birth, Circumcision, Purification and the Adoration of the Magi, as these are known from the

[1] See D. B. Botte, *Les origines de la Noël*.
[2] A. Wilmart, 'Un sermon de Saint Optat pour la fête de Noël', *Revue des sciences religieuses* 2 (1922), 271–302.

gospels of Matthew and Luke. The most frequent theme of these texts is Christ's double nativity (eternal and temporal); and the consideration of his temporal nativity leads on naturally to praise of Mary's virginal maternity and of her role in the plan of salvation.[3]

In time the feast of 1 January, eight days after 25 December, came to be celebrated as the commemoration of the Circumcision and the Purification since Luke recounts that Christ was circumcised and named eight days after his birth (Luke II.21). By the fourth century the commemoration of the Purification had become an independent feast, celebrated forty days after the birth of Christ in accordance with the stipulation in the law of Moses that a woman should be purified forty days after the birth of a male child (Leviticus XII.1–4). The feast of the Purification was first introduced in the East and was kept on 14 February, forty days after the Eastern feast of Christmas on 6 January; this then seems to have led in some areas to an analogous celebration on 2 February, forty days after 25 December. As a result the feast of 1 January now had a single subject, the Circumcision of Christ. In Rome and in the churches of the West, however, there does not seem to have been a feast of the Purification until it was introduced from Byzantium in the seventh century. Elsewhere, by the fifth century the widespread adoption of the Western date of Christmas on 25 December had led to a cycle of feasts comprising Christmas, Circumcision (1 January), Epiphany (6 January) and Purification (2 February). In Byzantium the feast of the Purification on 2 February was introduced in 542 by Justinian, and it was called the *Hypapante*, 'the meeting' (of Christ and Simeon). Despite its later name, therefore, the origins of the feast of the Purification of Mary demonstrate that it was a dominical feast, originating in the division of the complex feast of Christmas into its component parts. In Byzantium it subsequently became a feast of Simeon.

A separate feast of Mary, closely connected with the Christmas cycle, is attested in the fifth century and seems to have originated before the Council of Ephesus in 431. It appears certain that the sermon preached by Proclus before Nestorius, responsible for the beginning of the controversy which led to the Council, was for a feast of the Virgin. Vailhé adduced evidence to show that this feast was that of the Annunciation on 25 March,[4] but Jugie has shown that, although the object of the feast was almost identical with that of the Annunciation, it was a movable feast, celebrated in the period

[3] J. Leclercq, 'Aux origines du cycle de Noël', p. 10.
[4] S. Vailhé, 'Origines de la fête de l'Annonciation', *Échos d'Orient* 9 (1906), 138–45.

before Christmas.[5] It was probably kept on the Sunday before Christmas, forming part of the then developing liturgical season of Advent, and its object was Mary's divine maternity in general and, especially, the virginal conception.[6] The feast was celebrated in Constantinople, Palestine, Syria, Asia Minor, Egypt and Gaul, and it may have originated with the construction of a basilica in Nazareth. Even though 25 March was the obvious date on which to celebrate the virginal conception once Christmas had been fixed on 25 December, the establishment of the feast on this date was delayed by the differences concerning the date of Christ's Nativity. By c. 530, however, the feast of Mary's conception of Christ had been transferred in Byzantium to 25 March.[7]

In the seventh century and the eighth four more feasts of Mary were established in the Eastern church. From c. 450 onwards 15 August had been kept as a feast in honour of Mary in Jerusalem,[8] and in c. 600 this date was chosen by the Byzantine emperor Maurice as the date on which Mary's death and assumption were to be celebrated throughout his empire. The feast of the Nativity of Mary was probably kept by the first half of the seventh century.[9] Mary's presentation in the temple seems to have been celebrated from the end of the seventh century in Greece and perhaps from the fifth century in Jerusalem.[10] The feast of the Conception of Mary, on 9 December, had been instituted by the eighth century.[11] This feast was in origin principally a commemoration of the annunciation to Joachim and Anna of the conception of Mary, as related in the apocryphal *Proteuange-lium*, but it included also the miracle of the conception in a sterile pair and the passive conception of Mary. The ideas behind all four new Eastern feasts

[5] Jugie, 'La première fête mariale', and 'Homélies mariales byzantines II'.

[6] Jugie, 'La première fête mariale', p. 131.

[7] A sermon of Abraham of Ephesus was most probably preached on this date between 530 and 550 (see M. Jugie, 'Homélies mariales byzantines I', PO 16 (1922), 425–589, at 434–9; and Romanus (*fl. c.* 540) wrote a hymn for the same feast (see R. A. Fletcher, 'Three Early Byzantine Hymns and their Place in the Liturgy of the Church at Constantinople', *Byzantinische Zeitschrift* 51 (1958), 53–65).

[8] See Capelle, 'La fête de la Vierge'.

[9] See Lafontaine-Dosogne, *Iconographie de l'enfance de la Vierge* I, 25. The feast is attested by two eighth-century sermons by Andrew of Crete.

[10] S. Vailhé, 'La fête de la Présentation de Marie au Temple', *Echos d'Orient* 5 (1901–2), 221–4; see also M. J. Kishpaugh, *The Feast of the Presentation of the Virgin Mary in the Temple* (Washington, DC, 1941), p. 36.

[11] Jugie, *L'Immaculée Conception*, p. 135.

27

originated in the apocryphal narratives about Mary's birth and death, and three of the feasts (the Assumption, Nativity and Conception) are analogous to feasts of Christ.

In the West there is ample evidence for the celebration of a feast of Mary in the period immediately preceding Christmas. In the Milanese and Ravennan churches it was celebrated on the Sunday before Christmas,[12] and the decrees of the Council of Toledo in 656 fixed the Spanish feast on 18 December.[13] Up to then the feast had been a movable one in Spain, presumably kept on the Sunday before Christmas, but the Council was reluctant to continue to celebrate it in this way. The Spanish bishops seem to have known of the Byzantine feast of 25 March and admitted that this was the logical date on which to celebrate the virginal conception, but they refused to observe it on this day as it would always fall during Lent or during the paschal celebrations, a time when the church had traditionally not observed the feasts of saints. The movable feast on the Sunday before Christmas is also attested in two early monastic *ordines*, where it is entitled *Conceptio Sanctae Mariae* (no. xv, from the second half of the eighth century, and no. xvii, from the end of the eighth century).[14] *Conceptio* here is to be taken in its active rather than its passive sense, describing Mary's conception of Christ, not Anna's conception of Mary, and the feast has nothing to do with the Byzantine feast of the passive conception of Mary, normally entitled *Conceptio Sanctae Annae*.

Rome, however, did not celebrate the feast of Mary in Advent, but, instead, 1 January was kept as a Marian feast, at least at the end of the sixth century.[15] A mass for this feast-day was, arguably, composed between 560 and 590.[16] The Roman prayers for this mass seem to have been used later for the Gallican feast of Mary on 18 January;[17] this Gallican feast was celebrated from the sixth century at the latest, as it is mentioned by Gregory of Tours (*c.* 540–90). The Roman feast of Mary on 1 January appears no longer to have been celebrated in the papal liturgy during the papacy of Gregory the Great (590–604), however, and it was replaced by a

---

[12] Jugie, 'Homélies mariales II', pp. 311–13.

[13] Jugie, 'La première fête mariale', pp. 144–6.

[14] *Les Ordines romani du haut moyen âge*, ed. M. Andrieu, 5 vols. (Louvain, 1931–61) III, 95 and 175; see also B. Billet, 'Culte et dévotion à la Vierge'.

[15] See D. B. Botte, 'La première fête mariale dans la liturgie romaine' and Frénaud, 'Le culte de Notre-Dame', pp. 159–66.

[16] See Frénaud, 'Le culte de Notre-Dame', p. 164.

[17] Chavasse, *Le sacramentaire gélasien*, pp. 381–2 and 651–6.

Missa in octabas domini. Despite this, it seems to have survived in the *tituli*, the principal old churches of Rome, until the mid-seventh century, when the Byzantine feasts of the Assumption and the Annunciation were introduced. The prayers for 1 January were then re-used in the liturgy for the new celebrations, and 1 January received a mass explicitly composed for the octave of Christmas, in which the Marian character was far less marked.

Around 640 the Byzantine feast of 2 February, under the title of *Natale Sancti Symeonis* (or *Hypapante* in Greek) was introduced in some of the principal churches of Rome, as was the Assumption with the title *In natale* or *In festivitate Sanctae Mariae*.[18] Both feasts were then adopted into the papal liturgy, probably during the pontificate of Theodore I (642–9), and the celebration of the Purification was solemnized by a procession. The Annunciation, called *Adnuntiatio domini*, was introduced in Rome *c.* 650. It is obvious from these early titles that neither the feast of 2 February nor that of 25 March was regarded as a Marian feast; 2 February was a feast of Simeon, or of Christ and Simeon, and 25 March a feast of the Lord.[19] Around 660–70 the feast of the Nativity of Mary was introduced in Rome and was celebrated by the pope from *c.* 680–95 onwards. Pope Sergius (687–701) extended the procession already in use on 2 February to the feasts of 25 March, 15 August and 8 September. The titles of the feasts of 2 February and 25 March were soon altered to emphasize their Marian significance, that of 2 February becoming *Purificatio Sanctae Mariae* and that of 25 March becoming *Adnuntiatio* (or, occasionally, *Conceptio*) *Sanctae Mariae*. The title of the feast of 15 August was also changed to *Dormitio* or *Sollemnia de pausatione Sanctae Mariae* and, in the eighth century, to *Adsumptio*.[20] This happened even though the liturgy for the day shows the compilers' extreme reserve regarding the subject of Mary's assumption. By the end of the seventh century, therefore, four Marian feasts – the Purification, Annunciation, Assumption and Nativity – were being celebrated in Rome.

---

[18] *Ibid.*, pp. 375–402; Frénaud, 'Le culte de Notre-Dame', pp. 172–4; and Chavasse, 'Les plus anciens types du lectionnaire', p. 30.

[19] See Chavasse, *Le sacramentaire gélasien*, pp. 376–7.

[20] On the titles of the feasts, see *ibid.*, pp. 376–9, and Jugie, *Le mort et l'assomption de la Sainte Vierge*, pp. 197–8.

MARIAN FEASTS IN ANGLO-SAXON ENGLAND: THE SEVENTH AND EIGHTH CENTURIES

These four new Roman feasts were introduced into England only gradually and sporadically. We can trace their adoption in England through various texts: in particular, the third of Aldhelm's *Carmina ecclesiastica* (*In ecclesia Mariae a Bugge exstructa*), the *Martyrologium Hieronymianum Epternacense*, the Calendar of St Willibrord, the Walderdorf Calendar, Bede's works and the Würzburg Lectionary.

The third of Aldhelm's *Carmina ecclesiastica*, datable to *c.* 690, has been taken as evidence of how 'quickly the observance of the [Blessed Virgin Mary's] four festivals, introduced into the Roman liturgy by this pope [Sergius], was taken up by the Anglo-Saxons'.[21] The lines in question read:

> Istam nempe diem, qua templi festa coruscant
> Natiuitate sua sacrauit uirgo Maria,
> Quam iugiter renouant Augusti tempora mensis,
> Diuiditur medio dum torrens Sextilis orbe;
> Qui nobis iterum restaurat gaudia mentis,
> Dum uicibus redeunt solemnia festa Mariae
> Et ueneranda piis flagrant altaria donis.[22]

These lines clearly establish that Aldhelm knew a feast of Mary in mid-August. This is not, however, a Roman feast, as the Romans celebrated the death, not the birth, of Mary in mid-August.[23] It could be suggested that *natiuitas* here is merely a synonym of *dies natalis* which, while literally meaning 'birthday', was always used of the death-days of the saints (implying their 'birth' into eternal life). I have been unable, however, to find any instance of *natiuitas* used in this sense. Augustine, for example, declares that the church celebrates the *natiuitas* of Christ and John the Baptist only, whereas she celebrates the *natalis* of the other saints.[24] It

---

[21] Mayr-Harting, *The Coming of Christianity*, p. 187.

[22] *Aldhelmi opera*, ed. Ehwald, p. 17, lines 59–65: 'With her own birth the Virgin Mary consecrated this very day, on which the dedication of Bugga's church gleams brightly — the day which the month of August perpetually renews, when torrid Sextilis [i.e. the Roman month of August] is divided in the midst of its rotation [i.e. on 16 August]. It restores once again the joys in our minds when the feast of St Mary returns at its accustomed time, and the holy altars are redolent with the holy gifts [of incense]' (trans. M. Lapidge and J. L. Rosier, *Aldhelm: The Poetic Works*, p. 49).

[23] See above, p. 29.

[24] *Sermo* cclxxxvii: *In natali S. Ioannis Baptistae*, PL 38, 1301–2, at 1301.

would seem, therefore, that we cannot equate *natiuitas* in the poem with *natalis*, and hence that Aldhelm must be referring to Mary's birthday. The question therefore arises: was this a real feast or does Aldhelm merely have a confused impression of the Roman feast? The latter was the opinion of Ehwald, who deduced that the feast was not yet established in Aldhelm's time.[25] The Aldhelm reference cannot, however, be understood in isolation, since there are five other early insular witnesses to a commemoration of the nativity of Mary in the middle of August: the *Martyrologium Hieronymianum Epternacense*, the Calendar of St Willibrord, the Walderdorf Calendar, and two Irish martyrologies, that of Oengus and that of Tallaght. All these texts record a commemoration of the nativity of Mary on 16 August. A brief description of each of these texts is necessary before discussing their bearing on Aldhelm's reference.

The *Martyrologium Hieronymianum Epternacense* (now Paris, Bibliothèque Nationale, lat. 10837) was copied at the beginning of the eighth century and is thought by its editors to be an insular version of the Hieronymian Martyrology.[26] Its entry for 16 August reads *Natiuitas Sanctae Mariae* and it also commemorates the Gallican feast of the Deposition of Mary on 18 January and the Purification (called here the feast of Simeon) on 2 February. The *Martyrologium Hieronymianum Epternacense* seems to have been compiled from two versions of the Hieronymian Martyrology: a copy like the 'standard' texts of the Berne and Weissenburg copies and a breviate version of the same martyrology.[27] Some of the entries in the source resembling the Berne and Weissenburg copies had been misplaced by a day.

The Calendar of St Willibrord was also written at the beginning of the eighth century, probably by an Anglo-Saxon scribe at Echternach, and is bound up with the *Martyrologium Hieronymianum Epternacense*.[28] It is not a liturgical calendar, but one for private devotional use. It contains the feast

[25] *Aldhelmi opera*, p. 17, note to line 60: 'Videmus igitur de festi die Aldhelmi temporibus nondum constitisse in ecclesia.'

[26] The manuscript is described by Lowe, *Codices Latini Antiquiores*, V, no. 605, and the martyrology is ed. G. B. de Rossi and L. Duchesne, *Martyrologium Hieronymianum*, Acta Sanctorum, Nov. II.i (Brussels, 1894). See also H. Delehaye, *Commentarius perpetuus in Martyrologium Hieronymianum*.

[27] See H. J. Lawlor, *The Psalter and Martyrology of Ricemarch*, HBS 47 (London, 1914), xxv–xxxiii.

[28] The manuscript is described by Lowe, *Codices Latini Antiquiores* V, no. 606a, and K. Gamber, *Codices Liturgici*, no. 414. The calendar is ed. Wilson, *The Calendar of St Willibrord*.

of the Assumption on the Gallican date of 18 January, the Purification on 2 February (entitled *Sancti Symeonis patriarchae*), a feast of Mary on 16 August and the feast of the Nativity of Mary on 9 September. Textually the calendar is closely connected with the *Martyrologium Hieronymianum Epternacense*; it contains, for example, many of the Campanian saints who distinguish this version of the Hieronymian Martyrology. The entry for 16 August in this calendar now reads merely 'sanctae mariae', but it is preceded by an erasure, and a second contemporary hand has added *natiui* on the line above (that is, the one relating to 15 August). Of the erased letters only the final one, *s*, can be distinguished, and it has an abbreviation mark over it. This could have been the final letter of *depos* (for *depositio*), as Wilson suggested.[29] The *s* does not seem to be in the same hand as that of the main scribe, which suggests that it was also written over an erasure. Wilson therefore postulated that the original entry was *natiui*, that this was erased and replaced by *depos*, and that this was again erased, because of the feast of the Assumption in the calendar on 18 January, and *natiui* restored after consultation with the *Martyrologium Hieronymianum Epternacense*.

The Walderdorf Calendar (a fragment written in Anglo-Saxon half-uncial, *c.* 750) is thought to have some connection with Boniface, since it comes from his area of missionary activity.[30] It has an erasure at 15 August and the entry 'orationes et preces in natiuitate sanctae Mariae' on 16 August. As the fragment contains the months of July and August only, entries for the other Marian feasts are not preserved. The Walderdorf Calendar is closely related to the *Martyrologium Hieronymianum Epternacense* and is, therefore, connected with the Calendar of St Willibrord; neither is derived directly from the other, however, and both go back ultimately to a common original.[31]

The Martyrology of Tallaght and the Martyrology of Oengus are Irish texts, both apparently composed in the community of Tallaght.[32] The Latin Martyrology of Tallaght appears to date from *c.* 750 in its original form; Oengus's text, composed *c.* 800, derives from it and is written in Old

[29] Wilson, *The Calendar of St Willibrord*, p. 37.

[30] See P. P. Siffrin, 'Das Walderdorffer Kalendarfragment'; it is described by Lowe, *Codices Latini Antiquiores* VIII, no. 1052, and Gamber, *Codices Liturgici*, no. 412. The other calendar associated with Boniface, now Munich, Bayerisches Hauptstaatsarchiv, Raritätenselect 108 (see Gamber, *Codices Liturgici*, no. 413), is a fragment for May and June only and hence does not contain any Marian feast.

[31] Siffrin, 'Das Walderdorffer Kalendarfragment', p. 219.

[32] *The Martyrology of Tallaght*, ed. Best and Lawlor and *Félire Oengusso*, ed. Stokes.

Irish verse.[33] Tallaght has *Assumptio Sanctae Mariae* on 14 August and *Natiuitas Sanctae Mariae* on 16 August, and Oengus has a feast of the Commemoration of Mary on 15 August and a feast of her Nativity on 16 August. These two martyrologies, which are closely related to each other, are also related to the *Martyrologium Hieronymianum Epternacense*. This relationship can be seen more clearly in Tallaght, a much fuller text (Oengus is limited by its stanzaic form). Tallaght seems to have been derived from two versions of the Hieronymian Martyrology, one of which was 'the Epternach manuscript, though perhaps at second hand'[34] and the other a text like those in the Berne and Weissenburg manuscripts. The use of these two closely related sources, which often have the same entries but assigned to different days, has given rise to numerous doublets. Of these, the entries in the middle of August form one.

From the foregoing description of these texts it is evident that they are all related in some way to the *Martyrologium Hieronymianum Epternacense*. It is the entry for 16 August in this text that must, therefore, be examined. As I have pointed out, the *Martyrologium Hieronymianum Epternacense* dislocates many entries and of these, I believe, its entry for 15 August is one. It could be argued, as it was by Wilson, that the entry represents an insular feast of the Nativity which dies out soon after the introduction of the Roman feast,[35] but there are two arguments against this. The first is that it seems an unlikely coincidence that an insular feast of Mary's Nativity should fall within a day of the Eastern and Roman feast of Mary's death. The second is that the *Martyrologium Hieronymianum Epternacense* also has an entry for 2 February, another Eastern and Roman feast. As I have shown earlier, the feast of 2 February was introduced at about the same time as that of 15 August,[36] and the Assumption and Purification are generally found together in documents which do not contain the two later feasts of the Annunciation and the Nativity. Since the *Martyrologium Hieronymianum Epternacense* contains the feast of 2 February, it ought also to contain the feast of 15 August; and, since we know from other entries in

[33] On these texts, see J. Hennig, 'The Irish Counterparts of the Anglo-Saxon Menologium', *MS* 14 (1952), 98–105; 'Studies in the Tradition of the Martyrologium Hieronymianum in Ireland', *Studia Patristica* 1 (1957), 104–11; and 'Studies in the Latin Texts of the Martyrology of Tallaght, of Félire Oengusso and of Félire Hui Gorman', *Proc. of the R. Irish Acad.* 69C (1970), 45–112.

[34] *Martyrology of Tallaght*, ed. Best and Lawlor, p. xxiii.

[35] Wilson, *The Calendar of St Willibrord*, p. 37.

[36] See above, p. 29.

the *Martyrologium Hieronymianum Epternacense* that feasts were often mis-placed by a day, it seems more than probable that the entry on 16 August represents the Roman feast of 15 August. The use of *natiuitas* instead of *natalis* can be explained, as Delehaye suggested, by a wrong expansion of *nat* (to *natiuitas* instead of *natalis*),[37] and this wrong expansion may be due to the fact that the compiler of the *Martyrologium Hieronymianum Epter-nacense* had already included a commemoration of the death of Mary on the Gallican date of 18 January. That the entry for 16 August was a mistake is also supported by the evidence of scribal alteration in the Calendars of Willibrord and Walderdorf.

If, therefore, the entry in the *Martyrologium Hieronymianum Epternacense* can be explained as a mistake, what are we to make of the Aldhelm entry? The sources dependent on the *Martyrologium Hieronymianum Epternacense* are all martyrologies or calendars, and, although all the entries record feasts which were celebrated liturgically somewhere, all would not have been celebrated by the compilers of these texts. Some of the entries would have been of historical rather than liturgical interest. An error such as the wrong expansion of *nat* is more easily explicable if the compiler had no texts with which to celebrate the feast. Aldhelm, however, is undoubtedly referring to the celebration of a feast in mid-August. If this were a feast of Mary's Nativity it would seem that we were, after all, dealing with a real, liturgically celebrated feast. I think, however, that the lines in Aldhelm should be interpreted differently. The church described in the poem was dedicated to Mary, as can be seen from the title of the poem and the following lines:

> Quo regnante nouum praecelsa mole sacellum
> Bugga construxit, supplex uernacula Christi,
> Qua fulgent arae bis seno nomine sacrae;
> Insuper absidam consecrat Virginis arae.
> Praesentem ergo diem cuncti celebremus ouantes
> Et reciproca Deo modulemur carmina Christo![38]

The lines quoted earlier, which begin 'Istam nempe diem, qua templi festa coruscant', take up the 'praesentem diem' of these lines, and it is evident that Aldhelm is referring to the day on which the church was dedicated.

---

[37] *Commentarius perpetuus in Martyrologium Hieronymianum*, p. 446.

[38] *Aldhelmi opera*, ed. Ehwald, p. 16, lines 38–43: 'During his [i.e. Ine's] reign Bugga, a humble servant of Christ, built (this) new church with its lofty structure, in which holy

The liturgical feast on this day is, therefore, the feast of the anniversary of the church's dedication. Aldhelm then goes on to note the particular suitability of this day, as it is the day of Mary's birthday. It is extremely unlikely that the liturgical celebration of Mary's nativity would be chosen as the day on which to dedicate a church: the anniversary of the day of a church's dedication was a very important feast in the calendar of that church, with its own proper. This would have conflicted with the proper for the nativity, had there been one. I believe, therefore, that the feast referred to by Aldhelm was the dedication feast and that the day had been chosen because it was thought to be the date of Mary's nativity and therefore a suitable date on which to dedicate a church to her. The reference to the nativity is, then, commemorative or historical in character, not liturgical, and it seems reasonable to assume that it derives in some way from an immediate ancestor of the *Martyrologium Hieronymianum Epternacense*.

Instead of demonstrating the prompt adoption of the Roman feasts in Anglo-Saxon England, therefore, the passage in Aldhelm seems to show that he knew of an erroneous one in mid-August. His poem and the texts dependent on the *Martyrologium Hieronymianum Epternacense*, some of which are considerably later than Aldhelm, show that the feasts of Mary were introduced rather more slowly into Anglo-Saxon England than has been thought. As we know that Aldhelm at some stage in his life made a journey to Rome, it is perhaps surprising that he was ignorant of the feast of the Nativity.

Both the *Martyrologium Hieronymianum Epternacense* and the Calendar of Willibrord note a feast of Mary on the Gallican date of 18 January, the former having the entry *Depositio Sanctae Mariae*, the latter *Adsumptio Sanctae Mariae*. Wilson conjectured that this was originally an insular feast and that it subsequently spread to Gaul.[39] However, Gregory of Tours already knew of this feast, which was originally entitled *Festiuitas Sanctae Mariae*, and it is indisputably a Gallican feast. With the introduction of the feast of the Assumption in Rome the title of the Gallican feast was changed to *depositio* or *adsumptio*, as the Roman title was applied to the Gallican feast. The date of 18 January was retained initially but in time the feast in January disappeared altogether and Gaul celebrated the feast of the

altars gleam in twelve-fold dedication; moreover, she dedicates the apse to the Virgin. Therefore let us all rejoicing celebrate this present day and let us chant hymns in turn to Christ the Lord' (trans. Lapidge and Rosier, *Aldhelm: The Poetic Works*, p. 48).

[39] Wilson, *The Calendar of St Willibrord*, p. 19.

Assumption on 15 August.[40] That the *Martyrologium Hieronymianum Epternacense* and the Calendar of Willibrord enter the feast under the recent, and not the primitive, Gallican title indicates that it was not an old, established feast in England. As we have no English liturgical evidence for its observance, it is probably another purely commemorative entry.

The Calendar of Willibrord is the sole witness to a feast of Mary's Nativity on 9 September (elsewhere celebrated on 8 September). The entry reads *Natiuitas sanctae mariae hierosolymis*. While the dislocation of this feast by a day appears at first sight to be related to the misplacing of the feast of the Assumption, I suspect that the two are not, in fact, related. This feast of the Nativity on 9 September is not attested in any of the related documents (the *Martyrologium Hieronymianum Epternacense*, the Walderdorf Calendar, or the martyrologies of Tallaght and Oengus) and the word *hierosolymis* suggests that the compiler himself did not celebrate the feast, but knew that it was celebrated in Jerusalem. The date may be an error for 8 September or it could possibly have been the date on which the feast was kept for a while in Jerusalem, as Wilson argued: 'The Armenians, who derived, at any rate, their ancient lectionary system from Jerusalem, appear to have in some places kept the feast of Our Lady's Nativity on September 9.'[41] The *Martyrologium Hieronymianum Epternacense* and the Calendar of Willibrord note the feast of 2 February under the title of a feast of Simeon. The Annunciation is not marked in either text, and this also suggests that it was not via Rome that the compiler of the Calendar of Willibrord knew of the feast of the Nativity. The Annunciation was introduced in Rome before the Nativity, and we should, therefore, normally expect to find it in any document containing the Nativity.

Bede's works testify that he probably knew all four Roman feasts. He composed a homily for the feast of the Purification[42] and a hymn *In natali sanctae Dei genitricis*.[43] All four feasts are entered in Bede's martyrology, although only the Purification and the Annunciation are attested in the most reliable manuscripts, whose text does not extend beyond 25 July.[44] Bede also provides the earliest evidence for the knowledge in England of the procession of 2 February:

[40] See Jugie, *Le mort et l'assomption de la Sainte Vierge*, pp. 200–1.

[41] Wilson, *The Calendar of St Willibrord*, p. 39.

[42] *Bedae Venerabilis opera homiletica*, ed. Hurst. pp. 128–33.

[43] *Bedae Venerabilis opera rhythmica*, ed. Fraipont, pp. 433–4.

[44] See Quentin, *Les martyrologes historiques*, pp. 49–50.

Sed hanc lustrandi consuetudinem bene mutauit christiana religio, cum in mense eodem die sanctae Mariae plebs uniuersa cum sacerdotibus ac ministris hymnis modula deuotis per ecclesias perque congrua urbis loca procedit, datasque a pontifice cuncti cereas in manibus gestant ardentes. Et augescente bona consuetudine, id ipsum in caeteris quoque eiusdem beatae matris et perpetuae uirginis festiuitatibus agere didicit, non utique in lustrationem terrestris imperii quinquennem, sed in perennem regni caelestis memoriam.[45]

The Würzburg Lectionary, now Würzburg Universitätsbibliothek, M. p. th. f. 62, was written *c.* 750 'by a scribe in the pure insular tradition, to judge by the script and decoration'.[46] The manuscript contains an epistolary and an evangeliary which reflect the state of the Roman liturgy before and after *c.* 650 respectively.[47] The epistolary contains no Marian feast and thus reflects an earlier state of liturgical development than does the evangeliary, which contains the feasts of 2 February and 15 August. The Purification is obviously an addition inserted out of place in the exemplar of the evangeliary, since it is out of place in this copy, coming several Sundays after the feast of St Valentine on 14 February. The entry is untitled and merely specifies the gospel reading for the feast (Luke 11.22–32).[48] The feast of 15 August is entitled *Natale Sanctae Mariae*.[49] Because of the contents of the manuscript, Lowe surmised that it was written while the scribe was on a visit to Rome; had this been the case, however, one would have expected a Roman exemplar of *c.* 750 to include the feasts of the Annunciation and the Nativity, both well established in Rome by this date. The manuscript, therefore, was copied probably in England or in an Anglo-Saxon centre in Germany from an exemplar which

---

[45] *Bedae Venerabilis opera didascalica: De temporum ratione liber*, ed. C. W. Jones, CCSL 123B (Turnhout, 1977), p. 323: 'But the Christian religion rightly changed this practice of expiating when in the same month on the feast day of St Mary all the people together with their priests and ministers with devout hymns went in procession through the churches and suitable places in the city, and all carried in their hands burning wax candles given by the pope. With the growth of that good custom, he instructed that they do it also on the other feasts of the same blessed mother and perpetual virgin, not by any means for the five-yearly expiation of the earthly empire, but in perennial memory of the heavenly kingdom.'

[46] Lowe, *Codices Latini Antiquiores* IX, no. 1417; Gamber, *Codices Liturgici*, nos. 1001 and 1101.

[47] See G. Morin, 'Le plus ancien Comes ou lectionnaire de l'église romaine', *RB* 27 (1910), 41–74, and 'Liturgie et basiliques de Rome au milieu du viie siècle d'après les Listes d'Evangiles de Würzburg', *RB* 28 (1911), 296–330.

[48] Klauser, *Das römische Capitulare Evangeliorum* I, 18.   [49] *Ibid.*, p. 35.

had left Rome in the middle of the seventh century, and the scribe's failure to include the feasts of the Annunciation and the Nativity suggests that they were not well known in that part of England or Germany in which he wrote. By the end of the first half of the eighth century the feasts of Mary were clearly spreading in England, although they were not yet firmly established. The feasts appear to have been introduced rather slowly and gradually, with much initial confusion, most of which can be traced back to the *Martyrologium Hieronymianum Epternacense* or its ancestors.

MARIAN FEASTS IN ANGLO-SAXON ENGLAND: c. 750–c. 900

From the second half of the eighth century onwards the initial confusion in Marian feasts seems to be at an end, and later sources seem to follow the Roman pattern. Four texts and a liturgical calendar illustrate this development.

Three feasts of Mary are included in an antiphonary which is part of a *libellus precum* which was compiled by Alcuin *c.* 790, drawing, presumably, on the antiphonary in use at York.[50] The feasts of the Virgin are those of the Purification and Assumption and a feast in the period immediately preceding Christmas, which Constantinescu assigns to the feast of Mary on 18 December.[51] There is no English evidence for knowledge of this feast, however, and it is more likely to be for the movable feast of Mary on the Sunday before Christmas, attested in some monastic *ordines*, or for Advent or Christmas.[52]

The Metrical Calendar of York, which was probably composed at York in the second half of the eighth century, commemorates the feasts of the Purification, Annunciation, Assumption and Nativity:[53]

---

[50] The complete manuscript has not yet been printed, but the antiphonary is edited and discussed by Constantinescu, 'Alcuin et les "libelli precum"'. Constantinescu knew of only one manuscript of this collection (Bamberg, Stadtbibliothek, Misc. Patr. 17 (B. 2. 10), fols. 133–62, but another, Escorial B. 4. 17, has since been found. Donald Bullough is now preparing a full edition of this important florilegium.

[51] *Ibid.*, p. 55.   [52] See above, p. 28.

[53] Ed. A. Wilmart, 'Un témoin Anglo-Saxon du calendrier métrique d'York', *RB* 46 (1934), 41–69. The lines quoted are 9, 17, 47–8 and 51–2 of Wilmart's edition (see also Quentin, *Les martyrologes historiques*, pp. 120–30): 'On the second [of February] Christ was offered to the temple'; 'On the twenty-fifth [of March] the conception of Christ deservedly delights'; 'On the fifteenth [of August] the mother of God is known to approach / A virgin borne among the angelic hosts'; 'The eighth of September was dedicated with honour / on which the now happy Virgin Mary deserved to be born.'

Et quartas nonas Christus templo offerebatur.   (Purification)

Octauis merito gaudet conceptio Christi.   (Annunciation)

Sancta dei genetrix senas ter constat adire,
Angelicos uecta inter coetus uirgo Kalendas.   (Assumption)

Idus Septembris senas dedicabat honore,
Quis meruit nasci felix iam uirgo Maria.   (Nativity)

Æthelwulf's poem, composed in Northumbria at an unknown cell of Lindisfarne 803 x 821, and called by its editors *De abbatibus*, mentions four feasts of Mary which were introduced in the cell during the abbacy of Sigbald (*ob.* 771).[54] It appears that the feasts were unknown in the cell before Sigbald's abbacy, as Æthelwulf says that Sigbald:

> ac fratres precibus mulcet sollempnia festa
> ad letos caelebrare pie genetricis honores.[55]

The feasts in question are listed as follows:

> sanctam cumque diem sacrauit uirgo Maria,
> qua uolitans caelos meruit penetrare per altos,
> uel qua presenti generata redditur orbi,
> uel qua prepulchrae susceptat gaudia uitae,
> uel qua celsithronum meruit generare tonantem.[56]

Campbell, the most recent editor of this poem, identified these feasts as the Assumption, the Nativity of Mary, the Annunciation and the Nativity of Christ.[57] More recently, Mayr-Harting has suggested identifying them with the Assumption, Nativity of Mary, Purification and Annunciation.[58] This latter identification would seem to be corroborated by the order in which the feasts are enumerated, as the sequence 15 August/8 September/25 March/25 December seems less likely than 15 August/8 September/2 February/25 March. Christmas was never regarded as a Marian feast and the

---

[54] *Æthelwulf 'De abbatibus'*, ed. Campbell.

[55] *Ibid.*, p. 39, lines 468–9: 'he pressed the monks gently with prayers to celebrate solemn festivals for joyfully honouring the pious mother' (trans. Campbell, p. 38).

[56] *Ibid.*, p. 37, lines 460–4: 'and when the Virgin Mary blessed the sacred day on which she had it granted to her to rise up and penetrate the lofty skies, or that upon which she was born and given to the present world, or that on which she received the joys of a life which was very lovely, or that on which she had it granted to her to bear the thunderer high-enthroned . . .' (trans. Campbell, p. 36).

[57] *Ibid.*, p. 36, n. 5.   [58] Mayr-Harting, *The Coming of Christianity*, p. 308, n. 70.

list is explicitly stated to be of feasts associated with Mary. Mayr-Harting's identification, however, also raises a problem, since Æthelwulf's description of the Purification does not seem appropriate. A better solution is perhaps to take the third feast ('uel qua prepulchrae susceptat gaudia uitae') as the feast on the Sunday before Christmas, the feast of Mary's divine maternity, which also preserves the chronological sequence. The Purification may not have been included since it could have been viewed as a feast of Simeon or of Christ, as it often was. The four feasts mentioned by Æthelwulf, therefore, are probably the feasts of the Assumption, the Nativity, the Sunday before Christmas and the Annunciation.

Commemoration of the Annunciation, Assumption and Nativity are entered in the *Old English Martyrology*, a text composed in England some time before the end of the ninth century.[59] The Purification is missing as there is a gap in the text for February. Finally, the ninth-century calendar in Oxford, Bodleian Library, Digby 63, 40r–45v, contains all four feasts of Mary, entitled here *Ypapanti domini* (2 February), *Adnunciacio Sancte Marie* (25 March), *Adsumptio Sancte Marie* (15 August) and *Natiuitas Sancte Marie* (8 September).[60] By 900, then, the four Roman feasts of the Virgin had been consolidated in England.

MARIAN FEASTS IN ANGLO-SAXON ENGLAND: THE TENTH AND ELEVENTH CENTURIES

A metrical calendar which was probably composed in England in the early tenth century, but with Irish connections, and which is preserved in four manuscripts (London, British Library, Cotton Galba A. xviii, Cotton Tiberius B. v, vol. I, Cotton Julius A. vi and Oxford, Bodleian Library, Junius 27), commemorates the four Marian feasts in question:

> In quadris Christus templo deducitur archus.　(Purification)
>
> Octauis Dominum uirgo conceperat alma.　(Annunciation)
>
> Bis nonis uirgo Maria transiuerat astra.　(Assumption)
>
> Nascitur in senis uirgo perpulchra Maria.　(Nativity of Mary)

This calendar, in some manuscripts, also has another feast of Mary on

---

[59] *Das altenglische Martyrologium*, ed. Kotzor. For the date, see the discussion by Cross, 'Legimus in ecclesiasticis historiis'.

[60] *English Kalendars before A. D. 1100*, ed. Wormald, no. 1.

2 May: 'Concipitur uirgo Maria cognomine senis.'[61] The Martyrology of Tallaght has a feast of Mary on 3 May (*Mariae uirginis conceptio*) and one on 7 May (*Conceptio Mariae .i. utero*),[62] and Oengus has a feast on 3 May, which is described as 'the great feast of the Virgin Mary'.[63] The feast in the English text seems therefore to reflect an Irish tradition, but, as Grosjean has shown, this feast was never actually celebrated in Ireland.[64] It originated in a mistaken reading in the version of the Hieronymian Martyrology used by the compiler of the Martyrology of Tallaght. The saint properly commemorated on this day was St Marianus of Numidia and the omission of a contraction mark seems to have resulted in the reading *Mariae*. Oengus, not knowing anything of the feast, writes merely 'great feast', but later writers interpreted it as Mary's conception. The dislocation in the English text, which has 2 May rather than 3 May, is common in this metrical calendar, whose form allows only one entry for each day.

All four main feasts of Mary are mentioned in the Old English *Menologium*, which was composed probably between 965 and 1000 and which lists the feasts which were to be kept by the English people:

> And þæs embe ane niht
> þæt we Marian   mæssan healdað
> cyninges modor,   forþan heo Crist on þam dæge
> bearn wealdendes   brohte to temple.   (19b–22; Purification)

> Hwæt, ymb feower niht   fæder onsende,
> þæs þe emnihte   eorlas healdað,
> heahengel his,   se hælo abead
> Marian mycle,   þæt heo meotod sceolde
> cennan, kyninga betst,   swa hit gecyðed wearð
> geond middangeard;   wæs þæt mære wyrd
> folcum gefræge.   (48–54a; Annunciation)

---

[61] P. McGurk, 'The Metrical Calendar of Hampson: A New Edition', *AB* 104 (1986), 79–125. The five lines quoted are 33, 84, 227, 251 and 122: 'On the second [of February] Christ the Lord is brought from the temple'; 'On the twenty-fifth [of March] the kindly virgin conceived the Lord'; 'On the fifteenth [of August] the Virgin Mary passed over the stars'; 'The very beautiful Virgin Mary was born on the eighth [of September]'; 'On the second [of May] the Virgin, Mary by name, is conceived.'

[62] *Martyrology of Tallaght*, ed. Best and Lawlor, pp. 39–40.

[63] *Félire Oengusso*, ed. Stokes, p. 122.

[64] P. Grosjean, 'Notes d'hagiographie celtique, I: La prétendue fête de la Conception de la Sainte Vierge dans les églises celtiques', *AB* 61 (1943), 91–5.

Swylce þæs ymb fif niht   fægerust mægða
wifa wuldor,   sohte weroda god
for suna sibbe,   sigefæstne ham
on neorxnawange;   hæfde nergend þa
fægere fostorlean   fæmnan forgolden
ece to ealdre.   (148–53a; Assumption)

Septembres fær,   and þy seofoþan dæg
þæt acenned wearð   cwena selost
drihtnes modor.   (167–9a; Nativity of Mary)[65]

The same four feasts are entered also in all of the Anglo-Saxon calendars printed by Francis Wormald and, especially in the later texts, are often marked by capital letters and coloured inks.[66] From the end of the tenth century onwards some of the calendars mark vigils, most commonly for the Assumption.

Around 1030 two new Marian feasts were introduced into Anglo-Saxon England: the feast of the Conception of Mary (8 December) and the feast of her Presentation in the Temple (21 November).[67] The manuscripts in which these feasts occur are of great importance for what they tell us about the introduction and dissemination of the feasts, since much confusion has been caused by inaccuracies in the dating of the manuscripts.

The feasts are noted in three eleventh-century calendars: London, BL,

[65] 'Menologium', *Anglo-Saxon Minor Poems*, ed. Dobbie, pp. 49–55: 'And [it is] one night after that we celebrate Mary's festival, the mother of the king, because she brought Christ, the son of the Lord, to the temple on that day.

Lo, four nights after men celebrate the equinox, the father sent forth his archangel, who announced salvation to Mary the great, that she would have to bring forth the creator, the best of kings, as it was made known throughout middle earth; that famous event was well known to peoples.

Also, after five nights the fairest of maidens, the glory of women, because of the relationship to her son, sought out the God of hosts, a triumphant home in paradise; then the creator had given the Virgin a fair reward for fostering, for ever and ever.

. . . September's course, and on the seventh day the most blessed of queens, the mother of the Lord, was born.'

[66] *English Kalendars before 1100*.

[67] On these feasts, see F. A. Gasquet and E. Bishop, *The Bosworth Psalter* (London, 1908), pp. 43–53; Bishop, 'On the Origins of the Feast of the Conception', in his *Liturgica Historica*, pp. 238–59; Mildner, 'The Immaculate Conception in England'; Davis, 'The Origins of Devotion'; and Van Dijk, 'The Origin of the Latin Feast of the Conception'.

Cotton Vitellius E. xviii, Cotton Titus D. xxvii and Cambridge, Corpus Christi College 391.[68] The first two manuscripts were written at Winchester and the third at Worcester. Titus D. xxvii belonged to Ælfwine and was written when he was a dean of New Minster (1023–32), but the entries for the feasts of 8 December and 21 November seem to have been added later and were dated by Edmund Bishop to the period of Ælfwine's abbacy of the New Minster (1032–57).[69] They were added in a hand very similar to the main hand, which also added many of the obits, but they begin further to the left, among the numerals, and do not, therefore, seem to be part of the original manuscript. Vitellius E. xviii is probably also a New Minster manuscript, although it seems to have been transferred to the Old Minster at a fairly early stage in its history. The hand of this calendar closely resembles the one which wrote 20r–68r of Titus D. xxvi, once part of the same manuscript as Titus D. xxvii, and the two are probably roughly contemporary.[70] Edmund Bishop, following Wanley and Hampson, dated Vitellius E. xviii *c.* 1030, presumably on the basis of the tables it contains (these run from 1030 to 1145), but Wormald, without giving any reasons, dates it *c.* 1060.[71] Ker dates it s. xi[med].[72] In Vitellius E. xviii the entries for the feasts of the Conception and the Presentation are in the original hand. Titus D. xxvii and Vitellius E. xviii have the same wording: *Oblatio Sanctae Marie in templo domini cum esset trium annorum* for 21 November and *Conceptio Sancte dei genitricis Mariae* for 8 December. CCCC 391, the so-called 'Portiforium of St Wulstan' has the same entry for 8 December, but none for 21 November. The manuscript evidence suggests, therefore, that the feasts were first introduced into England at Winchester *c.* 1030.

It is noteworthy that these are not the only innovations in Vitellius E. xviii. As Davis points out, the Eastern feasts of St John Chrysostom (27

---

[68] BL, Cotton Vitellius E. xviii is described by Ker, *Catalogue*, pp. 298–301 (no. 224), and its calendar is ed. Wormald, *English Kalendars before* A. D. 1100, no. 12. Titus D. xxvii is described by Ker, *Catalogue*, pp. 264–6 (no. 202), and its calendar is ed. Wormald, *English Kalendars before* A. D. 1100, no. 9. CCCC 391 is described by Ker, *Catalogue*, pp. 113–15 (no. 67), and its calendar is ed. Wormald, *English Kalendars before* A. D. 1100, no. 17.

[69] *Liturgica Historica*, p. 239, n. 1.

[70] For the similarity of hands, see T. A. M. Bishop, *English Caroline Minuscule* (Oxford, 1971), p. 23.

[71] Bishop, *Liturgica Historica*, p. 239, and Wormald, *English Kalendars before* A. D. 1100, p. 155.

[72] Ker, *Catalogue*, p. 298.

January) and St Catherine (25 November) are also found for the first time in this calendar.[73] The feast of St Catherine is not found in any other English calendar until a century later, and that of St John Chrysostom only in two calendars of *c.* 1060. The dates of these two feasts and of the feasts of the Presentation and the Conception of Mary fall on the same day as, or within a day of, the Eastern feasts and it appears that there was direct influence from the East. The date of 8 December is an obvious one, given that Mary's nativity was celebrated on 8 September, but the date of the Presentation is not related to any other date and the coincidence can only be explained by direct influence from the East.

For this reason the suggestion advanced by Thurston and, following him, Mildner and Southern, that the feast of 8 December could have been an English innovation, introduced on the analogy of the feast of the conception of John the Baptist, cannot be accepted.[74] More plausible is Bishop's suggestion that the Greek influence on Anglo-Saxon England could have come via the many Greek monks in southern Italy.[75] There were also Anglo-Saxons in Constantinople[76] and we know of one Greek monk, named Constantine, at Malmesbury *c.* 1030.[77]

While these entries prove that the feasts were known in England, they do not prove that they were celebrated liturgically. However, various prayers (episcopal benedictions and a proper mass) for the feasts survive in four manuscripts and prove that the entries in the calendars mark liturgical feasts and are not merely expressions of devotional interest. The four manuscripts are:[78] London, BL, Harley 2892 (a pontifical–benedictional

---

[73] Davis, 'The Origins of Devotion', pp. 377–8.

[74] H. Thurston, 'The Irish Origins of Our Lady's Conception Feast', *The Month* ns 89 (1904), 449–65; Mildner, 'The Immaculate Conception', p. 92; and R. W. Southern, *St Anselm and his Biographer* (Cambridge, 1963), p. 293. Southern argued that 'it seems quite possible that the original justification was simply the incongruity of giving John the Baptist, whose conception was widely celebrated in the Anglo-Saxon church, a liturgical honour denied to the Virgin', but, while this may have been the reason for the introduction of the feast in the East, it is very unlikely to have been true of Anglo-Saxon England.

[75] Bishop, *Liturgica Historica*, p. 258.

[76] A. A. Vasiliev, 'The Opening Stage of the Anglo-Saxon Immigration to Byzantium in the Eleventh Century', *Annales de l'Institut Kondakov (Seminarium Kondakovianum)* 9 (1937), 39–70.

[77] *Willelmi Malmesbiriensis monachi de gestis pontificum Anglorum*, ed. Hamilton, pp. 415–16.

[78] *The Canterbury Benedictional*, ed. Woolley; *The New Minster Missal*, ed. Turner; *The*

from Christ Church, Canterbury, of the first half of the eleventh century, but after 1023); Le Havre, Bibliothèque municipale, 330 (a missal from the New Minster, Winchester, s. xi^med); London, BL, Add. 28188 (a pontifical–benedictional from Exeter, dated by Ker to the second half of the eleventh century and by Drage, more specifically, to the third quarter);[79] and Oxford, Bodleian Library, Bodley 579 (the 'Leofric Missal', written in north-east France in the second half of the ninth century, with additions made in Glastonbury in the tenth century and in Exeter in the eleventh). In the first three manuscripts, the texts are all in the original hand, but in the Leofric Missal the mass for the Conception was added by the scribe whom Drage, in her detailed description of the manuscript, designated scribe 10; it is part of a series of masses which he inserted into gaps left by the original scribes.[80] He was probably one of the canons of Exeter Cathedral and was one of the latest of the scribes who made additions to the book. His work seems to have begun before Leofric's death (in 1072), as the hand which Drage thinks is Leofric's occurs with that of scribe 10 elsewhere in the book. In other words, the mass for the Conception was probably added at Exeter about the time of, or shortly after, the Conquest.

The celebration of the feast of the Conception at Exeter is explicable by the connections between Exeter and Winchester: in his drive to build up the almost non-existent cathedral library which he acquired in 1050, Leofric had copies made of many Winchester manuscripts. The benedictional, with its blessing for the feast of the Conception, is one of these,[81]

Leofric Missal, ed. Warren; BL, Add. 28188 is unedited, but see Prescott, 'The Structure of English Pre-Conquest Benedictionals', p. 130. See below pp. 82–7 on these texts. Le Havre 330 has not hitherto been used as evidence for the introduction of the feast of the Conception, as it was dated by Delisle to 1120 and was, therefore, used as a witness to the re-introduction of the feast of the Conception in twelfth-century England.

[79] Ker, *Catalogue*, p. lvii, and E. Drage, 'Bishop Leofric and the Exeter Cathedral Chapter', p. 81.

[80] E. Drage, 'Bishop Leofric and the Exeter Cathedral Chapter', p. 359.

[81] Prescott, 'The Structure of English Pre-Conquest Benedictionals', p. 130. Bishop, *Liturgica Historica*, p. 239, had already argued that the Exeter Benedictional followed pre-Conquest Winchester usage; see also Hohler, 'Some Service Books of the later Saxon Church', pp. 73 and 224, n. 56. According to Prescott, p. 130, the Exeter Benedictional predates the Sampson Pontifical and the Canterbury Benedictional and was probably compiled in the early eleventh century (the manuscript of the Sampson Pontifical is from the early eleventh century). If this were so, then the blessing for the feast of the Conception would have to be a later addition, which is very unlikely, or we

and the mass for the feast in the Leofric Missal must also have come from a Winchester source, as it is identical with the mass in the New Minster Missal, except that the latter has an extra prayer. The presence of the feasts of the Conception and of the Presentation in the Canterbury Benedictional is probably due to the fact that the Canterbury Benedictional is in some sense a Winchester collection.[82] Textually, it is closely connected with the Winchester benedictional in Add. 28188 and with the benedictional in the Sampson Pontifical, another Winchester collection. The Winchester calendar was transferred to Canterbury in the first half of the eleventh century, but Korhammer has shown that this transfer had been effected by 1010 x 1020, the date of the calendar in London, BL, Arundel 155.[83] This is too early for the feasts of the Conception and Presentation, which must, therefore, have come to Canterbury independently of, and later than, the rest of the Winchester calendar.[84]

The inclusion of the feast of the Conception in the Exeter Benedictional, which is copied from a Winchester source, suggests that it was also celebrated in the Old Minster (the cathedral priory) in Winchester. A feast kept only in the New Minster would not normally have needed a bishop's benediction, so the Exeter Benedictional was probably copied from an Old Minster manuscript.

The feast of the Conception seems, therefore, to have spread from Winchester, where it was probably kept in both the Old and the New Minsters, to Christ Church, Canterbury, and to Exeter. It is probable that the feast of the Presentation was also liturgically celebrated in Winchester,

would have to push the date of the introduction of the feast back to the beginning of the century. Dr Prescott kindly informs me (in a letter of 29 June 1988), however, that, while the order of composition Sampson-Exeter-Canterbury is impossible, the order Sampson-Canterbury-Exeter is a possibility, although only further work on the texts in both benedictionals can settle the question.

[82] *Ibid.*, pp. 132–3.

[83] P. M. Korhammer, 'The Origin of the Bosworth Psalter', *ASE* 2 (1973), 173–87.

[84] Van Dijk ('The Origin of the Latin Feast of the Conception', p. 259) suggested that the spread of the feast of the Conception from Winchester to Canterbury was linked with Ælfsige, a Winchester monk closely connected with the history of the feast of the Conception, who became abbot of St Augustine's, Canterbury, in 1061. However, this theory is based largely on an incorrect dating of the St Augustine's martyrology in London, BL, Cotton Vitellius C. xii. This manuscript dates from the very end of the eleventh century or the beginning of the twelfth, not *c.* 1070, as Van Dijk thought. The evidence of the Christ Church manuscript, Harley 2892, points to the feast having been first introduced in Canterbury at Christ Church, not St Augustine's.

as the benedictions for it in the Canterbury Benedictional seem to originate in Winchester, and we have, of course, the calendar evidence from there. The feast of the Conception may have been celebrated in Worcester, but the only evidence is the calendar entry in the Portiforium of Wulstan (CCCC 391), and this does not indicate that the feast was actually celebrated there. It is perhaps easy to overestimate the importance of the feast outside Winchester, where it was indubitably significant. The only evidence for Canterbury is the Benedictional, but no sacramentary from Canterbury survives from the period 1030–70 and it is difficult, therefore, to judge the importance of the feasts in Christ Church. The Benedictional does seem to have been prepared specifically for Christ Church, however, and the inclusion of the two feasts was presumably deliberate. In the case of Exeter, the Benedictional is copied from a Winchester exemplar, and there is evidence of material appropriate only to Winchester being copied unthinkingly at Exeter.[85] The mass, on the other hand, must have been added to the Leofric Missal with a considered purpose and we can probably assume, therefore, that the feast was liturgically celebrated there.

THE NORMAN CONQUEST AND MARIAN FEASTS

The Conquest would probably have brought no immediate changes in the persistence of the feasts, as at first the English clergy were left undisturbed in their positions. One indirect result seems to have been a further spreading of the feast of the Conception, if we can trust a legend concerning Ælfsige first reported by Anselm in his collection of Marian miracles. Freeman and Southern have both examined the historical background of the Ælfsige legend and accept it as fundamentally true.[86] It is unlikely to be a late fabrication, as Abbot Anselm lacked the knowledge of English history evident in the story of the miracle, which seems to have come from a written Ramsey source. It relates how Ælfsige (who had been a monk of the Old Minster, Winchester, until appointed abbot of St Augustine's in 1061 and acting-abbot of Ramsey in 1062) was sent to Denmark:

Tempore quo normanni angliam inuaserunt, erat quidam abbas elsinus nomine constitutus, in ecclesia sancti augustini anglorum appostoli in qua ipse requiescit, ceterique successores sui. Angliam autem subiectam normannis audientes dani,

---

[85] Bishop, *Liturgica Historica*, p. 240.
[86] Freeman, *The Norman Conquest* IV, 749–52 (Appendix P) and Southern, 'The English Origins of the "Miracles of the Virgin"'.

47

arma preparant ut ad eiciendos eos ab anglia conuenirent. Cumque talia dux potentissimus normannorum guillelmus audisset, elsinum supradictum abbatem accersitum in daciam destinauit, ut inquireret si huius rei fama uera esset an falsa. At ille concitus in daciam uenit, peracturus iussa regis atque se obtutibus presentauit regis, deferens ei munera missa a rege guillelmo, ibique detentus est tempore non parvo. Postquam ibi fecisset multum temporis, petitam a rege licentiam redeundi accepit, maremque ingrediens cum sociis, ueloci cursu peruolat equora ponti. Cumque sic eum quiete nauigareret, ecce subito tempestas ualida in mari exorta est et cum spes salutis siue abeundi uel euadendi abesset, conuersi ad dominim sic flagitabant auxilium: O deus potentissime miserere nostri in hoc examine, ne maris tempestate absorti, sociemur in penis eternis. Cumque talia et multa similia perorassent, ecce subito quendam conspiciunt, pontificatus infula decoratum proximum naui. Qui conuocans ad se elsinum abbatem, his eum uerbis affatur: Si periculum maris uis euadere, si in patriam uis sanus redire, promitte mihi coram deo, quod conceptionis matris Christi diem sollempniter celebrabis ac obseruabis. Tunc ille: quomodo inquit faciam, uel in quo die? Nuntius inquit: In vi idus decembris die celebrabis, et predicabis ubicumque poteris, quatinus ab omnibus celebretur. Et quali inquit seruicio iubes uti in hoc festo? Cui ille: Omne seruicium quod dicitur inquit in eius natiuitate, dicetur et in conceptione. Sic ubi natalicium in natiuitate dicitur, conceptio in hac celebratione dicetur. Postquam autem abbas audisset, uento prospero flante anglicis littoribus adiungitur. Mox cuncta quae uiderat, uel audierat, quibuscumque potuit, innotuit. Statuitque in ramesiensi ecclesia cui ipse praeerat, ut hoc festum omni anno sollempniter vi idus decembris celebraretur.[87]

[87] *Miracula Sanctae Virginis Mariae*, ed. E. F. Dexter, University of Wisconsin Stud. in the Social Stud. and Histories 12 (Madison, Wis., 1927), pp. 37–8. 'At the time when the Normans invaded England, there was a certain abbot, Ælfsige by name, installed in the church of St Augustine, the apostle of the English, in which he himself is buried and the rest of his successors. However, the Danes, hearing that England was subject to the Normans, prepared arms in order to unite to throw them out of England. And when William the mighty duke of the Normans heard this, he summoned the aforementioned Abbot Ælfsige and sent him to Denmark, to find out if the report of this event was true or false And he [the abbot] came in haste to Denmark, in order to carry out the commands of the king and presented himself before the king, bringing to him gifts sent by King William, and he was detained there for some time. After he had spent much time there, he asked and received permission from the king to return home, and setting out on the sea with his companions he flew swiftly over the smooth surface of the sea. And when he was sailing calmly in this way, suddenly a violent storm rose in the sea and, when hope of safety or getting away or escaping disappeared, they turned to God and thus called for help: "O Almighty God, have pity on us in this ordeal lest, devoured by the sea, we are united in eternal punishment." When they had finished speaking this and many similar prayers, suddenly they saw a person, decorated with episcopal insignia, near the ship.

From this account we can deduce that Ælfsige knew of the feast of the Conception but did not celebrate it with his monks at Ramsey. That he knew of the feast is not surprising, as he had been a monk of the Old Minster and was a close associate of Archbishop Stigand, who, as bishop of both Winchester and Canterbury in plurality, probably celebrated the feast. That Ælfsige had not already introduced the feast at Ramsey, where he had been abbot for some four years at the time of the Conquest, may imply that he had met with some opposition and needed supernatural help. His position as acting-abbot may not have given him sufficient authority to enforce this observance without such heavenly aid.

An interesting aspect of this story is the liturgical instructions given by the bishop in the apparition. He specifies that the services are to be those of the Nativity of Mary, with *conceptio* substituted for *natiuitas*. If Ælfsige had celebrated the feast at Winchester and knew of its observance at Christ Church he may have been acquainted with the mass for the feast in the New Minster Missal (Le Havre 330). It is possible that the stress on the use of the Nativity services may have been a deliberate attempt to change the emphasis of the feast. The use of the mass for the Nativity would remove the apocryphal bias and the stress on the miraculous annunciation of Mary's birth in the Winchester and Canterbury texts for the feast. Instead, it would have a hallowed text, of unquestioned orthodoxy, implying that the object of the feast was doctrinally no different from that of the feast of the Nativity. The legend reads like an attempt to counter objections to the celebration, and was later used for precisely this purpose. Ælfsige moved in the circle of the Conqueror, and objections could have been formulated here at an early date. Both the supernatural command and the liturgical

He called Abbot Ælfsige to him and addressed him in these words: "If you wish to escape from the danger of the sea, if you wish to return to your native country safely, promise me in the presence of God that you will solemnly celebrate and observe the feast-day of the conception of the mother of Christ." Then the abbot said: "How am I to do this or on what day?" The messenger said: "You will celebrate it on the eighth day of December, and will preach wherever you can, that it may be celebrated by everybody." Ælfsige said: "And what sort of divine service do you command us to use on this feast?" He replied to him: "Let every service which is said at her nativity be said also at her conception. Thus, when her birthday is mentioned at her nativity, let her conception be mentioned in this other celebration." After the abbot heard this, he reached the English shore with a favourable wind blowing. Soon he made known everything he had seen or heard to whomever he could, and he ordered in the church at Ramsey, over which he had presided, that this feast be solemnly celebrated on 8 December.'

49

specifications seem designed to meet opposition to the innovation as well as the apocryphal content of the liturgy of the feast.

The two feasts seem to have been abolished soon after the date of Ælfsige's vision. In 1070 Stigand was deposed by papal legates and Lanfranc became the new archbishop. He instituted a reform of the Canterbury calendar, abolishing many of the feasts peculiar to Anglo-Saxon England. The feasts of the Presentation and the Conception seem to have been among the casualties, as there is no mention of either in Lanfranc's *Constitutions*.[88] The feasts also seem to have been abolished by the new Norman abbot at Winchester, Walchelin, as the New Minster calendar in London, British Library, Arundel 60, of the second half of the eleventh century, has neither feast. Nor is there any evidence that the feast continued to be celebrated at Exeter. It has been suggested that the feast of the Conception lived on at Ramsey, whence it was transferred to Fécamp when Herbert of Losinga, who had been a monk of Fécamp, became abbot of Ramsey. The evidence assembled by Fournée to support this argument is not convincing, however, as the feast occurs only in twelfth-century documents from Fécamp.[89] These are more likely to be witnesses to Fécamp's adoption of the twelfth-century English feast. It is probable that the feast died out in Ramsey after Ælfsige's death (Ælfsige fled to Denmark in 1070, when Stigand was deposed, but returned in 1080 and was abbot of Ramsey until his death in 1087).

CONCLUSIONS

By the end of the Anglo-Saxon period, then, the feasts of the Purification, Annunciation, Assumption, Nativity of Mary, Presentation in the Temple and Conception were being celebrated in England – the first four throughout the country, the Presentation and Conception in a few centres. The feasts of the Purification, Annunciation, Assumption and Nativity of Mary were introduced gradually in England in the course of the seventh century and the eighth, with some initial confusion, most which can be traced back to an ancestor of *Martyrologium Hieronymianum Epternacense*. The feasts of the Presentation and Conception were first introduced *c.* 1030 in Winchester and spread from there to Canterbury and Exeter. These two

[88] *Decreta Lanfranci (The Monastic Constitutions of Lanfranc)*, ed. D. Knowles (London, 1951).
[89] See J. Fournée, 'L'abbaye de Fécamp'.

feasts were not celebrated anywhere else in Western Europe at this date and their adoption must be the result of Eastern influence on Anglo-Saxon devotion. That Winchester monks were willing to adopt the two new feasts is an important manifestation of their developed interest in the Virgin in the late Anglo-Saxon period in particular.

3

The cult of the Virgin in the liturgy

The growth of the cult of the Virgin in the liturgy of the early Middle Ages in the West can be divided into two periods: the first is centred on the introduction of the four principal feasts, largely in the seventh and eighth centuries, while the second, from the tenth century onwards, saw extra devotional practices being developed and disseminated. This pattern, which was general throughout the West, can also be discerned clearly in the English evidence.

THE SEVENTH AND EIGHTH CENTURIES

Mary's role in the early Anglo-Saxon liturgy must have been intimately linked to the introduction in England of the four Roman feasts, as this naturally gave rise to a need for mass and Office texts for these days. We cannot, unfortunately, chart the gradual introduction of such texts in Anglo-Saxon manuscripts of the seventh, eighth and ninth centuries because there is a dearth of liturgical books from this period, with only fragments of sacramentaries and very little material related to the Divine Office surviving.[1] Since the feasts of the Purification, Annunciation, Assumption and Nativity of the Virgin were introduced from Rome, however, it is probable that texts from there also found their way to England to supplement the liturgical material imported by the missionaries and by Anglo-Saxon book-collectors such as Benedict Biscop.

When liturgical books become more plentiful in the tenth and eleventh centuries, we find that almost all the masses for these feasts are taken from the Gregorian sacramentary: this is the case in, for example, the New

[1] See Gneuss, 'Liturgical Books in Anglo-Saxon England', p. 94, and Mayr-Harting, *The Coming of Christianity*, pp. 272–5.

The cult of the Virgin in the liturgy

Minster Missal from Winchester, although, as with most of these later books, there is some admixture of Gallican elements.[2] The Gregorian masses are also likely to have been available in the earlier period. These masses do not, in general, testify to a very advanced state of Marian devotion, demonstrating instead the type of reserve which Bishop regarded as characteristic of the Roman rite, its 'soberness and sense'.[3] Mary figures only as the mother of God, whose intercession is implored and whose pure virginity is invoked, and many of the texts originally came from the liturgy for the feasts of holy virgins.[4] The emphasis is firmly Christological, except in the Assumption text, *Veneranda nobis*, which alludes to the Virgin's assumption in surprisingly explicit terms: 'Veneranda nobis, Domine, huius est diei festiuitas, in qua sancta Dei genetrix mortem subiit temporalem, nec tamen mortis nexibus deprimi potuit, quae filium tuum dominum nostrum de se genuit incarnatum: per.'[5] This celebration is out of keeping with the rest of the mass for the feast and its Marian-centredness is a clear departure from the view of the Virgin which concentrates on her relationship to Christ in the context of biblical events.

As with the mass texts, we can assume that texts for the Office would also have been imported into England. We know, for example, that John, precentor of St Peter's in Rome, came to Wearmouth in 679–80 to teach singing to the cantors there:[6] by that date all four feasts of the Virgin had been established in Rome and it is natural to suppose that John's teaching would have included chants for the mass and Office of these days. The Roman Marian chants, thus introduced by teachers and manuscripts (which until the ninth century, at the earliest, would have contained only the words, with no music), had been composed from the second half of the seventh century onwards, building on the developed repertory of Marian chants already available for the Advent and Christmas periods. These Advent and Christmas antiphons and responds, in celebrating the coming of the Saviour and Mary's virgin birth, had drawn principally on the

[2] *The Missal of the New Minster*, ed. Turner.
[3] Bishop, 'The Genius of the Roman Rite', in his *Liturgica Historica*, pp. 1–19, at 19.
[4] See Frénaud, 'Le culte de Notre-Dame'.
[5] Deshusses, *Le sacramentaire grégorien*, pp. 262–3, and see also the discussion by B. Capelle, 'L'oraison "veneranda" à la messe de l'assomption', in his *Travaux liturgiques* III, 387–9: 'Honoured by us, O Lord, is the feast of this day, on which the blessed mother of God underwent temporal death, but could not, however, be oppressed by the bonds of death, who had given birth to your son, our incarnate lord.'
[6] *Venerabilis Baedae opera historica*, ed. Plummer I, 240–1.

53

gospels, particularly on the beginnings of Luke and Matthew, on the Old Testament prophecies, the Psalms and, as Barré has shown, on Caelius Sedulius and on sermons for the Christmas season, especially the Pseudo-Augustinian African sermons available in contemporary homiliaries.[7] All of these diverse elements were consolidated and 'le formulaire marial de l'Avent et de Noêl se présente comme un tout, remarquablement homogène et trés équilibré dans l'organisation interne de ses diverses parties'.[8] These Advent and Christmas antiphons were probably composed in the second half of the sixth century,[9] and in tone and vocabulary are far more fervent in their attitude towards the Virgin than is the Gregorian sacramentary. Their Marian fervour derives largely from the African texts, which had themselves been heavily influenced by oriental sources. The homogeneity evident in them is, however, lacking in the chants for the four feasts of the Virgin. These depend on the Advent and Christmas chants to some extent (completely, in the case of the Annunciation), as well as drawing again on the same sources, in a few cases on Greek antiphons and, especially for the feast of the Assumpion, on the Song of Songs.[10] Despite the differences, many of them demonstrate the same willingness to celebrate Mary as do the Advent and Christmas texts, and Barré compares the fullness and lyricism of the liturgy for the Assumption with that of Christmas, pointing out, too, that 'Le thème central en est toujours le même, et la joie déborde à nouveau en cette "exaltation" suprême de la Mère bénie du Sauveur'.[11]

The masses and the antiphons which were probably introduced into England would, then, have complemented each other in their treatment of the Virgin, expressing both reserve and exuberance. The one extensive early group of Marian antiphons connected with England is, however, very unlike any other collection: it thus raises interesting questions about the nature of the liturgical texts available in Anglo-Saxon England. The antiphons in question are contained in the fourth book of a devotional

---

[7] Barré, 'Antiennes et répons', pp. 160–207.

[8] *Ibid.*, p. 204: 'The Marian formulary for Advent and Christmas appears as a whole, remarkably homogeneous and very balanced in the internal organization of its different parts.'

[9] *Ibid.*, p. 204.   [10] *Ibid.*, pp. 207–45.

[11] *Ibid.*, p. 234: 'The central theme is still the same in it and joy overflows anew in the supreme "exaltation" of the blessed mother of the Saviour.'

anthology, *De laude Dei*, which was compiled by Alcuin at York *c.* 790.[12]
This fourth book includes a selection of ninety-three antiphons, headed *De antiphonario*, covering the period (with some notable omissions) from Advent to Pentecost and the feast of the Assumption. The collection as a whole corresponds with no other and Rankin argues that:

> Comparison of the hundred or so liturgical texts assembled by Alcuin in his *De laude Dei* (under the heading *De antiphonario*) with chant repertories from other European regions suggests that Gregory's directions to gather together the best of Roman, English, Frankish and other liturgical material had, generally speaking, been followed in England, if not invariably: Alcuin's collection includes texts of demonstrably Roman, Gallican and possibly Hispanic provenance, and many which have no concordances elsewhere and may represent native English compositions just as well as an older layer, now lost, of Roman chant.[13]

The feasts of the Virgin included are those of the Purification and Assumption and, Constantinescu argues, the Spanish Marian feast of 18 December, but there are no rubrics in the manuscript. The three Purification antiphons do not refer to the Virgin, but this is amply compensated for in the last section of *De antiphonario*, where fourteen antiphons celebrate her:

80 Porta facta coeli, uirgo Maria facta est filia Dei.

81 Benedicta tu inter mulieres, per quam maledictio matris Aeuae soluta est.

82 Exaltata es, sancta Dei genitrix, super choros angelorum ad coelestia regna.

83 Gaude et laetare, sancta Dei genitrix, quae uero uirginali hospicio coelo, terris infernisque terribilem Dominum nobis propicium meruisti.

84 Vere benedicta imperatrix et gloriosa castitatis regina, quae cum honore uirginitatis gaudium matris habes.

85 Salue, sancta parens, gratia plena Maria, in quo decus angelicae integritatis cunctis uenerandum praefulget.

86 Te iusta laude praedicamus, salutis nostrae genitrix, cuius uterus intemeratus coelesti sponso thalamus est consecratus.

87 Gloriosa semper uirgo, uirga radicis Iesse, de qua uitae flos processit, intercede pro nobis.

88 Beatam praedicant omnes angeli, cui angelorum et hominum regem procreare donatum est.

89 Beata es, Maria, quae meruisti Dominum Iesum portare in utero.

---

[12] See Constantinescu, 'Alcuin et les "libelli precum"', pp. 38–55, and Bullough, 'Alcuin and the Kingdom of Heaven', pp. 4–8.

[13] Rankin, 'Liturgical Background', p. 322.

90 Sancta Maria, semper uirgo, domina sanctarum uirginum et omnes sancti angeli, orate pro nobis.

91 Deprecamur te, mater Iesu.

92 Te laudant angeli, archangeli, et clamant martyres sancti: Beata es, uirgo Maria, inter mulieres et benedicta.

93 Sancta Maria, nos laudamus te, gloriosa, glorificamus te, corona regni coronata es, intercede pro nobis, quia beata es. [14]

Bullough suggests that, despite the liturgical ordering of the collection, this section may not have been derived from the Office for the Assumption, as 'none of Alcuin's passages occurs in precisely the same form in any known antiphonary'[15] and 'after the first text in the group . . . the emphasis is on the ever-virginity of Mary and her motherhood of God'.[16] This latter objection, however, is not compelling, as texts for all the feasts of Mary tend naturally to extol her in her most central role, that of virgin

---

[14] Constantinescu, 'Alcuin et les "libelli precum"', pp. 49–51:

80 She is made the gate of heaven, the Virgin Mary is made the daughter of God.

81 Blessed are you among women, through whom the curse of the mother Eve is dissolved.

82 Blessed mother of God, you are exalted above the choirs of angels to the celestial domains.

83 Rejoice and be glad, O blessed mother of God, who by your truly virginal hospitality obtained for us the favour of the Lord who is feared in heaven, earth and hell.

84 Truly blessed empress and glorious queen of chastity, who possesses the joy of a mother with the honour of virginity.

85 Hail, holy parent, Mary full of grace, in whom the virtue of angelic integrity shines out, venerated by all.

86 We laud you with just praise, mother of our salvation, whose undefiled womb is consecrated as the bridal chamber of the heavenly bridegroom.

87 O glorious ever virgin, a rod from the root of Jesse, from whom the flower of life came forth, intercede for us.

88 All angels proclaim her blessed, to whom it was granted to beget the king of angels and men.

89 Blessed are you, Mary, who deserved to bear in your womb the Lord Jesus.

90 Holy Mary, ever virgin, mistress of holy virgins, and all holy angels, pray for us.

91 We pray to you, mother of Jesus.

92 Angels and archangels praise you, and the holy martyrs cry out: 'Happy are you, O virgin Mary, amongst women and blessed.'

93 We praise you, O glorious one, we glorify you, you are crowned with the crown of the kingdom, intercede for us, for you are blessed.

[15] 'Alcuin and the Kingdom of Heaven', p. 7.   [16] *Ibid.*, p. 8.

mother of God. In addition, antiphon no. 82, 'Exaltata es, sancta Dei genitrix, super choros angelorum ad coelestia regna', does occur in the ninth-century antiphonary of Compiègne and very frequently in later antiphonaries as a text for the feast of the Assumption and was clearly explicitly composed for this occasion.[17] It was also known to Paschasius Radbertus as an antiphon for the Assumption, as he refers to it in *Cogitis me*.[18] The section, therefore, does seem to have been intended for this feast. Although parts of many other of the fourteen texts can be paralleled, no other antiphon occurs in the same form in later antiphonaries for the Office and the sources of this section of *De antiphonario* present a particular problem. Constantinescu argues that the antiphons were inspired, or composed, by Ildefonsus of Toledo and adduces parallels in the sermons printed under Ildefonsus's name by Migne.[19] Many of the parallels are of the most general nature, however, and do not constitute proof of common authorship. The sermons, moreover, are not by Ildefonsus: he did not compose any of the sermons attributed to him in PL 96 and the text most frequently adduced by Constantinescu, *Sermo* ii, is thought to be the work of Paschasius Radbertus, because of the many similarities between it and *Cogitis me*.[20] The parallels between *Sermo* ii and the antiphons prove, if anything, the influence that liturgical texts had on the author of the sermon, not that it was composed by the same author. There is nothing to suggest, then, that the antiphons were composed in Spain.

Although only one of the texts (no. 82) is exactly paralleled in other antiphonaries, many of the others are either close to well-attested Marian antiphons in structure and content or else appear to depend on the same type of source. Antiphons nos. 80 and 81 recall 'Paradisi porta per Euam

---

[17] Barré, 'Antiennes et répons', p. 224 (no. 99).

[18] *Der Pseudo-Hieronymus-Brief IX 'Cogitis me'*, ed. Ripberger, p. 77.

[19] 'Alcuin et les "libelli precum"', p. 49, nn. 130–42; the sermons are in PL 96, 239–84.

[20] H. Barré, 'Le sermon "Exhortatur" est-il de Saint Ildefonse?', *RB* 67 (1957), 10–33, at 10–13; A. Braegelmann, *The Life and Writings of Saint Ildefonsus of Toledo*, The Catholic University of America, Studies in Mediaeval History ns 4 (Washington, DC, 1942), 158–63; and R. Maloy, 'The Sermonary of St Ildephonsus', *Classical Folia* 25 (1971), 137–99 and 243–301. Bullough, 'Alcuin and the Kingdom of Heaven', p. 8, points to the dubious attribution of these sermons, but says nevertheless that a Spanish origin is not implausible for the antiphons.

clausa est, et per Mariam iterum patefacta est, alleluia'[21] and 'Paradisi portae per te nobis apertae sunt, quae hodie gloriosa cum angelis triumphas.'[22] The 'gaude et laetare' of antiphon no. 83 is frequent also, as in 'In prole mater, in partu uirgo, gaude et laetare, Virgo mater Domini.'[23] Antiphon no. 86 is similar to 'Maria uirgo, semper laetare, quae meruisti Christum portare caeli et terrae conditorem, quia de tuo utero protulisti mundi Saluatorem.'[24] Other Marian antiphons include the phrases 'Te laudant angeli', 'Dei genitrix, intercede pro nobis' and 'Te laudamus, Dei genitrix.'[25] Two texts (nos. 84 and 85) are dependent on the *Carmen Paschale* of Caelius Sedulius, which had already served as a source for antiphons for the Christmas period, as, for instance: 'Genuit puerpera regem, cui nomen aeternum, et gaudia matris habens cum uirginitate pudoris, nec primam similem uisa est, nec habere sequentem, alleluia.'[26] This and the *De laude* antiphons clearly follow the wording of a passage of Caelius Sedulius:

> quae uentre beato
> Gaudia matris habens cum uirginitatis honore
> Nec primam similem uisa es nec habere sequentem:
> Sola sine exemplo placuisti femina Christo.[27]

The first antiphon of the *De laude* group (no. 80) is very close to a passage in the African Pseudo-Augustinian *Sermo* cxcv, a text which had already served as source for other antiphons: this sermon includes, in a speech of

21 See Barré, 'Antiennes et répons', p. 225, no. 102: 'The gate of paradise was closed by Eve, and was opened again by Mary, alleluia.'
22 *Ibid.*, p. 225, no. 103: 'The gates of paradise were opened to us by you, who glorious today triumph with the angels.'
23 *Ibid.*, p. 225, no. 101: 'Mother in offspring, virgin in birth, rejoice and be glad, virgin mother of God.'
24 *Ibid.*, p. 224, no. 100: 'Virgin Mary, rejoice always, who deserved to bear Christ, author of heaven and earth, because you brought forth from your womb the saviour of the earth.'
25 *Ibid.*, p. 185, no. 45; p. 196, no. 59; p. 196, no. 60.
26 *Ibid.*, pp. 179–80, no. 37: 'The woman in childbirth gave birth to the king, whose name is eternal, and, having the joy of a mother with the virginity of purity, her like was not seen beforehand, nor did she have a follower.'
27 *Sedulii opera omnia*, ed. Huemer, pp. 48–9, lines 66–9: 'who, having in your blessed womb the joys of a mother together with the dignity of virginity, neither was your like seen before, nor do you have a follower: you, without a model, were the only woman to please Christ'.

Mary's, 'Porta facta sum coeli; ianua facta sum Filio Dei', and later in the same text she is termed 'filia Dei'.[28] Similarly, *Sermo* cxciv, probably a seventh-century Italian text drawing on African Christmas homilies, includes 'Maledictio Euae in benedictionem mutatur Mariae . . .'[29] Antiphon no. 84 recalls a passage in a Christmas homily by Peter Chrysologus: 'Vere benedicta uirgo, quae et uirginitatis possidet decus, matris et pertulit dignitatem. Vere benedicta, quae et superni conceptus meruit gratiam, et sustulit integritatis coronam. Vere benedicta, quae et diuini germinis suscepit gloriam, et regina totius exstitit castitatis.'[30] The *De laude* texts, then, seem to draw on the same type of source as the earlier antiphons, as well as probably drawing directly on the earlier antiphons themselves.

We do not, of course, know whether these Assumption antiphons were composed as a group or whether they were collected together from different sources, which could have been composed at different times in different centres. They give an impression of coherence, with elements such as pleas for Mary's intercession, celebration of her especially blessed status and an exuberant joy at her ever-virgin state running through the group, but it must also be admitted that these themes are perhaps rather predictable in such a context and cannot be taken as proof of single authorship. Insofar as sources and analogues point to a place of origin, Rome appears most likely, as the antiphons seem to reflect a similar milieu and the availability of the same type of source material as the Roman antiphons for Advent and Christmas analysed by Barré. The emphasis on Mary's royalty ('benedicta imperatrix et gloriosa castitatis regina', 'corona regni coronata es') would also fit Rome, as it was there that the iconography of *Maria regina* was developed.[31] Given the degree of ardour which they show, a date at the end of the seventh or the beginning of the eighth century (in other words, very shortly after the introduction of the feast) would be most likely, as Rome was then heavily influenced by the East, where Marian fervour was always stronger. Later Roman books do not contain this group, but since our

[28] PL 39, 2107–10, at 2107 and 2108: 'I have been made the door of heaven, I have been made the entrance of the son of God.'

[29] PL 39, 2104–7, at 2105: 'The curse of Eve is changed into the blessing of Mary.'

[30] PL 52, 584: 'Truly blessed virgin, who both possesses the honour of virginity and bears the dignity of a mother. Truly blessed, who deserved the grace of a celestial conception and bore up the crown of integrity. Truly blessed, who received the glory of the divine offshoot and became the queen of all chastity.'

[31] See below, p. 146.

earliest Roman witnesses date from no earlier than the eleventh century,[32] these texts could represent an early tradition, superseded by more recent compositions. The early history of the Office antiphonary is very obscure, especially in Rome, and we do not know to what extent separate traditions existed; the *De laude* Assumption texts may well be our sole witness to a lost strand, similar to but different from the texts which have come down to us.[33]

In addition to the Assumption antiphons, *De laude Dei* includes, in its series of ten *O* antiphons, two which allude to Mary: 'O uirgo uirginum', a very widespread and old text which draws on Sedulius, and the otherwise unknown 'O Joseph . . .'[34] It also contains what Constantinescu terms 'une bénédiction métrique prononcée à vêpres le 18 décembre',[35] which he considers Spanish and perhaps by Ildefonsus of Toledo:

> Gaude nouo partu saeclis   clarissima uirgo
> Gloria summo Deo teneant   terrestria pacem
> Lux noua enituit
> Coelorum gloria terris
> Saluet nos sophia Patris.[36]

There is no other evidence for knowledge of the Marian feast of 18 December in England, however, and the text is more likely to be for the feast of Mary on the Sunday preceding Christmas, as this is attested in some early monastic *ordines*,[37] or to be an Advent or Christmas text, as its content suggests.

[32] See H. Hucke, 'Gregorian and Old Roman Chant', *The New Grove Dictionary of Music and Musicians*, 20 vols., ed. S. Sadie (London, Washington DC and Hong Kong, 1980) VII, 693–7.

[33] All of the antiphons quoted here as analogues are contained in the twelfth-century antiphonary of St Peter's in Rome, Vatican City, Biblioteca Apostolica Vaticana, S. Pietro B. 79, one of the two Old Roman antiphonaries extant, as well as in the Gregorian or Roman-Frankish books: they presumably belong to one of the oldest strata of Assumption texts and were probably composed in Rome.

[34] See below, p. 187.   [35] 'Alcuin et les "libelli precum"', p. 42, n. 91.

[36] *Ibid.*, p. 42:

> Rejoice, brightest virgin, in the new birth for the world:
> Let all things earthly possess peace in glory to the highest God.
> A new light shone out,
> Glory of the heavens for the earth,
> May the wisdom of the Father save us.

[37] See above, p. 28.

As *De laude Dei* is a devotional florilegium, we cannot place too much emphasis on those occasions which are omitted in the collection, but it is noticeable that only the two earliest of the four main Marian feasts are included. The Annunciation is lacking in many other antiphonaries, as texts from Advent and Christmas were used for this feast, but the absence of the Nativity of Mary is perhaps an indication of the date when the exemplar left Rome. The Nativity was the last of the four feasts to be introduced in Rome (*c.* 660–70) and its Office antiphonary was presumably, therefore, the last to be formed.

The *De laude Dei* texts, then, are almost our only positive proof of the nature of the early Anglo-Saxon liturgy for feasts of the Virgin, although much else can be surmised. The uniqueness of this antiphonary's Assumption texts should serve as a warning, however: it is not what we might have expected and implies that the early Anglo-Saxon liturgy was indeed diverse and complicated.

THE BENEDICTINE REFORM PERIOD

Apart from *De laude Dei*, there is no body of evidence as to how the Virgin was celebrated in the liturgy of the early Anglo-Saxon church, but it seems that the masses and Offices for the four feasts were the only liturgical manifestation of devotion to Mary in the early centuries. When liturgical manuscripts become more numerous in the tenth and eleventh centuries, all of them, where it is within their scope, provide for these occasions. The feasts also gradually gained in importance throughout the Anglo-Saxon period, with calendars and liturgical manuscripts testifying to the addition of vigils and octave celebrations, and, as with other feasts, the liturgy was embellished with tropes and sequences imported during the Benedictine reform. Thus the original part of the Leofric Missal, for example, includes a mass for the vigil of any Marian feast, masses for the Purification and the Annunciation, for the vigil and feast of the Assumption and for the Nativity.[38] The New Minster Missal contains masses for the vigil and feast of the Purification, the feast of the Annunciation and the vigils and feasts of the Assumption and Nativity.[39] The texts used for the four feasts are almost all taken from the Gregorian sacramentary, with some extra elements. The Gregorian sacramentary contains very few proper prefaces

---

[38] *The Leofric Missal*, ed. Warren.   [39] *The Missal of the New Minster*, ed. Turner.

and, where the English books contain extra prefaces, they have been added from other sources, probably Gallican. The Marian benedictions in the Anglo-Saxon benedictionals came from Gallican sources too, when they were not composed in England, as they were not a feature of the Roman liturgy.[40] But these four feasts of the Virgin were also augmented by new celebrations and it is to these that we must now turn. In England, almost all of these additions to the established round of Marian devotions appear to date from the middle of the tenth century onwards and they are attested largely in texts from centres of reformed monasticism.

The 'Regularis concordia'

The *Regularis concordia*, the rule for the reformed monasteries written *c.* 970, prescribes a mass for Mary on Saturdays, texts for which can be found in Anglo-Saxon sacramentaries: 'Hoc semper attendendum ut sexta feria de cruce, sabbato de Sancta Maria, nisi festiua aliqua dies euenerit, Missa celebretur principalis.'[41] We do not know whether the introduction of the Saturday mass in England predates the *Regularis concordia*, but the celebration of such a votive mass to Mary goes back to the innovations Alcuin brought about on the continent at the end of the eighth century. He seems to have been the first to compose a votive mass to the Virgin, which was included in his sacramentary along with his other votive masses.[42] These votive masses and others taken from the Gelasian sacramentary formed a supplement to the sacramentary which Alcuin produced by integrating Gelasian masses into the Gregorian sacramentary sent to Charlemagne by Hadrian. They were not included in the 'official' Frankish sacramentary, the *Hucusque*, edited soon afterwards, probably by Benedict of Aniane, but this did not prevent their widespread adoption. Alcuin himself does not seem to have assigned the votive masses to particular days (except that of the Trinity to Sunday), but this was done within a few

---

[40] See Prescott, 'The Structure of English Pre-Conquest Benedictionals'. The two main types of benedictional are the 'Gallican' and the 'Gregorian', both of which were compiled in Gaul. The benedictions for the feasts of Mary were taken from both types and new benedictions were also composed. See the tables in Prescott, pp. 134–55, and below, pp. 84–8.

[41] *Regularis concordia*, ed. Symons, p. 20: 'It must always be borne in mind that the principal Mass shall be of the Cross on Fridays and of St Mary on Saturdays, unless a feast-day occurs' (trans. Symons, p. 20).

[42] Barré and Deshusses, 'A la recherche du Missel d'Alcuin', pp. 17–32.

decades of his death, and the mass to Mary was then assigned to Saturday. Barré and Deshusses consider that the main reason for this was its position after the mass to the Cross, which, in memory of Good Friday, was assigned to Friday: 'Certes, on invoquera le repos sabbatique, où la Compassion du Calvaire, mais ces considérations apparaissent beaucoup trop tardivement pour être retenues comme décisives.'[43] Alcuin's votive masses may have been introduced in England before the Benedictine reform, since it is probable that he himself would have sent copies to York, as he did to Saint-Vaast and Fulda. The mass itself is firmly within the tradition of orthodox, sober Marian devotion: Mary is important only as virgin mother of God and her intercession is implored because of this, but there is no mention of anything outside this role.[44]

The *Regularis concordia* also prescribes a further Marian devotion: after Lauds and Vespers, when the psalms for the king and queen and benefactors have been sung, 'cantent antiphonam de cruce, inde antiphonam de sancta Maria et de sancto cuius ueneratio in praesenti colitur ecclesia aut, si minus fuerit, de ipsius loci consecratione'.[45] The *Regularis concordia* does not specify what this antiphon is and it is probable that it was not an antiphon in the normal sense of the word (a short, usually scriptural, sentence recited before and after the psalms and canticles in the divine Office), but a votive antiphon or suffrage. Suffrages, also called commemorations or memorials, were usually appended to Vespers and Lauds and consisted in their fullest form of an antiphon, versicle, respond and collect.[46] The early tenth-century southern English collectar and capitulary, Durham, Cathedral Library, A. IV. 19, preserves a series of such suffrages, which in the manuscript are termed antiphons, and here they are composed of an antiphon and collect or an antiphon, versicle and collect, as in the following examples, which depend on familiar liturgical texts, rearranged for this new context:

[43] 'A la recherche du Missel d'Alcuin', p. 28: 'Certainly, the rest on the sabbath or the compassion of Calvary will be appealed to, but these considerations appear much too late to be accepted as decisive.'

[44] PL 101, 455.

[45] *Regularis concordia*, ed. Symons, p. 14: 'they shall sing the antiphons of the Cross, of St Mary and of the saint whose name is honoured in that church or, if there be none such, of the dedication of that church' (trans. Symons, p. 14).

[46] See Batiffol, *History of the Roman Breviary*, p. 145, n. 4, and A. Hughes, *Medieval Manuscripts for the Mass and Office: A Guide to their Organization and Terminology* (Toronto, 1982), p. xxxi.

AN'

Maria uirgo, semper laetare quae meruisti christum portare, caeli et terrę conditorem, et de tuo utero protulisti mundi saluatorem. v'. defusa est gratia in labiis tuis, propterea benedixit te.

OREMUS

Famulorum tuorum quesumus, domine, delictis ignosce, ut qui placere de actibus nostris non ualemus, genitricis filii tui domini nostri iesu christi intercessione saluemur. per.

AN'

Beata mater et innupta uirgo, gloriosa regina mundi.

OREMUS

OR'. Concede nos famulos tuos, quesumus, domine deus, perpetua mentis et corporis sanitate gaudere, et gloriosa beatae mariae semper uirginis intercessione, a presenti liberari tristitia et futura perfrui laetitia. per.[47]

The mid-eleventh-century Exeter collectar, London, BL, Harley 2961, prescribes a Marian suffrage, again termed an antiphon, from the first Sunday of Advent to the vigil of Christmas:

De sancta maria usque uigiliam domini decantanda est ad matutinam hęc antiphona.
Spiritus sanctus iń te descendit maria. v'. Aue maria gratia plena.
AD VESPEROS. *ant.* Ne timeas maria inuenisti.
v'. Diffusa est.

Collecta

Deus, qui de beatę marię uirginis utero uerbum tuum angelo annunciante carnem

---

[47] *Rituale Ecclesiae Dunelmensis: The Durham Collectar*, ed. U. Lindelöf and A. H. Thompson, Surtees Society 140 (Durham, 1927), 151: 'AN'. Virgin Mary, rejoice always because you deserved to bear Christ, author of heaven and earth, and brought forth the saviour of the world from your womb.

v'. Grace is poured forth from your lips, therefore he has blessed you.

LET US PRAY. Forgive, we beseech, O Lord, the offences of your servants, so that we, who cannot please you because of our deeds, may be saved by the intercession of the mother of your son, our lord, Jesus Christ.

AN'. Blessed mother and unmarried virgin, glorious queen of the world.

LET US PRAY. Grant to us your servants, we beseech you, O Lord God, that we may enjoy perpetual health of mind and body, and, through the intercession of the blessed Mary ever virgin, we may be delivered from present sorrow and possess eternal joy.'

suscipere uoluisti, presta supplicibus tuis ut, qui uere eam dei genetricem credimus, eius apud te intercessionibus adiuuemur.[48]

It is not only the evidence of these manuscripts which suggests that the *Regularis concordia* is here enjoining the recitation of a suffrage of Mary and the Cross. London, BL, Cotton Tiberius A. iii, a mid-eleventh-century Canterbury manuscript, contains an Office of Mary and to Lauds and Vespers it appends a series of suffrages.[49] Tolhurst is probably right in suggesting that 'this text of the office of Our Lady is so arranged that its Vespers and Lauds are substituted for the suffrage [of Mary] and that the other suffrages, with some additions, follow immediately after these hours'.[50] The suffrages which follow this Office of Mary consist of what is probably an antiphon, followed by a versicle and a collect. As with the prescription of the Saturday mass, the recitation of daily suffrages demonstrates the important role assigned to the Virgin in the *Regularis concordia*, while, in extending the suffrage to a full Office of Mary, Tiberius A. iii testifies to her increasing significance within the liturgical life of one Anglo-Saxon house, Christ Church, Canterbury.

Offices of the Virgin

This Canterbury Office of the Virgin is not the only form of Marian Office introduced in England in the eleventh century. The early history of the Offices of Mary is obscure and it is complicated by the fact that early allusions, and many modern commentators, do not distinguish between the various forms this devotion could assume.[51] There are at least three

---

[48] *The Leofric Collectar* I, ed. Dewick, cols. 4–5:
'*This antiphon concerning holy Mary is to be sung up to the vigil of the Lord at Matins.* The Holy Spirit descended upon you, Mary. v.' Hail Mary, full of grace.
AT VESPERS. Ant. Do not be afraid, Mary, you have found . . .
v.' Poured forth . . .
Collect
O God, who was pleased that, at the message of an angel, your word should take flesh in the womb of the blessed virgin Mary, grant to us your suppliants that we, who believe her to be truly the mother of God, may be helped by her intercession with you.'

[49] *Facsimiles of Horae de Beata Maria Virgine*, ed. Dewick, cols. 19–48.

[50] *The Monastic Breviary of Hyde Abbey*, ed. Tolhurst VI, 121.

[51] For the history of the Marian Office, see Bishop, 'On the Origin of the Prymer', in his *Liturgica Historica*, pp. 211–37, at 224–8; Leclercq, 'Formes successives' and 'Formes

types of Marian Office (which can also be called a *cursus* or, like the suffrage, a *memoria*): (i) an Office consisting of a single text which could be said at any time; (ii) the Little Office of Mary as a fully developed daily Office of all the hours; and (iii) the Saturday votive Office of Mary, which seems to have owed its origin to the Saturday votive mass of Mary. Although we have no tenth-century texts, it is certain that the first and third of these devotions were in existence by the tenth century, as the continental evidence collected by Bishop proves.[52]

The earliest mention of the Office is a continental one, in a story told about Berengerius, bishop of Verdun from 940 to 962, who discovered the provost of his cathedral saying *Beatae Mariae memoria* alone in the church.[53] Almost contemporary is the reference to Bishop Udalric of Augsburg, who daily recited Offices of Mary, of the Cross and of All Saints.[54] Both of these references seem to be to private devotions which probably consisted of a single text which could be said at any time. The third tenth-century reference is to a Saturday Office, which was said at Einsiedeln, a monastery dedicated to Mary, *c.* 970. This was said in choir by all of the monks on Saturdays from the octave of Easter to Advent and consisted of three lections.[55]

The Verdun and Einsiedeln references are, then, roughly contemporary references to two different types of Marian Office, but we should not infer that the practice as such originated in these centres. The Offices of Mary were modelled on the Offices of the Dead and of All Saints, and many other Offices were coming into being at the same time: the Office of the Cross, of the Trinity and of St Benedict, to name but a few. The diversity of the texts used in the early Marian Offices suggests a simultaneous development in different centres: fifteen different eleventh- and twelfth-century Offices of Mary have so far been published.[56] The dissemination of the practice from a single centre would probably have involved the diffusion of an Office with uniform texts, not the compilation of many Offices with different texts. By the middle of the eleventh century the Office of Mary

anciennes'; Canal, 'Oficio parvo de la Virgen' and 'El Oficio parvo de la Virgen de 1000 a 1250'; *The Monastic Breviary of Hyde Abbey*, ed. Tolhurst VI, 120–9.

[52] *Liturgica Historica*, pp. 225–6.   [53] *Ibid.*, p. 225.   [54] *Ibid.*

[55] *Ibid.*, pp. 225–6.

[56] In *Facsimiles of Horae de Beata Maria Virgine*, ed. Dewick; Leclercq, 'Formes successives' and 'Formes anciennes'; Canal, 'Oficio parvo de la Virgen' and 'El Oficio parvo de la Virgen de 1000 a 1250'.

was well established, as the letters of Peter Damian and surviving texts show.[57]

The earliest English texts of Offices of Mary date from the eleventh century and are contemporary with the earliest surviving continental ones. We have, however, one piece of evidence which, if authentic, indicates that a private Office of Mary was recited in England in the second half of the tenth century. This is a note preserved in a twelfth-century manuscript written by Ordericus Vitalis, now Alençon, Bibliothèque municipale, 14, where it follows immediately a copy of Wulfstan of Winchester's *Vita S. Æthelwoldi* and hymns and a mass in honour of the saint:

De horis peculiaribus
Praeterea beatus pater Adelwoldus horas regulares et peculiares sibi ad singulare seruitium instituit, quas in tribus cursibus ordinauit . . . Est enim primae psalmodiae cantilena ad laudem beatae Dei genitricis semperque uirginis Mariae procurata; secunda autem ad honorem beatorum apostolorum Petri et Pauli omniumque nostri saluatoris humanitati praesentialiter famulantium; tertia uero ad suffragia omnium sanctorum postulanda, ut eorum pia intercessione protecti, multiformem uersipellis Antichristi et membrorum eius fallacium expugnare, et Christo remunerante coelestium praemiorum palmam mereamur accipere. Quae uidelicet horae plerisque in locis habentur ascriptae, et ideo in hoc codicello sunt praetermissae.[58]

In his discussion of the various *uitae* of St Æthelwold, Winterbottom suggested that the version in this manuscript was a rewriting of the Wulfstan *uita* by Ordericus Vitalis, mainly because Ordericus was considered responsible for the hymns which follow the *uita* in the manuscript.[59] Gneuss,

[57] For Peter Damian, see Batiffol, *A History of the Roman Breviary*, pp. 147–9.
[58] PL 137, 107; quoted by Barré, *Prières anciennes*, p. 133: 'Concerning the special hours:
Furthermore the blessed father Æthelwold established for his sole use regular and special hours, which he arranged in three *cursus*. The song of the first psalmody provides for the praise of the blessed mother of God and ever-virgin Mary; the second, on the other hand, for the honour of the blessed apostles Peter and Paul and of all the servants who ministered to the humanity of our Saviour; the third in truth asking for the support of all the saints that, protected by their pious intercession, we may deserve to overcome the manifold deception of the crafty Antichrist and of his members and to receive, by the reward of Christ, the palm of celestial prizes. These hours namely are to be had written down in very many places and therefore they are omitted in this note.'
[59] M. Winterbottom, 'Three Lives of St Ethelwold', *MÆ* 41 (1972), 191–201, at 198–9.

however, has pointed out that one of the three hymns occurs in two eleventh-century English manuscripts and cannot, therefore, have been written by Ordericus.[60] If the hymns are not to be attributed to Ordericus, then the note *De horis peculiaribus* may also antedate him and it is possible that it draws on authentic tradition. Despite the writer's assertion that the hours have been preserved in several places, it is not possible to identify such a sequence of three Offices today.

Whether or not Æthelwold recited an Office of Mary, it appears certain that the Marian Office in England originated in such a private devotion. Titus D. xxvii of *c.* 1030 preserves three Offices, of the Trinity, the Cross and Mary, which give us some idea of the sort of devotion to which the author of the note on Æthelwold was referring. All three cannot be Æthelwold's Offices, as only the Office of Mary occurs in both the note and the manuscript, but it is not impossible that the Marian Office is his. The very small format of the manuscript and the nature of its contents (prayers, devotions, computistical texts and other miscellaneous items) suggest that it was the private vade-mecum of Ælfwine, its owner, and the three Offices it contains seem to be private devotions which could be said at any time.[61] Although in the manuscript they seem very short, they would have taken some time to recite, especially as they include all 176 verses of Psalm CXVIII. They are of a similar format, with the same psalms, but are provided with appropriate antiphons, versicles, responds and hymns. Each Office is followed by a series of four prayers, that of Mary being followed by a further five short *preces sanctae*, four of which are either addressed to or mention Mary.

IN HONORE SANCTAE MARIAE (81v–82r)

Deus in adiutorium meum intende. Domine. Gloria. Sicut erat.
A'. Aue Maria.
Deus in nomine tuo.
Confitemini Domino. Beati inmaculati usque in finem.
Quicumque uult. A'. Aue Maria, gratia plena, dominus tecum, benedicta tu in mulieribus, alleluia.
CAPITULUM. Ab initio ante secula creata sum, et usque ad futurum seculum non desinam, et in habitatione sancta coram ipso ministraui.

---

[60] H. Gneuss, review of M. Winterbottom, *Three Lives of English Saints*, N&Q ns 20 (1973), 479–80.
[61] See the descriptions of Titus D. xxvi + xxvii in the *Liber Vitae*, ed. Birch, pp. 251–83.

R'. Beata es, Maria, quae omnium portasti creatorem Deum; genuisti qui te fecit et in aeternum permanens uirgo.

V'. Aue Maria, gratia plena: Dominus tecum. Genuisti.

HYMNUS. Aue maris stella.

V'. Post partum uirgo.

A'. Succurre, sancta. Magnificat.

Succurre, sancta genitrix Christi, miseris ad te confugientibus, adiuua et refoue omnes qui in te confidunt, ora pro totius mundi piaculis, interueni pro clero, intercede pro monachorum choro, exora pro sexu femineo.

Kyrie el. Christe el. Kyrie el.

Pater noster. Et ne nos inducas.

Credo in Deum. Carnis resurrectionem.

Beata mater. Post partum uirgo. Aue Maria. Specie tua. Domine exaudi.

COLLECTA. Auerte, quesumus, Domine, iram tuam.

ALIA. Famulorum tuorum, quaesumus, Domine, delictis ignosce.

ITEM. Supplicationes seruorum tuorum.[62]

---

[62] Leclercq, 'Formes anciennes', pp. 101–2, collated with the manuscript:

'O God, come to my assistance.

O Lord [make haste to help me]

Glory [be to the Father and to the Son and to the Holy Spirit] As it was [in the beginning, is now, and ever shall be, world without end]

A'. Hail Mary . . .

Lord in your name [Ps. LIII]

Let us give thanks to the Lord [Ps. CXXXV]

Blessed are the blameless [Ps. CXVIII] *to the end.*

Whoever wishes . . . [Athanasian Creed]

A'. Hail Mary, full of grace, the Lord is with you, blessed are you among women, alleluia.

CAPITULUM. From the beginning and before the ages . . . I have ministered. [Ecclesiasticus XXIV. 14]

R'. Blessed are you, Mary, because you bore God, creator of all things; you gave birth to him who made you and you remain for ever a virgin.

V'. Hail Mary, full of grace: the Lord is with you.

R'. You gave birth . . .

HYMN. Hail, star of the sea.

V'. A virgin after the birth . . .

A'. Succour, holy. Magnificat.

Succour, holy mother of Christ, the wretched who flee to you, help and comfort those who trust in you, pray for the sins of the whole world, mediate for the clergy, intercede for the choir of monks, beseech on behalf of the female sex.

Kyrie el. Christe el. Kyrie el.

Our Father . . .   And lead us not . . .

I believe in God . . .   Resurrection of the body . . .

The four prayers which follow this Office are the Carolingian prayer, *Singularis meriti*, the *Oratio Alchfriðo* which first appears in the Book of Cerne, a prayer which seems to have been composed in Winchester by elaborating another prayer to Mary and a fourth prayer which does not occur elsewhere.[63]

The Office itself draws entirely on the liturgy for the feasts of Mary, emphasizing her virgin maternity and her powers of intercession. The antiphons are all from the Offices for the feasts and even *Succurre sancta genitrix*, whose ultimate source is the Pseudo-Augustinian *Sermo* ccviii of Ambrosius Autpertus, probably comes from them. The *capitulum* from Ecclesiasticus XXIV. 14, in which Wisdom, as a figure of the Virgin, speaks of her eternal nature, was also associated liturgically with Mary, having been used as an epistle in Marian masses from an early date.[64]

In addition to this private Office, we have the full pre-Conquest Office of Mary in Tiberius A. iii and another which was added to a tenth-century manuscript, London, BL, Royal 2. B. v very shortly after the Conquest: both cater for all the hours.[65] Both will be considered here, as the latter is clearly a manifestation of Anglo-Saxon rather than Norman piety. The Tiberius Office forms part of a large collection of texts written about the middle of the eleventh century, probably in Christ Church, Canterbury, while the Royal text is preserved on leaves added to a tenth-century psalter, almost certainly between 1066 and 1098.[66] These dates were suggested by Dewick on the basis of the prayer prefixed to the Office, which contains an appeal for the restoration of land which had been donated to the house of the suppliants. The house was dedicated to Mary, as the prayer makes clear, and the circumstances point to the Nunnaminster, St Mary's. Part of their land had been given to the Norman, Hugh FitzBaldric, and this seems to be the only instance of the alienation of lands from a religious house in this period.

Both of these Offices have a very similar arrangement of psalms which,

Blessed mother. A virgin after the birth. Hail Mary. By your beauty. Lord, help.
COLLECT. Turn away, we beseech, your anger, o Lord.
ANOTHER. Forgive, we beseech, o Lord, the offences . . .
ALSO. The supplications of your servants.'
[63] See below, pp. 95–113.
[64] B. Capelle, 'Les épîtres sapientales des fêtes de la Vierge', in his *Travaux liturgiques*, III, 316–22.
[65] Both Offices are ed. Dewick, *Facsimiles of Horae de Beata Maria Virgine*.
[66] Dewick, *Facsimiles of Horae de Beata Maria Virgine*, pp. xi–xii.

unlike the psalms of the Divine Office, do not vary with the days of the week. Many of the hymns of the two Offices are identical, as they are those used in the Divine Office for Marian feasts, but they are assigned to different hours in each Office. The collects in both are drawn from the Gregorian sacramentary, and the antiphons, versicles and responds again come chiefly from the Offices for the feasts of Mary, but a different selection is made in each Office, although they have some texts in common. Both Offices make abundant use of Ecclesiasticus XXIV, which had already been used in Titus D. xxvii. The two Offices differ completely in their readings, however: Royal 2. B. V draws all its readings from the Song of Songs, which was already associated liturgically with Mary through its use in the readings for the feast of the Assumption, while Tiberius A. iii uses Ambrosius Autpertus, the legend of Theophilus and an unknown text.[67]

The readings in Tiberius A. iii are adapted for their function as part of the Office and seem to have been chosen for their stress on Mary's powers of intercession. The first reading, from Ambrosius Autpertus, has received an addition at the end ('Offer . . . ') in which Mary's help is solicited:

Quas igitur tibi laudes sancta dei genitrix Maria fragilitas humana persoluet, que solo mirabili commercio recuperandi nobis aditum inuenisti. Accipe itaque quascumque exiles, quascumque meritis tuis impares gratiarum actiones, et cum susceperis uota, culpas nostras orando excusa. Offer preces pro nobis quos cernis offensos ante oculos conditoris: sic quoque, pia domina, pro nobis insiste orationibus in celis ut deleas quicquid deliquimus in terris. Tu autem.[68]

The second reading is drawn from the legend of Theophilus:

Recordare nostri, sancta Dei genitrix Maria, qui ad te recta fide confugimus et pura conscientia memoriam tuam celebramus et deprecare pro nobis apud misericordem dominum, impetrans nobis sine fine mansura perhennis uite gaudia. In te, piissima, omnes speramus, ad te oculos nostros die noctuque leuamus, que sola dominum portasti et in eternum uirgo permansisti. Obsecramus te, domina, ergo

---

[67] The Ambrosius Autpertus was identified by Dewick, *Facsimiles of Horae de Beata Maria Virgine*, p. xviii, and the Theophilus by Barré, *Prières anciennes*, p. 132.

[68] *Facsimiles of Horae de Beata Maria Virgine*, ed. Dewick, col. 20: 'Therefore, holy Mary, mother of God, human frailty pays tribute to you who discovered for us the way to recovery by a single miraculous commerce. Accept, therefore, the acts of thanksgiving, however feeble and however unequal to your merits, and when you have received our vows, by our prayers forgive our faults. Offer up prayers for us whom you see odious before the eyes of the creator: in like manner, O pious lady, continue with prayers for us in heaven that you may efface whatever we do wrong on earth.'

lacrimosis suspiriis ut nostre deuotionis obsequia sint tue pietati accepta, quatinus digni in tuis inueniamur laudibus. Tu autem.[69]

Recordare ergo et nostri, sancta Dei genitrix, qui ad te uigilamus pura fide et confugimus, et non derelinquas pauperrimum ouile, sed deprecare pro eo apud misericordem deum, et intercede ut conseruetur incommodis et sine calumnia. In te enim speramus omnes christiani, ad te confugimus, ad te oculos nostros die noctuque pandimus [*some manuscripts read* leuamus]. Te enim et eum, qui ex te carnem suscepit, dominum nostrum Iesum Christum, salutamus et glorifi-camus.[70]

The compiler has here inserted a reference to the Office (which he here and elsewhere calls a *memoria*), has substituted a plea for the joys of eternal life for a passage which is appropriate only to the Theophilus legend and has used a liturgical respond to emphasize Mary's uniqueness as mother and virgin. The last sentence of the source, which glorifies Christ as well as Mary, is omitted and another entreaty to Mary substituted.

The source of the last reading has not yet been traced, but it is also found in the twelfth-century psalter of Westminster, Paris, Bibliothèque Nationale, lat. 10433:

O Maria, omni laude dignissima, regina celorum, domina angelorum, interuen-trix peccatorum, conuertere quesumus ad salutem miseriarum nostrarum. Tuis intercessionibus tuo quoque patrocinio nos committimus obsecrantes ut dum humili te obsequio frequentamus in terris, tu, gloriosa domina, sedula prece nos digneris adiuuare in celis. Et sicut tu meruisti uirtute altissimi obumbrari, sic nos

---

[69] *Ibid.*, cols. 20–1: 'Call to mind, blessed Mary, mother of our God, that we have recourse to you with good faith and we celebrate your memorial with a pure conscience and intercede for us with the merciful Lord, obtaining for us joy without end in the mansion of eternal life. In you we all hope, o kindest one, to you we raise up our eyes day and night because you alone bore the lord and remained a virgin for eternity. We implore you, lady, therefore, with tearful sighs, that the services of our devotion may be accepted by your piety, that we may be found worthy in your praises.'

[70] Meerssemann, *Kritische Glossen op de Griekse Theophilus-Legende*, p. 31: 'Call us to mind, therefore, also, blessed mother of God, because we keep vigil to you with pure faith and we have recourse to you, and do not abandon the poorest sheep-fold, but beseech for it with the merciful God, and intercede that it be kept from troubles and without malicious attack. In you truly we hope, all we christians, we have recourse to you, we open our eyes to you day and night. Truly we greet and glorify you and him, who received flesh from you, our Lord, Jesus Christ.'

mereamur spiritus sancti gratia inluminari, per eum qui ex te natus est Christum dominum nostrum. Tu autem.[71]

All three texts are notable for their ardent praise of Mary, concentrating on her central roles as virgin and mother, and for their trust in her powers of intercession. This is the only Anglo-Saxon Marian Office we have which adapts the texts chosen to their place in the Office: the antiphon for the Nativity 'Cum iocunditate natiuitatem . . . ', for example, is changed to 'Cum iocunditate memoriam sancte Marie celebremus ut ipsa pro nobis intercedat ad dominum Deum nostrum.'[72] The following collect has also been adapted: 'Concede quesumus, omnipotens Deus, ut qui beate Dei genitricis semperque uirginis Marie commemorationem specialiter deuotione colimus, per hec temporalia festa que agimus, ad eterna gaudia peruenire mereamur.'[73] The compiler's use of Ambrosius Autpertus is not limited to the reading at Nocturns and the liturgical antiphon which we also find in Titus D. xxvii and Royal 2. B. V: he also goes back to the source of this antiphon and adapts it slightly to create a new text: 'Sancta Maria, succurre miseris, iuua pusillanimes, refoue flebiles, ora pro populo, interueni pro clero, intercede pro deuoto monachorum choro: sentiant omnes tuum leuamen quicunque celebrant tuam sanctam memoriam. Adsiste parata uotis poscentium et repende omnibus optatum effectum. Sentiant.'[74] The Tiberius Office also provides our earliest text of the

---

[71] *Facsimiles of Horae de Beata Maria Virgine*, ed. Dewick, col. 21: 'O Mary, most worthy of all praise, queen of the heavens, mistress of the angels, mediatress of sinners, turn and save us from our miseries, we beseech you. We entrust ourselves to your intercession and also to your advocacy, imploring that, while we celebrate your divine service on earth, you, glorious lady, with assiduous prayer deign to help us in heaven. And as you deserved to be overshadowed by the power of the Most High, so let us deserve to be enlightened by the grace of the Holy Spirit, through him, who was born from you, Christ, our Lord.'

[72] *Ibid.*, col. 22: 'Let us celebrate with joy the memorial of holy Mary, that she may intercede for us to the Lord, Jesus Christ.'

[73] *Ibid.*, col. 31: 'Grant, we beseech you, almighty God, that we, who celebrate with particular devotion the commemoration of the blessed mother of God and ever-virgin Mary by means of these temporal feasts which we keep, may deserve to attain eternal life.'

[74] *Ibid.*, cols. 32–3: 'Holy Mary, succour the wretched, help the faint-hearted, comfort the sorrowing, pray for the people, mediate for the clergy, intercede for the devout choir of monks: let all experience your comfort who celebrate your holy memorial. Stand ready for the prayers of those who beseech you and give to all of us the longed-for outcome.'

antiphon exhorting Mary to rejoice: 'Gaude Dei genitrix uirgo inmaculata. Gaude que gaudium ab angelo suscepisti. Gaude que genuisti aeterni luminis claritatem. Gaude mater. Gaude sancta Dei genitrix uirgo, tu sola mater innupta. Te laudat omnis factura domini. Pro nobis supplica.'[75] Apart from its introductory prayer, the Office in Royal 2. B. V consists entirely of liturgical texts or texts already used in the liturgy of Marian feasts, like the Song of Songs. The use of the Song of Songs and a marked preference for the liturgy of the feast of the Assumption result in an emphasis on Mary's assumption, but the most remarkable aspect of the Office is the prefatory prayer:

Dominator omnium, domine, quesumus qui omnem diligis iustitiam, et iniuriam seruorum tuorum uindicas, adesto nobis in presenti tribulatione, et tua nos letifica consolatione, et presta, per merita et intercessionem gloriosę genitricis tuę semper uirginis Marię in cuius atrio magestati tue famulamur, sanctisque tuis angelis et archangelis patriarchis quoque ac prophetis, cum beatis apostolis martiribus et confessoribus uirginibusque sanctis intercedentibus, ut nobis miserearis, quia in angustia positi sumus et de nullo auxilio humano confidimus. Ideo, domine Deus, succurre nobis et uindica iniuriam quam patimur. Tu quoque, sancta Maria semper uirgo, adesto angustię nostre et erue de manu inimici nostri possessionem huic sanctę ecclesię tuę oblatam et in tuorum famulorum alimoniam collatam. Presta igitur, domina, ut non gaudeat inimicus qui non timuit tuam inuadere possessionem. Redde ei secundum opera malitię suę, quia nostra in te sperantia corda perturbauit et domus tue reuerentiam pro nihilo reputauit. Annue quoque ut omnes ei consentientes ultionis tue uindictam sentiant et quia te contempserunt cum obprobriis et suppliciis intellegant. Te quoque sancte Machute confessor et te, uirgo ueneranda sancta Eadburga, oramus, quatinus nostram Deo commende-tis tribulationem et inimicorum nostrorum praua consilia ad perpetuam sibimet ipsis dampnationem commutetis nobisque ęternam misericordiam eius impetretis, qui cum patre et spiritu sancto uiuit et regnat.[76]

---

[75] *Ibid.*, col. 29; see also Wilmart, 'Les méditations d'Etienne de Salley sur les joies de la Vierge Marie', in his *Auteurs spirituels*, pp. 317–60, at 330–1: 'Rejoice immaculate virgin, mother of God. Rejoice because you have received joy from the angel. Rejoice because you have given birth to the brightness of eternal life. Rejoice, O mother. Rejoice, holy mother of God, you alone are a virgin, O unmarried mother. All the work of the Lord praises you. Entreat for us.'

[76] *Facsimiles of Horae de Beata Maria Virgine*, ed. Dewick, cols. 1–2: 'Lord, master of all, we beseech you, who love all justice and avenge the wrong [done to] your servants, assist us in the present distress and gladden us with your consolation and, through the merits and intercession of your glorious mother ever-virgin Mary, in whose hall we serve your greatness, and with the intercession of the angels and archangels, the

This prayer is transcribed in large letters before the Office and Dewick is undoubtedly right in suggesting that the Office itself was said with this 'intention'.[77] The Nunnaminster is regarded as Mary's possession and she is asked to punish those who have deprived it, and her, of its lands and those who have consented to this. Mary is addressed as the local saint and her intervention in human affairs is taken for granted.

It is probable that the Canterbury and Winchester Offices were for liturgical celebration rather than private use as in the case of the Titus Office, even though Dewick thought that:

There are several features in the Office of our Lady in Tiberius A. iii which suggest that it was to be said privately and not publicly. The form of absolution, *Misereatur et propitius sit mihi omnipotens dominus* implies this, and the three benedictions at Matins seem to be peculiar forms composed for private use. The Litany too differs considerably in detail from that found in the Psalter of Christ Church, Canterbury (Arundel 155). It may also be noticed that large script is used for all the liturgical forms except the anthems and responds.[78]

Against this, however, can be cited the fact that most of the forms are plural, while the different forms of the benedictions and the litany can be explained as a deliberate attempt to produce texts solely for this Office, just as other texts are deliberately adapted to make them appropriate to this context. The benedictions, for example, read: 'Pater de celis Deus fauente sancta Maria conferat nobis dona salutaria'; 'Beata interueniente Maria benedicat nos trinitas sancta'; 'Intercessio sancte Marie uirginis obtineat

patriarchs and the prophets also, with the blessed apostles, martyrs and confessors and holy virgins, grant that you may have pity on us because we are placed in difficulty and we trust in no human help. Therefore, O Lord God, help us and avenge the wrong which we suffer. You also, holy Mary, ever virgin, be present in our difficulty and rescue from the hand of our enemy the possession offered to this holy church and bestowed for the support of your servants. Grant, therefore, O lady, that the enemy may not rejoice who feared not to seize your possession. Repay him according to the works of his malice because he confounded our hearts, hoping in you, and considered as nothing the reverence of your house. Grant also that all agreeing to it may realize and comprehend the punishment of your vengeance because they defied you with disgraces and humiliations. We pray to you and also to St Machutus, confessor, and you, revered virgin, St Eadburg, that you commend our distress to God and that you change the evil plans of our enemies into perpetual damnation for themselves and obtain for us the eternal mercy of him who lives and reigns with the Father and the Holy Spirit.'

[77] *Ibid.*, p. xii.   [78] *Ibid.*, p. xiv.

nobis gratiam indiuidue trinitatis.'[79] As Tolhurst has pointed out, Lauds and Vespers are also followed by suffrages which would have been said in choir.[80] The opening prayer in Royal 2. B. V establishes its conventual nature from the beginning and it appears to be a votive Office said by the whole community with a specific aim.

While the Offices themselves suggest liturgical use, the manuscripts in which they occur are not liturgical. Tiberius A. iii is a large miscellaneous collection, including the *Regula S. Benedicti* and the *Regularis concordia*, material relating to the Rule, prognostics, devotions, Ælfric's *Colloquy* and homiletic material, and many of the items are in Old English or were glossed in the vernacular.[81] It seems to have been compiled to preserve texts of interest and could perhaps have been used as a teaching book, but it is very unlikely to have been used in choir. Royal 2. B. V is equally unlikely to have been used in the liturgy as it contains a glossed psalter with Latin scholia.[82] It was probably a reference or, again, a teaching book. The Offices seem to have been copied into both of these books merely as a record, and not for use from these manuscripts. It is possible that the recitation of these Offices was not permanent but ephemeral, undertaken, as with the Winchester Office, for a particular intention. The *Regularis concordia* makes provision for the adoption of such extra practices in cases of particular need: 'Si autem pro qualibet necessitate quid extra communem regularis consuetudinis usum addendum fuerit, tamdiu agatur quoadusque negotium pro quo agitur Christi opitulante gratia melioretur.'[83] The manuscripts do not specify whether the Offices were to be recited daily or on Saturdays only.

None of these three English Marian Offices occurs in any other manuscript and this raises a problem with regard to the origin of the texts. Were they composed in England? The negative evidence of their non-

---

[79] *Ibid.*, cols. 20–1: 'O Father, God of the heavens, bestow on us saving gifts, by the favour of holy Mary; May the holy Trinity bless us, by the intercession of holy Mary; may the intercession of the holy virgin Mary obtain for us the grace of the indivisible Trinity.'

[80] *The Monastic Breviary of Hyde Abbey*, VI, 121.

[81] Ker, *Catalogue*, pp. 240–8 (no. 186).

[82] *Ibid.*, pp. 318–20 (no. 249).

[83] *Regularis concordia*, ed. Symons, p. 5: 'And if, in case of need, any practice be added over and above the common monastic use and custom, let it be continued only until, with the help of Christ's grace, the matter for which it was undertaken be settled' (trans. Symons, *ibid.*).

occurrence elsewhere, the fact that one of the prayers following the short Winchester Office seems to have been composed there and that the prefatory prayer in the full Winchester Office was certainly also composed there may not be enough to prove that the Offices were composed in England, but it certainly suggests that they were. The onus of proof rests with those who would wish to argue otherwise. If, then, the Offices were composed in England, they provide valuable evidence for English Marian piety, showing us, by the type of texts drawn upon and by the different emphases (intercession in Tiberius A. iii, the Assumption in Royal 2. B. V), the nature of the Marian piety of the compilers.

A third type of Marian Office, a short Saturday Office, is preserved in the Portiforium of St Wulstan, Cambridge, Corpus Christi College 391, which, Hughes argues, was written in 1065 and which seems to have been copied from a Winchester source.[84] This Office, which is again referred to in the text itself as a *memoria*, has texts for the hours of Matins, Lauds, Prime, Terce, Sext and None. Prime, Terce, Sext and None have only one antiphon each, all of which are drawn from the Offices for the feasts of Mary. Lauds consists of two antiphons and Matins of three lections, each followed by a respond and versicle. This text can hardly be regarded as a complete Office: it is, rather, a commemoration consisting only of a Marian antiphon to be said at most hours but with the addition of three lections and the same number of responds and versicles at Matins. In the lections Mary is assigned a most active role in the salvation of mankind: the salvation of the world depends on her and it is she who is described as assisting the entire world and opening up the kingdom of heaven. Honoured in heaven by God, angels and saints, she is appealed to now as mother of man, *mater piissima*, and lauded with imagery which proclaims her as elevated above all other saints, culminating in the assertion that whatever good the universe has comes from her. In terms of originality of treatment and emphasis on Mary's autonomy, this Office goes far beyond those in Tiberius A. iii and Royal 2. B. V:

Ant. Ortus conclusus es . . .

Lectio I. Sacrosancta et uenerabilis Deus genitricis Mariae memoriam congruae diuinis laudibus catholica frequentat aecclesia, quia eius sine intermissione salutari indiget auxilio. Nam reuerentia quae matri defertur, illi etiam qui eam talem fecit ut uirgo et mater esset exhibetur. Ideo ergo totis desideriis totisque preconiis eius insistamus laudibus ut et matrem sentiamus nobis piissimam

---

[84] *The Portiforium of St Wulstan*, ed. Hughes II, vi–vii.

77

filiumque eius iudicem serenissimum. Haec est uirgo quae antiquum diabolice deditionis cyrographum aboleuit totoque seculo subuenit et caeleste regnum patefecit, dum per spiritum sanctum Dei filium concepit.

R'. Veni electa mea . . . v'. Specie tua . . .

Lectio II. Opere pretium quippe est, ut intentis celebratur laudibus in terris, cui oficiossime angeli famulantur in celis. Nam si eam ille praecipuus Gabriel humiliter salutaris honorabat in terris, multo amplius eam super caelos exaltata, et, ut ita dicam, in throno Dei collocatam, nunc cum sanctis omnibus honorat laudibus dignissimis. Haec est sola cui nulla uirgo potest comparari, quia tanta est ut quanta sit non possit enarrari. Hanc sancti expectabant patriarche. hanc preconebant prophete, omnesque quos spiritus sanctus attingerat optebant uidere.

R'. Ista est speciosa . . . v'. Specie tua et pulchritudine tua

Lectio III. Haec tanta tamque sancta regia uirgo, digno exiit uenerari preconio, cuius constat mundus saluatus suffragio. Haec, inquam, est fenestra caeli, aurora solis aeterni, ianua paradysi, ueri et arca propitiatorii. Haec est uirgo, domina regum, decus mulierum, gemma uirginum, lux sanctorum, congratulatio angelorum, consolatio miserorum, refugium peccatorum, omniumque reparatio credentium. Quicquid igitur boni mundus habet, ab illa habet, ex qua salutis nostrae initium manet. Haec nobis suis semper subuenire dignetur ueneratoribus, atque piae sacris precibus a uitiis purget omnibus, seque considerare et collaudare donet in celestibus.

R'. Super salutem . . . v'. Valde eam . . . [85]

---

[85] *Ibid.* II, 60–1:

Ant. 'You are a closed garden . . .

Lection I. The catholic church fitly celebrates the sacrosanct memorial of the honoured Mary, mother of God, with divine praises because it needs her saving help without interruption. For the reverence which is offered to the mother is shown also to him who so made her that she might be a virgin and mother. Therefore with all longings and all commendations we continue with praises of her that we may experience her as a most pious mother to us and her son as a most favourable judge. This is the virgin who destroyed the old signed document of diabolical surrender and came to the assistance of the entire world and opened up the heavenly kingdom when she conceived the son of God through the Holy Spirit.

R'. Come, my chosen one . . .   v'. By your beauty . . .

Lection II. It is certainly worthwhile that she is celebrated by eager praises on earth, whom angels serve zealously in heaven. For if that chief messenger of salvation, Gabriel, honoured her humbly on earth, then much more when she is exalted above the heavens, and, so to speak, placed on the throne of God, does he honour her now together with all the saints with most fitting praises. She is unique to whom no virgin can be compared because she is so great that how great she is may not be fully set forth. The holy patriarchs hoped for her, the prophets heralded her and all whom the Holy Spirit had touched longed to see her.

The brevity of this Office shows that it was said in addition to the normal Office for the day. Both a Friday Office of the Cross and this Office follow the usual Saturday Office in the manuscript. The three lections occur elsewhere: in three later English Offices (in the twelfth-century Winchcombe Breviary in Valenciennes, Bibliothèque municipale, 116, the breviary of Hyde Abbey of *c.* 1300 and the Hereford Breviary of the fifteenth century) and, most notably, in a group of manuscripts centred around the monastery of Saint-Sépulchre in Cambrai, where they occur, however, as one text.[86] The earliest of the French manuscripts dates from the end of the eleventh century. There are more French manuscripts of the text than there are English; the French manuscripts have a final doxology lacking in the English; and the French text is purer, without the scribal mistakes in the Wulstan Portiforium (e.g. the first sentence, which should read 'Sacrosanctam et uenerabilis Dei . . .'). These factors, together with the lack of divisions in the French manuscripts, prompted Barré to suggest that the lections were composed in Saint-Sépulchre, as a single text.[87] None of these arguments is necessarily compelling, however. The presence of the text in a mid-eleventh-century English manuscript, which itself seems to have been copied from an earlier Winchester manuscript, is an obvious objection to a French origin: it would be strange if an English manuscript predated all French witnesses, had the text been composed in France. The French texts are largely centred on Cambrai and could as easily go back to one English manuscript imported into Cambrai as to a text composed there. The question of whether the text was originally a single, undivided text or

R'. She is beautiful . . .   V'. Your splendour and your beauty . . .
Lection III. This so great and so holy royal virgin, according to whose decision the world's salvation is established, has gone forth to be venerated by a worthy herald. She is, I say, the window of heaven, the dawn of the eternal sun, the door of paradise and the chest of the true propitiator. She is the virgin, the lady of kings, the ornament of women, the jewel of virgins, the light of saints, the rejoicing of angels, the consolation of the wretched, the refuge of sinners and the restoration of all believers. Whatever of good the universe has, therefore, it has from her from whom the beginning of our salvation flows. May she deign always to help us, her venerators, and piously by her prayers purify us from all faults and may she grant that we contemplate and praise her highly in heaven. R'. More than health . . .   V'. Greatly . . .'

[86] For the French manuscripts, see Barré, 'Un plaidoyer monastique pour le samedi mariale', p. 376.

[87] *Ibid.*, p. 377.

three lections tells us nothing about the origin; it could be argued that, since it was obviously written to propagate the Marian Office, as the first sentence shows, it was composed specifically as part of the Office, in which case the division into three lections is merely a natural consequence of its place there. Its occurrence in an Office book seems, indeed, to be more faithful to the original design than does its presence in a legendary, as in the earliest French manuscript. The scribal mistakes in the Wulstan version, which Barré regards as an argument for the priority of the French, could all be due to the history of the transmission of the text in England; an uncorrupted text could have been exported to France, or the Latin could have been corrected there.

The Saturday Office in the Wulstan Portiforium is accompanied by a Friday Office of the Cross which also has three lections, not so far known to occur elsewhere and strikingly similar to the Saturday Office in style and treatment.[88] These two texts have every appearance of being composed by the same author: had that author been French, we would expect the Friday lections also to occur in French manuscripts.

The earliest French manuscript contains two further texts, which Barré thinks were added at a slightly later date; the first of these, *Quare omni sabbato memoria sanctae Mariae celebratur*, is another attempt to propagate the Saturday Office of Mary. This text obviously draws on the *Sacrosancta* in themes and vocabulary but cannot, as Barré points out, be by the same author:

A l'encontre des *Lectiones* [*Sacrosancta*], le plaidoyer pour le samedi n'accumule pas les vocables en l'honneur de la Vierge, et il est centré sur le thème *Mater misericordiae*, que celles-ci ignorent. Plus développé, il est seul également à faire appel aux examples tirés des *Miracula* et à se montrer explicite sur la célébration du samedi. Il marque donc une maturation de pensée, qui confirme l'antériorité des *Lectiones*. De plus, il est d'un style rythmé très étudié.[89]

The dissemination of the later text from Saint-Sépulchre is not open to question and is not complicated by any English evidence. It looks as if the

[88] *The Portiforium of St Wulstan*, ed. Hughes II, 59–60.

[89] 'Un plaidoyer monastique pour le samedi mariale', p. 377: 'Contrary to the procedure of the *Lectiones* [*Sacrosancta*], the plea for Saturday does not pile up terms in honour of the Virgin and it is centred around the theme of the Mother of Mercy, of which they are ignorant. More developed, it is also alone in appealing to examples drawn from the *Miracula* and in being explicit on the celebration of Saturday. It therefore shows a maturing of thought, which confirms the pre-existence of the *Lectiones*. In addition, it is in a very studied rhythmical style.'

later text is a deliberate attempt to modernize and improve the *Sacrosancta* and it seems probable that the monks of Saint-Sépulchre felt the earlier text to be inadequate. It is possible, therefore, that the *Quare omni sabbato* was composed to supersede a text imported from England which did not altogether satisfy the piety and the stylistic demands of the French monks.

There is nothing in the texts of the three Marian lections inconsistent with an English origin, and, more particularly, with a Winchester origin. The list of Marian epithets, so atypical of the later French text, recalls the long Winchester prayer in London, BL, Arundel 60, and the ardent veneration of Mary and the trust in her powers of intercession which the readings display corresponds with that shown in other Winchester texts. I would suggest, therefore, that the readings for the Office of Mary were composed in Winchester, probably in the first half of the eleventh century, along with those for the Office of the Cross, as it is from a Winchester exemplar that the Wulstan Portiforium is thought to have been copied,[90] and as this centre provides a suitable context for the readings.

Even if these readings were composed in England, however, this does not imply that the Saturday Office as such originated in England. Although the Wulstan Portiforium is our earliest known text of a Saturday Office, the Customary of Einsiedeln, of *c*. 970, prescribes: 'per totam quinquagesimam paschalem infra ebdomadam fiant tres lectiones similiter; sexta quoque feria et septima, si sanctorum natalitia non affuerint, de sancta Cruce et sancta Maria tres eodem modo compleantur . . . Hoc quoque de sancta Cruce et sancta Maria non dimittatur usque in Aduentum Domini.'[91] Interestingly, the abbot of Einsiedeln between 964 and 996 was Gregory, an Englishman, and there may be some connection between the Einsiedeln Office and the English one. Such a connection can only be conjectural, however, as we do not have sufficient evidence to settle the question.

---

[90] *The Portiforium of St Wulstan*, ed. Hughes II, vi–vii.

[91] Quoted by Bishop, in his *Liturgica Historica*, p. 226, n. 1: 'Throughout all the fifty days of Easter three lections take place during the week in a similar fashion; and on the sixth and seventh day, if the feasts of the saints do not occur, in the same way three may be completed concerning the holy cross and holy Mary . . . Also this concerning the holy cross and holy Mary may not be abandoned until the Advent of the Lord.'

New texts for the feasts of Mary

In addition to the composition of new Offices, the introduction of the feasts of the Virgin's Conception and Presentation in the Temple naturally necessitated the composition of texts for these occasions, and a mass for the Conception and benedictions for both days survive. The mass is extant in two manuscripts, the New Minster Missal, Le Havre 330, and as an addition to the Leofric Missal, Bodley 579: both share three prayers, with a fourth in the New Minster Missal:

Deus, qui beate Mariae uirginis conceptionem angelico uaticinio parentibus predixisti, presta huic presenti familiae tuae eius presidiis muniri, cuius conceptionis sacra sollempnia congrua frequentatione ueneratur.

Secreta

Sanctifica, domine, muneris oblati libamina, et beate Dei genitricis saluberrima interuentione, nobis salutaria fore concede.

Postcommunio

Repleti uitalibus alimoniis et diuinis reparati mysteriis, supplices rogamus, omnipotens Deus, beate Mariae semper uirginis cuius uenerandam colimus conceptionem pia interuentione, a squalorum erui inmanium dominatione.[92]

Only the first of these prayers contains more than a mere mention of the occasion of the feast, alluding to the angel's announcement of Mary's birth to Joachim and Anna, an event recounted, of course, only in the apocrypha. It is illuminating to compare this mass with that for the feast of the Conception of John the Baptist, also among the additions to the Leofric

---

[92] *The Missal of the New Minster*, ed. Turner, p. 190:
'O God, who foretold the conception of the blessed virgin Mary to her parents by an angelic prophecy, grant to this your family here present to be strengthened by her protection, the sacred fitting festival of whose conception is honoured by a celebration.
Secreta
Sanctify, O Lord, the offerings of the offered gift, and by the most saving intervention of the blessed mother of God, grant that they may lead to our salvation.
Postcommunio
Filled with the vital sustenance and restored by the divine mysteries, we, humble petitioners, ask, O omnipotent God, by the pious intervention of the blessed Mary ever virgin, whose venerable conception we celebrate, to be rescued from the domination of monstrous and foul deeds.'

Missal. Just as the original author of the *Proteuangelium* appears to have modelled his legend on the story of John the Baptist, so the author of these prayers modelled his texts on those used for the Conception of John the Baptist, although the assertions of Mary's holiness appear to be independent. Of John also it was said that his birth had been announced by an angel: 'Deus, qui hodierna die sanctum Iohannem preconem ueritatis angelico concipiendum ministerio preuidisti . . . '[93] The fact that the proper of the Marian mass parallels that for the equivalent feast of John the Baptist is also doctrinally revealing, suggesting that the question of Mary's freedom from original sin did not arise in the mind of the author: it was never thought that John had been conceived without original sin, although it was believed that he had been born without it, but the orthodoxy of celebrating his conception was not, in this period, questioned. These prayers indicate that the apocryphal legends surrounding Mary's origin had achieved a status comparable with the canonical account of the origin of John the Baptist.

The extra text in the New Minster Missal, a unique preface, raises a question as to the meaning of the feast, however:

per Christum dominum nostrum. Cuius uirginis matris conceptionis sollempnia deuotis mentibus recolentes, tue magnificentiae preconia non tacemus, quam ante ortum ita sanctificasti, ante conceptum sic sancti spiritus illustratione et uirtute altissimi obumbrasti, ut templum domini, sacrarium spiritus sancti, mundi domina, celi regina, sponsa Christi, et unici filii Dei foeta mater effici, et post partum uirginitatis insigniis perpetualiter meruisset decorari. Et ideo.[94]

The problem hinges on the understanding of *conceptio*, that is, on whether the active or passive conception of Mary is being described here. But since there are clear verbal echoes in the second sentence of the account of the

---

[93] *The Leofric Missal*, ed. Warren, p. 267: 'O God, who on this day foresaw that John the herald of truth was to be conceived by a message of an angel . . .'

[94] *The Missal of the New Minster*, ed. Turner, p. 190 and *Corpus praefationum*, ed. Moeller, p. 62 (no. 202): 'through Christ our lord. Honouring anew the solemnity of the conception of his virgin mother with devout minds, we do not stay silent respecting the celebration of your great deeds, who sanctified her thus before her birth; likewise before conception you overshadowed her by the enlightenment of the Holy Spirit and the power of the Highest One so that as a result she had merited to be made the temple of the Lord, the sanctuary of the Holy Spirit, the mistress of the world, the queen of heaven, the spouse of Christ and the fruitful mother of the only son of God and after the birth to be adorned perpetually with the honours of virginity.'

Annunciation in Luke 1.35 ('Spiritus sanctus superueniet in te et uirtus altissimi obumbrabit tibi'), the conception referred to in *ante conceptum* must be Mary's conception of Christ, not Anna's of Mary. *Ante ortum*, on the other hand, seems to refer to the birth of Mary herself, before which, the preface asserts, she was sanctified. Paschasius Radbertus in the ninth century had already argued that Mary had been sanctified before her birth,[95] so this idea was not a new one, but it is important to note that the prayer says only *ante ortum* and does not specify at what point this took place. If the *conceptio* of the first sentence, however, is the passive conception of Mary by Anna, i.e. that of the feast of 8 December, then *ante ortum* might refer back to this and the prayer could then be taken as suggesting sanctification at conception. This is not, of course, the doctrine of the Immaculate Conception, which involves a preservation of Mary from all original sin, not a sanctification. If, on the other hand, the *conceptio* of the first sentence is Mary's conception of Christ, then there is no indication of when before birth this sanctification took place. While it may seem far-fetched to propose that the author of the prayer used *conceptio* in two different senses, the former reading nevertheless seems to me more likely. The celebration of Christ's conception by Mary is something which can be a feature of the liturgy of all Marian feasts, not just that of the Annunciation, but it is ordinarily prefaced with a reference to the feast of the day, in this case that of Anna's conception of the Virgin.

The unique prayers in the Exeter Benedictional, BL, Add. 28188, fol. 161, which were also probably composed in Winchester,[96] place more stress on the Virgin's role in the scheme of salvation:

Sempiterna[m] a Deo benedictionem uobis beate Marie uirginis pia deposcat supplicatio, quam concipiendam omnipotens, ex qua eius conciperetur unigenitus, angelico declarauit preconio, quam et uobis iugiter suffragari benigno, ut est benignissima, sentiatis auxilio. Amen.

Quique illam ante conceptum presignauit nomine spiritus sancti obumbratione, uos diuinam gratiam mente annuat concipere in sancte trinitatis confessione, atque ab omni malo protectos deifica confirmet sanctificatione. Amen.

Sancta uero Dei genitrix Maria uobis a Deo pacis et gaudii optineat incrementum, ut quibus felix eiusdem beate uirginis partus extitit salutis exordium,

---

[95] See above, p. 22.

[96] Bishop, in his *Liturgica Historica*, p. 239 and Prescott, 'The Structure of English Pre-Conquest Benedictionals', p. 130.

sit etiam ipse Iesus Christus premium in celis uite permanentis sempiternum.[97]

Here again there is ambiguity: the mention of the conception of Christ in the first part of the benediction suggests that the announcement by the angelic message could refer to the Annunciation, but the very similar phrasing in other Winchester prayers undoubtedly refers to Anna's conception of Mary, indicating that this is also what is intended here. In the second part of the blessing, however, the reference does seem to be to the Annunciation, as once again there is an echo of Luke's account of the overshadowing of the Virgin by the Holy Spirit: the marking out by name presumably alludes here to Gabriel's greeting at the Annunciation. The last prayer is modelled on the liturgical prayer *Famulis tuis* for the feast of the Nativity and the *partus*, which is the beginning of salvation, is Mary's giving birth to Christ, not her own birth from Anna.[98]

The benedictions for the feast of the Presentation and the Conception found in Harley 2892 (a Canterbury manuscript, whose texts were probably again composed in Winchester),[99] show clearly that the author was drawing on the apocryphal narratives of Mary's birth and childhood:

Benedictio de presentatione sancte Marie

Benedictionum celestium uos dominus imbre locupletet et sanctuaria cordium

[97] Quoted by Bishop, in his *Liturgica Historica*, p. 240, and *Corpus benedictionum pontificalium*, ed. Moeller II, 811 (no. 1987):
'May the pious supplication of the blessed Virgin Mary request everlasting benediction from God for you, whose conception the Omnipotent announced by an angelic message and from whom was conceived his only-begotten son and whom you may perceive to support you perpetually with kind help, as she is most kind. Amen.
May he who designated her by name before the conception by the overshadowing of the Holy Spirit, grant you to conceive divine grace with your mind in the acknowledgement of the holy Trinity and may he strengthen and protect you from all evil by his deifying blessing. Amen.
Truly, may the holy Mary, mother of God, obtain for you an increase of peace and joy from God so that to you for whom the happy birth of the same blessed Virgin was the beginning of salvation, Jesus Christ himself may also be the everlasting reward of enduring life in heaven.'

[98] Used, for example, in *The Missal of the New Minster*, ed. Turner, p. 157: 'Famulis tuis quaesumus domine caelestis gratiae munus impertire. ut quibus beate uirginis partus extitit salutis exordium: natiuitatis eius uotiua sollempnitas pacis tribuat incrementum' ('We beseech you, O Lord, bestow on your servants the gift of heavenly grace, that as our salvation began by the child-bearing of the blessed Virgin, so this votive celebration of her nativity may grant us an increase of peace').

[99] Prescott, 'The Structure of English Pre-Conquest Benedictionals', pp. 132–3.

85

uestrorum sue habitationis uisitatione perlustret, qui beatam Mariam angelico oraculo concipiendam predixit. Amen.

Et que illum qui panis est angelorum in sui uteri habitaculo meruit baiulare, uos diu hic adiuuet uiuere et post celica regna feliciter penetrare. Amen.

Et sicut sibi congaudetis honoris gratia celebrantes hunc diem, quo templum Dei, sacrarium spiritus sancti in aula Dei est presentatum, ita uos faciat purificatis neuis contagiorum unico filio suo presentari et in albo beati ordinis dignanter ascribi. Amen.[100]

Benedictio in die conceptionis sancte Dei genitricis Marie

Caelestium carismatum inspirator terrenarumque mentium reparator, qui beatam Dei genitricem angelico concipiendam preconauit oraculo, uos benedictionum suarum ubertate dignetur locupletare et uirtutum floribus dignanter decorare. Amen.

Et qui illam prius sanctificauit nominis dignitate, quam edita gigneretur humana fragilitate, uos uirtutum copiis adiuuet pollere et in nominis sui ueneranda confusione infatigabiliter perdurare. Amen.

Obtineat uobis gloriosis intercessionibus prospera tempora, iocunda et pacifica, et post presentia secula gaudia sine fine manentia, cuius uenerande conceptionis frequentamini magnifica sacramenta. Amen.[101]

---

[100] *The Canterbury Benedictional*, ed. Woolley, p. 116, and *Corpus benedictionum pontificalium*, ed. Moeller I, 155 (no. 374): 'May the Lord enrich you with a shower of heavenly blessings and purify the sanctuary of your heart with the visitation of his dwelling, who foretold the conception of the blessed Mary with angelic prophecy. Amen.

And may she, who deserved to carry in her womb him who is the bread of angels, help you to live long here and afterwards to enter happily the heavenly kingdom. Amen.

And as you rejoice together in thanksgiving for the honour, celebrating this day on which the temple of God, the sanctuary of the Holy Spirit, is presented in the hall of God, so may he cause you to be presented to his only son when purified of all the blots of contagion and deservedly to be registered in the order of the blessed.'

[101] *Ibid.*, pp. 118–9, and *Corpus benedictionum pontificalium*, ed. Moeller I, 161 (no. 387): 'May the inspirer of celestial gifts and restorer of earthly minds, who proclaimed the conception of the blessed mother of God by an angelic prophecy, deign to enrich you with the abundance of his blessings and to adorn you, as you have deserved, with flowers of virtues. Amen.

And may he help you to be strong with an abundance of virtues who sanctified her beforehand with the dignity of her name, who was born and brought forth of human frailty, and to endure indefatigably in the venerable acknowledgement of his name. Amen.

May she, by her glorious intercession, obtain for you successful times, pleasant and peaceful, and, after the present ages, lasting joys without end, the splendid sacraments of whose venerable conception you are celebrating. Amen.'

The reference here to the angel's announcement of Mary's name (and in this case it must be the announcement to Joachim and Anna which is referred to) seems to depend on the *Liber de natiuitate Mariae*, the post-Carolingian retelling of the *Gospel of Pseudo-Matthew*, as it is only in this apocryphon that the angel reveals Mary's name.[102] The second prayer for the Conception states that Mary was sanctified by her name before being born of human frailty, but again it seems that this did not involve a preservation from original sin. The first to formulate the concept of the Immaculate Conception was Eadmer of Canterbury (*c.* 1060–*c.* 1128)[103] and he was not anticipated in the Anglo-Saxon texts. The close connection between the feasts of the Conception and the Presentation in the Temple, introduced in Winchester at the same time, is evident in the benedictions for the Presentation, which refer to the angelic annunciation of Mary's birth in words very similar to the first blessing for the Conception. Many of the texts for the feast of the Conception, then, manifest a confusing ambiguity in the use of the word *conceptio*, but this probably does not indicate confusion on the part of the authors so much as a desire to mark the feast of Anna's conception of Mary with a celebration, even though a doctrinal basis for this celebration had not yet been formulated. The authors frequently fell back, therefore, on praise of Mary in her fundamental role as mother of God, her *conceptio Christi*, but alluded too to the apocryphal account of her own conception by Anna.

In addition to the mass and benedictions for the two new feasts, texts were also composed for the four long-established Marian feasts. Such new prayers are concentrated in the benedictionals, which, as Prescott has shown, constitute 'one of the most notable Anglo-Saxon liturgical achievements',[104] with a large number of new texts being composed in Winchester. The most important collections for new Marian benedictions are those from Exeter and Canterbury, both of which probably originated in Winchester.[105] The new benedictions for the four Marian feasts celebrate the Virgin as 'uirgo beatissima', 'interuentrix piissima, quae regina uirtutum floret dignissima', 'domina mundi et regina caeli' and emphasize

---

102 *Evangelia Apocrypha*, ed. Tischendorf, pp. 113–25. For a discussion of the date of this text, see Beyers, *De natiuitate Mariae*, p. 42.

103 See *Eadmeri monachi Cantuariensis tractatus de conceptione sanctae Mariae*, ed. H. Thurston and T. Slater (Freiburg-im-Breisgau, 1904).

104 Prescott, 'The Structure of English Pre-Conquest Benedictionals', p. 120.

105 *Ibid.*, pp. 130–3.

above all her virginal maternity, in time-honoured phrases: 'uirgo ante partum, uirgo in partu, uirgo permansit inuiolata post partum' and, with an echo of Sedulius: 'sola sine exemplo mater existens et uirgo gignere meruit Deum et hominum Saluatorem mundi'.[106] She conceived, according to the Canterbury Annunciation blessing, through the ear in believing Gabriel ('quae dum archangelo credidit per aurem concipiens'), preserving her chastity: 'uirginalem non perdidit pudicitiam'.[107]

The other liturgical genre practised in Winchester was that of the preface and the New Minster Missal contains a number of unique prefaces, largely for English saints. These new texts include one for the vigil of the feast of the Nativity of the Virgin, which praises her as the door to eternal life: this text occurs nowhere else and was presumably composed in Winchester:

VD: Et beatae Mariae festa cum ieiuniorum et hostiarum muneribus praeuenire, per quam semper nobis digneris subuenire. Ipsa quoque nobis lucis aeternae ianuam aperiat, quae ianua uitae facta, salutis auctorem uirgo edidit incorrupta. Quem laudant angeli.[108]

CONCLUSIONS

By the end of the Anglo-Saxon period, then, the English church was celebrating not only the principal feasts of the Virgin, with the extra feasts of her Conception and Presentation in the Temple, and composing texts for all these occasions, but they had also adopted new, optional devotional

---

[106] *The Canterbury Benedictional*, ed. Woolley: 'most blessed Virgin', p. 108; 'most merciful mediator, who blooms as the most worthy queen of virtues', p. 108; 'lady of the world and queen of heaven', p. 90; 'virgin before the birth, virgin in birth, she remained an inviolate virgin after the birth', p. 105; 'alone, without a precedent, being a mother and as a virgin she deserved to give birth to the God of men and the Saviour of the world', p. 108.

[107] *Ibid*: 'who, when she believed the archangel, conceiving through the ear . . .', p. 90; 'she did not lose her virginal chastity', p. 105.

[108] *The New Minster Missal*, ed. Turner, p. 157, and *Corpus praefationum*, ed. Moeller, p. 76 (no. 244): '[It is truly meet and just, right and for our salvation, that we should at all times and in all places give thanks to thee, holy Lord, Father almighty, eternal God] and anticipate the feast of blessed Mary with gifts of fasts and sacrifices, through whom always may you deign to help us. May she also open for us the door of eternal light, a stainless virgin, who, being the door of life, brought forth the author of our salvation, whom angels praise.'

practices which testify to a strong interest in Mary. They recited votive masses and Offices to the Virgin, the latter probably both in choir and in private, and they had added short Marian suffrages to the Divine Office. The Offices of Mary in Anglo-Saxon manuscripts seem, moreover, to have been composed in England, although the devotions themselves probably began more or less simultaneously in different countries. The Saturday Office of Mary, too, can reasonably be claimed as an English composition and is the earliest known text of such an Office, although we have an earlier continental reference to the devotion. The diffusion of these practices in Anglo-Saxon England is difficult to judge. Most of the evidence comes from Winchester and the Worcester manuscript which contains the Saturday Office of Mary was copied from a Winchester exemplar. As with the feasts of the Conception and the Presentation in the Temple, the surviving evidence suggests that Winchester was the centre of Marian devotion in late Anglo-Saxon England. It was here that new Marian devotions were eagerly appropriated and texts composed.

4

Private prayer to Mary

Private prayer has always been a feature of Christian life. In the early period, such prayer was addressed to the Father, Son or Holy Ghost. Subsequently, as their cults grew in the early church, prayers were addressed to the saints. Belief in the saints' powers of intercession encouraged appeals to them, and there can be little doubt that prayers to Mary, too, were uttered from an early date, although they are first attested in public rather than private contexts.[1] A fourth-century Greek papyrus of the prayer later translated into Latin as *Sub tuum praesidium confugimus, sancta Dei genitrix*, is extant[2] and, also from the fourth century, in the West we find the Virgin addressed in poems and homilies, especially in the African Christmas homilies of the followers of Augustine, which often concentrated on Mary's role in the Incarnation.[3] These homilies were incorporated in many of the early homiliaries and seem to have been widely disseminated. The number of Marian prayers in the liturgy grew rapidly too, as texts composed for feasts associated with the Virgin were added to the Marian texts of the Christmas cycle: in the second half of the sixth century, for example, a mass with a pronounced Marian emphasis was celebrated in Rome on 1 January.[4] The seventh-century Spanish *Orationale Visigothicum*, to take a totally different region, contains thirty-five *Orationes de festiuitate gloriae sancte matris uirginis* for the Marian feast of 18 December,

---

[1] For a very full treatment of prayers to Mary, see Barré, *Prières anciennes*.

[2] O. Stegmüller, 'Sub tuum praesidium. Bemerkungen zur ältesten Überlieferung', *Zeitschrift für katholische Theologie* 74 (1952), 76–82.

[3] See Leclercq, 'Aux origines du cycle de Noël', p. 10, and Barré, *Prières anciennes*, pp. 22–3 and p. 29.

[4] See above, p. 28.

although only four of these address Mary directly.[5] The Gallican liturgy included a Marian mass on her feast of 18 January. Marian masses were also, of course, incorporated into the Gregorian and Gelasian sacramentaries. By the time Christianity was established in England, prayers to the Virgin would have been familiar, therefore, from the liturgy, poetry and homilies, as well as being occasionally incorporated in such genres as saints' lives and biblical commentaries.

THE EARLY ANGLO-SAXON PERIOD

The earliest Anglo-Latin prayers to Mary are attested, as in other areas, by being included in a variety of other literary forms. The earliest surviving is a passage in Aldhelm's poem, *In basilica beatae Mariae semper uirginis* (*c.* 685), and this already testifies to a strong belief in the efficacy of prayer to the Virgin:

> Femina praepollens et sacra puerpera uirgo,
> Audi clementer populorum uota precantum,
> Marcida qui riguis umectant imbribus ora
> Ac genibus tundunt curuato poplite terram,
> Dum ueniam fuso lacrimarum fonte merentur
> Et crebris precibus delent peccamina uitae![6]

A similar faith in Mary's powers of intercession is evident in a passage concerning St Wilfrid (*ob.* 709) in Stephen's *Vita S. Wilfridi* and Bede's similar account of the same incident.[7] Stephen recounts how Wilfrid was taken ill and almost died on a return journey from Rome. On the fifth day of his illness, however, St Michael appeared to him saying:

Ego sum Michael summi Dei nuntius, qui misit me ad te indicare, quod tibi adduntur anni uitae pro intercessione sanctae Mariae genetricis Dei semperque uirginis et pro subditorum tuorum lacrimis, ad aures Domini peruenientibus; et

[5] *Oracional Visigotico*, ed. J. Vives, Monumenta Hispaniae Sacrae, Series Liturgica 1 (Barcelona, 1946), nos. 202–36.

[6] *Aldhelmi opera*, ed. Ehwald, p. 13: 'Excellent lady and holy virgin mother: listen mercifully to the petitions of these people praying, who moisten their withered faces with streams of tears and, on bended leg, strike the earth with their knees, seeing that they deserve forgiveness from the flowing fountain of their tears and obliterate the sins of their life with their continual prayers' (*Aldhelm: The Poetic Works*, trans. Lapidge and Rosier, p. 47).

[7] *The Life of Bishop Wilfrid*, ed. Colgrave, p. 122; *Venerabilis Baedae opera historica*, ed. Plummer I, 329.

hoc tibi erit signum, quod ab hac die in dies melioratus sanaberis et ad patriam tuam peruenies, tibique substantiarum tuarum carissima quaeque redduntur, et in pace uitam consummabis. Paratus quoque esto, quia post .iiii. annorum spatium iterum uisitabo te. Iam enim memento quod in honore sancti Petri et Andreae apostolis domos aedificasti, sanctae uero Mariae semper uirgini intercedenti pro te nullam fecisti. Habes hoc emendare et in honorem eius domum dedicare.[8]

This story is interesting as it would appear to be a deliberate corrective: Wilfrid's neglect of Mary is castigated and the implication of the tale is that Mary's intercession is more effective than that of Peter and Andrew. It cannot be without significance that the pope with whom Wilfrid had just spent several months in Rome was Sergius (687–701), a man noted for his devotion to Mary, and this can hardly be unconnected with his dream.[9] The reproof was not without effect, and Wilfrid made good his omission by dedicating a church to Mary in the monastery of St Andrew at Hexham, as well as by ordering gifts to be sent to the church of Santa Maria Maggiore in Rome after his death.

Although several of Bede's homilies and his commentary on Luke deal with Mary, these texts are not punctuated by prayer to her as are, for example, the African Marian homilies of the fifth and sixth centuries.[10] The only text in which Bede appeals explicitly for Mary's intercession is the hymn *In natali sanctae Dei genitricis* and even this text is chiefly Christocentric. The first two verses are addressed to Christ and it is only in the third that Bede turns to Mary:

> et tu, beata prae omnibus,
> Virgo Maria, feminis,

[8] *Ibid.*, p. 122: 'I am Michael the messenger of the most high God, who sent me to tell you that years of life have been added to you by the intercession of St Mary, mother of God and ever virgin, and by the lamentations of your followers, which have reached the ears of the Lord; and this shall be a sign to you: from this day you will begin to grow better day by day, and you will reach your native land; and all the most precious of your possessions will be returned to you, and you will end your life in peace. Also be prepared; for after the space of four years I will visit you again. Now remember that you have built churches in honour of the Apostles St Peter and St Andrew; but you have built nothing in honour of St Mary, ever virgin, who is interceding for you. You have to put this right and to dedicate a church in honour of her' (*The Life of Bishop Wilfrid*, p. 123).

[9] See Levison, *England and the Continent*, p. 57.

[10] See, for example, Pseudo-Augustine, *Sermo* cxx (PL 39, 1984–7).

> Dei genetrix inclita,
> Nostris faueto laudibus. [11]

Later in the hymn Bede praises Mary as a concrete, earthly figure:

> Pudica cuius uiscera,
> Sancto dicata Spiritu,
> Dauidis ortum semine
> Regem ferebant saeculi.
>
> Beata cuius ubera
> Summo repleta munere
> Terris alebant unicam
> Terrae polique gloriam. [12]

Scheffzyck has pointed out that the way in which Bede extols Mary here had a significant influence on 'die poetische Erfassung der menschlich-mütterlichen Züge Mariens'. [13] The main part of the hymn recounts the events of Mary's life as told in the New Testament and the final verses contain an appeal for Mary's intercession with Christ to accept the hymn of praise. As a plea for intercession this is minimal, a feature in keeping with Bede's emphasis on Christ rather than Mary.

The *uita* of Leoba (*ob.* 779), an Anglo-Saxon nun who became abbess of Bischofsheim in Germany, was written *c.* 836 by Rudolf, a Fulda monk, and again provides evidence of an appeal to Mary, this time with a specific request:

Interea saeuit tempestas, et uentorum furorem domorum tecta non sustinent, crebrisque fulminum ictibus terra tremescit, tenebrarum quoque densitas' et continua coruscationum per fenestras irruptio maximum timidis horrorem ingeminant. Tum populus omnis, tanti terroris inmanitatem non ferens, ad altare cucurrit et beatam uirginem ab oratione excitat periculis opponendam. Primaque eam Tecla, consanguinea eius, his uocibus adorsa est: 'O dilecte dilecta, in te opes populi huius, in te uotorum summa consistit. Surge ergo et pro nobis dominam tuam sanctam Dei genitricem inuoca, ut eius intercessione ab huius tempestatis discrimine liberemur.' Ab hanc uocem illa ab oratione surrexit, et quasi ad

---

[11] *Opera rhythmica*, ed. Fraipont, p. 433: 'And you, Virgin Mary, glorious mother of God, blessed above all women, favour our praises.'

[12] *Ibid.*: 'Whose chaste womb, consecrated to the Holy Spirit, brought forth the king of the world, born from the seed of David. Whose blessed breasts, filled with the highest gift, nourished for the world the unique glory of earth and sky.'

[13] Scheffczyk, *Das Mariengeheimnis*, p. 135.

colluctationem uocaretur, cappam qua erat induta abiciens, fores aecclesiae confidenter aperuit, atque in limine consistens, signo sanctae crucis edito, furenti tempestati nomen summae maiestatis opposuit, extensisque manibus in caelum, terno clamore Christi clementiam inuocauit et per intercessionem ac merita sanctae Mariae uirginis propitium eum populo suo uelociter adesse precabatur. [14]

The phrase 'dominam tuam' is interesting here in that it suggests Leoba's personal devotion to the Virgin, who is, of course, the obvious patron of a virgin nun.

Alcuin (*ob.* 804), as well as composing liturgical prayers to Mary, also wrote a series of tituli for churches and altars, including some dedicated to the Virgin. These fervid inscriptions, whose epithets reveal an exalted concept of Mary's status, were intended to prompt prayer in the minds of those reading them in the churches:

> Virgo Maria, dei genitrix tu intacta tonantis.
> Tu regina poli, uitae spes maxima nostrae . . . [15]

> Virgo Maria dei genitrix, castissima uirgo,
> Lux et stella maris, nostrae regina salutis [16]

> Tu mihi dulcis amor, decus, et spes magna salutis.

---

[14] *Vita Leobae*, ed. G. Waitz, p. 128: 'In the meantime the storm raged, the roofs of the houses were torn off by the violence of the wind, the ground shook with the repeated shocks of the thunderbolts, and the thick darkness, intensified by the incessant flicker of lightning which flashed through the windows, redoubled their terror. Then the mob, unable to endure the suspense any longer, rushed to the altar to rouse her from prayer and seek her protection. Thecla, her kinswoman, spoke to her first, saying: "Beloved, all the hopes of these people lie in you: you are their only support. Arise, then, and pray to the Mother of God, your mistress, for us, that by her intercession we may be delivered from this fearful storm." At these words Leoba rose up from prayer and, as if she had been challenged to a contest, flung off the cloak which she was wearing and boldly opened the doors of the church. Standing on the threshold, she made a sign of the cross, opposing to the fury of the storm the name of the High God. Then she stretched out her hands towards heaven and three times invoked the mercy of Christ, praying that through the intercession of Holy Mary, the virgin, He would quickly come to the help of his people' (*The Anglo-Saxon Missionaries in Germany*, trans. Talbot, pp. 219–20).

[15] *Alcuini carmina*, ed. Dümmler, p. 325 (no. XII, lines 5–6): 'Virgin Mary, you (are) the undefiled mother of God the Thunderer, you (are) the queen of the sky, greatest hope of our life . . .'

[16] *Ibid.*, p. 336 (no. IV, lines 1–2): 'Virgin Mary, mother of God, most pure virgin, light and star of the sea, queen of our salvation . . .'

Auxiliare tuum seruum, clarissima uirgo.
Vox mea te lacrimis pulsat, mens ardet amore . . .[17]

Alcuin's Marian vocabulary is fairly conventional by this date, showing the influence of liturgical texts in particular.

THE PRAYER-BOOKS OF THE EIGHTH AND NINTH CENTURIES

The evidence thus far shows that prayer addressed directly to Mary, asking for her intercession, was an accepted feature of early Anglo-Saxon religious life. The Bede hymn was intended for liturgical use, but the other prayers are in a sense incidental to the literary form in which they occur. From the second half of the eighth century onwards, however, we find prayers explicitly composed for private devotion and recorded in collections intended as aids in such devotion. The origin of these prayer-books is obscure and, although the earliest manuscripts are English, Wilmart thought that an ascription of the genre to the British Isles would be too simplistic: 'il n'est pas interdit de croire que les premiers textes de cette catégorie ont été composés en divers pays, au début du moyen âge, sous l'empire des mêmes besoins'.[18] But it has also been argued that such collections are indeed an English development, influenced by the Irish interest in private prayer and confession, even though no similar Irish collections survive:[19] the English books certainly seem to owe much to Irish influence, as one would expect at this period, and two of them preserve texts of the *Lorica* of Laidcenn, a seventh-century Irish prayer, and have many other Irish connections.[20] It is not impossible, then, that the impulse to gather these devotional texts into distinct collections was originally an insular one. There is no doubt, at any rate, that the surviving English collections are English in origin, rather than being imported from

---

[17] *Ibid.*, p. 313 (no. XC, lines 6–8): 'You are sweet love, grace and the great hope of salvation for me. Help your servant, brightest virgin; my voice batters you with tears, my mind burns with love.'

[18] A. Wilmart, 'Prières à Sainte Anne, à Saint Michel, à Saint Martin, censées de Saint Anselme', in his *Auteurs spirituels*, pp. 202–16, at 210: 'The belief that the first texts of this type were composed in different countries, at the beginning of the Middle Ages, in response to the same needs, is not precluded.'

[19] Bestul, 'Continental Sources of Anglo-Saxon Devotional Writing', pp. 104–11.

[20] See Bishop, 'Liturgical Note' and 'Spanish Symptoms', in his *Liturgica Historica*, pp. 165–202; Sims-Williams, 'Thought, Word and Deed'; Hughes, 'Some Aspects of Irish Influence'.

elsewhere, and they are one manifestation of a drive to compile different types of material useful in the devotional life, evident in the eighth and ninth centuries.[21] They clearly show the influence of the two main types of piety to which England was exposed, the Roman and the Irish. Four of these collections, dating from the end of the eighth century and the beginning of the ninth, survive: London, BL, Harley 7653; BL, Royal 2. A. XX, the Royal Prayer-Book; BL, Harley 2965, the Book of Nunnaminster; and Cambridge, University Library, Ll. 1. 10, the Book of Cerne.

Harley 7653 is now a fragment of seven leaves, written at the end of the eighth or the beginning of the ninth century, probably for a woman, as there are many feminine forms.[22] It contains a litany, the beginning of which is missing, and seven prayers. The Royal Prayer-Book, of the end of the eighth century, is a Mercian florilegium composed of gospel extracts, canticles, prayers, hymns and a litany; it also includes a short prayer in Greek and a series of prayers by Moucan, who was probably a Welshman.[23] The Book of Nunnaminster, written at the end of the eighth or the beginning of the ninth century, concentrates especially on the Passion of Christ: it begins with the different evangelists' accounts of the Passion and there follows a series of prayers, including a long cycle on the life of Christ and his Passion.[24] Other prayers, less relevant to the central theme of the manuscript, occur both before and after this core of texts. The fourth book, the Book of Cerne (to which monastery it later belonged), is another southern manuscript, written at the beginning of the ninth century. It consists of a collection of gospel extracts (the Passion and Resurrection according to each of the evangelists), an acrostic spelling Æthilwald, a long series of mainly penitential prayers, a breviate psalter and a Harrowing of Hell text.[25] The decoration of the book has affinities with manuscripts connected with Canterbury, but it is generally considered to be a Mercian manuscript: however, as Dumville points out, it should be remembered that Canterbury remained part of the Mercian empire throughout the first quarter of the ninth century.[26] The manuscript 'is not an original or

[21] See Bestul, 'Continental Sources', pp. 106–9.
[22] *The Antiphonary of Bangor*, ed. Warren II, 83–6.
[23] *The Book of Cerne*, ed. Kuypers, pp. 200–25; on Moucan see Hughes, 'Some Aspects of Irish Influence'.
[24] *An Ancient Manuscript*, ed. Birch.   [25] *The Book of Cerne*, ed. Kuypers.
[26] See Alexander, *Insular Manuscripts: 6th to the 9th Century*, p. 84; Dumville, 'Liturgical Drama', p. 395, n. 5.

homogeneous collection of prayers, but was derived directly or indirectly from more than one source'[27] and the core of the collection may have been compiled by Æthilwald, bishop of Lindisfarne from 721 to 740.[28] Dumville defines this core as the acrostic, gospel extracts, hymns, breviate psalter and the Harrowing of Hell text: it did not, on his reckoning, include the prose prayers. All of these manuscripts have texts in common with at least one other manuscript of the group, and the three complete collections are similarly structured, with gospel extracts followed by prayers. The Royal, Nunnaminster and Cerne books share some prayers from a cycle on the life of Christ which, Sims-Williams points out, is not found 'at all in the Carolingian and later continental collections, a fact which leads one to suppose that the cycle was a late-eighth- or early-ninth-century development which occurred after Alcuin's departure for the continent and consequently enjoyed a purely English popularity'.[29]

Harley 7653 has no prayer to the Virgin, nor is she mentioned in what remains of the litany, even though this includes a large number of female virgin saints. The Royal Prayer-Book similarly has no prayer to Mary, but there does, however, appear to have been an intention to include one, since on fol. 46 we find the title *Oratio sanctae Mariae matris domini nostri*, followed by a prayer to the Trinity. Kuypers saw no incongruity in this, but Barré has pointed out that the same title also occurs in a Trier psalter and here it is followed by the prayer to Mary which we also find in the Book of Nunnaminster and the Book of Cerne.[30] This prayer, then, must have been in the exemplar from which the Royal scribe was copying and it was, therefore, probably circulating in England in the second half of the eighth century. Some of the prayers in the Royal Prayer-Book invoke Mary among other saints: the long *Oratio sancti Hygbaldi abbatis* includes the words 'Sancta Maria semper uirgo beata et gloriosa dei genitrix intercede pro me, cum omnibus simul sacris uirginibus . . .';[31] Mary is also invoked in the concluding *Deprecatio*: 'Benedictio sanctae Mariae cum filiabus suis sit super me.'[32] The *Precatio ad sanctam Mariam et sanctum Petrum et ad ceteros*

---

[27] *The Book of Cerne*, ed. Kuypers, p. xviii.

[28] See Bishop, 'Spanish Symptoms', in his *Liturgica Historica*, pp. 192–7; Dumville, 'Liturgical Drama', pp. 393–4.

[29] Sims-Williams, 'Ephrem the Syrian', p. 209.   [30] Barré, *Prières anciennes*, p. 64.

[31] *The Book of Cerne*, ed. Kuypers, p. 208: 'Holy Mary, ever virgin, blessed and glorious mother of God, together with all the sacred virgins, intercede for me . . .'

[32] *Ibid.*, p. 209: 'May the holy blessing of Mary with her daughters be upon me.'

apostolos begins: 'intercede pro me sancta Maria beatissima et gloriosa dei genitrix domini nostri Iesu Christi . . .'[33] Prayers to the Virgin alone presumably grew out of this type of text, with the Marian portions being separated from the rest and then expanded.

In the Book of Nunnaminster this process is complete, as it includes an independent prayer to Mary. The Marian text comes between prayers to Michael and to John the Baptist, as do the prayers to her in the Book of Cerne, whereas in the later books Mary is placed before the angels, in accordance with the liturgy: 'Ecce exaltata es super choros angelorum . . .'[34] The Nunnaminster prayer appears both here and in the Book of Cerne followed by a prayer to John the Baptist so similar in construction that it is probably the work of the same hand, or else one is an imitation of the other:

Sancta Maria gloriosa Dei genetrix et semper uirgo, quae mundo meruisti generare salutem, et lucem mundi caelorumque gloriam obtulisti sedentibus in tenebris et umbra mortis, esto mihi pia dominatrix, et cordis mei inluminatrix, et adiutrix apud Deum Patrem omnipotentem, ut ueniam delictorum meorum accipere, et inferni tenebras euadere, et ad uitam aeternam peruenire merear. Per.[35]

Sancte Iohannes baptista, qui meruisti saluatorem mundi baptizare tuis manibus in fluuio Iordanis, esto mihi pius interuentor apud misericordem Deum redemtorem nostrum, ut me a peccatorum tenebris eripiat et ad lucem caelestis gratiae perducat, qui tollit peccata mundi et regnum caelorum adpropinquare promisit, cui honor et gloria per omnia saecula saeculorum. Amen.[36]

The main difference between these two prayers is the difference in quantity and quality between the epithets applied to Mary and to John the Baptist: Mary is 'pia dominatrix', 'inluminatrix' and 'adiutrix', John merely 'pius

[33] *Ibid.*, p. 218: 'Most blessed holy Mary, glorious mother of God, our lord Jesus Christ, intercede for me . . .'

[34] PL 78, 798.

[35] Barré, *Prières anciennes*, p. 65: 'Glorious and ever-virgin holy Mary, mother of God, who deserved to give birth to salvation for the world and offered the light of the world and the glory of the heavens to those sitting in darkness and the shadow of death, be to me a kind patroness and enlightener of my heart and helper before God, the omnipotent Father, so that I may deserve to receive forgiveness for my offences and to escape the darkness of hell and attain to eternal life.'

[36] *An Ancient Manuscript*, ed. Birch, p. 88: 'St John the Baptist, who deserved to baptize the Saviour of the world in the river Jordan with your own hands, be a kind intercessor for me in the presence of the merciful God our redeemer, so that he may rescue me from

interuentor'. These epithets transfer into the feminine the kind of
appellations originally used of one of the Trinity. Although not as effusive
as the first prayer to Mary in the Book of Cerne, this prayer shows a
developed concept of the importance of Mary's role and sets a pattern of
appeals for her help at judgement.

The Book of Cerne contains three prayers to Mary (nos. 56–8), one of
which is identical to that in Nunnaminster. Barré considered that all three
were English and that all date from the second half of the eighth century.[37]
The first of these consists largely of a virtuoso piling-up of near synonyms:

Sancta Dei genetrix semper uirgo, beata, benedicta, gloriosa et generosa, intacta et
intemerata, casta et incontaminata Maria, inmaculata, electa et a Deo dilecta,
singulari sanctitate praedita atque omni laude digna, quae es interpellatrix pro
totius mundi discrimine, exaudi, exaudi, exaudi nos, sancta Maria. Ora pro nobis
et intercede, et auxiliare ne dedigneris. Confidimus enim et pro certo scimus quia
omne quod uis potes impetrare a filio tuo Domino nostro Iesu Christo, Deo
omnipotente, omnium saeculorum rege, qui uiuit cum Patre et Spiritu sancto in
saecula saeculorum. Amen.[38]

Bishop describes this prayer thus:

As a prayer to the Blessed Virgin it certainly has some noteworthy features: the
accumulation on the one appellative 'Dei genetrix semper uirgo' of eleven
adjectives, besides three adjective clauses; the triple 'exaudi'; the very confident
expression 'we trust and know for certain you can obtain from your son everything
that you wish'. These three items make up, it may be said, the whole prayer,
which may read to some as betraying a mind overstrung, to others only as if
evincing a desire to outdo a forerunner.[39]

the darkness of sins and bring me to the light of heavenly grace, who takes away the sins
of the world and promises the approach to the kingdom of heaven, to whom be honour
and glory for ever and ever. Amen.'

[37] Barré, *Prières anciennes*, p. 70.

[38] *Ibid.*, pp. 67–8: 'Holy, ever-virgin mother of God, happy, blessed, glorious and noble,
untouched and pure, chaste and undefiled Mary, immaculate, chosen and beloved by
God, endowed with singular sanctity and worthy of all praise, who are the mediator for
the whole world when faced with danger, hear, hear, hear us, holy Mary. Pray and
intercede for us and do not scorn to help. For we trust and we know for certain that you
can obtain everything that you wish from your son, our Lord Jesus Christ, the
omnipotent God, king of all ages, who lives with the Father and the Holy Spirit without
end. Amen.'

[39] 'Spanish Symptoms', in his *Liturgica Historica*, p. 174.

There has been some discussion of the sources of this prayer. Bishop implies that it owes much to Spanish influence, particularly to the *Liber de uirginitate perpetua Sanctae Mariae* of Ildefonsus, bishop of Toledo (*c.* 607–67),[40] and Mayr-Harting, too, argues that this, 'the most remarkable of Cerne's prayers to the Blessed Virgin', offers a 'particularly clear case of Spanish influence': 'The expressions by Hildephonsus of confidence in the Virgin's power, his urgent repetitions, and his piling-on of adjectives are echoed in the Cerne prayer.'[41] We have, however, no manuscript evidence that this work of Ildefonsus was known outside Spain before the tenth century,[42] and neither the similarity of style nor that of sentiment between Cerne 56 and the Spanish treatise is so close as to admit of no explanation other than direct influence. There is nothing in Cerne 56 comparable to the dependence shown by the third Cerne prayer (58) to the Virgin on the second (57), for example, and the vocabulary shared by it and *De uirginitate perpetua* is not distinctive enough to differentiate them from other Marian texts of this period. Ildefonsus's style is based on the *Synonyma* of Isidore of Seville, a work which was known early in Ireland and exercised a stylistic influence there also.[43] Indeed, Bishop pointed out that 'the *De uirginitate perpetua* shews the same sort of florid elocution, in which triads and quaternions are the soberest forms, that meets us so often in early Irish Latinity'.[44] It is perhaps more likely, then, that Cerne 56 was composed independently of the work of Ildefonsus, but in an Irish-influenced milieu exposed to the same type of stylistic influence. The intense Marian fervour evident in the Cerne prayer was also not peculiar to Spain: it resembles, for example, that in the antiphonary which seems to have been used at York and which was copied by Alcuin into his devotional anthology *De laude Dei.*[45] Suggestions of Spanish influence in this are difficult to substan-

---

[40] *Ibid.*, pp. 174–8; but see Sims-Williams, 'Ephrem the Syrian', pp. 216–17.

[41] Mayr-Harting, *The Coming of Christianity*, p. 186.

[42] *De uirginitate beatae Mariae*, ed. Garcia, pp. 7–54; J. N. Hillgarth, 'The East, Visigothic Spain and the Irish', *Studia Patristica* 4 [= Texte und Untersuchungen 79] (1961), 442–56, at 446, n. 2.

[43] See *De uirginitate beatae Mariae*, ed. Garcia, pp. 244–7, for Isidore's influence on Ildefonsus and J. N. Hillgarth, 'Visigothic Spain and Early Christian Ireland', *Proceedings of the Royal Irish Academy* 62C (1962), 167–94, at 172, for Isidore and the Irish.

[44] 'Spanish Symptoms', in his *Liturgica Historica*, p. 176.

[45] See Constantinescu, 'Alcuin et les "libelli precum"', pp. 49–51.

tiate.[46] It should be remembered that this very period was one in which Roman devotion to the Virgin was influenced by a succession of Syrian and Greek popes, several of whom were particularly noted for their devotion to Mary (e.g. Sergius and John VII): Roman liturgical texts introduced in England at this period would probably have reflected this upsurge in Marian devotion. The following antiphons from *De laude Dei* can be compared in ardour and in their appeals for intercession to Cerne 56: 'Vere benedicta imperatrix et gloriosa castitatis regina, quae cum honore uirginitatis gaudium matris habes'; 'Gloriosa semper uirgo, uirga radicis Jesse, de qua uitae flos processit, intercede pro nobis'; 'Sancta Maria, nos laudamus te, gloriosa, glorificamus te, corona regni coronata es, intercede pro nobis, quia beata es.'[47] The Cerne prayer, then, may well be the product of an insular, liturgically-influenced devotional impulse, rather than a Spanish one.

The second prayer in Cerne is the *Sancta Maria gloriosa* of the Book of Nunnaminster and the third, headed *Oratio Alchfriðo ad sanctam Mariam*, is clearly based on the Nunnaminster one (it is unlikely to have been the other way round, as Alchfrith also adapts other prayers):

Sancta Maria gloriosa Dei genetrix et semper uirgo, quae mundo meruisti generare salutem, exaudi me et miserere mihi nunc et ubique propter honorem et gloriam excellentissimae uirginitatis tuae. Te deprecor humiliter, esto mihi saluatrix et adiutrix apud omnipotentem Deum et dominum nostrum Iesum Christum, ut ipse me pius pastor et princeps pacis a peccatorum maculis emundet, et ab inferni tenebris eripiat, ut ad uitam perducat aeternam. Qui per te, castissima uirgo Maria, uenit in mundum inmundissimum, et humanum genus suo sanguine saluauit et a morte leuauit, et inferni claustra destruxit et caelestis regni ianuas' aperuit, ille me per misericordiam suam in hoc saeculo saluare et emundare et seruare dignetur, et post finem huius uitae labentis aliquam partem aeternae beatitudinis in sanctorum societate concedat Iesus Christus dominus noster.

[46] See Bullough, 'Alcuin and the Kingdom of Heaven', pp. 7–8; Rankin, 'The Liturgical Background of the Old English Advent Lyrics', p. 322. See also above, p. 57.

[47] Constantinescu, 'Alcuin et les "libelli precum"', pp. 49–51: 'O truly blessed empress and glorious queen of chastity, who possess the joy of a mother with the honour of virginity'; 'O glorious ever virgin, a rod from the root of Jesse, from whom the flower of life came forth, intercede for us'; 'Holy Mary, we praise you, glorious one, we glorify you, you are crowned with the crown of the kingdom, intercede for us because you are blessed.' See also above, pp. 55–6.

Illi honor et gloria cum Patre et Spiritu sancto per infinita saecula saeculorum. Amen.[48]

Alchfrith, the author of this prayer, seems to have been an anchorite in the area of Lindisfarne towards the end of the eighth century. A letter of his, which draws on two sermons by Columbanus, is preserved in two eleventh-century English manuscripts: the addressee is Hyglac, who probably lived *c.* 780 in Northumbria and was the teacher of the poet Æthelwulf.[49] Two other prayers which Alchfrith addressed to God, Cerne 47 and 48, are extant and both take Cerne 17 as their starting-point, but differ conspicuously from their source: 'Prayers 47 and 48, as compared with 17, are marked by sobriety and restraint. In 17 there is a pious abandon that surrenders itself to an overpowering consciousness of guilt and seems to lose the sense of proportion.'[50] Prayer 17 shows a marked affinity with texts which we know to be Irish, displaying the qualities of 'all heart and much fluency with little mind',[51] which Bishop thought characteristic of Irish piety, and it is, therefore, reasonable to assume that it was composed in Ireland or in a sphere of Irish influence. The more subdued type of spirituality evident in the changes which Alchfrith makes to his source displays, according to Kuypers and Bishop, the influence of the Roman sacramentaries in use in England. There can be no simple distinction between the areas of Irish and Roman influence, therefore: Alchfrith's spirit may have been more akin to the Roman, but his sources in these prayers and in his letter to Hyglac are Irish, with the heightened language and exaggerated self-abasement often found in Irish prayer. The

[48] Barré, *Prières anciennes*, pp. 69–70: 'Holy Mary, glorious mother of God and ever virgin, who deserved to give birth to salvation for the world, hear me and have mercy on me now and everywhere through the honour and glory of your most excellent virginity. I pray to you humbly be my salvatrice and my helper before Almighty God and our Lord Jesus Christ, that the kind shepherd and prince of peace himself may purify me from the stains of sins and rescue me from the darkness of hell and lead me into eternal life. He who through you, o most chaste virgin Mary, came into the most unclean world and saved mankind with his blood and rose from death and destroyed the locks of hell and opened the doors of the heavenly kingdom, may he in his mercy deign to save and cleanse and guard me and, after the end of this fading life, may Jesus Christ our Lord grant me some part of the eternal happiness in the fellowship of the saints. To him be honour and glory with the Father and the Holy Spirit for ever and ever. Amen.'

[49] See Levison, *England and the Continent*, pp. 295–302; *De abbatibus*, ed. Campbell, pp. xxvii–xxviii; Hughes, 'Some Aspects of Irish Influence', p. 59.

[50] *The Book of Cerne*, ed. Kuypers, p. xix.

[51] Bishop, 'About an Old Prayer Book', in his *Liturgica Historica*, pp. 384–91, at 385.

adaptation of the prayer to Mary shows verbal similarities with Alchfrith's other works. Levison has pointed to the parallel with the letter to Hyglac: 'Qui . . . inferni claustra destruxit et caelestis regni ianuas aperuit . . . Ipsi honor et gloria'[52] and the description of Mary as 'castissima uirgo' is paralleled in the second prayer to God: 'Obsecro te domine Iesu Christe . . . per Mariam matrem tuam et castissimam uirginem'.[53] A comparison of Cerne 58 with its source shows that he expands mainly by adding passages relating to Christ, not Mary. Only the first two sentences in Alchfrith's text develop the Marian content by an appeal to Mary to listen to his prayer and to have mercy on him. The long Christological passages correct the balance of the prayer and the effect resembles the restraining influence which Alchfrith brings to the source of his prayers to God. His spirit is not that of the Roman church as described by Bishop – 'frigid and unmoved before the enthusiasm by which the Eastern or barbarian mind was carried away'[54] – yet it cannot be accused of showing the wild abandon of Cerne 56.

These three early insular prayers are considered by Barré to be especially important for the history of Marian devotion because 'il existe alors fort peu d'autres témoignages explicites du recours à l'intercession de la Vierge Marie'.[55] In Cerne 56 this belief in Mary's powers of intercession is especially striking and the ability to demand everything from her son is attributed to her. All three texts laud Mary as the virgin mother of God, as we would expect, and Cerne 56 ascribes a unique holiness to her. Numerically, too, both Nunnaminster and Cerne show Mary's importance in comparison with other saints. Nunnaminster has sixty-four prayers and of these only three are addressed to individual saints: one each to Michael, Mary and John the Baptist. Cerne contains seventy-four prayers and the three addressed to Mary are equalled only by the three to Peter. The Royal Prayer-Book contains no prayers to individual saints, so the apparent intention to include one to Mary is also significant.

We know that Alchfrith's prayer was composed in Northumbria, and this also, of course, proves that the Nunnaminster prayer was circulating there by *c.* 780 at the latest. It is possible that the Irish-influenced Cerne 56 is Northumbrian also, but Kathleen Hughes has shown that Mercia, too,

---

[52] *England and the Continent*, p. 300.   [53] *The Book of Cerne*, ed. Kuypers, p. 144.

[54] Bishop, 'A Liturgical Note', p. 280.

[55] *Prières anciennes*, p. 70: 'There are at that time very few other explicit witnesses to recourse to the intercession of the Virgin Mary.'

was very much under Irish influence (although most of her evidence relates to the seventh, not the eighth century)[56] and it could, therefore, have originated there. The Book of Cerne in its present form seems to be a Mercian production and it may have drawn on local as well as Northumbrian sources. The small number of early prayer-books does not allow many generalizations about the spread of devotion to the Virgin, but it is nevertheless clear that it flourished in Northumbria in the second half of the eighth century and that several ninth-century Mercian compilers were interested and pious enough to incorporate prayers to the Virgin in their devotional florilegia.

THE TENTH AND ELEVENTH CENTURIES

Glastonbury

The eighth-century efflorescence of Marian prayers is followed by a gap: if anything was composed in the ninth and the beginning of the tenth centuries, nothing survives. A second flowering of Marian devotion, this time in the south of England in the latter half of the tenth century (the Benedictine reform period), is, however, heralded by a text composed by Dunstan, one of the initiators of the reform movement, when he was abbot of Glastonbury (c. 940–956) and before he became archbishop of Canterbury. Two Anglo-Saxon manuscripts (Cambridge, Trinity College, O.1.18 (1042), a late tenth- or early eleventh-century copy of Augustine's *Enchiridion* and Cambridge, Trinity College B.14.3. (289), a copy (from the same period) of Arator's *De actibus apostolorum* preserve a poem composed of 'a series of prayers by Dunstan to God the Father, to Christ, to the Holy Ghost, to the Virgin, to the prophets and to the Church Fathers and apostles'.[57] Dunstan's authorship is established by the telestich INDIGNVM ABBATEM DVNSTANVM XPE RESPECTES, spelt out by the final letters of each line. As Lapidge points out, no one else would address Dunstan as 'indignus'.[58] The poem is written in the hermeneutic style and Dunstan seems to have written it as a 'deliberate challenge to his readers' wits':[59]

---

[56] 'Some Aspects of Irish Influence', pp. 60–1.
[57] Lapidge, 'The Hermeneutic Style', p. 109.
[58] *Ibid.*, p. 96.   [59] *Ibid.*

Gaudia quam implores caelesti semine neuiS
Nuntius angelico ut me famine, uirgo, salutaT
Explosis natum es concepto crimina natA
Regmina qui trinum retinet mihi mystica numeN,
Intuitusque pii dignetur cernere uisV
Soluere tu proprium rogo quo dare longa per ȩuuM.[60]

Mary's complete sinlessness is here made the basis of a request that she intercede for the forgiveness of Dunstan's sins. Dunstan's assertion that Mary was born without stain is particularly interesting, although it is difficult to know how rigorously it should be interpreted. Such pictorial language was often applied to Mary, and this insistence on her unblemished birth may not have been intended as a theological statement of her freedom from original sin. Nevertheless, such descriptions generally state only that she was *immaculata* or *intemerata*, without specifying that she was born thus: Dunstan's poem appears to be the first such statement in England and may, therefore, indicate Carolingian influence. It is significant also that Mary is the only saint to whom Dunstan addresses a prayer singly and that this is placed directly after the prayers to the Trinity. Apart from the reference to Mary's birth without sin, the prayer is sober and Christological and it is not until the eleventh century that there is a marked development in emotionalism in Anglo-Latin prayers.

Canterbury

Even though Dunstan's prayer appears to have been written in Glastonbury and not Canterbury, this latter city is one where we would also expect his influence to be apparent, but there is little evidence of this in Canterbury manuscripts. Paris, Bibliothèque Nationale, lat. 8824, the Paris Psalter of *c.* 1030, may have been written in Canterbury, although perhaps for a woman not connected with the Canterbury diocese.[61] This manuscript has parallel versions of the Psalter in Latin and Old English, the latter probably

---

[60] *Ibid.*, p. 108: 'Virgin, whom the messenger salutes in angelic speech, you were born without stain: I ask that you implore him – who, born from the conception of celestial seed holds the mysterious command as trinal deity – to forgive me my sins, that he may deign to grant longlasting joys through his own eternity and to look upon me with the sight of his holy vision' (trans. Lapidge, *ibid.*, p. 111).

[61] Temple, *Anglo-Saxon Manuscripts 900–1066*, p. 100; I am grateful to Jane Toswell for pointing out this prayer to me.

by Alfred, followed by canticles, a litany and a series of prayers. It contains a prayer to Mary and all the saints, in which Mary heads a list of the groups whose intercession is implored and in which she is the only saint to be mentioned by name:

Sancte Marie semper uirginis sanctorumque omnium archangelorum, angelorum, patriarcharum, prophetarum, apostolorum, martirum, confessorum, monachorum, uirginum et omnium simul sanctorum tuorum, domine, suffragia imploramus ut eorum intercessionibus a cunctis, domine, liberemur offensis peccati atque maculis per te, fili dei qui uiuis . . .[62]

Otherwise, only London, BL Arundel 155, a psalter from Christ Church, Canterbury, of the first half of the eleventh century, contains a copy of the beginning of the *Oratio Alchfriðo*, glossed in Anglo-Saxon:

La þu halige 7 wuldorfulle godes moder 7 simle mæden ðu middanearde gearnudest cennan hælend, gehyr (me) 7 gemiltsa min nu 7 æfre for wyrþscipe haligre 7 oferhlifigendestran mædenhades þines þe ic bidde eadmodlice beo þu me ic bidde hælestre 7 fultumgestre mid gode ælmihtigum.[63]

Abingdon

From Abingdon we have one Marian text, added, probably between 1030 and 1044, to Cambridge, University Library, Kk.3.21, a copy of Boethius's *De consolatione Philosophiae* written in Abingdon c. 1000.[64] The poem consists of a set of Latin verses, written in the form of a circular maze, which can be read in either of two ways: by following the path of the maze, which gives one arrangement of lines, or according to the circles, which

---

[62] 'We implore, Lord, the prayers of holy Mary, ever virgin, and of all the holy archangels, angels, patriarchs, prophets, apostles, martyrs, confessors, monks, virgins and of all your saints also, that through their intercession, Lord, we may be set free from all offences of sin and from stains, through you, son of God, who lives . . .'

[63] F. Holthausen, 'Altenglische Interlinearversionen', p. 254: 'O you holy and glorious mother of God and ever virgin, you deserved to give birth to the Saviour here on earth, hear me and have mercy on me now and for ever through the honour of your holy and pre-eminent virginity. I pray to you humbly, be for me, I beg, a salvatrice and helper with Almighty God.'

[64] See my 'Assumptio Mariae'; the incipits are printed and the manuscript is described by Ker, *Catalogue*, p. 58.

gives a different arrangement.[65] The seven concentric circles reflect the sevenfold heaven into which, the author prays, Siweard, the dedicatee of the verses, will be introduced. This Siweard was probably the Siweard who was abbot of Abingdon from 1030 to 1044 and later acted as archbishop of Canterbury. The verses are a prayer to Mary on his behalf, the description of her exalted state in heaven after the assumption serving to show the efficacy of appealing to her. It is not clear from the work whether the author envisages a corporal assumption of Mary, although he would perhaps have made this explicit, had he intended it. Mary was presumably chosen as the future psychopomp of Siweard at least partly because she was the patron saint of Abingdon, Siweard's monastery, and, as such, *protectrix* of its inhabitants, but also because of the majesty and eminence attributed to her. In this poem she is exclusively the queen reigning in heaven, extolled by angels, patriarchs and prophets:

ASSUMPTA EST MARIA AD CAELESTIA, ALLELUIA!
Mater uirginea nunc caelica regnat in aula,
Agminis aeterni millena milite septa.
Angelici ciues, magna comitante caterua,
Assumptae matri occurrunt, simul et paradoxam
Progenitam super exaltant prosapia Dauid,
De sua caeligenis conciue tam generosa
Angelicisque choris resonantibus alleluia.
Alleluia Deo tibi soluimus, est quia sumpta.
Assumpta caelo laudetur uirgo Maria!
Ad thronum maiestatis hanc extulit almi
Ingeniti unigena, tum congaudentibus illic,
Caelicola felix quia terque quaterque beata.
Alma chorus patriarcharum pariterque prophetae
Exultant et apostolico cetui sociantur.
Regi quo regum famulus sit pronus in aethre,
Ast tibi, uirgo, decus, laus, gloria magnificata,
Ante deum super attollique sic meruisti.
Insere Siweardum caeli septemplicis aula!

---

[65] I am grateful to Miss Barbara Raw for pointing this out to me. Such labyrinthine designs can also be found in Carolingian manuscripts: see H. Leclercq, 'Labyrinthe', *Dictionnaire d'archéologie chrétienne et de liturgie* VIII (Paris, 1928), cols. 973–82, and W. Haubrichs, *Ordo als Form: Strukturstudien zur Zahlenkomposition bei Otfrid von Weissenburg und in karolingischer Literatur*, Hermaea: Germanistische Forschungen ns 27 (Tübingen, 1969), 285–93.

Augustamque potentatus summi ante tribunal
Laudibus alternis reboant: 'Aue, uirgo Maria'.
Accipe deuotum tuum et famulatus honorem,
Mater et alma dei genitrix, felixque Maria.
ASSUMPTA EST MARIA AD CAELESTIA, ALLELUIA!

Virgo petit caelum; facit exultatio uersum.
Lege sua si mentis adhuc modus utitur in me,
Et dextre si forte meae non error habundat,
Hanc, ut res protestatur, sapientia struxit
Vrbem, septenus quam sic septemplicis orbis
Ambitus ambit, eamque aditis patentibus unus
Exitus, introitus aperit, claudensque recludit.
Hanc tibi nunc, Siwearde pater, pro munere dedi,
Officiosus in officio, tibimetque parebo,
Testificans tibi maiorem sub Christo et amorem,
Qui minus adtendit dantur sibi quanta sed ex quo.
His praelibatis, Christo uale, uiue, ualeto. Amen.[66]

[66] 'Assumptio Mariae', pp. 424–5: 'Mary is assumed into heaven, alleluia. The virgin mother now reigns in the court of heaven, surrounded by a thousand soldiers of the eternal army. The angel citizens, with the accompaniment of a great throng, meet the mother after the assumption and at the same time they exalt the marvellous offspring above the race of David, with dwellers in heaven and angelic choirs re-echoing alleluia for their fellow-citizen, so noble is she. We say alleluia to you, O God, because she is assumed. Assumed into heaven, let the virgin Mary be praised! The only-begotten son of the kindly unbegotten one has raised her to the throne of majesty; then, amid their rejoicing there, you are a happy inhabitant of heaven, because threefold, fourfold blessed. The kindly chorus of patriarchs and likewise the prophets exult and join the apostolic gathering. At which let your servant kneel to the king of kings in heaven, but to you, O glorified virgin, let there be honour, praise and glory, you who have thus deserved to be raised up before God. Introduce Siweard into the hall of the sevenfold heaven. Before the tribunal of the highest majesty they [laud] the august one with alternate praises, re-echoing "Ave, virgin Mary". Accept your devoted servant and the honour of service to you, mother and kind mother of God and happy Mary. Mary is assumed into heaven, alleluia.

The Virgin seeks out heaven; exaltation inspires my verse. If mental control still exercises its law in me, and if, perchance, my right hand does not err excessively, as the facts bear witness wisdom has structured this city, which a sevenfold circle surrounds, and one and the same exit and entrance opens it with open approaches and closing, closes it again. To you, father Siweard, I have given this as a gift, I, dutiful in my duty to you, and I shall obey you, bearing witness to you my greater love under Christ, who does not attend to how much is given but from where. These things having been said, rejoice, live and rejoice in Christ. Amen.'

Winchcombe

The mid-eleventh-century psalter in Cambridge, University Library, Ff. 1.23 probably comes from Winchcombe, as St Kenelm is prominent in the litany, and it includes three Marian prayers: Cerne 57, the last lines of Cerne 56 and another prayer which is otherwise found only in a thirteenth-century Italian psalter:

Dei genitrix domina mea beata Maria, te deprecor per Christum Iesum dominum, ut miserearis mihi peccatori famulo tuo N., quia multiplicata sunt peccata mea super numerum arene maris, et non habeo ubi confugiam nisi ad te, domina mea, sancta Maria. Ideo flexibiliter peto ut [ad] dominum Deum nostrum pro me intercedere digneris, quatenus per tuas sanctas orationes omnia peccata mea dimittere dignetur. Per.[67]

As Barré points out, the 'non habeo ubi confugiam nisi ad te' echoes the legend of Theophilus,[68] and it is possible that the whole prayer, a simple plea for forgiveness, is also inspired by this legend. The evidence does not allow us to decide whether or not this is an English composition, although the use of the Theophilus legend is certainly compatible with an English origin, as it was well known in Anglo-Saxon England.

Other Centres

No new Marian prayers survive in Worcester manuscripts, but Cambridge, Corpus Christi College, 391, the Wulstan Portiforium, includes a copy of the *Oratio Alchfriðo* and an incomplete text of the Carolingian prayer to Mary, *Singularis meriti*, with the incipit altered to *Singularis gratiae*. This change from merit to grace, also found in other English manuscripts, is interesting and suggests a wish to emphasize Mary's sanctification. Both Oxford, Bodleian Library, Douce 296, a mid-eleventh-century Crowland psalter, and London, BL, Harley 863, an Exeter psalter from the second half of the eleventh century, also include the Carolingian prayer *Singularis*

---

[67] Barré, *Prières anciennes*, p. 131: 'Mother of God, my lady, blessed Mary, I pray to you through Christ Jesus our Lord, that you may have pity on me, your servant N., a sinner, for my sins are multiplied above the sands of the sea and I have no one to whom I may have recourse except you, my lady holy Mary. Therefore, bending down, I ask you that you may deign to intercede with the lord our God for me in order that he may deign to forgive all my sins through your holy prayers.'

[68] *Ibid.*, p. 131 n. 24.

meriti (*gratiae* in Douce 296) and Vatican City, Reg. lat. 12, the eleventh-century Bury St Edmunds psalter, contains another Carolingian prayer, beginning 'Sancta Maria, genetrix domini nostri Iesu Christi, semper uirgo gloriosa', with the otherwise unattested addition:

Ob id precor te, regina caelorum, ut interuenias pro peccatis meis ad unicum Dei Filium, qui per te nasci dignatus est ad redimendum genus humanum. Sit Deo Patri gloria eiusque soli Filio una cum sancto Spiritu in saecula saeculorum. Amen.[69]

Winchester

The most interesting group of Marian prayers is, without any doubt, the texts collected in Winchester manuscripts of the eleventh century. Here, the eleventh century saw a remarkable development in prayer to the Virgin, with more important new prayers composed than in any other centre: more significant than the numerical importance, however, is the scale and nature of the devotion displayed in some of these texts. As with new liturgical texts, then, Winchester appears to have been the only centre where an innovative spirit resulted in the production of new, progressive texts. The interest in Mary appears to go back to Æthelwold himself and must have been fostered by the major role of the Virgin in the liturgical life of the monasteries in the city.

Titus D. xxvi is a small prayer-book written between 1023 and 1035 for Ælfwine, dean of New Minster, which seems later to have passed into the ownership of a woman, perhaps a nun, as some of the prayers are corrected with feminine forms. It contains a prayer to Mary and the saints, beginning: 'Sancta uirgo uirginum, succurre. Sancta Dei genitrix, intercede. Sancta Maria cum sanctis uirginibus Dei, feliciter exaudi, que inter Cherubim et Seraphim adsumpta, agnum Dei inmaculatum sequeris . . .'[70] and a litany with six invocations to Mary: 'Sancta Maria, ora. Sancta

---

[69] *Ibid.*, p. 130; A. Wilmart, 'The Prayers of the Bury Psalter', *Downside Review* 48 (1930), 198–216, at 205: 'For this I beg you, queen of the heavens, that you should intercede for my sins to the only son of God, who deigned to be born of you in order to redeem mankind. Glory be to God the Father and to his only Son together with the Holy Spirit for ever and ever, Amen.'

[70] Barré, *Prières anciennes*, p. 134: 'Holy Virgin of virgins, help. Holy mother of God, intercede. Holy Mary, together with the holy virgins of God, listen favourably, because you are assumed amongst the Cherubim and the Seraphim, you follow the immaculate lamb of God . . .'

Maria, intercede pro me misero peccatore. Sancta Maria, adiuua me in die exitus mei ex hac praesenti uita. Sancta Maria, adiuua me in die tribulationis meae. Sancta Dei genitrix, ora. Sancta uirgo uirginum, ora.'⁷¹ Its companion manuscript, Titus D. xxvii (both were probably part of the same manuscript originally), contains four prayers to Mary, which follow its Marian Office and were presumably intended to be said after it. The first is the Carolingian prayer *Singularis meriti*, the third the *Oratio Alchfriðo*, while the second is unique and the fourth occurs only in Winchester: both were probably composed there. The second is the first English prayer to appeal in detail for Mary's help in this life, as well as at death, addressing her with the innovative 'solamen et refocillatio omnium credentium' and trusting in her intercession:

ORATIO AD DEI GENITRICEM

Sancta et intemerata uirgo Maria, solamen et refocillatio omnium credentium, ex qua auctor nostrae salutis incarnari dignatus est, submissis te interpello suspiriis et deuotissima exoro interuentione, ut ad proprium pro me intercedas misero et proboroso filium, quatinus quicquid in meis actibus prauum ac anime sospitati est contrarium deleat et abstergat, quicquid utile proficuumque hoc plantet consolidetque, ne humani generis callidissimus aduersator de meo letetur interitu, sed tuo iuuamine expulsus tristetur, meque per tua sancta suffragia taliter Christi componat gratia, ut mente pariter et corpore perseuerem incorrupta, humilis et mansueta, fidei, spei caritatisque donis fulcita prefulgidis, omnibusque Christi ita obtemperans iussis, ut cum mihi dies sorsque uenerit supprema, in collegio beatorum spirituum tibi iugiter suppeditantium merear annumerari, te mitissima mundi polique regina interueniente et Christo filio tuo annuente, qui cum coaeterno patre et almo pneumate uiuit et gloriatur unus omnipotens Deus per cuncta climata saeculi. Amen.⁷²

---

⁷¹ *Ibid.*, p. 134: 'Holy Mary, pray. Holy Mary, intercede for me, a wretched sinner. Holy Mary, help me on the day of my departure from this present life. Holy Mary, help me on the day of my distress. Holy mother of God, pray. Holy Virgin of virgins, pray.'

⁷² *Ibid.*, pp. 136–7: 'Holy and pure virgin Mary, solace and reviver of all believers, of whom the author of our salvation deigned to be incarnated, I appeal to you with humble sighs and I beseech you by your most devoted intervention that you may intercede for me, a wretched and shameful man, to your own son, that he may destroy and wipe away whatsoever is shameful in my deeds and harmful to the welfare of my soul, that he may plant and make firm whatsoever is useful and beneficial, so that the most cunning opponent of the human race may not rejoice in my ruin, but, expelled with your help, may be downcast and so, through your holy prayers, may the grace of Christ so reconcile me that I may persevere incorrupt in mind and equally in body, humble and gentle, supported by the brightly shining gifts of faith, hope and charity, and so obeying all the

111

The fourth prayer is closely related to a prayer to Mary and all the saints found in an Office for the veneration of the cross in the eleventh-century Italian psalter of Nonantola. Barré argues convincingly that the Winchester text is based on the Nonantola one, as the former contains an echo of the litany in Titus D. xxvi: 'Sancta Maria, adiuua me in die exitus mei ex hac praesenti uita.'[73] There is no reason for the Nonantola text, had it been based on the Winchester one, to omit this passage, while it is understandable that a Winchester redactor should add it. It seems probable, therefore, that the Winchester text depends on the Nonantola one, although it is also possible that both go back to a lost common source. The Titus prayer abbreviates the part of the Nonantola text dealing with the cross and the saints and it expands the source chiefly by a reference to the scene at the Crucifixion where Christ recommends Mary to John and by an increased number of supplications. These include a prayer 'pro rege nostro': this feature is very much in keeping with English piety, as prayer for the royal family is a major feature of the *Regularis concordia*.[74] It is followed by five short *preces sanctae*, the first of which is addressed to Mary:

O uirgo uirginum Dei genitrix Maria mater domini nostri Iesu Christi, regina angelorum et totius mundi, oraculum aeternae uitae, claritas caelorum, quae nec primam similem uisa es nec habere sequentem, per pretiosum sanguinem filii tui unigeniti domini nostri Iesu Christi, quem in pretium nostrae salutis effudit; et per sanctam et uenerabilem et salubrem crucem eius in qua adfixus stare dignatus est pro salute generis humani qui est fabricator mundi, et inter mortis supplicium, quod ipse Dei filius sponte pro nobis in cruce pati uoluit, te suo discipulo sancto Iohanni commendauit dicens: Ecce mater tua, adiuua nos; et per gloriosam resurrectionem eius adiuua me miserum et peccatorem sanctis meritis tuis et gloriosis precibus tuis in infirmitate corporis mei et animae meae nunc laborantem, et in hora exitus mei ex hac praesenti uita, et in omnibus tribulationibus et angustiis meis et in omnibus necessitatibus meis in hoc saeculo et in futuro, illius ad laudem et gloriam et honorem qui me miserum creauit, quem tu sacratissima et castissima et sanctissima et beatissima omnium feminarum uirgo Dei genitrix

commands of Christ that, when the the day of my final destiny has come to me, I may deserve to be immediately counted in the company of the assembly of blessed spirits with you, through your intercession, mildest queen of earth and heaven, and with the assent of Christ your son, who, one omnipotent God, lives and is glorified with the coeternal Father and the kind Spirit throughout all regions of the world. Amen.'

[73] *Ibid.*, pp. 135–6.
[74] On the monastic reform prayers for the royal family, see E. John, 'The King and the Monks in the Tenth-Century Reformation', in his *Orbis Britanniae*, pp. 154–80, at 177.

Maria, mundi saluatorem et redemptorem de tuo sancto et intemerato uirginali utero edidisti; et per illius amabile nomen et maiestatis suae nomen, quod Deus omnium saeculorum a cunctis christianis fidelibus uocatur et creditur, et per illius sanctissimum amorem, intercede pro nobis, et pro rege nostro, et pro famulo tuo, et pro fratribus quoque et sororibus nostris, qui se in meis orationibus commendauerunt, et pro omnibus qui in tribulatione et in captiuitate sunt, et pro omni populo christiano, et pro animabus omnium fidelium defunctorum apud Deum, quia ipse est saeculi uita et redemptio nostra et salus nostra et omne gaudium nostrum et refugium nostrum, in omni tribulatione et angustia quae circumdederunt nos, et omnis consolatio nostra, qui ex te nasci dignatus est unigenitus summi Patris filius dominus noster Iesus Christus. Sit crucifixo domino Deo nostro decus et imperium, honor et potestas et gloria et gratiarum actio in saecula sempiterna. Amen.

Preces sanctae. Sancta mater Christi Maria, esto mihi adiutor famulo tuo, ut per tua sacra suffragia caelestia adipisci merear gaudia. Per.
Item. Fili Dei uiui et fili sanctae Mariae uirginis, sicut uis et sicut tu scis et sicut potes, sic miserere mei indigno misero peccatori.
Alia. Qui cognoscis omnia occulta, a peccatis meis munda me, et per sacram tuae intemeratae matris semper uirginis Mariae interuentionem tempus mihi concede, ut repenitens plangam quod peccaui. Miserere mei, Christe, saluator mundi.
Item alia. Multa et innumerabilia sunt, Domine, peccata mea; intercedente sancta Maria cum omnibus sanctis, indulge et miserere mei, quia peccaui tibi nimis.
Oratio. Domine Iesu Christe tibi flecto genua mea, tibi corde credo, tibi confiteor omnia peccata mea; miserere mihi miserrimo peccatori. Amen.[75]

[75] Barré, *Prières anciennes*, pp. 137–8: 'O virgin of virgins, mother of God, Mary, mother of our lord Jesus Christ, queen of the angels and of all the world, mercy-seat of eternal life, brightness of the heavens, you who seem never to have had an equal before or since, by the precious blood of your only-begotten son, our lord, Jesus Christ, which he shed as the price of our salvation, and by his holy and honoured and health-giving cross on which he, who is the maker of the world, deigned to stand fastened for the salvation of mankind, and during the suffering of death, which he himself, the son of God, wished voluntarily to suffer for us on the cross, he commended you to his disciple St John saying: "Behold your mother", help us; and by his glorious resurrection help me, a miserable, suffering sinner, by your holy favours and by your glorious prayers, in the infirmity of my body and of my soul, now and in the hour of my departure from this present life, and in all my tribulations and difficulties and in all my needs in this world and in the next, to the praise and glory and honour of him who created me, a wretched one, to whom, the saviour of the world and the redeemer, you, most sacred and most pure and most holy and most blessed of all women, O virgin Mary, mother of God, gave birth from your holy and chaste womb; and through whose lovable name and the name of his majesty, in that he is called and is believed to be God of all ages by all Christians, and through whose

London, BL, Arundel 60, a psalter written in Winchester *c.* 1060, has additions of the late eleventh century which include the *Singularis meriti* and the fourth Marian prayer in Titus D. xxvii, but more interesting is one of the original texts, a prayer to Mary on 145r-147v which Barré considered to be 'une composition personelle de quelque moine de Newminster'.[76] It is a long prayer, based mainly on the legend of Theophilus, an archdeacon who humbly declines a bishopric, but then finds himself consumed by envy of the new bishop. He signs away his soul to the devil but later repents and prays to the Virgin, who wrests back from the devil the deed which Theophilus had signed in his own blood.[77]

Sancta et inmaculata Dei genitrix uirgo Maria, clementissima et misericordissima et piissima Domini mei mater gloriosa, et super sidera excelsa, que sola sine exemplo placuisti femina Christo, et perdito mundo subueniens sola intulisti salutem, intemerata ac uirginum uirgo dignissima et omnium potentissima, cunctarum domina mulierum, cui nichil difficile est apud Deum, subueni misero

> most holy love, intercede for us and for our king and for your servant and for our brothers and sisters also, who have commended themselves in my prayers, and for all who are in distress and in captivity, and for all Christian people, and for the souls of all the faithful dead in the presence of God, because he himself is the life of the world and our redemption and our salvation and all our joy and our refuge, in all the distress and difficulties which surround us, and all our consolation, who deigned to be born from you, the only-begotten son of the highest Father, our lord Jesus Christ. Esteem and mastery, honour and power and glory and thanksgiving be to our crucified lord God for ever and ever. Amen.
>
> *Holy prayers.* Holy mother of Christ, Mary, be a helper to me your servant, that I may deserve to attain heavenly joys through your holy intercession.
> *Also.* Son of the living God and son of the holy virgin Mary, as you wish and as you know how and as you are able, so have mercy on me an unworthy, wretched sinner.
> *Another.* You who know all secrets, cleanse me from my sins, and through the sacred intervention of your pure mother, the ever-virgin Mary, grant me time that I may, repenting, bewail that I have sinned. Have mercy on me, Christ, saviour of the world.
> *Another also.* Many and innumerable, Lord, are my sins; be kind to me and have mercy on me, through the intercession of holy Mary and all the saints, because I have sinned against you very much.
> *Prayer.* Lord Jesus Christ to you I bend my knees, I believe in you with my heart, I confess to you all my sins, have mercy on me, a most wretched sinner. Amen.'

76 Barré, *Prières anciennes*, p. 139: 'a personal composition of a monk at the New Minster, Winchester'.
77 For an edition of the Theophilus legend, see Meerssemann, *Kritische Glossen op de Griekse Theophilus-Legende.*

peccatori, uiro iniquo, homini pleno peccato. Succurre, queso, michi indignissimo et scelestissimo, que genuisti agnum purgantem crimina mundi. Cognosco iniquitates meas, scio scelera mea, confiteor peccatum meum, nimiumque me perpendo indignum, et omni polluto sordidiorem inspicio. Sed tu, queso, pietate inconparabilis et uenerabilis uirgo, mitiga furorem et auerte iram domini Dei mei sanctissimis precibus tuis. Submoue celestem quam mereor uindictam, et tuam quam non mereor infer medelam. Porrige dexteram et subleua iacentem. Eripe captiuum, solue compeditum, ne forte de meo gaudeat interitu inimicus. Sentiat ergo, sentiat serpens et draco malignus uirtutem tuam, et nichil in decipiendo me preualere cognoscat astuciam suam, qua me cotidie querens ut deuoret, occultis machinationibus, etiam in sibi famulantibus et obedientibus [MS odientibus], me dolositate, simulatione et fraude, ac callidissimis argumentis, inpetere non cessat. A cuius me laqueis et insidiis libera, felicissima domina, precibus tuis, et dimicantem aduersarium contra me a me, queso, repelle orationibus tuis.

Scio enim, o semper beatissima et domina benedicta, christianorum protectio et refugium sempiternum, licet errata corrigere, et pro admissis licet sceleribus penitere, corde certissimum teneo et ore confiteor, mitius duco gratiusque complector uniuersa reorum in presenti supplicia perpeti, quam in perpetuum indulgentia carere peccati. Sed memor sum, o piissima domina, eorum qui ante me lapsi per penitentiam surrexerunt, ut per utriusque testamenti exempla manifestatur . . . [Here follows a list of Old and New Testament penitents.] His igitur et aliis huiuscemodi prouocatus et informatus exemplis accessi, quamuis audacter, sed non diffidenter, interpellaturus amplissimam bonitatem tuam, obtestans et inprecans, si forte audeo, te dominam meam, per Deum et Dominum omnium Iesum Christum filium tuum, quem nimis infelix grauiter offendere miser ipse non timui – quod me modis omnibus penitet – ut tuis michi subuenias precibus et orationibus piis succurras, quatinus, meorum michi omnium per te uenia peccatorum concessa, illus altissimi Filii aeterni Dei et singularis Domini mei gratiam merear inuenire et inuentam habere et habitam perhenniter retinere. [A profession of faith follows.]

Hanc ergo fidem rudimentis ecclesiasticis michi traditam, inclita domina et inextricabiliter benedicta, corde credo, ore confiteor, ueneror et amplector tota mentis intentione. Hanc pro me dignare, alma Dei genitrix, offerre Deo confessionem, ut reatus mei recipiat satisfactionem.

Tu es enim post Deum uia errancium, uita morientium, spes periclitancium, portus fluctuancium, requies laborantium, fons sitiencium, consolacio tristantium, mediatrix Dei et hominum, uirgo felicissima et fecundissima mater, et tutissimum praesidium christianorum, tutela et firmamentum ad te confugientium, paratissimum ac solidissimum christianorum patrocinium. Scio enim – et ueraciter scio – quia aput te uera medicina infirmancium, recuperatio desperatorum, o liberatrix hominum, Domini mei mater beatissima, afflictorum piissima consolatrix, ruenciumque promptissima subleuatrix, que sola facta es ianua uite, sola tulisti discrimina uite, sola lactasti precium uite. Aput te est namque refugium nostrum, aput te refrigerium nostrum, aput te recuperatio uite nostre. Suscipe, deprecor, uotum meum et offer illud domino Deo meo, quia tua precatio omni prece ualentior, tua oratio omni oratione acceptior, tua peticio omni thiamıamıate gracior.[78]

[78] Barré, *Prières anciennes*, pp. 140–2: 'Holy and immaculate virgin Mary, mother of God, most gentle and most merciful and most holy, glorious mother of my God, and elevated above the stars, the only woman, without an example, who pleased Christ and alone brought salvation, coming to the assistance of the ruined world, pure and most worthy virgin of virgins, and most powerful of all, mistress of all women, for whom nothing is difficult before God, help me a wretched sinner, a wicked man, a man full of sin. Aid me, most undeserving and wicked, I beg you who gave birth to the lamb who cleanses the sins of the world. I recognize my iniquities, I know my wickednesses, I confess my sin and I judge myself very unworthy and I consider myself more base than all defilement. But you, I beg, virgin incomparable and honoured in piety, soften the fury and avert the anger of the lord my God with your most holy prayers. Banish the divine punishment which I deserve and introduce your remedy which I do not deserve. Offer your right hand and lift up the fallen. Rescue the captive, release the fettered, in case the enemy rejoice at my destruction. May he feel, therefore, may the serpent and wicked dragon feel your power, and may he not learn that his cunning has any power to deceive me, whereby daily seeking to devour me with secret tricks, even in the guise of his own minions and time-servers, he never ceases to assail me with deceit, pretence and fraud, and with the readiest arguments. Most fortunate lady, free me from his traps and trickery with your prayers and, I beg, repel from me with your prayers the opponent fighting against me.

For I know, O always most happy and blessed lady, protection of Christians and ever-lasting refuge, although I hold it most certainly in my heart and confess it with my mouth to correct my faults and to do penance for the crimes I have committed, I consider it more merciful and I more willingly embrace the endurance of all the punishment of the guilty in this present life than for all eternity to be deprived of the remission of sins. But I am mindful, O most pious lady, of those who fell before me and rose up through penance, as is clearly shown through examples from both Testaments . . . Stimulated and instructed, therefore, by these examples and others of that nature, I have reached the point, albeit boldly, but not without confidence, of calling upon your most great goodness, imploring and invoking, if, perchance, I dare, you, my lady, through the God and lord of all, Jesus Christ your son, whom I, very unhappy and wretched, did not fear to offend very gravely – and of this I repent in every way – that you come to my assistance with your prayers and help me with your pious prayers, so that, with all my sins pardoned through your favour, I may deserve to obtain the grace of him, the highest son of the eternal God and of my sole lord and, having obtained it, to possess it, and, having possessed it, to retain it for ever.

Therefore, glorious and indescribably blessed lady, I believe with my heart this faith handed down to me from the beginnings of the church, I confess it with my mouth, I

While this text draws freely on the *Penitentia Theophili*, the actual legend of Theophilus is not mentioned. Instead, the author of the prayer chiefly uses those portions of the text in which Theophilus prays to God or Mary. The first paragraph of the prayer, a confession of sins and an appeal for help, while broadly similar to Theophilus's initial recognition of his fault and his pleas to Mary, is the most free in construction, with echoes of the liturgy and of the second prayer in Titus D. xxvii.[79] The original parts of this paragraph show that the author's confidence in Mary's powers bordered on the excessive: 'perdito mundi subueniens sola intulisti salutem' and 'cui nichil difficile est apud Deum'. Most of the Old and New Testament examples in the second paragraph are from the Theophilus legend, but the phrasing of the prayer is independent. The Creed in the third paragraph is again based on the confession of faith which Mary requires of Theophilus before assisting him, but the structure of the second half, with its alternating proofs of Christ's perfect humanity and divinity, is original to the prayer. It also expands the details of the Crucifixion – 'flagellatum, illusum, consputum, spinis coronatum, crucifixum propter nos' – and it is interesting to see an emphasis on the affective details of the Passion in a poem of such advanced Marian devotion. The last (incomplete) paragraph of the prayer is mainly composed of a list of Marian epithets, most of which are derived from the Theophilus text. Although the content of this prayer is almost entirely taken from the *Penitentia Theophili*, its form is to be attributed to the author. It shows a high degree of rhetorical skill and the writer has a particular fondness for parallel clauses and sentences – for

honour and I embrace it all with the attention of my mind. Deign, O kind mother of God, to offer to God this confession for me, that he may receive amends for my guilt.

For you, after God, are the right way for the erring, the life of the dying, the hope of those in danger, the haven of the storm-tossed, rest for the toiling, a spring for the thirsty, the consolation of the sad, the mediatress between God and man, the most happy virgin and most fruitful mother and safest support of Christians, guardian and mainstay of those who have recourse to you, readiest and soundest defence of Christians. For I know and I truly know that in you is the true medicine of the infirm, the recovery of the despairing, O deliverer of men, most blessed mother of my lord, most pious consoler of the afflicted and most prompt supporter of the falling, who alone was made the door of life, alone swept away the dangers of life, alone suckled the price of life. In you is our refuge, in you our consolation, you are the restoration of our life. Receive, I implore, my prayer and offer it to the lord my God, because your prayer is more powerful than every prayer, your prayer is more acceptable than every prayer, your request is more pleasing than all sacrifice . . .'

[79] See Barré, *Prières anciennes*, p. 140.

example, the long series of sentences beginning 'Penitentia . . .' or the concluding description of Mary's powers: 'tua precatio omni prece ualentior, tua oratio omni oratione acceptior, tua peticio omni thiamate gracior'.

An estimation of the value of this text as a witness to English devotion to Mary is not easy because of its dependence on the Theophilus legend, as it is always difficult to distinguish imitation from reminiscence in medieval devotional texts. Prayers almost always echo 'sources' – Benedicta Ward, for example, writes of the prayers of Anselm: 'In such spontaneous effusions, words and phrases already known are recalled to the memory as they are prayed in the heart, becoming the present prayer of the one who uses them.'[80] Such a use of another text is mostly unconscious: 'reminiscences are not quotations'.[81] In the case of this prayer, however, it appears almost certain that the author was deliberately copying his source: his prayer, in other words, is closer to a literary exercise than a spontaneous outpouring. This does not nullify the significance of the fact that the piece chosen as model was a Marian text, and the prayer must be regarded as an outstanding monument of late Anglo-Saxon devotion to Mary, especially as the passages not directly dependent on the *Penitentia Theophili* display the same ardent veneration of Mary. The whole text suggests a willingness to welcome and assimilate one of the most advanced products of Marian devotion available in contemporary Europe. Bestul even regards the text as 'not so much different in scale from such prayers of Anselm as the prayer to the Virgin "Maria, tu illa . . ."'[82] Even the most extravagant of the epithets applied to Mary in the Theophilus legend are incorporated in the prayer in Arundel 60. This legend seems to have been one of the most important texts inspiring devotion to Mary in late Anglo-Saxon England; Ælfric summarized it in his homily for the Assumption in *Catholic Homilies I*, the Canterbury Office of the Virgin in Tiberius A.iii takes one of its readings from it, there is a reminiscence of it in the prayer to Mary in the Winchcombe Psalter and this prayer is almost entirely dependent on it.

In contrast to this prayer from Arundel 60, the other Anglo-Latin prayer to Mary which is based directly on a source, the fourth prayer to Mary in Titus D. xxvii, is much more restrained and Christocentric. In this prayer it

[80] *The Prayers and Mediations of St Anselm*, trans. B. Ward (Harmondsworth, 1973), p. 27.

[81] J. Leclercq, *The Love of Learning and the Desire for God*, trans. C. Misrahi (London, 1978), p. 94.

[82] Bestul, 'St Anselm and the Continuity of Anglo-Saxon Devotional Traditions', p. 23.

is Christ who is 'saeculi uita et redemptio nostra et salus nostra et omne gaudium nostrum et refugium nostrum', whereas in the prayer in Arundel 60 Mary is 'uita morientium . . . liberatrix hominum . . . refugium nostrum'. Nevertheless, even in the Titus prayer we find a piling-up of epithets to describe Mary: 'sacratissima omnium feminarum' in the source, for example, becomes 'sacratissima et castissima et sanctissima et beatissima' in Titus.

Only one of the Anglo-Latin prayers seems to be reflected in the vernacular texts, with two of the anonymous homilies echoing the conclusion of Cerne 56: 'Confidimus enim et pro certo scimus quia omne quod uis potes impetrare a filio tuo Domino nostro Iesu Christo.' The first is a passage in the *Sermo ad populum dominicis diebus* in London, Lambeth Palace 489 (probably an Exeter manuscript from the third quarter of the eleventh century): 'and eac we sceolon biddan þa halgan fæmnan Sancta Marian ures drihtnes moder, þæt heo us geþingie to hyre leofan bearne, hyre scippende, and to urum scippende (þæt is god ælmihtig), forþam ðe heo mæg abiddan æt him eall, þæt heo wyle'.[83] A similar passage occurs at the end of Assmann X, a translation of the *Gospel of Pseudo-Matthew* adapted for use as a homily for the feast of the Nativity of the Virgin: 'Nu we geare witan, þæt heo mæg æt hire þam deoran sunu biddan, swa hwæt swa heo wile, and beon ðingere to urum drihtne . . .'[84] At least Cerne 56, then, was widespread enough to be echoed in two homilies of the late Anglo-Saxon period. Ælfric's works, even those Marian homilies which end with pleas for the Virgin's intercession, show no knowledge of these private prayers, but seem to be based rather on the liturgy, as in, for example, the conclusion to the Second Series homily for the Assumption: 'Uton nu geornlice biddan. þa eadigan marian. þe nu todæg wæs ahafen. and geuferod. bufon engla ðrymme. þæt heo us ðingige. to ðam ælmihtigan gode. se ðe leofað and rixað. on ealra worulda woruld.'[85]

---

[83] *Wulfstan*, ed. Napier, p. 299: 'and we must also entreat the holy virgin St Mary, mother of our Lord, that she intercede for us to her beloved child, her creator, and to our creator (that is Almighty God) because she can ask of him everything that she wishes'.

[84] *Angelsächsische Homilien und Heiligenleben*, ed. Assmann, p. 137: 'Now we know well that she can ask of her dear son whatever she wishes and be an intercessor to our Lord.'

[85] *CH II*, p. 259, lines 134–7: 'Let us now fervently pray to the blessed Mary, who was today raised and exalted above the hosts of angels, that she intercede for us to the Almighty God, who liveth and reigneth for ever and ever' (trans. *Homilies*, ed. Thorpe II, 445).

CONCLUSIONS

The prayer-books of the Anglo-Saxon period, then, contain a significant number of prayers to the Virgin. These form two groups: the first consists of three prayers which are found in manuscripts from the end of the eighth and the beginning of the ninth centuries and which were probably composed in Northumbria in the second half of the eighth century; the second, larger, group dates mainly from the eleventh century and comes from the south of England (Canterbury, Abingdon and, above all, Winchester). The first group occurs in florilegia of private prayer, the second principally as additions to psalters. These two groups coincide with the two periods in which Anglo-Saxon devotion to the Virgin is strong, as can be seen from other texts and from artistic evidence. In the early texts Mary's intercession is implored – in one of them in urgent terms hardly surpassed in any of the later texts – and her merits lauded: she has deserved to bear Christ, has been chosen by God, and in Cerne 56 an extravagant list of adjectives celebrates her virtues and exalted state.

In the later period these early texts were still copied, although only the last lines of Cerne 56 survive in an eleventh-century manuscript, and Carolingian influence is evident in the relatively wide dissemination of the prayer *Singularis meriti*. In all of the later books, prayers to Mary come directly after prayers to one or all of the Trinity, and sometimes to the cross, and before those to the angels and the other saints. This arrangement parallels that of the litanies of the saints from the ninth century onwards. Some eleventh-century manuscripts which we could expect to include prayers to the Virgin fail to do so, however: the prayers added in the eleventh-century to the Vespasian Psalter and the prayer-book London, British Library, Cotton Galba A. xiv, for example, lack Marian texts. Of the new prayers composed in the eleventh century, those from Winchester are by far the most important. They are more expansive, more detailed in their requests, and contain a much wider range of Marian epithets. The Arundel 60 prayer, in particular, heralds the later Middle Ages and the popular contrast between a stern God and an all-merciful Virgin with its request that she avert the anger of God with her prayers. The implication is, of course, that there is a clash between the Virgin and her son, with her will not conforming to his. A specific concern with the day of death is also more evident in these later texts, with many pleas for intercession centring on this. In contrast to the effusiveness and the intensity of the Winchester texts, those from other centres contain little more than simple pleas for intercession, although in the case of the Abingdon texts this is incorporated in a description of the Virgin's assumption. Once again, then, Winchester emerges as the most important centre of the late Anglo-Saxon cult of the Virgin.

5

Marian dedications, relics and pilgrimage in Anglo-Saxon England

In this chapter I shall examine the Marian dedications of the cathedrals and monastic churches of Anglo-Saxon England. I have not attempted to study the dedications of the ordinary churches, as it has proved impossible to discover the majority of them. In addition, I shall look at the evidence of relics of Mary and the question of pilgrimage to Walsingham, the only Marian pilgrimage in England thought to date from the pre-Conquest period.

DEDICATIONS

The fullest enumeration of Anglo-Saxon church buildings is contained in the *Domesday Book* of 1086, but this document is, unfortunately, extremely uneven in its records for the different counties of England, being very detailed in some cases, much more sketchy in others. The detailed accounts include records of churches of all types and, despite the fact that such lists were not drawn up for all counties, the number of churches mentioned is 2,061, most of which must have been pre-Conquest.[1] There were undoubtedly hundreds more which were not assessed and therefore not included. Many of the churches, both those included and excluded, must have been small, rather insignificant buildings, and we have no way of knowing the dedications of the majority of them, as they are described by localization rather than by name. It would be an impossible exercise to seek to identify the original dedication of each of these churches and to date their foundation, which would be necessary if we were to attempt to trace

[1] See S. Keynes, 'Anglo-Saxon Architecture and the Historian', in M. Biddle, R. Cramp, M. McC. Gatch, S. Keynes and B. Kjølbye-Biddle '*Anglo-Saxon Architecture* and Anglo-Saxon Studies: A Review', *ASE* 14 (1985), 293–317, at 294–8.

any chronological development in Anglo-Saxon church dedications. *Domesday Book*, then, is not of great help for this purpose. The two surveys of English church dedications are also virtually unusable in this regard, as they are not compiled on historical principles.[2] While the Taylors note the dedications and assign rough dates to the buildings in their catalogue of churches which incorporate Anglo-Saxon work, the total number of churches accepted in volume III is only 267.[3] Of these, fifty-six are dedicated to the Virgin: between a quarter and a fifth, a large proportion. While a percentage figure based on the Taylors' data undoubtedly has some significance, what has survived from Anglo-Saxon times is naturally an arbitrary selection of what once existed and is not sufficient to give us an adequate idea of developments or trends in church dedications. The position with respect to the great bulk of ordinary Anglo-Saxon churches is, therefore, unfavourable. However, conditions are far more favourable with regard to cathedrals and monasteries. The dedications of the English cathedrals are well documented in almost every case, as are the dates of their foundations, and the history of the monastic houses has been admirably illuminated by Knowles and Hadcock.[4] Their work forms the basis of this chapter.

In drawing up the lists of monastic houses I have departed somewhat from the organization of Knowles and Hadcock. Their first section, a list of Benedictine houses, covers only those houses which were founded or refounded at the time of the Benedictine reform, and the houses which remained extinct from the ninth century are relegated to their Appendix I, which lists all houses existing at any period before 1066. Appendix I also includes institutions of secular clergy, which have not been included here, except for the cathedrals. The lists given in this chapter, therefore, include all monastic houses which existed at any period before 1066, but those printed in italics by Knowles and Hadcock and characterized as 'insignificant, doubtful or disproved' have been omitted. Cells and priories dependent on large monasteries have also been omitted. Where it is

---

[2] F. A. Foster, *Studies in Church Dedications, or England's Patron Saints* (London, 1899) and F. Bond, *Dedications and Patron Saints of English Churches* (London, 1914). A very valuable survey of the seventh- and eighth-century dedications can be found, however, in Levison, *England and the Continent*, pp. 259–65.

[3] H. M. Taylor and J. Taylor, *Anglo-Saxon Architecture* I and II (Cambridge, 1965) and H. M. Taylor, *Anglo-Saxon Architecture* III (Cambridge, 1978).

[4] Knowles and Hadcock, *Medieval Religious Houses*.

possible, but not certain, that a house refounded in the tenth century existed at an earlier period (as with Cerne, for example), I have given only the definite later date. I have replaced Knowles and Hadcock's alphabetical order by a chronological one, dividing the houses by the dates of their foundations into hundred-year blocks. Where Knowles and Hadcock list a house as pre-1066, I have taken this to mean eleventh century although it is, of course, possible that it existed earlier.

Knowles and Hadcock are not entirely consistent with regard to the nunneries of Anglo-Saxon England. Most of the early nunneries (seventh and eighth century) seem to have been double monasteries under the rule of an abbess – indeed, Stenton considers that 'it is doubtful whether any houses for women only were ever founded in this period'.[5] However, some of these foundations are included under Benedictine monasteries in *Medieval Religious Houses*, some under nunneries. Instead of preserving their categories, therefore, I have chosen to list them all under nunneries, as they were under the rule of an abbess and seem to have been founded primarily for women.

The sixth- and seventh-century monasteries of the Celtic fringe also present a problem with regard to their dedications. Most of these monasteries were later known under the name of their founder or could be seen as dedicated to him. These houses may have had no original dedication, like many of the Irish monasteries in which 'dedications were not usual, but they were not unknown'.[6] In listing these foundations, therefore, I have included them with those houses whose dedications we do not know.

Many of the houses of the Benedictine reform had existed earlier, but in most cases we know only the tenth-century dedications. It would be foolhardy to assume that this was also the original dedication, as we know of several cases where this was certainly not the case.[7] These houses, therefore, have been entered at the date of their original foundation, where this is known, but have been listed with the houses whose dedication is unknown, and have been entered again under the tenth century with the dedication which is firmly attested in this period. Where a house continued into the tenth century, or was refounded with the same dedication, it has been listed only under the date of the original foundation, as the dedication

[5] Stenton, *Anglo-Saxon England*, p. 161.

[6] J. Ryan, *Irish Monasticism: Origins and Early Development* (Dublin, 1931), pp. 288–9.

[7] See below, pp. 133–5.

is in this case a reflection of the piety of the earlier age, not the tenth century. For the seventh- and eighth-century churches I have checked Knowles and Hadcock against the list of dedications given by Levison in Appendix V of *England and the Continent in the Eighth Century*.

CATHEDRALS

s. vii

Hexham	Andrew
Rochester	Andrew
Winchester	Holy Trinity, Peter and Paul
Hereford	Mary
Lichfield	Mary
North Elmham	Mary
London	Paul
Lindisfarne	Peter
Worcester	Peter (later changed to Mary)[8]
York	Peter
Dorchester	Peter and Paul
Lindsey	Peter and Paul
Canterbury	St Saviour's (later known as Christ Church)

Unknown: Dunwich,[9] Leicester

s. viii

Selsey	Mary
Sherborne	Mary

s. x

Wells	Andrew
Hoxne	Æthelberht
Durham	Cuthbert
St Germans	Germanus

[8] See below, pp. 133–4.
[9] The Anglo-Saxon name is *Domnoc*, which is either Dunwich or Felixstowe. See D. Whitelock, 'The Pre-Viking Age Church in East Anglia', *ASE* 1 (1972), 1–22, at 4, n. 2.

Crediton   Mary[10]

Unknown: Ramsbury

s. xi

Exeter   Peter (later changed to Peter and Mary)[11]

MONASTERIES

s. vi

Canterbury   Peter and Paul (later known as St
                                      Augustine's)

Unknown: Bodmin, Much Dewchurch, Padstow, Partney, St Asaph,
St Goran, St Keverne, St Kew, St Neot, St Piran

s. vii

Hexham	Andrew
Pegham	Andrew
Lastingham	Mary?
Reculver	Mary
Jarrow	Paul
Chertsey	Peter
Ithanacester	Peter
Lindisfarne	Peter
Monkwearmouth	Peter
Ripon	Peter
Westminster	Peter
Malmesbury	Peter and Paul

Unknown: Abingdon, Bardney, Barrow-on-Humber, Bosham, Breedon-
on-the-Hill, Brixworth, Burgh Castle, Bury St Edmunds, Castor, Colling-
ham, Crayke, Fladbury, Frome, Gateshead, Hoo, Icanho, Muchelney,

---

[10] The present church at Crediton is dedicated to the Holy Cross, but the evidence suggests
that the pre-Conquest church was dedicated to Mary. See J. Hill, 'The Exeter Book and
Lambeth Palace Library MS 149: The Monasterium of Sancta Maria', *American Notes and
Queries* ns 1 (1988), 4–9, at 4–5.

[11] See below, p. 135.

Nursling, Peterborough,[12] Soham, Stamford, Tadcaster, Tetbury, Tilbury, Woking

s. viii

St Albans	Alban
Oundle	Andrew
Crowland	Bartholomew[13]
St Benet of Hulme	Benedict
Bradford-on-Avon	Laurence
Glastonbury	Mary
St Michael's Mount	Michael
Bishop's Cleeve	Michael
Bamburg	Peter
Breedon	Peter
Cookham	Peter
Minster-in-Thanet	Peter and Paul

Unknown: Barwick-in-Elmet, Beddington, Dacre, Daylesford, Deerhurst, Evesham, Kidderminster, Stratford-on-Avon, Tewkesbury, Tisbury, Twyning

s. ix

Athelney	Peter and Paul

Unknown: Berkeley, Dingerein

s. x

New Minster, Winchester	Christ and Peter?[14]
Huntingdon	Mary
Cranborne	Mary and Bartholomew
Ramsey	Mary and Benedict
Tavistock	Mary and Ruman
Horton	Mary[15]

Unknown: Bedford

---

[12] See Levison, *England and the Continent*, p. 260.
[13] *Ibid.*, p. 262. There seems to be no early evidence for Mary as a patron saint.
[14] See below, p. 132.   [15] See below, pp. 132–3.

s. x: Refoundations

Abingdon	Mary
Deerhurst	Mary
Malmesbury	Mary
Thorney	Mary[16]
Westbury-on-Trym	Mary
Crowland	Mary and Bartholomew
Winchcombe	Mary and Kenelm
Cerne	Mary and Peter
Exeter	Mary and Peter[17]
Ely	Mary, Peter and Æthelthryth[18]
Pershore	Mary, Peter and Paul
Muchelney	Peter and Paul
Peterborough	Peter, Paul and Andrew[19]
Winchester, New Minster	Saviour, Mary and All Saints?[20]

s. xi

Burton-upon-Trent	Benedict (later Mary and Modwenna)
Buckfast	Mary?
Horton	Mary
Stow	Mary
Eynsham	Mary (Andrew and Eadburg)
Coventry	Mary, Peter and Osburg
Abbotsbury	Peter

s. xi: Refoundations

Bury St Edmunds	Edmund

---

[16] The monastery at Thorney seems to have been dedicated to Mary (and Christ, who is mentioned in almost all dedications), but the church in the monastery was dedicated to the Trinity, with altars to Mary, Peter and Benedict. See the foundation charter, S 792, *The Early Charters of Eastern England*, ed. Hart pp. 166–7 (no. VII).

[17] See below, p. 135.

[18] Knowles and Hadcock, *Medieval Religious Houses*, p. 64, give Æthelthryth only. For SS Mary and Peter, see Hohler, 'Les saints insulaires', p. 296. Mary as patron saint is also attested by the authentic charter of Edgar to Ely, S 780 (BCS 1268).

[19] Hohler, 'Les saints insulaires', p. 296.   [20] See below, p. 132.

NUNNERIES

s. vii

Barking	Mary
Folkestone	Mary?
Minster (Sheppey)	Mary
Minster-in-Thanet	Mary
Tynemouth	Mary
Much Wenlock	Michael
Bath	Peter
Leominster	Peter
Whitby	Peter
Gloucester	Peter and Paul?[21]

Unknown: Burton-upon-Trent, Carlisle, East Dereham, Ebchester, Ely, Hackness, Hanbury, Hartlepool, Lyminge, Repton, South Shields, Thorney, Threekingham, Wareham, Watton, Weedon, Withington

s. viii

| Winchcombe | Peter |

Unknown: Oxford, Wimborne

s. ix

Shaftesbury	Mary
Wilton	Mary and Bartholomew
Chester	Peter and Paul

Unknown: Eltisley, Polesworth

s. x.

Romsey	Mary
Winchester (Nunnaminster)	Mary
Amesbury	Mary and Melor
Wherwell	Holy Cross and Peter
Chichester	Peter

Unknown: Reading

s. xi

| Chatteris | Mary |

[21] Levison, *England and the Continent*, p. 261.

It is evident from these lists that dedications to Mary were by no means uncommon even in the very earliest period of Anglo-Saxon Christianity. Of the fifteen bishops' seats dedicated in the seventh century, three were to Mary: North Elmham, Hereford and Lichfield. The only two bishoprics created in the eighth century, Sherborne and Selsey, were both dedicated to her. Only Crediton, of the sees created in the tenth century, was dedicated to Mary, but in some cases the dedications of these new cathedrals reflected the piety of a preceding century, as already existing churches were raised to bishops' seats (e.g. Wells). All of the new tenth-century sees, except for Durham, were founded in the first half of the century, before the Benedictine reform. The only new pre-Conquest eleventh-century see was established in the monastery at Exeter, to which Leofric transferred his seat in 1050; this monastery appears to have been dedicated already to Mary and Peter.

The most widespread dedication for both cathedrals and monasteries in the early period was to Peter, as we might expect in view of the Roman missionaries and other contacts. Only Reculver and, perhaps, Lastingham (we know of a church dedicated to Mary in the monastery, but we have no evidence for the monastery itself)[22] were dedicated to the Virgin in the seventh century. However, we know that in some cases monasteries dedicated to another saint contained a church dedicated to Mary: SS Peter and Paul (later St Augustine's) in Canterbury is an example of this.[23] In the eighth century only Glastonbury, refounded in 705 by Ine of Wessex, was dedicated to Mary, and the only ninth-century monastery whose dedication we know was not dedicated to her.

Unlike the monasteries, the nunneries were very frequently dedicated to the Virgin, whose suitability as the patron saint of a predominantly female house is obvious. Of the nine seventh-century foundations whose dedications we know, four are to Mary: Sheppey, Barking, Minster-in-Thanet and Tynemouth. Folkestone, for which we have only later evidence of the Marian dedication, may also have been dedicated to her in this period. This association of Mary with the nunneries is not attested in the eighth century, in which we know the dedication of only one double house (Winchcombe, dedicated to Peter like all the houses associated with Offa),[24] but continued in the ninth with, Wilton, dedicated to Mary and

---

[22] *Ibid.*, p. 263.   [23]*Ibid.*   [24] *Ibid.*, p. 257.

Bartholomew, Shaftesbury, dedicated to the Virgin, and the Nunna-minster in Winchester, also dedicated to her.

Levison's conclusion that the seventh- and eighth-century English dedications are 'overwhelmingly Roman'[25] in character is undoubtedly true, but one may question his conjecture that the Marian dedications were connected with relics of Mary: 'It is impossible to trace the origins and wanderings of relics of St Mary which these dedications suggest; one may imagine for example that Gregory's disciples brought relics from Santa Maria Maggiore.'[26] While there is evidence of Marian relics from the fifth century onwards in Jerusalem and Constantinople, there is no mention of them in Rome in this period. Relics of the Virgin were a relatively late development, much later than the relics of the martyrs, as the widespread belief in the absence of her body from her tomb presented an obvious difficulty to the discovery of any remains. Bede mentions that Augustine and his companions brought with them 'sanctorum etiam apostolorum ac martyrum reliquias',[27] but says nothing about any Marian relics. The early Marian churches in England were perhaps dedicated simply in imitation of the Italian churches familiar to the Roman missionaries. The angelic instruction given to Bishop Wilfrid to dedicate a church to Mary, which was quoted in Stephen's *Vita S. Wilfridi* and in Bede's *Historia ecclesiastica*, doubtless also had an effect on the number of houses dedicated:

Ego sum Michael summi Dei nuntius, qui misit me ad te indicare, quod tibi adduntur anni uitae pro intercessione sanctae Mariae genetricis Dei semperque uirginis et pro subditorum tuorum lacrimis, ad aures Domini peruenientibus; et hoc tibi erit signum, quod ab hac die in dies melioratus sanaberis et ad patriam tuam peruenies, tibique substantiarum tuarum carissima quaeque redduntur, et in pace uitam consummabis. Paratus quoque esto, quia post .iiii. annorum spatium iterum uisitabo te. Iam enim memento quod in honore sancti Petri et Andreae apostolis domos aedificasti, sanctae uero Mariae semper uirgini intercedenti pro te nullam fecisti. Habes hoc emendare et in honorem eius domum dedicare.[28]

Dedications to Mary, therefore, had always been a feature of church life, but in the tenth century the number of Marian dedications increased dramatically. Some predate the Benedictine reform: Mary was included in the dedication of Æthelstan's foundation for secular clerics at Milton Abbas in 933 and it is thought that she was also included in the dedication of the

---

[25] *Ibid.*, p. 34.   [26] *Ibid.*, p. 36.   [27] *Opera historica*, ed. Plummer I, 63.
[28] *The Life of Bishop Wilfrid*, p. 122; for translation see above pp. 91–2, n.8.

New Minster in Winchester. The New Minster dedication is confusing, however, with differences between texts. The Trinity, Mary and Peter are named in Edward's charter of 903, but this is spurious in its present form,[29] and authentic charters of 925 x 933, 940 and 959 name respectively the Saviour, God and Peter, and Peter only. It appears, then, that the Virgin may not have been included in the original dedication. When the secular clerics were expelled and the house refounded and rededicated, Mary became part of the dedication, as is evident from both the text and the illumination of Edgar's charter of 966: 'nostro saluatori eiusque genitrici semper uirgini Mariae et omnibus apostolis cum caeteris sanctis'.[30] Æthelgar, the Abingdon monk who was appointed first abbot of the reformed New Minster in 964 by Æthelwold, regarded Mary as his special patron, and this may reflect the influence of Æthelwold, his abbot at Abingdon.[31] Indeed, with the Benedictine reform, Marian dedications seem to have become almost an obligatory feature of the English monasteries. Of the fourteen houses refounded in the tenth century, five were dedicated to Mary and seven more to Mary and another saint. Only Peterborough and Muchelney did not include Mary in their dedications, so far as we know. Muchelney seems to have been refounded already in 939 by Æthelstan, probably as a house for secular clerics, and the Benedictine abbey presumably retained the earlier dedication to SS Peter and Paul. All the new tenth-century foundations whose dedications we know (Huntingdon, Cranborne, Ramsey and Tavistock) were dedicated to Mary or to Mary and another saint, except perhaps Horton. The early history of Horton is very confusing, but Knowles and Hadcock say that there was a tenth-century foundation dedicated to St Wolfrida, which was destroyed by the Danes in 997.[32] Wolfrida seems to be Wulfthryth, mother of St Edith. In the eleventh century another abbey was founded on the site which, it is clear from the charter, was dedicated to Mary: 'Sancta Marian to wurðmynte ðe seo stowe ys fore gehalgod.'[33] Horton would be unique among

[29] S 370 (BCS 602). On the dedication, see *Liber Vitae*, ed. Birch, p. viii.

[30] S 745 (BCS 1190): 'for our Saviour and for his mother Mary ever virgin and for all the apostles together with the other saints'; see also below, pp. 158–9, on the illumination.

[31] *Liber Vitae*, ed. Birch, p. 10: 'atque suae specialis domine celi terraeque reginae Dei genitricis Mariae' ('and of his especial lady, queen of heaven and earth, Mary, mother of God').

[32] Knowles and Hadcock, *Medieval Religious Houses*, p. 68.

[33] A. J. Robertson, *Anglo-Saxon Charters* (Cambridge, 1939), p. 220: 'In honour of St Mary for whom the place is dedicated.'

the tenth-century foundations if it were dedicated to an Anglo-Saxon saint alone; moreover it would also be unique in being dedicated to a living Anglo-Saxon woman, who appears to have been abbess of Wilton from *c.* 965 to 1000.[34] It is possible, therefore, that the tenth-century foundation, if there was one, also had the Marian dedication attested only for the eleventh-century house. In the eleventh century Stow, Eynsham and Coventry included Mary in their dedications. Burton-upon-Trent, founded at the beginning of the century, was exceptional in being originally dedicated to St Benedict, but this seems to have been quickly superseded by a dedication to SS Mary and Modwenna.[35] In *Domesday Book* the house is known as St Mary's. Abbotsbury, dedicated to Peter, was founded *c.* 1026 for secular canons and only later became Benedictine. Its dedication, therefore, does not reflect the Benedictine preference for Mary. We have no evidence from this period for the dedication of Buckfast Abbey, but it was later dedicated to Mary, and it is possible that this dedication dates from the eleventh century.

In some houses of the Benedictine reform the dedications were deliberately changed, as was the case with the New Minster. The dedication of Worcester cathedral and monastery seems to have been altered from Peter to Mary with the monastic revival. Robinson thought that the well-attested alteration in the name of Worcester cathedral was due to the construction of a new cathedral, dedicated to Mary, which would gradually have superseded the older building.[36] John has since argued that only the dedication of the cathedral was changed with the conversion of the community to monasticism, while the bishop's throne in the cathedral retained the dedication to St Peter.[37] His argument, however, is based on the *Altitonantis*, a spurious Worcester charter dated 964, though it may contain some genuine features.[38] From 966 onwards Mary was also added

---

[34] *The Heads of Religious Houses: England and Wales 940–1216*, ed. D. Knowles, C. N. L. Brooke and V. C. London (Cambridge, 1972), p. 222.

[35] Knowles and Hadcock, *Medieval Religious Houses*, p. 61, give Mary and Modwenna only; for the original dedication to Benedict see *Charters of Burton Abbey*, ed. P. H. Sawyer, Anglo-Saxon Charters 2 (1979), xliv.

[36] See J. A. Robinson, *St Oswald and the Church of Worcester*.

[37] John, 'St Oswald and the Church of Worcester', in his *Orbis Britanniae*, pp. 234–48, at 242.

[38] See the discussion by P. H. Sawyer, 'Charters of the Reform Movement: The Worcester Archive', *Tenth-Century Studies*, ed. Parson, pp. 84–93, at 85–7.

to Peter in the benediction on those who kept the terms of the Worcester charters, reflecting her new status as *protectrix* of the community.[39]

Before the Benedictine reform Malmesbury, too, had been dedicated to Peter, but its dedication was changed to Mary under the reforming abbot Ælfric (probably *c.* 965–77), as William of Malmesbury explained:

Hic est Elfricus qui, omnem curam ad beatam transferens Mariam, possessionem et nomen monasterii eius delegauit ditioni et, tacito interim beatissimi Petri nomine, ipsa sola loco uideatur imperare. Nec fastidiuit gloriosa domina illustris et praedicandi uiri munus; quinimmo usque hodie praesidet ecclesiae, sanctissimi Aldelmi communionem in potestate amplectens.[40]

In the case of Bath the evidence for a change of dedication is rather more flimsy. The dedication of Bath is usually described as St Peter's or, sometimes, SS Peter and Paul.[41] We have, however, one document which indicates a dedication to Mary, Peter and Benedict: this is the inscription in London, British Library, Cotton Claudius B. v, a manuscript given to Bath by Athelstan: 'Hunc codicem Ætheltsanus [sic] rex tradidit deo et alme Christi genetrici sanctisque Petro et Benedicto in Bathonie ciuitatis coenobio . . .'[42] Robinson argued that such a prominent abbey would probably not have been dedicated to Benedict in the time of King Æthelstan, suggesting that this dedication would be more likely after the Benedictine reform and that the inscription had, therefore, been added later.[43] The dedication to Mary also points to the reform period and it is possible that there was a short-lived attempt to change the Bath dedication to that typical of the monastic revival. Keynes, however, has argued that the inscription may well be contemporary and that Benedict could have

---

[39] John, 'St Oswald and the Church at Worcester', p. 243.

[40] *Willelmi Malmesbiriensis monachi de gestis pontificum Anglorum*, ed. Hamilton, p. 405: 'This is the Ælfric who, transferring all the care to the blessed Mary, made over the property and the name of the monastery to her authority so that, the name of the most blessed Peter having in the mean time become silent, she alone may be seen to govern the place. The glorious lady did not dislike the gift of the distinguished and praiseworthy man, but, on the contrary, she presides over the church to this very day, embracing the community of the most holy Aldhelm in her power.'

[41] For the variation see *Anglo-Saxon Writs*, ed. F. E. Harmer (Manchester, 1952), p. 134, n. 6.

[42] Quoted by Robinson, *The Times of St Dunstan*, p. 61: 'King Æthelstan gave this book to God and to the kind mother of Christ and to the saints Peter and Benedict in the monastery in the city of Bath . . .'

[43] *Ibid.*, p. 63.

been honoured at Bath in Athelstan's reign: 'this might seem surprising, but on the basis of our knowledge of conditions in Athelstan's reign we should certainly not exclude the possibility that a group of people who had taken monastic vows gathered at Bath and observed there the Rule of St Benedict'.[44]

Exeter also appears to have altered its dedication from Peter to Mary. The history of the successive foundations at Exeter is unclear, but the last house before the monastic reform)was dedicated to Peter. After the reform the house is described, although not invariably, as St Peter's and St Mary's, so it is probable that Mary was added to the dedication with the introduction of the monks in 968.[45] It is possible that even the dedication of St Saviour's, or Christ Church, Canterbury, was for a while altered. The bilingual Canterbury version of the *Anglo-Saxon Chronicle* in London, British Library, Cotton Domitian A. viii, written after the Conquest, includes under the year 995 a summary of the history of the see, which says that the cathedral was dedicated 'in honorem Iesu Christi, et S. Mariae matris eius'.[46]

The overwhelming number of dedications or rededications to Mary associated with the Benedictine reform suggests that this dedication was regarded almost as a hallmark of the reform, an outward sign of a truly monastic, celibate community. The uniformity was not absolute, as some older houses (St Alban's and St Augustine's, for example) retained their pre-reform dedications, but it is nevertheless very striking. It is surprising, therefore, that no contemporary source explicitly notes this aspect of the reform. The *uitae* of Dunstan, Æthelwold and Oswald make no reference to any deliberate policy, although the majority of houses founded by all three reformers were dedicated to Mary.

We have only one contemporary account, in Byrhtferth's *Vita S. Ecgwini*,[47] which, in effect, attempts to explain the dedication of a monastery. Ecgwine allegedly founded Evesham in the eighth century, but we do not know the original dedication of the house. In the tenth century it

[44] S. Keynes 'King Athelstan's Books', in *Learning and Literature in Anglo-Saxon England*, ed. Lapidge and Gneuss, pp. 159–65, at 162.

[45] Barlow, *The English Church 1000–1066*, pp. 213–14, n. 6.

[46] *Two of the Saxon Chronicles Parallel, with Supplementary Extracts from the Others*, ed. C. Plummer and J. Earle, 2 vols. (Oxford, 1892) I, 286; see also K. D. Hartzell, 'An Unknown Benedictine Gradual of the Eleventh Century', *ASE* 4 (1975), 131–44, at 136.

[47] *Vita quorundum Anglo-Saxonum*, ed. J. A. Giles, Caxton Society 16 (1854), 349–96. See also Lapidge, 'Byrhtferth and the *Vita S. Ecgwini*'.

was dedicated to Mary and Ecgwine. Byrhtferth seems to have composed his *Vita S. Ecgwini* from extremely scanty sources, elaborating them with the help of oral tradition.[48] The Marian part of the dedication is explained by a vision of Mary to Eoves, one of Ecgwine's swineherds, and then to Ecgwine himself. Byrhtferth does not connect the dedication to Mary in any way with the Benedictine reform, whose progress he had recorded in detail in his *Vita S. Oswaldi*. This suggests a lack of awareness of the near universality in the dedications to Mary, although it is, of course, possible that the dedication to Mary, in the case of Evesham, goes back to the first foundation in the eighth century, and that the legend predated the Benedictine reform. The names of Eoves and the other three swineherds do seem to preserve a basis of fact, as Lapidge has shown by recourse to place-name evidence.[49]

Although no contemporary attempts to explain the dedications, there must have been some reason for the trend. Poole in 1921 suggested that it was the result of continental influence:

there are many signs that the development of devotion to the Blessed Virgin Mary was greatly stimulated by the religious movement which is connected with Cluny. One cannot miss the significance of the fact . . . that when St Oswald returned to England from his training at Fleury and became bishop of Worcester, he rebuilt the cathedral church of St Peter and dedicated it anew in honour of St Mary. In the following century this dedication, from a rare one in England, became the most frequent.[50]

It is undoubtedly true that Carolingian influence was important for the Anglo-Saxon cult of Mary, but we have no evidence that this affected the dedications of churches. Fleury itself was dedicated to Benedict, Cluny to SS Peter and Paul, and Ghent, where Dunstan spent his exile, to Peter. Gorze, another continental house which influenced the English reform, was dedicated to the Roman martyr St Gorgonius. Moreover, the Marian dedications in England seem to have, in part, predated any significant continental influence on the reform. Glastonbury, the original centre of the movement, had been dedicated to Mary since its first foundation, but Æthelwold's foundation and dedication of Abingdon preceded Dunstan's exile abroad and Æthelwold's sending of a disciple to Fleury.

---

[48] Lapidge, 'Byrhtferth and the *Vita S. Ecgwini*', p. 348.   [49] *Ibid.*, pp. 347–8.
[50] R. L. Poole, 'The Beginning of the Year in the Middle Ages', *PBA* 10 (1921), 113–37, at 127.

One possible explanation would be that the newly reformed houses were dedicated in imitation of Glastonbury and Abingdon, the dedications being a proclamation of their affiliation. The accident of Glastonbury's existing dedication to the Virgin could also have been reinforced by the personal devotion of the leaders of the reform to her: Dunstan's prayer, where Mary is the only saint to be individually mentioned, suggests his attachment to her,[51] and Æthelwold seems to have composed an Office of the Virgin.[52] Æthelwold's personal devotion to the Virgin is also mentioned in the foundation charter of Thorney Abbey (c. 973), the church of which was dedicated to the Trinity, Mary, Peter and Benedict: these saints were chosen because Æthelwold trusted particularly in their intercession.[53] Mary as the virgin saint par excellence was also a suitable patron saint for a reformed monasticism which stressed celibacy above all; Peter, who had once had a wife, may have been regarded as less suitable. It is chiefly as a virgin mother that she is celebrated by Ælfric. That the majority of the reformed houses were dedicated to Mary would in itself have been instrumental in increasing devotion to her, since the patron saint of a house is given great prominence in the *Regularis concordia* and his or her intercession is frequently implored.[54] The pervasiveness of Marian dedications, while clearly a reflection of devotion to Mary, equally clearly becomes a cause of increased devotion.

As well as dedicating their churches to Mary, some Anglo-Saxons also seem to have constructed their buildings according to a plan particularly associated with the Virgin in the Middle Ages: the round church.[55] Influential in this development were: the round church over the supposed tomb of the Virgin in the valley of Josaphat; the round Blachernae chapel in Constantinople, probably of the seventh century, which contained the relic of Mary's girdle; and the rededication of the Pantheon to Mary and the martyrs c. 610. Although not all round churches had Marian dedications, many did. Hexham is the first Anglo-Saxon church which fits into this widespread pattern: built by Wilfrid c. 705–9 (in response to his dream admonishing him for neglecting to dedicate a church to the Virgin), it

---

[51] See above, pp. 104–5.   [52] See above, pp. 67–8.
[53] S 792; Hart, *The Early Charters of Eastern England*, no. VII, p. 167.
[54] *Regularis concordia*, ed. Symons, pp. 14, 31 and 35.
[55] See R. Krautheimer, 'Sancta Maria Rotunda', in *Studies in Early Christian, Medieval and Renaissance Art* (London and New York, 1969), pp. 107–114 and Gem, 'Towards an Iconography of Anglo-Saxon Architecture', pp. 7-12.

appears to have been a round or polygonal structure and Gem points to a striking resemblance to Adamnan's account of Arculf's description of the church dedicated to Mary in the valley of Josaphat.[56] Wilfrid could also have been acquainted with continental examples of round or polygonal churches (the difference is immaterial in this context). In the later Anglo-Saxon period, Abingdon's new church, built under Æthelwold *c*. 960 and dedicated to Mary, seems to have been 'a tower-like rotunda with surrounding ambulatory and with an apsidal chancel to the East',[57] which resembles the ninth-century Carolingian royal chapel at Aachen. The church of Mary and Edmund in Bury St Edmunds, dedicated in 1032, seems to have been similar in plan to that at Abingdon, and St Augustine's in Canterbury began to construct a rotunda *c*. 1049 under Abbot Wulfric, which again seems to be connected with the Virgin.[58] Anglo-Saxon church architects, then, were clearly familiar with and copied the tradition of associating round churches with Mary.

RELICS

By the tenth and eleventh centuries many English churches and monasteries must have been in possession of relics of Mary. We have three eleventh-century lists of relics in England, from Winchester, Bath and Exeter.[59] The Marian relics which they include are typical of those which we find all over Europe by this time: fragments of her clothing, her hair and her sepulchre, as well as some of her milk. The Winchester lists were added in the mid-eleventh century to London, British Library, Stowe 944 (the *Liber uitae* of the New Minster) and they include part of Mary's tunic and her sepulchre.[60] The Bath lists were added in the second half of the eleventh century to Cambridge, Corpus Christi College 111, but the relics themselves must have been older, as the monks no longer knew the contents of the reliquaries:

Ðis se haligdom þe ælsige abb. 7 þa gebroðra þe mid him wæron fundon on þam

---

[56] 'Towards an Iconography of Anglo-Saxon Architecture', pp. 11-12.
[57] *Ibid.*, p. 8.
[58] *Ibid.*, pp. 9–11.
[59] On the question of relics in Anglo-Saxon England, see M. Förster, *Zur Geschichte des Reliquienkultes*.
[60] *Liber Vitae*, ed. Birch, pp. 158–63.

scrinon þa þa heom tweonode hwæt haligdomes hi hæfdon. Þa fæston hi to 7 undydon þa scrina 7 fundon ealswa hit heræfter sægð.[61]

The contents of this reliquary included 'of sancta marian reafe' and 'of sepulchrum sancte marie', as well as 'de capillo sancte Marie, de lacte sancte Marie' and, once again, 'de uestimento sancte marie'. Another Latin list in the same manuscript also includes, twice, 'de uestimento Sancte Marie'. The Exeter list, which takes the form of a 'kirchliche Aussprache',[62] was added in Exeter in the second half of the eleventh century to a tenth-century Breton gospel book, Oxford, Bodleian Library, Auct. D. 2. 16, but the relics are again older as part of them had been given to Exeter by Athelstan. These relics include 'Of þam girlan þære heofenlican hlæfdian sca. Marian' and 'Of þam heafodclaðe þære ilcan Godes moder 7 of hire fexe'.[63] The Marian relics, perhaps partly because they seem to have been almost ubiquitous by the eleventh century, do not appear to have excited the kind of relic-theft which more recent saints, with only one authenticated set of bones, precipated in England.

WALSINGHAM AND MARIAN PILGRIMAGE

The only centre of Marian pilgrimage thought to have originated before 1066 is that of Walsingham. There are two pieces of evidence which suggest that this may go back to the year 1061. The first is a note added in an early fifteenth-century book which reads 'anno domini mᵒ sexagesimo primo capella beate marie de Walsyngham in comitatu Norff. fuit fundata et incepta'.[64] The second is the Pynson ballad, published *c.* 1496, which begins:

> Of this chapell se here the fundacyon,
> Bylded the yere of Crystes incarnacyon,

---

[61] *Two Chartularies*, ed. W. Hunt, p. lxxv: 'This is the collection of relics which Abbot Ælfsige and the brothers who were with him found in the shrines when they were uncertain what relics they had. Then they fasted and opened the shrines and found as follows . . .'

[62] Förster, *Zur Geschichte*, p. 58.

[63] *Ibid.*, p. 70: 'from the garment of the heavenly lady St Mary'; 'from the headdress of the same mother of God and from her hair'.

[64] Quoted from Dickinson, *The Shrine of Our Lady*, p. 4, n. 1: 'in the year of the Lord one thousand and sixty-one the chapel of blessed Mary in Walsingham was founded and begun in the county of Norfolk'.

> A thousande complete syxty and one,
> The tyme of sent Edward kyng of this region.[65]

The ballad relates that Mary showed in a dream her house in Nazareth to a widow Rychold and instructed her to build one like it in Walsingham. The place in which it was to stand was revealed by the failure of a heavenly dew to cover two spots in a meadow. When the carpenters attempted to erect the church on the first site 'no pece with oder wolde agre with geometrye', and on the following night Mary herself moved the house to the second site.

Only the note and the ballad attach a date to the foundation and both of these sources are late. The only other evidence is a twelfth-century pipe roll and an undated charter in the Walsingham cartulary.[66] The charter is the foundation charter of Walsingham priory, established by a Geoffrey de Favarches to take care of the chapel which his mother had built at Walsingham. This priory, to judge by the list of priors in the Walsingham cartulary, seems to have been established *c.* 1153.[67] The pipe roll of 1130–1 says that a William de Hocton rendered account of ten gold marks to marry the widow of Geoffrey de Favarches, taking over control of her land and the wardship of her son. It has been deduced that this Geoffrey was father of the Geoffrey who founded the priory and that the widow was the Rychold of the ballad. This would suggest that the church at Walsingham could not have been built until the first half of the twelfth century.[68] Hall, on the other hand, argues

why . . . should this 1130–1 widow be Rychold. The old documents never mention the name and she could just as well be the 1061 widow of the Ballad whose son Geoffrey, after going on the First Crusade, gave the undated charter; and it was his widow who married William de Hocton in 1139–1 . . . The fact remains that the Pynson Ballad alone gives the date, 1061, and it might as well be accepted.[69]

Against this can be set the date of the foundation of Walsingham as a priory for Augustinian canons, 1153 (Hall has to argue that the foundation of Geoffrey's charter was not Augustinian and that the house was later taken over by them), and Dickinson's compelling suggestion that 'Rychelde's

---

[65] *Ibid.*, p. 125.
[66] *Ibid.*, pp. 4–7 and Hall, *English Mediaeval Pilgrimage*, pp. 107–8.
[67] Dickinson, *The Shrine of Our Lady*, p. 4.   [68] *Ibid.*, p. 4.
[69] Hall, *English Mediaeval Pilgrimage*, pp. 107–8.

erection of the Holy House may have been inspired by her son's visit to the Holy Land (which is mentioned in the foundation charter)'.[70] On the whole, it seems probable that the only Marian pilgrimage which has been assigned to the pre-Conquest period was, in fact, a later development.

[70] Dickinson, *The Shrine of Our Lady*, p. 7.

6

The Virgin as portrayed in Anglo-Saxon art

As with the liturgy and prayer, we can discern in Anglo-Saxon England two principal periods when a flourishing devotion to Mary resulted in the production of depictions of her in art. In time and place these periods coincide with the other types of Marian evidence and, indeed, with the two high-points of Anglo-Saxon culture in general: the first, based in Northumbria and Mercia, stretches from the end of the seventh century to the beginning of the ninth, and the second, located in the southern centres of the Benedictine reform, dates from the middle of the tenth century to the end of the Anglo-Saxon period. As we might expect, the early representations tend to be included mainly in scenes whose theological import is Christological: Mother and Child scenes, the Annunciation and the Adoration of the Magi, in particular. These are also prominent in the Benedictine reform period, as are depictions of the Virgin in Crucifixion scenes, but, in addition, we find a larger number of autonomous images, which occasionally draw on the Marian apocrypha rather than on the gospels. Most Anglo-Saxon portrayals of Mary depend on early Christian art, which established patterns for succeeding generations.

THE VIRGIN IN EARLY CHRISTIAN ART

As with other manifestations of the cult of the Virgin, the first centuries of our era offer little evidence of artistic treatment. The early portrayals of Mary are intimately related to the Infancy cycle and there was little interest in this until the date of Christmas had been fixed.[1] It is not until the third century that we begin to find images of Mary, originally always in

[1] See above, pp. 25–6.

conjunction with Christ.[2] Not surprisingly, they show the same kind of assimilation of contemporary, often imperial, imagery, as do other types of Christian art.[3] The earliest surviving painting of the Virgin is perhaps one in the catacomb of Priscilla, probably of the first half of the third century, where a woman nurses a child:[4] similar nursing mothers are common in pre-Christian Roman art. While these figures would seem to represent the Virgin and Child, the iconography of the whole scene is puzzling and has been disputed. If this is really Mary, then this first depiction is of a naturalness and liveliness not often attained, or, indeed, aimed at, in the early church.

When Christmas first began to be celebrated as a major feast, it was a composite commemoration, covering the entire Nativity cycle as related in the gospels. The most common image in the early church for this whole sequence of events was that of the Adoration of the Magi, which was dogmatically important as 'the iconographic sign that indicates the principal argument in favour of the salvation of each believer: the fact of the Saviour's Incarnation and his work on earth'.[5] The Adoration of the Magi thus frequently appears on sarcophagi as 'a sign of the Incarnation – Redemption'[6] and it is also, of course, a natural image for the heathen recognizing Christ. The earliest depictions tend to be fairly naturalistic, with the three Magi approaching the Virgin, who is seated on a chair with the child on her lap.[7] In the fifth century we begin to find more hieratic versions of the scene, with the child now depicted as the divine *Logos*: he is nimbed, with his right hand raised in blessing and a scroll in his left hand. An angel is usually present, either as a guide to the Magi or to usher them into the divine presence, while the Magi are now often differentiated as representatives of the three ages of man, presenting their gifts in veiled hands, in accordance with court ceremonial. In these treatments the accent has moved from naturalism to a hieratic emphasis on the dignity and glory of God and his mother. A further development, probably of the sixth century, is the frontal, central Virgin and Child, who do not acknowledge

---

[2] An excellent introduction to the Virgin in art can be found in two studies by Schiller, *Iconography of Christian Art* and *Die Ikonographie*.
[3] See Grabar, *Christian Iconography*.
[4] See Schiller, *Iconography of Christian Art*, I, 13.
[5] Grabar, *Christian Iconography*, p. 12.   [6] *Ibid.*, p. 13.
[7] On the Adoration of the Magi see Schiller, *Iconography of Christian Art*, I, 94–114, and Becker, *Franks Casket*, pp. 125–34 (Appendix III).

the Magi: here the Magi and any other figures tend to be grouped symmetrically around the central throne. These depictions stress the dogma of the divine child and the *Theotokos*: their function is to convey a theological idea, one of majesty and power.

During the fourth and fifth centuries the other scenes of the Infancy cycle begin to be represented also. Many of them find a place in a very important, though iconographically unusual, cycle of mosaics which was commissioned by Pope Sixtus III for the church of Santa Maria Maggiore in Rome and executed between 432 and 440.[8] The iconography of the Infancy cycle on the triumphal arch is thought to have been designed to celebrate the victory of orthodoxy over Nestorianism at the Council of Ephesus in 431, when Mary's right to the title *Theotokos* was affirmed. The Virgin appears here, in the first Roman church dedicated to her, in the Annunciation, the Presentation in the Temple, the Adoration of the Magi and the Flight into Egypt: she is depicted throughout as an imperial lady in diadem and pearls, flanked by angels. Such cycles of biblical scenes became common in different media from this period onwards.

Of the individual scenes found in early Christian art, the most common early type of Annunciation is one with a seated Virgin, generally spinning, while Gabriel, with one hand stretched out towards Mary, stands beside her or advances towards her. Mary's head is usually covered by a veil as a symbol of her virginity and she is frequently accompanied by a maid, who has no place in Luke's account of the event. A slightly later type of Annunciation has a standing Virgin, again holding a spindle, with Gabriel advancing towards her. The Annunciation is very often accompanied by a second image of Christ's conception: the Visitation. This can be depicted with Mary and Elizabeth embracing or with the two women speaking to each other, and Grabar has shown that the Visitation was the Christian equivalent of the parental embrace which was a standard image of conception in the pre-Christian royal biographical cycles.[9] The Annunciation and Visitation were, then, originally 'two parallel images of the same theme of conception, the second being added – in conformity with common iconographic tradition – to show the first witness to Christ's conception'.[10]

The earliest depictions of the birth of Christ lack the Virgin: the Child is

---

[8] See Schiller, *Iconography of Christian Art*, I, 26–8 and throughout.

[9] Grabar, *Christian Iconography*, pp. 130–1.

[10] *Ibid.*, p. 131.

represented in the manger accompanied by the ox and the ass, or by the animals and a shepherd. Mary and Joseph appear regularly only from the fifth century onwards, reflecting perhaps the increase in Marian devotion after the Council of Ephesus.[11] The most common image of the Nativity from the sixth century on shows a cave, with Mary reclining on a couch, the child in an altar-like manger with the ox and the ass on either side, and a seated Joseph resting his head on his hand. Joseph's head is often averted from the child, probably as a means of expressing that he is not the father;[12] the altar-manger prefigures the Crucifixion. Many nativities include one or more midwives, sometimes the Salome of the apocrypha, with her withered hand, or the midwives bathing the child, frequently in a font or chalice-shaped basin. Some of the very early images have a seated Virgin, presumably as a means of conveying her painless childbirth:[13] this goes back to the fourth-century Roman sarcophagi.

Very few portrayals of the Presentation in the Temple survive until the eighth century, apart from that in the Santa Maria Maggiore mosaics.[14] In the fifth-century mosaic the Virgin, preceded by Joseph and an angel and followed by two more angels, holds the child, and she is being met by Simeon, Anna and a large group. The sacrificial doves stand on the temple steps. In some eighth- and ninth-century images we find a modified version of this representation of the scene, but, particularly in the West, a different iconography dominates from the eighth century onwards. In it Mary hands the child, who is usually shown above an altar, to Simeon; Joseph and Anna are also often present. The altar again foreshadows Christ's sacrifice and the emphasis in the whole scene is on the presentation, not the meeting with Simeon.[15]

The earliest surviving depiction of the flight into Egypt also occurs on the Santa Maria Maggiore triumphal arch, but, again, it differs from the later iconography. It shows Mary, Joseph and the child, flanked by four angels, being greeted by Aphrodisius and his followers in Egypt, in an episode drawn from the New Testament apocrypha. From the sixth century

---

[11] Schiller, *Iconography of Christian Art*, I, 61.

[12] Grabar, *Christian Iconography*, p. 130.

[13] See E. Mâle, *Religious Art in France: The Twelfth Century. A Study of the Origins of Medieval Iconography*, trans. M. Mathews (Princeton, 1978), pp. 63-4.

[14] See D. C. Schorr, 'The Iconographic Development of the Presentation in the Temple', *Art Bulletin* 28 (1946), 17–32, and Schiller, *Iconography of Christian Art* I, 90–4.

[15] See above, p. 29, on the change of name of the feast.

the common image is of Mary holding the child and seated on an ass which is led by Joseph.

From the fifth century, too, we begin to have autonomous images of the Virgin and Child outside of any narrative context. In the sixth century these hieratic images, which probably originated in the East, commonly take the form of the Virgin and Child attended by angels: the *regina angelorum*.[16] The *Theotokos* often adorns the apse of churches from this period on, especially in the East: in the fifth century she seems to have been flanked by saints and donors, in the sixth, as in other contexts, by angels.[17] Also in the sixth century, apparently first in the Roman church of Santa Maria Antiqua, the crowned Virgin appears: she wears a high jewelled Byzantine crown, although in Byzantine art she is never thus depicted.[18] The Byzantine images of the type called the *regina angelorum* depict a veiled, not a crowned, Virgin; the crown is especially characteristic of Roman Marian iconography.

THE EARLIEST ANGLO-SAXON DEPICTIONS OF THE VIRGIN

These, then, were the main types of images of the Virgin which had developed by the sixth century. At the very end of that century St Augustine arrived in England (597) and from the beginning the missionaries brought images with them.[19] The first reference we have to a depiction of the Virgin in Anglo-Saxon England is in Bede's description of the works brought from Rome by Benedict Biscop between 675 and 686. These would appear to have been panel-paintings[20] and include an 'imaginem . . . beatae Dei genetricis semperque uirginis Mariae, simul et duodecim apostolorum'.[21] These thirteen panels appear to have been hung across the church of St Peter's, Wearmouth, from wall to wall, perhaps across the central arch marking the entrance to the sanctuary.[22] Both the churches at

---

[16] See Rademacher, *Die Regina Angelorum*, p. 26; Shepherd, 'An Icon', p. 93.

[17] Rademacher, *Die Regina Angelorum*, pp. 31–3; Shepherd, 'An Icon', p. 92.

[18] See M. Lawrence, 'Maria Regina', *Art Bulletin* 7 (1924–5), 148–61.

[19] *Historia ecclesiastica gentis Anglorum* I. 25, in *Venerabilis Baedae opera historica*, ed. Plummer, I, 46.

[20] Meyvaert, 'Bede and the Church-Paintings', p. 70; Dodwell, *Anglo-Saxon Art*, pp. 86 and 272.

[21] *Historia abbatum*, c. 6, in *Venerabilis Baedae opera historica*, ed. Plummer I, 369: 'an image of the blessed mother of God and ever virgin Mary, and also of the twelve apostles'.

[22] Meyvaert, 'Bede and the Church Paintings', pp. 72–4.

Wearmouth and at Jarrow also had images of scenes from the gospels, and these could well have included depictions from the Infancy cycle, perhaps particularly in the church dedicated to the Virgin at Wearmouth which was adorned with 'dominicae historiae picturas'.[23] In a poem written before 705 by Æthilwald, a pupil of Aldhelm, there is another reference to images of the Virgin brought back from Rome as gifts to a church.[24] They are described as having heads which shone golden in the light and this has been interpreted as bust-pictures or as gilded-glass pictures. These latter consisted of etched images produced in gold foil and then fused between layers of glass, and they often featured an orant Virgin.[25] On the other hand the gold may simply have been gold-painted haloes.[26]

Some idea of what these seventh-century Roman works were like can perhaps be gained from the one surviving seventh-century English depiction of the Virgin. This is a carving on one end of the wooden coffin of St Cuthbert, produced in Lindisfarne in 698 (pl. 1). The Virgin and Child here form part of a complex iconographical scheme, with figures (Christ, the Evangelist symbols, the apostles and archangels) being taken from different models and chosen 'in accordance with the requirements of literary texts',[27] probably prayers. Kitzinger thought it possible that all the figures 'stand for so many invocations which the monks of Lindisfarne were wont to chant in their prayers and which are here laid down in a permanent and visual form',[28] intended to secure protection for the relics. The different models used for the coffin all seem to have been of Mediterranean origin, mostly from the sixth or seventh centuries.

The Cuthbert Coffin shows the Virgin in a seated position, although without a chair; her face, like the child's, is turned directly to the beholder, but the lower parts of their bodies are seen in three-quarter view. The child sits across Mary's lap, blessing with his right hand and holding a scroll in his left; her left hand is on his left shoulder and her right hand on his knee. Both figures have haloes, the child's cruciform. This three-quarter view, with the child across Mary's lap, is very unusual: much more common in this period is an absolutely frontal image, with the child in the centre of

---

[23] *Historia abbatum*, c. 9, ed. Plummer I, 373: 'paintings of the history of the Lord'.
[24] *Aldhelmi opera*, ed. Ehwald, pp. 528–33 (lines 171–7).
[25] Dodwell, *Anglo-Saxon Art*, p. 107.
[26] See R. Deshman (reviewing Dodwell, *Anglo-Saxon Art*), *Art Bulletin* 68 (1986), 329–32, at 330.
[27] Kitzinger, 'The Coffin-Reliquary', p. 277.   [28] *Ibid.*, p. 279.

Mary's lap. There is, however, a striking parallel painted about a century later at an unidentified centre in the British Isles: the famous Virgin and Child in the Book of Kells (Dublin, Trinity College 58, 7v), where the bodies of the mother and child are again seated facing each other.[29] This 'complementary profiles' arrangement, as Kitzinger termed it in his discussion of the two images, is more marked in Kells, where the child is seen entirely in profile, his face looking up at his mother rather than out at the beholder.[30] The Kells image also brings the pair into a much more intimate relationship: Mary's left arm supports Christ's back and he touches her left wrist with his right hand and her breast with his left hand. The Virgin's breasts are clearly outlined beneath her garment. She is nimbed, although the child has no halo, and four angels surround her seat, three with staffs or flabella, one with a flowering branch. Kitzinger argued convincingly that the model of the Kells miniature was of Greek inspiration, executed perhaps in the hellenized Rome of the seventh century, and, similarly, that the carving's 'soft, fluid lines indicate that the model was of a fairly naturalistic kind'[31] and also Greek-inspired.

Kitzinger believed that both the Cuthbert and Kells portrayals derived from a common prototype, better preserved in Kells. The iconographical schemes behind the two depictions are clearly different, however, and they are much more likely to go back to two different types of models imported into the British Isles in the seventh or eighth centuries. The unnimbed Kells child, reaching to his mother's breast, touching her hand and looking up to her face, emphasizes Christ's humanity and its origin in Mary.[32] The flowering branch held by the angel perhaps alludes to Mary as the rod of Jesse. The Virgin's halo, on the other hand, indicates her role as *Theotokos*, as do the attendant angels. The Cuthbert Coffin, however, stresses primarily Christ's divinity, with the blessing child holding the scroll, his eyes fixed on the spectator. The different iconography is in each case designed to illustrate a particular point and it would appear, as Wright suggests, that 'the coffin and the miniature copied two separate models of essentially the same style, and with the unusual feature of showing the

---

[29] See reproduction in F. Henry, *The Book of Kells* (London, 1974), pl. 10.
[30] Kitzinger, 'The Coffin Reliquary', pp. 248–64.
[31] *Ibid.*, p. 263.
[32] See the discussion by Rosenthal, 'The Historiated Canon Tables', pp. 211–13.

seated Virgin in three-quarter view'.[33] The Cuthbert carving was also, of course, planned as part of the overall iconographical programme of the coffin: Mary is included, not only as one of the saints whose protection is invoked, but as part of the double theophany of the Lord. This is depicted with the Virgin and Child representing the Incarnation and with the Christ in majesty on the lid emphasizing his divinity and, perhaps, given the presence of the apocalyptic beasts, his Second Coming.[34] This double theophany, with all its suggestions of redemption, is eminently appropriate for a coffin.

Almost contemporary with the Cuthbert Coffin is the earliest surviving Anglo-Saxon depiction of the Adoration of the Magi. This is on the front of the Franks Casket of *c*. 700, an ivory box carved in low relief, now divided between the British Museum and the Museo Nazionale in Florence, which, 'with its heterogeneous content, its ambitious programme, its acquaintance both direct and indirect with late antique and early Mediterranean as well as native sources, must be the product of a major Northumbrian intellectual centre'.[35] The carving, even though it includes some very uncommon features, appears to be imitated from an oriental exemplar. Mary, seated on a throne with the child, is seen in three-quarters view, though there is no attempt to portray the lower parts of their bodies. Both are nimbed. The three Magi approach from the left, in conventional posture and dress, apart from their bonnet-style head-dress which is also found elsewhere on the casket. The form of the gifts is curious, but even more extraordinary is the bird which leads the Magi and which appears to be the Anglo-Saxon carver's equivalent of the angel who often appears in oriental Adoration scenes.[36] The other scene on the same panel is from the legend of Weland and a deliberate parallel may well be intended with the 'theme of redemption through a hero's birth latent in both scenes'.[37]

Evidence of another contemporary Adoration scene, this time a manuscript illumination, is provided by a ninth-century manuscript from

---

[33] D. H. Wright (reviewing Battiscombe, *The Relics of St Cuthbert*), *Art Bulletin* 43 (1961), 141–60, at 146.

[34] M. Werner, 'The Madonna and Child Miniature in the Book of Kells', *Art Bulletin* 54 (1972), 1–23 and 129–39, at 14–16.

[35] Webster, 'Stylistic Aspects of the Franks Casket', p. 28. The casket is reproduced and described by Beckwith, *Ivory Carvings*, no. 1, pls. 3–7, and in Becker, *Franks Casket*.

[36] Becker, *Franks Casket*, p. 77.

[37] Webster, 'Stylistic Aspects of the Franks Casket', p. 29.

Liège, an illustrated copy from an Anglo-Saxon manuscript of *c.* 700.[38] We cannot, of course, know how closely it reflects its source. With its haloed Mother and Child, the veiled hands of the Magi as they present their gifts and the cushioned throne and footstools, this miniature again emphasizes the divinity of the child and the reverence owed to him.

STONE CARVING IN THE EIGHTH AND NINTH CENTURIES

In the first half of the eighth century free-standing stone crosses begin to appear in Northumbria. The major monument on which the Virgin is prominent is the Ruthwell Cross in Dumfriesshire: this has the most elaborate schema of all the surviving early crosses, with figural panels on the two broad sides and around the cross-head, as well as Latin and Anglo-Saxon inscriptions.[39] The identification of the carvings is not always easy and commentators differ, but the large panels appear to depict, on the original east side, the Visitation, Mary Magdalen wiping Christ's feet, Christ healing the blind man, the Annunciation and the Crucifixion. On what was originally the west side, we find John the Baptist carrying the *Agnus Dei*, Christ recognized by the beasts in the desert, SS Paul and Anthony breaking bread in the desert, the flight into/out of Egypt and an obliterated panel at the bottom. The Visitation scene is of the familiar type of Mary and Elizabeth embracing, while the Annunciation shows the standing Virgin on the right and a striding Gabriel on the left, both nimbed. Gabriel leans towards Mary, while she draws back, her right hand raised to her chest in a gesture which seems to indicate fear. The placing of the Annunciation immediately above the Crucifixion panel is significant and is most probably intended to point to the coincidence of date of the two events, Christ's conception and death: 25 March was regarded as the 'historical' date of the Crucifixion, which was celebrated liturgically on the movable feast of Easter.[40]

---

[38] Antwerp, Plantin-Moretus Museum, M. 17. 4. Reproduced and described in Alexander, *Insular Manuscripts*, no. 65 and pl. 290.

[39] See F. Saxl, 'The Ruthwell Cross', *Journal of the Warburg and Courtauld Institutes* 6 (1943), 1–19; M. Schapiro, 'The Religious Meaning of the Ruthwell Cross', *Art Bulletin* 26 (1944), 232–45; R. T. Farrell, 'Reflections on the Iconography'; Ó Carragáin, 'The Ruthwell Crucifixion Poem'.

[40] É. Ó Carragáin, 'Liturgical Innovations Associated with Pope Sergius and the Iconography of the Ruthwell and Bewcastle Crosses', in *Bede and Anglo-Saxon England*, ed. R. T. Farrell, British Archaeological Reports 46 (Oxford, 1978), 131–47, at 131–4.

The figure of the Virgin in the Egypt panel on the original west side of Ruthwell conforms to the common iconography of the scene. Of the panel immediately below, almost nothing now remains, but it has been repeatedly suggested that it could have been a Nativity scene, corresponding to the Crucifixion on the same panel of the opposite face. Remnants of a profile figure can just be made out on the left of the panel.[41] This could belong to a seated Virgin as in, for example, the Nativity scene in the Rabula Gospels, but a profile, seated Virgin is very unusual in Nativity scenes, and it is possible that an Adoration of the Magi could have figured here. In function this would be very similar to a Nativity and would fit admirably into the theme of recognition of Christ which is so important on this side of the cross.

In the Anglo-Saxon images of the seventh and eighth centuries, the Virgin is represented in her role as *Theotokos*, but around the year 800 we begin to find monuments which testify to a greater degree of interest in Mary herself. The earliest surviving group of sculptures from Mercia, dated *c.* 800, includes a number of Marian images. This school begins with architectural sculpture and sarcophagi from Breedon, Peterborough, Fletton and Castor, the most famous being the Breedon sandstone friezes, but there are also figural panels of considerable importance. All of the surviving depictions of Mary belong to the group of figural works in Barnack stone; the latest detailed study attributes these relief carvings to a school probably centred either at Peterborough or at the Barnack quarry in Northhamptonshire, which produced these works at different stages of the first half of the ninth century.[42]

The Hedda Stone, a stone shrine-tomb in Peterborough which Jewell dates to the first decade of the ninth century, seems to be at the beginning of this Midlands tradition of figural sarcophagi, possibly derived from antique exemplars.[43] The carving is very worn, with six figures on each long side, animal ornament on the roof and rough ends: Christ, the Virgin and four apostles are featured on the front, six further apostles on the back. Mary is veiled and haloed and she holds a short plant stem, ending in a pointed leaf with two lobes at the base, in her left hand. On this monument, then, Mary is not present only as an image of the Incarnation,

[41] Ó Carragáin, 'The Ruthwell Crucifixion Poem', forthcoming.

[42] See Jewell, 'The Pre-Conquest Sculpture'; Cramp, 'Schools of Mercian Sculpture'.

[43] Cramp, 'Schools of Mercian Sculpture', p. 210 and pl. 57c; Jewell, 'The Pre-Conquest Sculpture', p. 285.

although the stem she holds probably alludes to her role as the rod of Jesse, bearing the fruit of Christ; she is also standing next to Christ, in a place of honour amongst the apostles.

A Breedon panel of the beginning of the ninth century has an angel who is likely to have been the Gabriel of the Annunciation and who would probably originally have been represented greeting the Virgin, who presumably stood in a neighbouring panel.[44]

More important is the figure in an arched panel in Breedon which, despite some iconographical peculiarities, is generally agreed to represent the Virgin.[45] The Breedon church was certainly dedicated to Mary at a later date[46] and perhaps in this period too, and the veiled figure is undoubtedly a female saint. It is a half-length, frontal figure, with banded drapery, veiled but without a halo, with deeply-drilled, staring eyes; the right hand, with disproportionately large (and characteristically insular) fingers, is raised in blessing and the left hand, covered by a triangle of drapery, holds a book (pl. II). The model may have been Byzantine: Jewell argues that the style of the drapery seems to derive from seventh-century Byzantine art and 'the hieratic frontality, and rigidly fixed staring gaze of the Virgin also derive from Byzantine art'.[47] Hieratic art is not restricted to the East, however, and a Western model cannot be ruled out. Such a portrayal of Mary without the Christ child is unusual for the period, as are the book she holds and, in particular, the blessing, which is most frequently associated with Christ and the apostles. The book can be paralleled in later depictions of Mary from Anglo-Saxon England, but not the attitude. When the Virgin is without the Christ child and not part of a narrative context, she is usually depicted as an orant, a pose which conveys a very different conception of her role. Jewell suggests that the English sculptor could have confused the attributes of the Virgin with those of another figure or that the panel had a companion piece representing Christ.[48] But had the latter been the case the two panels would have shown Mary and Christ in identical attitudes since the Virgin's 'attitude is more similar to that usually associated with

---

[44] Jewell, 'The Pre-Conquest Sculpture', pp. 268–76 and 286.

[45] Cramp, 'Schools of Mercian Sculpture', p. 210; Jewell, 'The Pre-Conquest Sculpture', pp. 259–65.

[46] On the dedication see Cramp, 'Schools of Mercian Sculpture', p. 210, and Jewell, 'The Pre-Conquest Sculpture', p. 238.

[47] Jewell, 'The Pre-Conquest Sculpture', p. 263.   [48] *Ibid.*, pp. 261–2.

Christ'.[49] It appears very unlikely that companion depictions of Christ and the Virgin would have shown them with identical attributes and attitudes, especially as Mary is not otherwise represented in the act of blessing in this period. The English artist may, then, have been adapting a depiction of, say, an apostle, taking over the 'masculine attributes',[50] but making it into an image of the Virgin. The demand for such a cult image in a church dedicated to Mary is readily understandable and it would doubtless have served as a focus of the community's devotion to her. If this was its purpose, then the blessing rather than the orant attitude is also appropriate. Such cult images undoubtedly found a place in ninth-century English churches: in the unknown church of the Lindisfarne cell described in Æthelwulf's poem *De abbatibus* (written between 803 and 821), for example, what appears to be a statue of Mary is mentioned:

> talibus exornata bonis, in uestibus albis,
> inclita, sed uario comptim permixta colore,
> a dextris uirgo et genetrix astare uideri
> rectoris, caelos, terris qui et numine portat.[51]

Jewell tentatively dates the panel to the decade 830–40 on the basis of its similarities with the Book of Cerne and its place in the stylistic development of the Breedon/Peterborough group.[52]

Another very important stone monument on which the Virgin is prominent is the slab in Wirksworth, Derbyshire, which seems to have once formed part of a stone shrine or sarcophagus and which has been variously dated from the second half of the seventh century to the first half of the ninth (pl. III).[53] Rosemary Cramp points out that there are clear stylistic similarities between it and the Bakewell school of stone crosses in the Peak District, which is probably to be dated to the first half of the ninth century, and she suggests that 'despite its antique iconography, [the slab] could be an offshoot of the Bakewell school'.[54] She sees the tradition of such

[49] Rice, *English Art*, p. 87.   [50] Cramp, 'Schools of Mercian Sculpture', p. 210.

[51] *De abbatibus*, ed. Campbell, pp. 181–9 (lines 202–5): 'Honoured by such good deeds, glorious in white robes, but with beautiful touches of various colours, the virgin mother of the ruler, who by his divinity carries heaven and earth, was seen to stand upon the right.'

[52] Jewell, 'The Pre-Conquest Sculpture', p. 287.

[53] See Kurth, 'The Iconography of the Wirksworth Slab', and Cockerton, 'The Wirksworth Slab'.

[54] Cramp, 'Schools of Mercian Sculpture', p. 224.

sarcophagi as perhaps beginning in Breedon or Peterborough towards the end of the eighth century under the influence of contacts with Eastern and continental art and then spreading northwards.[55]

The slab is in two registers and parts have been broken off at both ends. The upper register depicts the washing of feet, a lamb on a Greek cross surrounded by the symbols of the Evangelists, the death of the Virgin and an incomplete scene which is very difficult to interpret; the bottom one has an enigmatic scene which has been explained as the Nativity or as Christ's descent into hell, the Ascension, Annunciation and a further scene which is most probably the Presentation. The Annunciation has the seated Virgin on the right with the angel on the left, his hand extended in a gesture of speech or blessing. One of Mary's hands is raised, in an attitude perhaps intended to convey astonishment, and the whole composition can be compared to the Annunciation on the sixth-century throne of Archbishop Maximian in Ravenna or the sixth-century mosaic in the apse of the cathedral at Parenzo.[56] The Ascension scene has a man and a woman below Christ's mandorla, instead of the common iconography of all of the apostles with Mary, probably because of lack of space. Here they presumably represent Mary and Peter: this inclusion of the Virgin is normal from the sixth century onwards, despite the silence of the gospels. On the left of the Presentation scene a man and two women, who must be Joseph, the prophetess Anna and Mary, hand a smaller figure holding a scroll to a man on the right, Simeon. The scroll carried by the child is a common feature. The details of the scene can be paralleled in the lost early eighth-century mosaic of John VII and a lost fresco for the same period in Santa Maria Antiqua, which both showed Mary carrying the child, followed by Joseph and Anna, and being met by Simeon.[57]

The most intriguing of all the Marian scenes on the slab, however, is undoubtedly that representing the dead Virgin on a bier carried by two apostles. This corresponds so exactly to the apocryphal legend that there can be little doubt about the correctness of the interpretation, although no earlier treatment of the legend has survived. The iconography of the Dormition must have already been developed, however: even though the earliest surviving Eastern *Transitus* scenes date from the tenth century,

[55] *Ibid.*, pp. 219 and 224.
[56] Reproduced in Schiller, *Iconography of Christian Art*, I, pls. 71 and 72. See also Kurth, 'The Iconography of the Wirksworth Slab', p. 115.
[57] See Schiller, *Iconography of Christian Art*, I, 91.

Schiller suggests that the iconography of the legend would have been initiated in the East around 600, when the feast of the Assumption began to be celebrated, and that the evidence must then have been destroyed by the iconoclasts.[58] The *Liber pontificalis* records the donation of textiles depicting the Assumption by a number of popes, beginning with Hadrian I (771–5).[59] Apart from the slab, the next surviving *Transitus* images are three remaining scenes from a fresco cycle in the Roman church of Santa Maria Egyziaca, painted between 872 and 882.[60] The quality of the works indicates Eastern exemplars, although these have all been lost. They show Christ announcing her death to Mary, the raising up of the apostles on clouds and the apostles greeting each other in front of Mary's house. The Wirksworth slab, then, may well be a copy of an Eastern model from the pre-iconoclastic period. All of the other identifiable scenes on the slab follow an established iconography and it is probable that for this scene, too, the carver had an exemplar; many of the details of the carving resemble later treatments of the subject. The scene shows a figure bearing a palm (John, according to the apocrypha), preceding a bier borne by two apostles (Peter and Paul). On the bier lies the Virgin's body and underneath, attached by his hands, is stretched the Jew who wished to burn Mary's corpse. In a circle or cloud above are six heads, presumably angels. The Dormition image is unusual in that the other scenes on the slab all show parts of Christ's life: even the Annunciation is clearly Christological rather than Mariological in import. The death of Mary, however, cannot be viewed in the same light: Mary's assumption after death, which is signified by the palm, is, of course, a consequence of her role as *Theotokos* and its place above the Annunciation signifies this, but its inclusion in a Christological cycle is nevertheless a significant departure from the norm in such cycles.

From about the same period (*c.* 800) in Northumbria we have the Virgin

---

[58] Schiller, *Die Ikonographie* IV.2, 92.

[59] Le '*Liber pontificalis*', ed. L. Duchesne, 2nd ed., 3 vols. (Paris, 1957) I, 500: 'in ecclesia uero sanctae Dei genetricis ad Praesepe fecit uestes II super altare maiore: una ex auro purissimo atque gemmis, habentem adsumptionem sanctae Dei genetricis . . .' ('Truly in the church of the holy mother of God at the Praesepe he placed two cloths above the larger altar: one from the purest gold and gems, depicting the assumption of the holy mother of God . . .'). See also II, 14, 61 and 145.

[60] See Lafontaine, *Peintures médiévales*, pp. 29–35.

and Child on the remains of the Dewsbury cross shaft in West Yorkshire.[61] The group is treated here in a classical fashion, set 'within an architectural frame, with fluted columns, stepped bases and capitals, and tiny curling sprays rising from the capitals'.[62] The Virgin, veiled and haloed, is half turned and the Child is seated sideways on her lap, a scroll in his left hand, his right hand reaching to her breast. The arrangement of the figures is very similar to the Cuthbert Coffin in particular and it is the earliest example in stone of this type of portrayal. The combination of scroll, signifying the teacher, and of affectionate gesture, signifying the human relationship of mother and child, points to the twofold nature of Christ. The gaze of the Virgin, with drilled eyes, is hieratically directed at the beholder, as on the coffin, rather than at the Child. The Dewsbury cross also has a depiction of the Miracle of Cana, with Mary whispering to Christ as he blesses the water pots.[63]

At Hovingham in the North Riding of Yorkshire the Annunciation is portrayed on a ninth-century stone sarcophagus.[64] The style is influenced by Mercian figure sculpture, and the sarcophagus, with its groups of figures under plant arcades, derives from the Mercian sarcophagi. There are eight figures in all and the first two clearly represent the Annunciation, with Gabriel in the first arcade and the seated Virgin in the second. The nimbed angel holds a staff in his left hand and blesses with his right, stepping towards the Virgin. She is also nimbed and sits on a cushioned chair with a footstool, her hand raised to express either speech or surprise. Collingwood suggested that the next four figures might be evangelists and that the last two could be intended to represent the Visitation, but none of these is as clear as the Annunciation scene.

The end of a shrine-tomb in Oswaldkirk, possibly of the ninth century, has a standing Virgin with the nimbed, swaddled child in her arms[65] and another shrine-tomb from Bedale, again in Northumbria, also has the seated Mother and Child on one end, with another figure on the left bending towards them.[66]

---

[61] Collingwood, 'Anglian and Anglo-Danish Sculpture', pp. 163–4; Cramp and Lang, *A Century of Anglo-Saxon Sculpture*, pl. 2b.

[62] Cramp and Lang, *ibid.*

[63] Collingwood, 'Anglian and Anglo-Danish Sculpture', p. 165.

[64] Collingwood, 'Anglian and Anglo-Danish Sculpture', p. 337; Cramp, 'Schools of Mercian Sculpture', p. 210.

[65] Collingwood, *ibid.*, p. 380.   [66] *Ibid.*, p. 292.

The surviving Marian images from the earlier Anglo-Saxon period, then, all come from Northumbria and the Midlands. They include autonomous Virgin and Child images and the narrative scenes of the Annunciation, Visitation, Presentation in the Temple and the Adoration of the Magi, as well as, most surprisingly, what is probably the earliest surviving Western depiction of the Dormition. The oldest of all of the Anglo-Saxon portrayals, that on the Cuthbert Coffin, bears witness to the availability in England of an unusual iconographic type, more informal than is normal for this period, as does the Kells miniature with its intimate, tender relationship of the Child to his mother. In early ninth-century Mercia the Breedon panel and the Wirksworth slab testify to an interest in the Virgin which goes beyond the strictly Christological doctrines inherent in the Virgin and Child images. They are possibly from related centres, if the tradition of sarcophagi spread from Wirksworth to Breedon, and they provide evidence, otherwise lacking, of knowledge of Marian apocrypha and a developed degree of devotion to the Virgin in this area.

MANUSCRIPT ILLUMINATION OF THE EARLY TENTH CENTURY: THE ÆTHELSTAN PSALTER

There appear to be no surviving illuminations or sculptures of Mary from the last part of the ninth century and the beginning of the tenth. The first surviving illustrations of the Virgin after this gap are in the pages added in England at the beginning of the tenth century to the ninth-century continental psalter, London, BL, Cotton Galba A. xviii, often known as the 'Æthelstan Psalter'.[67] These contain four miniatures, namely: Christ with choirs of angels, patriarchs, prophets and the apostles with Mary; Christ with choirs of martyrs, confessors and virgins; the Ascension; and the Nativity (a detached leaf of the same manuscript, now Oxford, Bodleian Library, Rawlinson B. 484, fol. 85). The Nativity miniature is in two registers, with a central crib in the upper register, a seated Joseph on the left and a reclining Mary on the right; the lower register has the washing of the Child by two midwives.[68] The painting is firmly Christological and sacramental in import, with suggestions of Christ's Passion in the

---

[67] For the date of the miniatures see Keynes, 'King Athelstan's Books', p. 195.
[68] Reproduced in *Golden Age*, ed. Backhouse *et al.*, pl. 4b; discussed by Deshman, 'Anglo-Saxon Art after Alfred', pp. 183–6.

altar-shaped crib and of baptism and the eucharist. The unnimbed Mary, who is looking away from the Child and out at the spectator, her outstretched hands in a witnessing position, is here as a proof of Christ's human nature and to witness to his significance. The Ascension shows an enthroned Christ in a mandorla borne by two angels; below are the two half-length *uiri Galilei* pointing Christ out to the two groups of apostles and the central nimbed orant Virgin.[69] The prominence of the Virgin, directly beneath Christ's mandorla and separated from the apostles by a plant on either side, is striking. She functions here, as in all images of the Ascension in which she appears, both as a sign of the Incarnation and as a symbol of the church in prayer. Deshman has suggested that the source of this miniature was a Middle Byzantine model, pointing out that the combination of features found in the English illustration is paralleled most closely in Byzantine works of the post-iconoclastic period.[70]

THE BENEDICTINE REFORM PERIOD: WINCHESTER MANUSCRIPTS

The four Æthelstan Psalter miniatures testify to the eclecticism of its illuminators: earlier insular art, Carolingian and early Christian Mediterranean sources all appear to have been drawn upon. In this they herald the Benedictine reform of the second half of the tenth century in which, although, as has been argued, 'an intentional programme' of copying Carolingian sources becomes evident,[71] we find also a remarkable iconographic originality, a willingness to combine and synthesize. The one illumination in the New Minster Charter (London, BL, Cotton Vespasian A. viii, fols. 1–33), one of the earliest reform manuscripts, is a good example of this. The book probably dates from 966 and Wormald suggests that it was 'a sumptuous record', a 'solemn commemoration' of King Edgar's *priuilegium* to the New Minster in Winchester, which may have been intended to be kept on the altar there.[72] The miniature shows Edgar flanked by the Virgin and St Peter, presenting the charter to Christ seated above in a mandorla surrounded by angels (pl. IV). Following Kantorowicz,

---

[69] *Golden Age*, ed. Backhouse *et al.*, pl. 4a.
[70] Deshman, 'Anglo-Saxon Art after Alfred', pp. 186–90.
[71] Alexander, 'The Benedictional of St Æthelwold', p. 174.
[72] Wormald, 'Late Anglo-Saxon Art: Some Questions and Suggestions', *Collected Writings* I, pp. 109–10.

Deshman terms Mary and Peter an 'insular Deesis', Peter replacing the more usual John the Baptist.[73] The position of the saints is unusual, however: they are normally depicted flanking Christ in heaven, not the king on earth, and in the New Minster Charter 'the scale of the figures reverses the customary hierarchy: it is the donor, King Edgar, who is larger than the saints, rather than vice versa'.[74] Deshman explains that 'the location of these celestial intercessors on either side of King Edgar deliberately recalls the grouping of the Deesis of the Last Judgement [in the eleventh-century ivory of the Last Judgement in the University Museum of Archaeology and Ethnology in Cambridge] and assimilates him to Christ directly above him in heaven, and the king's larger scale calls attention to his superior rank as the *imago Christi*'.[75] The emphasis of the miniature, then, is on Edgar, but Mary and Peter are chosen to flank the king partly because of their importance as patrons of the New Minster and also because of the weight attached to their intercession on the Last Day.[76] The attributes held here by the two saints support this view: Mary's palm, symbol of victory, and her cross, symbol of Christ's Passion, an original combination of attributes, point to her role in the scheme of redemption. Peter bears the key to heaven in his right hand and the gospels, which set forth Christ's entrusting of this office to him, in his draped left hand. The New Minster Charter shows that in Winchester, the centre of the reform, Mary and Peter were honoured above all other saints. In this crucial reform document the Virgin, rather than any local or English saint, is given a very prominent place, paralleling all of the other indications of her importance to the reformed monks.

Veneration of the Virgin is very prominent in what is probably the most important of all reform manuscripts, the Benedictional of St Æthelwold (London, BL, Add. 49598). This, the most elaborately decorated of all benedictionals, was made in Winchester between 971 and 984, and Deshman argues that it was probably created to celebrate the coronation of Edgar and his queen in 973.[77] The book was clearly designed with enormous care and thought and, despite its dependence on Carolingian and

---

[73] Deshman, 'The Iconography', pp. 112–31, and see also 'Benedictus monarcha et monachus', p.224.
[74] Deshman, 'Benedictus monarcha et monachus', p.224.   [75] *Ibid.*
[76] Deshman, 'The Iconography', p. 230.
[77] *Ibid.*, p. 241; the facsimile edition is *The Benedictional of St Æthelwold*, ed. Warner and Wilson.

Byzantine models, is 'a very personalized product',[78] in which the different illuminations are related by a network of similarities and echoes. Deshman has demonstrated the extent to which the manuscript's illuminations are permeated with regal elements and has interpreted this in the light of the close connections between the Benedictine reform and King Edgar: 'The royal program of the manuscript expounds the political theology which Æthelwold created to legitimatize his alliance with King Edgar for the reform of the Anglo-Saxon monasteries. On the one hand, the Christ-like nature of the king is stressed in order to imbue him with spiritual significance; and, on the other, royal overtones are attributed to monasticism. This dual ideal of monastic royalty and royal monasticism is corroborated by contemporary written sources.'[79] Mary now appears in the Annunciation miniature for the first Sunday of Advent (5v), the day upon which the Annunciation pericope was read, Christmas (15v), the Octave of Christmas (22v), the Adoration of the Magi (24v), the Presentation in the Temple (34v), the Ascension (64v) and the Dormition (102v). In addition, the missing leaves must have included a miniature for the Nativity of the Virgin, which seems to be the earliest known instance in a liturgical manuscript.[80] Deshman very plausibly argues that Mary would also have had a prominent place in the sequence which begins the Benedictional.[81] This originally probably consisted of thirteen miniatures, with Christ in Majesty followed by twelve choirs. Mary is not in the choir of virgins, where she might be expected to hold the foremost place, and it is inconceivable, given her importance in the manuscript as a whole, that she was missing from the introductory series; Deshman therefore suggests that the missing first miniature had an insular Deesis, with Peter and Mary interceding with Christ, which seems probable in view of the similar Deesis in the New Minster Charter, or that 'she was represented at the head of the choirs of saints with some sort of Trinity, as in the later "Quinity" or in the John pages of the Grimbald Gospels, where there are also choirs of saints'.[82]

The most striking of the Mariological scenes are the Annunciation and the Assumption. The Annunciation (5v) shows a seated Mary under a

---

[78] D. H. Turner, 'Illuminated Manuscripts', in *Golden Age*, ed. Backhouse *et al.*, pp. 46–7, at 46.
[79] Deshman, 'The Iconography', p. 351.   [80] *Ibid.*, p. 201.
[81] *Ibid.*, pp. 112–3.
[82] In a letter dated February 1988.

baldachine with Gabriel on the left, holding a sceptre and making a speaking gesture: over Mary's head is the rubric *Sancta Maria* and the scene is entitled: 'Nuntius e caelo hic stat praedicando Mariae: / Ecce Deum paries hominemque simul benedicta' (pl. v). The scene is related to two Carolingian ivories of the Metz School, the Brunswick Casket and another casket in the Louvre, and all three probably derive ultimately from the same Metz School manuscript.[83] They share the baldachine over the Virgin, indicating her great dignity, and the Brunswick Casket and the Benedictional show her with her right hand on a book which rests on a lectern. This theme seems to originate with the casket and refers to Mary's reading the psalter, as she does in the *Gospel of Pseudo-Matthew*. Only in the Benedictional do we find the object in Mary's hand: a golden, oval-shaped object which replaces the spindles she carries in the two Metz ivories. Warner described it as a shuttle[84] and it is possible that the Anglo-Saxon artist wished to indicate weaving rather than spinning to conform to the *Gospel of Pseudo-Matthew*, in which Mary weaves the purple cloth for the temple veil. The other innovation in the miniature is the use of clouds surrounding Mary's head and Gabriel. Cloudy backgrounds are common in the Benedictional and appear to be derived from its models,[85] but there is no other Annunciation scene in which they are used in a comparable manner. The artist surrounds Mary's head with a nimbus of cloud instead of the conventional nimbus, and Deshman relates this to literary tradition, both to exegesis of the 'obumbrabit' of Luke's Annunciation account and to such Old Testament passages as Isaiah XLV.8 ('nubes pluant iustum') which were seen as prefigurations of the Incarnation.[86] The miniaturist, then, drew on these exegetical associations and 'the uniqueness of the artist's achievement in expressing these literary traditions in visual form is an indication of his unusual degree of originality and imagination'.[87] It shows that whoever was responsible for planning the manuscript was willing to depart from his artistic models in order to convey a theological point and clearly devoted much thought to finding a suitable visual vehicle for the moment of the Incarnation, as God entered Mary's womb.

The miniature for the Assumption (102v) is one of the most interesting

---

[83] Deshman, 'The Iconography', pp. 11–19 and 48.
[84] *The Benedictional of St Æthelwold*, ed. Warner and Wilson, p. xviii.
[85] Alexander, 'The Benedictional of St Æthelwold', p. 180.
[86] Deshman, 'The Iconography', pp. 16–18.
[87] *Ibid.*, p. 18.

in the entire manuscript. It is in two registers: in the bottom one stand nine apostles, those in front making speaking gestures; in the top register a haloed Mary lies on a bed, her hands outstretched, while a woman behind her adjusts her pillow and two further women by her bedside weep into their mantles, the foremost also making a speaking gesture (pl. VI). The hand of God lowers a crown in the middle of the top register and it is flanked by four angels, two making a gesture of reverence, one with draped hands and one holding a sceptre. The scene clearly illustrates the death of Mary as recounted in the apocryphal narratives: the discussion of the apostles occurs there, as do the attendant women.[88] This is the earliest surviving depiction of the death of the Virgin in a Western manuscript and also the earliest of her coronation, although the crowned Virgin is of course common in Italian, especially Roman, iconography from a much earlier period. We know, however, that manuscript depictions of the apocryphal story of Mary's death almost certainly existed before this time[89] and this naturally raises the question of whether or not the artist of the Benedictional was acquainted with such an illustrated text. Alexander argued that the miniature is 'an invention of the Winchester artist, put together from other scenes known to him'[90] and almost all of the elements of the composition can, in fact, be paralleled in other scenes in the Benedictional. There are similarities in composition with the Christmas miniature (the maid adjusting the pillow is found there); the hovering angels can be found in the baptism miniature; the apostles in the miniatures at the beginning of the manuscript are also similar; the crowning hand of God can be found in the Ascension scene; and the women weeping into their mantles can be found in other Winchester manuscripts, with the Harley Psalter (London, BL, Harley 2904) offering a particularly close parallel.[91] The Winchester artist, then, seems to have been responsible for the composition of the scene, as an illustration of a *Transitus* text. Deshman and Therel both argue that the artist was illustrating an episode in *Transitus* A where Mary and her three virgins have a conversation about death.[92] The difficulty with this

---

[88] O. Sinding, *Mariae Tod und Himmelfahrt* (Oslo, 1903), p. 66; O. Homburger, *Die Anfänge der Malerschule von Winchester im X. Jahrhundert*, Studien über christliche Denkmäler, ns 13 (Leipzig, 1912), 52; Deshman, 'The Iconography', pp. 83–9.

[89] See above, pp. 154–5.   [90] Alexander, 'The Benedictional of St Æthelwold', p. 179.

[91] See *ibid.*, p. 178, and Deshman, 'The Iconography', p. 86.

[92] Deshman, 'The Iconography', pp. 86–7; M. L. Therel, *A l'origine du décor du portail occidental de Notre-Dame de Senlis: La triomphe de la Vierge-Eglise* (Paris, 1984), pp. 53–4.

1 Durham Cathedral, St Cuthbert's Coffin; the Virgin and Child

11 Breedon, Leicestershire, Breedon church; the Virgin

III Wirksworth, Derbyshire; the Wirksworth Slab

IV London, British Library, Cotton Vespasian A. viii (New Minster Charter), 2v

v London, British Library, Add. 49598 (Benedictional of St Æthelwold), 5v;
the Annunciation

VI London, British Library, Add. 49598 (Benedictional of St Æthelwold), 102v;
the Dormition of the Virgin

VII Rouen, Bibliothèque municipale, 369 (Pontifical of Robert of Jumièges), 54v;
the Dormition of the Virgin

VIII London, British Library, Cotton Titus D. xxvii, 75v; the 'Quinity'

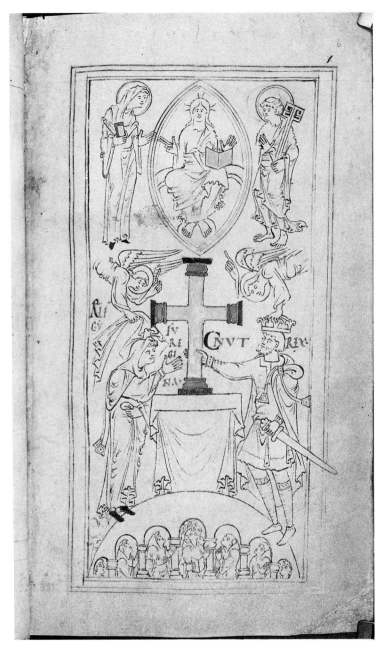

ix London, British Library, Stowe 944 (New Minster *Liber uitae*), 6r

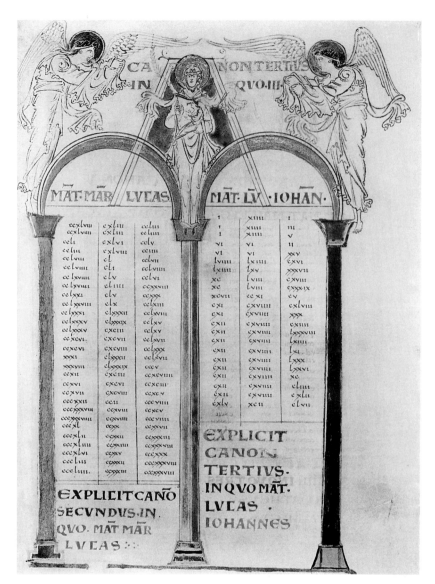

x New York, Pierpont Morgan Library, 869 (Arenberg Gospels), 11r; canon
tables with the Virgin and Child.

XI Rouen, Bibliothèque municipale, 274 (Sacramentary of Robert of Jumièges),
32v; the Nativity

XII Cambridge, Pembroke College 301, 2v; canon tables with the Virgin and saints

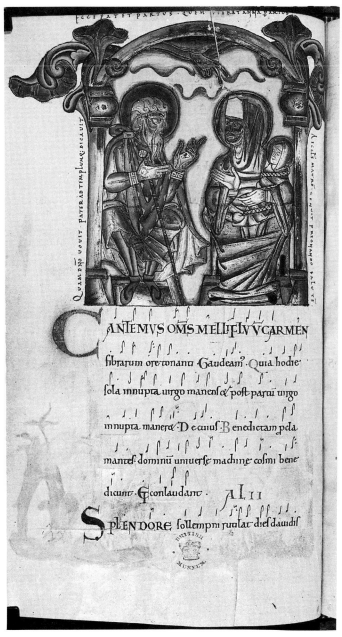

XIII London, British Library, Cotton Caligula A. xiv, 26v; Joachim and Anna
with the infant Mary

XIV New York, Pierpont Morgan Library, 709 (Judith of Flanders Gospels), 1v;
the Crucifixion

xv Oxford, Ashmolean Museum, walrus ivory; the Virgin and Child

XVI Cambridge, Museum of Archaeology and Ethnology, walrus ivory; the Last
Judgement

suggestion is the lack of evidence of knowledge of *Transitus* A in England: it is extant in only one manuscript, from Reichenau, and there is nothing to prove that it was known elsewhere.[93] The two accounts which undoubtedly circulated in England are *Transitus* B2 and *Transitus* C.[94] *Transitus* B2 describes the three virgins and the apostles as present at Mary's death, but there is no dialogue;[95] in *Transitus* C there is a conversation about death between Mary and 'omnes propinquos' in which she tells them not to weep, but the number is not restricted to the three virgins; the three women and the apostles are present at Mary's death.[96] Deshman's arguments, which rely on the scene in *Transitus* A in which Mary addresses some of the group of neighbours as 'virgines dei', are hardly compelling in view of the fairly close parallels with *Transitus* C and the lack of evidence for knowledge of *Transitus* A outside Reichenau. The Benedictional's miniature can probably be explained as an illustration of the apocryphal description of Mary attended by the three virgins and the apostles, with the stance of all the figures – Mary, the virgins and the apostles – being drawn from compositions already familiar to the artist. The eschatological overtones which Deshman finds in *Transitus* A are as prominent in *Transitus* C and cannot, therefore, be used to decide which of the two apocrypha was the source.

Deshman further points out that the inclusion of the Virgin in the Assumption miniature, as well as drawing on literary sources, was also 'certainly influenced by the older tradition of such figures in infancy scenes, for the maid adjusting the Virgin's pillow derived from the composition of the Nativity in the same manuscript'.[97] This links Mary's role as mother of God to her coronation and 'since in the two Anglo-Saxon pictures one of these servants humbly waits upon the Virgin at the very events where she renders and is rewarded for her maternal service to the Lord, we can hardly escape the conclusion that these servants of the mother of God symbolize the believers themselves who hoped to win her heavenly intercession through their devoted imitation of her humility'.[98]

As well as thus devising a visual image for the apocryphal story, the artist also incorporated into the miniature a concept which has no place in

---

[93] Ed. Wenger, *L'assomption de la très Sainte Vierge*, pp. 245–56.

[94] See pp. 17–19, 24 and 232–5.

[95] *Ein neuer 'Transitus Mariae'*, ed. Haibach-Reinisch, p. 74.

[96] *Transitus* C, in *Analecta Reginensia*, ed. Wilmart, §§ 5, 14 and 23.

[97] Deshman, 'Servants of the Mother of God', p. 59.   [98] *Ibid.*, p. 59.

the *Transitus*-narratives: the coronation of the Virgin, represented by the crown in the hand of God and the sceptre carried by the angel. The title *Maria Regina* was by now widespread in exegetical and devotional literature and the miniaturist may also have been acquainted with the Italian iconography of the crowned Virgin, but this seems to be the earliest depiction of a coronation. It has, however, been suggested that the crown has no connection with the concept of *Maria Regina*, but is the crown of life: 'Die Krone ist hier nicht die der Himmelskönigin oder des davidischen Königgeschlechts (*Madonna Regina*), sondern die Krone des Lebens, die nach Apk 2, 10 denen verheissen ist, die bis zum Tod treu sind.'[99] Schiller does not advert to the sceptre, however, and this second regal element clearly indicates a desire on the artist's part to express the idea of Mary as queen. Furthermore, the resemblances between this and the Christmas illumination, as Deshman points out, express the reason for the Virgin's regal status: they 'visualize the idea that Mary was crowned because of her role in the Incarnation'.[100] The concept is, moreover, a prominent one in connection with the feast of the Assumption. Paschasius Radbertus's epistle, *Cogitis me*, for example, which was intended to be read on the feast, stresses Mary's queenship and describes how her son led her to the throne prepared for her in heaven. Ælfric translated this passage in his First Series text for the day, where he also describes Mary as 'middangeardes cwen' and 'seo heofenlice cwen': 'hu miccle swiðor wenst þu þæt he nu todæg þæt heofonlice werod togeanes his agenre meder sendan wolde, þæt hi mid ormætum leohte and unasecgendlicum lofsangum hi to þam þrymsetle gelæddon þe hire gegearcod wæs fram frymðe middangeardes'.[101] The miniature, then, glorifies the Virgin as queen of earth and heaven. But this emphasis on Mary's royalty is not solely the result of the liturgical and devotional significance of the idea. It can also be related to the position of the queen in contemporary Anglo-Saxon England and the growing significance of her role: 'The medieval conception of a parallel between the organization of society in heaven and earth was the basis for the

---

[99] Schiller, *Die Ikonographie* IV.2, 102. 'The crown here is not that of the Queen of Heaven or of the race of David (*Madonna Regina*), but rather the crown of life, which according to Rev. II.10 is promised to those who remain true unto death.'

[100] In a letter dated 8 May 1987.

[101] *Catholic Homilies I*, ed. Thorpe: 'queen of the world', p. 438; 'the heavenly queen', p. 446; 'how much rather thinkest thou he would now today send the heavenly host to meet his own mother, that they with light immense and unutterable hymns might lead her to the throne which was prepared for her from the beginning of the world', p. 442 (trans. Thorpe).

belief in an archetypal correspondence between *Maria Regina* and terrestrial queens.'[102] Queens were of great importance in the progress of the monastic reform in England and their role in protecting the nunneries was laid down in the *Regularis concordia* itself.[103] Because they were of increasing consequence in England, it was natural to invest Mary with the symbols of royalty but this, of course, was a double-edged gesture: Mary's queenship also conferred a sacred aura on earthly queens and kings. The miniature, then, fits into the royal programme of the Benedictional: Mary's coronation also enhances the position of the Anglo-Saxon queen.

The Ascension scene in the Benedictional of Æthelwold is also Mariologically significant in that, while keeping the Western positioning of Mary to one side (rather than the Eastern central orant Virgin), she is nevertheless represented as the most important of the onlookers, leading one group of five apostles and clearly more dominant than Peter, who heads the other group.[104]

A manuscript which is clearly related to the Benedictional of St Æthelwold and executed shortly after it (*c.* 980), in the New Minster, Winchester, is the so-called Benedictional (properly a pontifical) of Robert of Jumièges (Rouen, Bibliothèque municipale, 369 (Y.7)). It has lost the miniatures of the Nativity and the Ascension which it once contained and only Pentecost, the Three Marys at the tomb and the Dormition of the Virgin survive. The last is a much simplified version of that in the Benedictional of St Æthelwold: Mary lies on a bed, her hands in an orant position, attended by four grieving women, while above her is suspended a crown, attached by rays to the hand of God in a roundel above (pl. VII). As Deshman points out, the narrative elements have disappeared here, an extra virgin (not in the apocrypha) has been added and we have simply the orant Virgin about to be crowned.[105]

A second manuscript showing the influence of the Æthelwold Benedictional is the St Bertin Gospels manuscript of the end of the tenth century, illustrated by an Anglo-Saxon artist working on the continent (Boulogne, Bibliothèque municipale, 11). The Annunciation in this manuscript, placed side-by-side with the Visitation under two rows of Christ's ancestors, has the Virgin seated beside a lectern, as in the Benedictional,

---

[102] Deshman, 'The Iconography', p. 232.
[103] *Regularis concordia*, ed. Symons, p. 2.
[104] See Deshman, 'The Iconography', p. 189, n. 197; reproduced in Rice, *English Art*, pl. 50b.
[105] Deshman, 'The Iconography', pp. 87–9.

and the Nativity scene shows the Virgin's pillow being arranged by a servant, a typically Anglo-Saxon feature.[106]

A creative reworking of models, which results in an accentuation of Mary's importance, is evident in a Winchester drawing of 1023–35 which derived from several different illustrations in the Utrecht Psalter, Utrecht, University Library, Script. eccl. 484.[107] The Winchester drawing accompanies the Office of the Holy Trinity in London, British Library, Cotton Titus D. xxvii, and it is essentially a combination of the *Gloria* and *Credo* illustrations and that before Psalm CIX in the ninth-century Utrecht Psalter. The *Gloria* drawing shows God seated within a mandorla, with the Virgin on his right, surmounted by the Dove and with the Child in her arms, and the lamb on his left; the *Credo* illustration has a similar figure of Mary (the upper half of whose body is enclosed in a mandorla), the Child and the Dove on the left of God in his mandorla and next to him an empty throne, a symbol of the divine Christ; and the psalm illustration depicts God the Father and God the Son in a mandorla, conversing, with two enemies forming a footstool. The Winchester artist combined elements from all of these to produce an image, the so-called 'Quinity', which has God the Father and God the Son seated in conversation, while Mary stands on the left, the Dove perched on her head and the Child in her arms (pl. VIII). All the figures are within a circular glory and at their feet are Satan, Arius and Judas. Here Christ's dual nature is represented, as human in Mary's arms and as enthroned deity conquering Satan. Mary is distinguished as human in that she alone stands and has no halo, but her importance is indicated by her presence within the glory, by the evident interest she displays in the divine conversation and by the crown she wears.

The Titus D. xxvii artist was also responsible for the presentation miniature in the New Minster *Liber uitae* of *c.* 1030 (London, BL, Stowe 944). This shows Cnut and his queen Ælfgifu, or Emma, presenting a cross to Christ who is enthroned above in a mandorla (pl. IX). It is very similar to the New Minster Charter, but in the *Liber uitae* Mary and Peter flank Christ in heaven, rather than the king on earth, as in the earlier

---

[106] Reproduced in *Golden Age*, ed. Backhouse *et al.*, pl. 42.

[107] See the discussions by E. Kantorowicz, 'The Quinity of Winchester', *Art Bulletin* 29 (1947), 73–85; M. D'Ancona, *The Iconography of the Immaculate Conception in the Middle Ages and Early Renaissance*, Art Bulletin Monographs 7 (Princeton, 1957), pp. 20–1; Schiller, *Iconography of Christian Art*, I, 8; and J. A. Kidd, 'The Quinity of Winchester Reconsidered', *Studies in Iconography* 7–8 (1981–2), 21–33.

miniature.[108] The *Liber uitae* stresses the dependence of the human couple on divine favour more strongly than the earlier illustration had done. Cnut is here being crowned by an angel, and a second angel veils Ælfgifu, while both angels point upwards to Christ's mandorla with their other hands. Beneath, in a half-circle at the bottom of the miniature, are the monks of the New Minster in prayer. Mary and Peter above are haloed, and she holds a book in her outer hand while Peter holds a large key. With the palms of their inner hands outstretched in witness and in prayer, they gesture towards Christ. Mary's book is again presumably the gospels, replacing the Child whom she usually holds. Visually, the similarity between the Virgin and Ælfgifu, one directly above the other, is striking. The theme of the miniature is intercession for the royal couple: that of the monks below and of Mary and Peter in heaven.[109] Cnut and Ælfgifu serve the church on earth, in this instance by the gift of an altar cross, and are rewarded by divine favour for their kingship, expressed in the angelic crownings and by saintly mediation. Again, then, the saints whose intercession is valued in Winchester are Mary and Peter.

CANTERBURY MANUSCRIPTS OF THE LATE TENTH AND
ELEVENTH CENTURIES

Whereas the Winchester manuscripts, apart from the Titus and *Liber uitae* drawings, portray Mary largely in narrative scenes related to liturgical feasts, the late tenth- and eleventh-century Canterbury manuscripts depict her in some very unusual images of the Incarnation. The Arenberg Gospels (New York, Pierpont Morgan Library, 869), written probably in the last decade of the tenth century in Canterbury, contains a series of historiated canon tables, two of which refer to the Incarnation. On 11r the Virgin stands in an alpha-shaped frame, the child on her left arm and a palm in her right hand, flanked by adoring angels (pl. x).[110] As Rosenthal shows, the 'rigorously frontal' Virgin appears to derive from contemporary English drawings unrelated in subject matter and the artist adapted the frontal female figure here as 'a critical feature of the iconography, since it suggests that she, in contrast to the profile child, is complete within the limits of

---

[108] See Wormald, 'Late Anglo-Saxon Art', *Collected Writings I*, p. 110; Deshman, 'The Iconography', pp. 230–1.

[109] Deshman, 'The Iconography', p. 230, and 'Benedictus monarcha et monachus', pp. 223–4.

[110] See Rosenthal, 'The Historiated Canon Tables', pp. 200–18.

her human nature'.[111] The profile child, stretching his hands out to the victory-palm held by Mary, emphasizes Christ's human nature and his future victory through that nature taken from his mother: 'The Arenberg iconography thus presents the Virgin as the instrument not only of the Incarnation but also of the Redemption of man.'[112]

A further Canterbury illumination with the profile child and the palm-branch is possibly related to this Arenberg image: this is the miniature at the beginning of the Gospel of John in the Grimbald Gospels of c. 1020 (London, British Library, Add. 34890).[113] This very elaborate icono-graphic programme has representations of the Last Judgement and the Incarnation on facing pages. In the central roundel of the *In principio* page, the enthroned Virgin and Child are depicted in a mandorla supported by angels: the child is seated sideways across Mary's lap, holding a book in one hand and blessing with the other, looking up at the palm-branch in Mary's hand. The Trinity sits in judgement in the three roundels at the top of the facing page, so that the means of redemption, the incarnate Christ, is here balanced against the Judgement.

The second Incarnation image in the Arenberg Gospels, on the verso of the first, is derived from the drawing illustrating the *Gloria* in the Utrecht Psalter.[114] The Arenberg image retains the Christ in the mandorla of the source; the Virgin again stands on his right, with the Dove sitting on her head, but she now holds a book; a ram stands on his left. There is an angel on either side. This image of the Second Person of the Trinity shows the resurrected, glorified Christ in heaven with Mary present as the beginning of his humanity and the ram denoting his Crucifixion. Mary carries the book of the gospels as the embodiment of the Word and 'her appearance in this epiphany of the Saviour, though necessary as a reference to the Incarnation, seems intended in addition to celebrate her as the Mother of God. She retains the halo which she possesses in the Arenberg image of the Incarnation, but which she lacks in the Utrecht model. Also the Son addresses Himself exclusively to His Mother, thus honoring her and acknowledging her as the instrument of His present Glory.'[115] The

---

[111] *Ibid.*, p. 210.   [112] *Ibid.*, p. 203.

[113] Reproduced in *Golden Age*, ed. Backhouse *et al.*, pl. XVI; see Rosenthal, 'The Historiated Canon Tables', p. 216, n. 37.

[114] The Arenberg image is reproduced in Temple, *Anglo-Saxon Manuscripts*, pl. 167; it is discussed by Rosenthal, 'The Historiated Canon Tables', pp. 219–46.

[115] Rosenthal, 'The Historiated Canon Tables', p. 241.

Arenberg drawing, therefore, although clearly derived from the continental psalter, demonstrates a greater emphasis on the Virgin and her role in the scheme of redemption. All three Canterbury images indicate a concentration on Mary in her principal role of *Theotokos*, but, by thus placing the Virgin and Child in new contexts, the artists reveal a conception of her significance which goes beyond that inherent in the traditional images.

The Bury Psalter (Vatican City, Biblioteca Apostolica Vaticana, Reg. lat. 12), probably made in Canterbury *c.* 1050, contains New Testament illustrations in addition to its cycle of psalter drawings.[116] The former include the Nativity, remarkable for the way in which Mary longingly extends her hands to the Christ child, the Adoration of the Magi and the Ascension with Mary and Peter, looking eagerly upwards, leading the two groups of apostles. On 62r, at the beginning of Psalm LI, is an historiated Q, with a crowned, veiled female figure seated on a broad throne; the inscription reads *Oliua fructifera* (Psalm LI. 10).[117] In two roundels at the sides are women bearing in their outer hands a cross-inscribed book and extending their inner hands towards the central figure. That figure holds a palm-branch in her right hand and a sceptre crowned with a trefoil in her left; at the base of the Q, forming the tail, is a dragon. The figure could be Mary or *Ecclesia*: one does not exclude the other, given the long tradition of parallels between the Virgin and the church, and the conquest of sin and evil, in the dragon, is appropriate to both. Here, then, the movement towards the crowned Virgin bearing a symbol of power is evident, in marked contrast to the earlier period when she almost invariably holds the Child.

MANUSCRIPTS ASSOCIATED WITH THE SACRAMENTARY OF ROBERT OF JUMIÈGES

There are several additional images of Mary in a group of related manuscripts whose place of origin has not yet been definitively established, but which has connections with Canterbury and Peterborough.[118] The

---

[116] See R. M. Harris, 'The Marginal Drawings of the Bury St Edmunds Psalter' (unpubl. PhD dissertation, Princeton Univ., 1960).

[117] Reproduced in Temple, *Anglo-Saxon Manuscripts*, pl. 262.

[118] On the connections between the following manuscripts see the descriptions in Temple, *Anglo-Saxon Manuscripts*, nos. 65, 72, 73 and 75.

most important of these is Rouen, Bibliothèque municipale, 274 (Y. 6), the Sacramentary of Robert of Jumièges (*c.* 1020), the most elaborately illustrated Anglo-Saxon sacramentary, with thirteen full-page miniatures. These include the Nativity, the Annunciation to the Shepherds with the Flight into Egypt, the Adoration of the Magi, the Crucifixion with Mary and John and the Ascension. A significant departure from the usual Anglo-Saxon iconography of the Nativity is the angel who hovers over the Virgin's bed, his left hand draped, the right extended in blessing (pl. XI). The dignity thus accorded the Virgin is most unusual: adoring angels are common in Byzantine nativities, but normally pertain to the Christ Child. Here the Child is in the lower register and the angel's blessing is clearly directed at Mary who is, in addition, attended by a nimbed midwife. The Ascension miniature in the Sacramentary is well known for its characteristically Anglo-Saxon iconography of the 'disappearing Christ',[119] but it is equally notable for its depiction of Mary: she stands below the apostles, nimbed and orant and surrounded by a mandorla. The mandorla around the Virgin at the Ascension occurs in only one other miniature, the Odbert Psalter (Boulogne, Bibliothèque municipale, 20) of *c.* 1000, which is one of the St Bertin manuscripts influenced by Anglo-Saxon iconography. In both miniatures Christ, too, is shown in a mandorla and the Virgin is therefore associated with him. Mary is normally accorded the mandorla in this period only when she is depicted with the Christ Child, and it is then an attribute of the Child rather than the Virgin, as in, for example, the Grimbald Gospels. Schiller interprets it in the Ascension scenes as an indication that Mary is here, to a greater extent than usual, seen in her role as *ecclesia*, arguing that the mandorla emphasizes the *ecclesia*-function implicit in the *Maria orans*: 'Auffallend ist, dass hier *Maria-Orans* von einer Mandorla umgeben und so mehr als üblich als Ekklesia hervorgehoben ist.'[120] However, given the veneration shown to the Virgin in late Anglo-Saxon England and evident in this manuscript in the innovation of the angel at the Nativity, it seems doubtful whether the mandorla is intended principally as a reference to the *ecclesia*-function of the Virgin. It would appear that Mary is singled out from the apostles and

---

[119] See M. Schapiro, 'The Image of the Disappearing Christ: The Ascension in English Art around the Year 1000', *Gazette des Beaux-Arts*, 6th ser. 23 (1943), 135–52.

[120] G. Schiller, *Die Ikonographie der christlichen Kunst III: Die Auferstehung und Erhöhung Christi*, 2nd ed. (Gütersloh, 1986), p. 157: 'It is striking that here *Maria-Orans* is surrounded by a mandorla and is therefore emphasized more than usual as *Ecclesia.*'

honoured by an attribute more often associated with one of the Trinity, as well as receiving a special angelic blessing at the Nativity.

Cambridge, Pembroke College 301 (*c.* 1020), part of the same group and again with some Canterbury connections, has a series of canon tables surmounted by figures. These begin with the *Agnus Dei*, evangelist symbols, Christ and the Virgin and continue with angels and apostles. The Virgin is again depicted with a mandorla (2v), nimbed, holding a book in the left hand and a lily-like sceptre in her right; below her are two female saints looking up, one holding a book, the other a cross (pl. XII). Ohlgren's description of the canon tables has a question-mark over the designation of this as an image of the Virgin,[121] but there can be little doubt: she fits naturally into the sequence of figures, which moves from Christ to the angels and apostles, following the order of a litany. The book is presumably the gospels, again standing for Christ, and the sceptre held aloft in Mary's hand is a symbol of royal power, with its flowering nature perhaps referring specifically to Mary as queen of virgins or to the rod of Jesse or to both simultaneously. As Schiller explains: 'From about the year 1000, the shoot as an attribute was often placed in the hand of the Virgin . . .; it was the symbol of Christ's human descent. In addition, the concepts of the shoot and the flower merge and in their various forms always refer to the whole prophecy. The shoot may be portrayed as a long, leaf-like stem, a short, sceptre-like shaft with a flower, later as a rose or flower signifying Christ.'[122]

Cambridge, Trinity College B. 10.4 (of the first quarter of the eleventh century), again associated with the same group of manuscripts, also has a series of canon tables, although here the figures do not follow the same clear order. On 12v are three nimbed female figures, holding books and flowers, which probably represent Mary and two saints, as in Pembroke College 301. On 18r, the initial page of the Gospel of Matthew, there is an elaborate initial L within a Winchester-type frame.[123] In the roundels in the centre of each side are three bearded men with books and, at the top, a nimbed woman with a flower and a book. This is again most probably the Virgin, presiding over the *Liber generationis*, the genealogy of Christ, and the Infancy gospel at the beginning of Matthew. The flower is probably

---

[121]*Insular and Anglo-Saxon Manuscripts*, ed. Ohlgren, no. 178 (p. 193).

[122] Schiller, *Iconography of Christian Art*, I, 15.

[123] Rice, *English Art*, pl. 60b.

again to be associated with Mary's virginity, or with the rod of Jesse, with the book perhaps symbolizing the *Logos*.

London, British Library, Harley 76 (*c.* 1020–30), another manuscript with some Canterbury connections, contains a further series of canon tables. On 9r a half-length Virgin, flanked by two women, holds a palm-branch topped by a trefoil.[124] The palm again probably alludes to the victory and redemption achieved through the human nature which Christ took from Mary and the trefoil also makes it into a type of sceptre, again a symbol of royal power. Mary's position above the acclaiming women proclaims her as *uirgo uirginum*.

THE NATIVITY OF THE VIRGIN

At the very end of the Anglo-Saxon period we find the first artistic reflections of the *Pseudo-Matthew* legend. In London, British Library, Cotton Caligula A. xiv, fols. 1–36, a troper dated *c.* 1050 which shows the influence of continental painting, we find two miniatures for the feast of the Nativity of the Virgin. On 26r the angel announces Mary's birth to Joachim, who is portrayed with his animals (a sheep, ram, ox and two goats).[125] Both Joachim and the angel hold scrolls. The titulus around the miniature reads:

> Credidit angelico Ioachim per nuntia uerbo
> Credens foecundam conceptu germinis Annam.
> Christum glorificat inopi qui semper habundat.[126]

On the verso Joachim and Anna, holding the infant Mary, sit within an architectural frame, from the middle of which the hand of God emerges from clouds, blessing the child (pl. XIII). The titulus reads:

> Ecce patet partus quem [. . .] erat Anna per artus
> Aecclesie matrem genuit pregnando salutem
> Quam Domino uouit pater ad templumque dicauit.[127]

---

[124] E. G. Millar, *English Illuminated Manuscripts from the Xth to the XIIIth Century* (Paris and Brussels, 1926), pl. 21.

[125] Reproduced in Temple, *Anglo-Saxon Manuscripts*, pl. 294.

[126] 'Joachim believed the announcement delivered by the angel, believing Anna fruitful in the conception of an offshoot. He glorifies Christ who always provides plenty for the needy.'

[127] 'Behold the offspring is manifest whom Anna had brought forth [. . .] through her loins. She begot the mother of the church, being heavy with our salvation, whom her father vowed to the Lord and dedicated to the temple.'

These seem to be the earliest surviving depictions of *Pseudo-Matthew* in a Western manuscript, although there is plenty of evidence of earlier treatments of the apocryphon in Rome and elsewhere in other media. According to the *Liber pontificalis*, Pope Leo III (*ob.* 816) commissioned a cycle of paintings based on the story of Joachim and Anna for a Roman church and presented a tapestry depicting the story of Mary to the church of Santa Maria Maggiore.[128] Some scenes from a cycle of frescoes painted between 872 and 882 in the Roman church of Santa Maria Egyziaca survive: these consist of Joachim in the wilderness, the maid's reproaches to Anna and the arrival in Bethlehem.[129] The oldest surviving Eastern cycle, in Kizil Cukur in Cappadocia, dates from 859 to 860 and probably relies on exemplars from before the middle of the ninth century.[130] The Anglo-Saxon miniatures, however, are not like the other early treatments in detail: there does not seem to be any early parallel for the hand of God blessing the infant Mary, for example. A striking feature about the Annunciation to Joachim, too, is the different animals depicted: sheep, goats and an ox. In *Pseudo-Matthew* Joachim's flocks appear to consist of sheep only, whereas in the Greek *Proteuangelium* the implication is that the flocks include all three animals: when the angel announces Mary's conception to him, Joachim orders ten lambs, twelve calves and a hundred kids to be slaughtered. This perhaps suggests an Eastern model for the Anglo-Saxon illumination, one which could have been designed originally to accompany the *Proteuangelium*.

THE VIRGIN AT THE CRUCIFIXION

Mary's role at the Crucifixion, in which she figures almost invariably in southern manuscripts of the tenth and eleventh centuries, is either that of witness, gesturing towards Christ on the cross, or that of mourner. In the Crucifixion scene in the Sherborne Pontifical, Paris, Bibliothèque Nationale, lat. 943, probably a Canterbury manuscript of the second half of the tenth century, for example, Mary and John stand impassively at either side of the cross: Mary's hands are raised to her chest, but not in a gesture of grief, and John's are in an orant posture.[131] In the Arenberg Gospels, Mary

---

[128] Schiller, *Die Ikonographie*, IV.2, 34.
[129] See Lafontaine, *Peintures médiévales*, pp. 20–8.
[130] Schiller, *Die Ikonographie*, IV.2, 33–4.
[131] Reproduced in Temple, *Anglo-Saxon Manuscripts*, pl. 134.

stands beside the cross, her hands in an orant position, with her right hand also holding the end of her veil, but here she looks up at Christ's face and the symmetrical arrangement of Mary and John at either side of the cross, which is usual in such depictions, is abandoned 'in order to place Mary closer to her Son and thus suggest, through this physical proximity as well as through the fixing of her glance directly upon His face, that the flesh of the sacrificial victim in the mass is indeed that born of the Virgin Mary'. [132] The alterations here introduced, although they serve to stress the closeness between Mary and her son, are doctrinally rather than emotionally significant. In Harley 2904, on the other hand, the Virgin is a stooped, grief-stricken figure, weeping into the end of her mantle, and imbued with what Wormald terms a 'lyrical mysticism which is not met with in contemporary European art'. [133] In the Judith of Flanders Gospels, New York, Pierpont Morgan Library, 709, of the middle of the eleventh century, Christ's body sags towards the Virgin's side of the cross and she 'lovingly raises the edge of her headcloth to wipe the wound in Christ's side, the impulsiveness of her tender gesture, unparalleled in this context, anticipating the highly emotional portrayals of the Crucifixion in the following centuries' (pl. XIV). [134] In these last two miniatures, then, Anglo-Saxon artists emphasize Mary's maternal anguish and affective participation in the passion.

IVORIES FROM THE TENTH AND ELEVENTH CENTURIES

Ivories depicting the Virgin also survive from the Benedictine reform period and show either the Virgin and Child or Mary standing at the foot of the cross. [135] Beckwith 15 is a panel, originally rectangular and probably attached to a book-cover, of the first half of the eleventh century, which has the enthroned and haloed Virgin and Child in a quatrefoil mandorla; the

[132] Rosenthal, 'The Historiated Canon Tables', p. 150; the miniature is reproduced in Temple, *Anglo-Saxon Manuscripts*, pl. 171.

[133] Wormald, 'The Survival of Anglo-Saxon Illumination after the Norman Conquest', *Collected Writings I*, pp. 153–68, at 156; the miniature is reproduced in Temple, *Anglo-Saxon Manuscripts*, pl. 142.

[134] Temple, *Anglo-Saxon Manuscripts*, p. 109.

[135] There are some eighth-century ivories portraying Mary which Beckwith considers to be Anglo-Saxon (Beckwith, *Ivory Carvings*, nos. 3, 5, 6 and 9), but convincing objections have been raised in each case; see H. Fillitz, (reviewing Beckwith, *Ivory Carvings*), *Kunstchronik* 27 (1974), 429–34.

Virgin's feet rest on a footstool, beneath which lies the serpent of sin (pl. xv).[136] The mandorla is supported below by two angels and there are the remains of two further angels above. Mary's right arm is raised, with the hand broken off, while Christ holds a book in his left hand and blesses with his right. This depiction of the *regina angelorum* is one which emphasizes the importance of the incarnation in the victory over sin and it is conceivable that the Virgin bore a palm-branch or a cross in her broken right hand to make this even more explicit.

A Virgin and Child enthroned on a rainbow within a mandorla comes perhaps from a school in the South Midlands.[137] The Virgin, without a halo, is seated on a rainbow as a sign of sovereignty or salvation; her left arm supports the haloed child and in her right hand she holds a branch-like sceptre. Between her left arm and the child's back is a book and the child, seen in profile, extends both hands, holding in them another book. The sceptre-branch probably both refers to Mary as the rod of Jesse and functions as a symbol of power, while the books allude to Christ as *Logos*. A bronze plaque from the York Museum, dated 1050–75 and with stylistic similarities to ivory carving, also shows the Virgin with the blessing profile Child sideways across her left knee.[138]

Mary's role in the Crucifixion ivories, as also in the manuscripts, is either that of witness, gesturing towards Christ on the cross, or that of mourner, her hand raised to her cheek as a sign of grief. The most striking of the latter type is the St Omer Virgin (*c.* 1000) which belonged to a Crucifixion group of which only the companion figure of John the Evangelist also survives.[139] Both hands, one holding the end of her cloak, are raised to Mary's face and her whole figure incorporates deeply felt anguish. A simplified version of this figure, probably from a similar group, is also preserved in copper alloy from the second half of the eleventh century.[140] The more impassive, acclaiming Virgin can be seen in, for example, Beckwith 17.

Mary and Peter flank a Christ in glory displaying his wounds in the

---

[136] Beckwith, *Ivory Carvings*, pl. 36, no. 15; see also *Golden Age*, ed. Backhouse et al., no. 122.

[137] Beckwith, *Ivory Carvings*, pl. 75, no. 40; Rice, *English Art*, p. 168.

[138] Rice, *English Art*, p. 235 and pl. 90a.

[139] Beckwith, *Ivory Carvings*, pl. 57, no. 25; *Golden Age*, ed. Backhouse et al., no. 119 and pl. xxvii.

[140] *Golden Age*, ed. Backhouse et al., no. 267 and pl. 267.

upper register of a late Anglo-Saxon ivory found in North Elmham (pl. XVI).[141] The ivory as a whole probably depicts the Last Judgement, with the lower register showing angels supporting a cross beneath which stand, presumably, the saved souls. Mary holds a book in her left hand, while Peter holds a key, and both raise their right hands, palms outwards, in a gesture of prayer and intercession. The top register is very similar to that of the New Minster *Liber uitae*, but the context has been moved here to the Last Judgement and Mary is shown as crowned in heavenly glory: the *regina coeli*. The two saints as intercessors on the Last Day are also prominent in several vernacular texts of the period.

THE VIRGIN IN MONUMENTAL ART

Few Marian images survive in monumental art, apart from Mary at the foot of the cross (as in the Breamore Rood in Hampshire and St Dunstan's church in Stepney, for example).[142] Mary and John the Evangelist at the foot of the cross are very much part of the southern sculptural tradition and are scarcely found at all in the northern half of England, where Stephaton and Longinus preponderate.[143] Apart from Crucifixion scenes, there is one panel and several crosses which show Mary with the Child. The Deerhurst plaque is thought to date from *c*. 1000 and is an extemely flat panel which was probably originally painted. It depicts a half-length standing female figure and Talbot Rice suggested that it could be an example of the Byzantine type known as the *Nicopea* where the Virgin holds in front of her a medallion containing Christ.[144] Several eleventh-century crosses include carvings of the Virgin and Child: the Shelford Cross (near Nottingham) has a frontal Virgin, with the Child, his face facing the spectator, seated across her knees, holding a book;[145] the damaged Sutton-on-Derwent panel again has a frontal Virgin with the profile Child across her knees, holding a book with one hand while reaching to Mary's breast with the other;[146] the Nunburnholme Cross has a frontal Virgin with the Child seated across her

---

[141] Beckwith, *Ivory Carvings*, no. 18.

[142] Rice, *English Art*, pl. 16a; see also pl. 9a.

[143] This can be seen in, for example, the notable absence of Mary and John from the Crucifixion scenes discussed in R. Bailey, *Viking Age Sculpture in Northern England* (London, 1980).

[144] Rice, *English Art*, p. 107, pl. 18a.

[145] Reproduced in Pattison, 'The Nunburnholme Cross', pl. XLIVa.

[146] *Ibid.*, pl. XLIVd.

knees, holding a book and looking out at the spectator.[147] At Inglesham in Wiltshire an eleventh-century carving has a 'complementary profiles' Madonna and Child, with the child blessing with his right hand and holding a book in his left hand.[148] Barbara Raw relates this to the iconography of the Book of Kells and the model of the Cuthbert Coffin: 'The reappearance of this iconographic type in the eleventh century, even though in an isolated example, would tend to support Kitzinger's theory that the model of the Cuthbert Coffin had "something of the status of a revered icon" and that it formed the basis for works of art long after the seventh century.'[149]

Apart from those which have survived, there is also some evidence for lost effigies of Mary. The Virgin with a choir of angels may have adorned the first storey of the tower built in the New Minster in Winchester in the 980s.[150] Abbot Ælfsige of Ely (996 x 999 to 1012 x 1016) had an image of the Virgin and Child made of gold and silver which, Dodwell surmises, must have been about seven feet in height.[151] The noblewoman Godgifu left a precious jewelled necklace to the statue of Mary in Coventry.[152] Many more such images must have existed. The very impressive Golden Virgin of Essen (made between 973 and 982) gives us some idea of these English images: it is made of wood covered by gold and is just under life-size.[153]

CONCLUSIONS

The artistic evidence, then, presents us with a wealth of Marian images in manuscripts, ivories and sculpture. Much more has clearly been lost, particularly in wall paintings, wood carvings and embroideries. Judging from what has survived, there appear to be two periods when interest in the

[147] See *ibid.*, pl. XLC, and J. T. Lang, 'The Sculptors of the Nunburnholme Cross', *Archaeological Journal* 133 (1976), 75–94.
[148] Reproduced and discussed in Raw, 'The Inglesham Virgin and Child'.
[149] *Ibid.*, p. 46.
[150] R. N. Quirk, 'Winchester New Minster and its Tenth-Century Tower', *Journal of the British Archaeological Association*, 3rd ser. 24 (1961), 16–54, but see Gem, 'Towards an Iconography', p. 16.
[151] Dodwell, *Anglo-Saxon Art*, p. 215; *Liber Eliensis*, ed. E. O. Blake, Camden Third Series (London, 1962), p. 132.
[152] Dodwell, *Anglo-Saxon Art*, p. 188; the source is William of Malmesbury's *Gesta pontificum*.
[153] See Schiller, *Die Ikonographie* IV.2, pl. 795.

Virgin is especially prominent: the beginning of the ninth century and the period of the Benedictine reform. The evidence from the ninth century is largely sculptural and is not very extensive, with nothing like the abundance of manuscript illumination which we find in the tenth and eleventh centuries. Nevertheless, it is possible to say that the images in Breedon and Wirksworth are inconceivable without a background of devotion directed specifically to the Virgin.

In the Benedictine reform period the ardent Marian piety which is evident in so many of the artistic monuments is of a piece with all the other witnesses which testify to the Marian enthusiasm of the south of England. The manuscript illuminations of the late tenth and eleventh centuries, in particular, demonstrate in a variety of ways the progress of the cult of Mary in Anglo-Saxon England. In some of the Crucifixion images she shares emotionally in the plight of her son on the cross, in a way which is new for the Middle Ages. She is celebrated to a much greater degree in her own right than was the case in the earlier period: sometimes by appearing as an autonomous figure, at other times by changes in the traditional images which reveal a conscious desire to honour her. There are suggestions, too, of a more deliberate participation of the Virgin in the scheme of redemption. The sense of power implicit in that more active role is expressed in several images of the crowned Virgin or in the attribute of the sceptre. In Winchester there is a distinct emphasis on Mary as mediator: in two of the most important and, probably, publicly displayed manuscripts we find Mary and Peter coupled as intercessors for the earthly rulers. It is striking, too, that England furnishes us with the earliest surviving treatment of the death of the Virgin and of the *Pseudo-Matthew* legend in Western manuscripts: this parallels the readiness that we find in the Anglo-Saxon liturgy to assimilate at an early stage any Marian devotional practice with which the monasteries came into contact.

7
The Virgin in Old English poetry

It is clear from the evidence of the liturgy, extra-liturgical devotions, prayers, dedications and art discussed in the preceding chapters that the cult of the Virgin was important in Anglo-Saxon England, in particular in the areas of Northumbria and Mercia from the late seventh to the first half of the ninth century and in the West-Saxon centres of the Benedictine reform, especially Winchester, in the late tenth and eleventh centuries. The vernacular material which survives in some abundance from the Anglo-Saxon period is a most valuable supplement to this Latin evidence, adding to our knowledge of how this cult was viewed by some of the thinking members of the society and of what Latin sources of Marian doctrine and narrative were circulating and how they were interpreted. By far the largest body of vernacular material is that of the homiletic corpus, but the Virgin is also discussed in the poetry. In contrast to the Latin evidence from Anglo-Saxon England, much of which can be dated and localized with some degree of certainty, it is difficult to be confident about attributing much of the vernacular material to any particular place or date: this is particularly true of the poetry, which is notoriously difficult to localize or date. Accordingly we cannot often be sure whether the vernacular literature conforms to the patterns of date and localization established by the other witnesses to the cult. Nevertheless, the poetic evidence is revealing both in what it includes and omits, and without the Old English *Advent* poem, in particular, a whole aspect of Marian thought would escape our knowledge.

ADVENT

Advent, or the *Advent Lyrics*, or *Christ I*, as the poem is variously called, is the first poem in the Exeter Book, a large collection of Old English poetry, religious and secular, written by one scribe in the late tenth century and given to Exeter by Bishop Leofric (*ob.* 1072).[1] The beginning of the manuscript, containing part of this work, is missing, but what remains consists of a series of expansions of antiphons sung at Vespers in the period before Christmas, usually before and after the *Magnificat*. Advent is followed in the Exeter Book by two works, *Ascension* and *Judgement Day* (or *Christ II* and *Christ III*), whose relation to it has been the cause of much controversy. Earlier theories that all three works were by Cynewulf have been discredited and now only the second, which concludes with his runic signature, is attributed to him.[2] Hill has shown that the three texts belong to very different types of poetry, requiring different levels of sophistication and learning, and that they are likely to have been quite separate in origin.[3] The order of the three works in the Exeter Book, with its chronological treatment of the life of Christ, is unlikely to have been merely accidental, however, and must be the result of careful scribal selection.[4]

The existing part of *Advent* can be divided into twelve sections on the basis of its antiphonal sources.[5] Sections I, II, V and VI are based on four of the group of seven Great 'O' antiphons which appear to have been composed by a common author and which share a common text structure; and IV depends on the antiphon *O uirgo uirginum*, which always accompanies the other seven in early liturgical books.[6] III, VIII and IX use antiphons often known as the monastic 'O's but which also occur in secular books and are found in what is now southern Germany, Switzerland and northern Italy.[7] VII seems to derive from an antiphon known only from the

---

[1] The manuscript, Exeter, Cathedral Library, 3501, is described by Ker, *Catalogue*, no. 116. There are many editions of *Advent*, including: *Codex Exoniensis*, ed. B. Thorpe (London, 1842); *Bibliothek der angelsächsischen Poesie*, ed. C. W. M. Grein, 2 vols. (Göttingen, 1857–8); *The Christ of Cynewulf*, ed. Cook; *The Exeter Book*, ed. Krapp and Dobbie; *Advent Lyrics*, ed. Campbell.

[2] See, for example, the discussion by K. Sisam, 'Cynewulf and his Poetry', in his *Studies*, pp. 1–28, at 10–11.

[3] T. D. Hill, 'Literary History and Old English Poetry: The Case of Christ I, II and III', *Sources of Anglo-Saxon Culture*, ed. Szarmach and Oggins, pp. 3–22.

[4] For the suggestion that *Christ II* was deliberately composed as a bridge between the other two poems, see C. Chase, 'God's Presence through Grace'.

[5] For discussion of the antiphons, see *The Christ of Cynewulf*, ed. Cook, pp. xxxv–xliii; E. Burgert, *The Dependence of Part I*; Burlin, *Old English Advent*; Rankin, 'Liturgical Background'.

[6] See Rankin, 'Liturgical Background', pp. 328–31.   [7] *Ibid.*, p. 332.

antiphonary included in Alcuin's devotional florilegium *De laude Dei*.[8]
X corresponds to an antiphon known only from two Italian antiphonaries,[9]
XI probably to a Trinity antiphon[10] and XII derives from *O admirabile
commercium*, an antiphon for Lauds on the Octave of Christmas.[11] As the
poet uses only four of the seven central 'O' antiphons, it has been argued
that three sections, based on the three remaining texts, are missing from
the beginning of *Advent*.[12] The author's deep familiarity with liturgical
sources suggests that he himself was a monk or cleric: Woolf suggested that
the purpose of the text might have been the practical one of providing
readings 'in the monastic refectory on the appropriate days of Advent'[13]
and Raw points out that 'their syntax suggests that they were intended for
some form of public devotion'.[14] It is hard to imagine such a meditative,
allusive poem being intended for a wider audience than a religious
community, however, and we have no evidence for the use of the vernacular
in reading aloud in any formal context in the monasteries. The lyrics are
perhaps more likely to have been intended for private reading.

The structure of *Advent* has been a cause of controversy, with opinions
ranging from Cook's view that, 'as the work is essentially lyrical in
character', the only unity necessary is 'secured through the character of the
Advent season to which the antiphons belong',[15] to Campbell's view that
'there is no structural progression in idea or emotion from one poem to the
next',[16] to Burlin's view that the work consists of three movements, the
second and third concluding with sections IV and VII, with 'evident
disjunctions' between the movements,[17] while the 'Marian sequence, with
its evident chronology and progression, functions as a backbone to the
structure'.[18] He sees the concluding sections of the first two movements as
similar, dramatically conceived descriptions of the historical Advent and

---

[8] As was pointed out by Hill, 'A Liturgical Source'.

[9] This source was discovered by S. Tugwell, 'Advent Lyrics 348–77 (Lyric No. X)', *MÆ* 39 (1970), 34; a second manuscript is indicated by Rankin, 'Liturgical Background', p. 332.

[10] *The Christ of Cynewulf*, ed. Cook, p. 108; Rankin, 'Liturgical Background', p. 326.

[11] S. Moore, 'The Source of *Christ* 416 ff', *MLN* 29 (1914), 226–7.

[12] Most recently by Rankin, 'Liturgical Background', p. 333.

[13] R. Woolf (reviewing *Advent Lyrics*, ed. Campbell), *MÆ* 29 (1960), 125–9, at 129.

[14] B. Raw, *The Art and Background of Old English Poetry* (London, 1978), p. 39.

[15] *The Christ of Cynewulf*, ed. Cook, p. xci.

[16] *Advent Lyrics*, ed. Campbell, p. 10.   [17] Burlin, *Old English Advent*, p. 175.

[18] *Ibid*, p. 177.

thinks that their dramatic mode 'invites a full stop'.[19] Most recently, Rankin has pointed out that the twelve lyrics follow the pattern of part of the liturgical year; lyrics I-X develop the themes of Advent, XI those of Christmas, and the more retrospective XII is based on an antiphon sung a week after Christmas.[20] The pattern Rankin discerns is in many ways similar to Burlin's view of the Marian sequence as a structural principle of the work: this progresses from the incomprehension of the dwellers of Jerusalem in IV to Joseph's doubts and Mary's resolution of them in VII to the accomplished Advent of IX, with its image of the Child at Mary's breast. Whether these depictions of human limitation in the face of divine mystery function as full stops seems, however, questionable. The lay-out of the poem in the Exeter Book suggests a different interpretation.[21] Here the work is divided into five parts or *fitte*: the beginning of the first one is lost, but the others begin at sections IV, VII, IX and XI. The two dramatic presentations of human perplexity act in the manuscript as the starting-points of *fitte* within which the mystery of the Incarnation is explored from different perspectives. Mary's role is the most tangible aspect of the Incarnation and the manuscript *fitte* move from her to the more incomprehensible and ineffable aspects. The kind of reading suggested by the Exeter Book lay-out is probably at least as valid as that of Burlin: both are possibly personal attempts to impose a structure on the work. It is because *Advent* itself is so loosely composed that diferent readers are able to view it so differently, and Hill's view of the overall structure is probably the most persuasive: he describes *Advent* as 'poetry in the "ruminative" mode' where the 'progression from one theme to another involves the association of related ideas'.[22] The themes are all facets of *Advent* and the poet moves from one to another through patterns of association.

One of the chief themes is that of Christ's temporal birth and in this the Virgin naturally plays a large part. Two sections of the poem are based on Marian antiphons (IV and IX) and are devoted almost exclusively to her role in the Incarnation, while the Joseph antiphon which lies behind VII is interpreted in such a way as to focus attention on Mary, and the poet returns to her also in some of the other sections. She is not mentioned in the fragmentary first section, which explores the image of Christ as the

---

[19] *Ibid.*, p. 175.   [20] Rankin, 'Liturgical Background', pp. 334–6.

[21] I am most grateful to Prof. E. Ó Carragáin for drawing the layout of the Exeter Book to my attention and for suggesting its importance in a reading of the poem.

[22] See T. D. Hill, 'Notes on the Imagery and Structure', p. 88.

cornerstone who is implored to come and to save mankind. In II, based on the *O clauis David* antiphon, which does not allude to Mary, the poet develops the account of Christ's rescue of mankind by describing his conception:

> Wæs seo fæmne geong,
> mægð manes leas, þe he him to meder geceas.
> Þæt wæs geworden butan weres frigum
> þæt þurh bearnes gebyrd bryd eacen wearð.
> Nænig efenlic þam, ær ne siþþan,
> in worlde gewearð wifes gearnung;
> þæt degol wæs, dryhtnes geryne.[23] (Lyric 2, lines 18b–24)

It is the *uirgo immaculata* and *electa* who is prominent here and her uniqueness is stressed in an anticipation of IV, the source for which declares 'nec primam similem uisa es, nec habere sequentem'.[24] In the light of the frequent statements in patristic and later texts that Mary merited to become the mother of God, the emendation of the manuscript reading *gearnung* to *geeacnung*, favoured by Cook, Grein and Burlin, seems unnecessary. In the prayer to the Virgin in the Book of Nunnaminster and the Book of Cerne, for example, we find 'quae mundo meruisti generare salutem'[25] and one of the *De laude Dei* antiphons for the Assumption reads: 'Beata es, Maria, quae meruisti Dominum Iesum portare in utero.'[26]

Section III takes as its starting-point the antiphon 'O Hierusalem, ciuitas Dei summi: leua in circuitu oculos tuos, et uide Dominum tuum, quia iam ueniet soluere te a uinculis.'[27] This is only one of the many liturgical texts which associate Jerusalem with prophecies of Christ's birth. One of the allegorical explanations of Jerusalem, albeit a relatively rare one, was the city as a figure of the Virgin, and Cook has suggested that the *Advent* poet

---

[23] *Advent Lyrics*, ed. Campbell, p. 49; he translates: 'The girl was young, a virgin free of sin, she whom he chose for a mother. It was accomplished without the love of a man that the bride was magnified by the birth of a child. Nothing approaching that, before or since, no such merit of woman existed in the world. Such a thing is miraculous, a mystery of God.'

[24] See below, p. 184, for this antiphon.

[25] Barré, *Prières anciennes*, p. 65: 'who deserved to give birth to salvation for the world'.

[26] Constantinescu, 'Alcuin et les "libelli precum" ', p. 50: 'Blessed are you, Mary, who deserved to bear in your womb the lord Jesus.'

[27] Quoted in *Advent Lyrics*, ed. Campbell, p. 51: 'O Jerusalem, city of the highest God; raise up your eyes round about, and see your lord, for he is about to come now to release you from your bonds.'

exploited this.[28] Although the spotlessness was part of the interpretation of Jerusalem as the church, as Cook indicates, the emphasis on it in lines 5b–8a may also be partly due to the Marian interpretation:

> Næfre wommes tacn
> in þam eardgearde   eawed weorþeð,
> ac þe firena gehwylc   feor abugeð,
> wærgðo ond gewinnes.[29]   (Lyric III, lines 5b–8a)

In lines 10–17a, the exhortation to Jerusalem to 'uide Dominum tuum', the Marian association is more evident, although again the passage is consistent in its reference to Jerusalem also:

> Sioh nu sylfa,   þe geond þas sidan gesceaft,
> swylce rodores hrof   rume geondwlite
> ymb healfa gehwone,   hu þec heofones cyning
> siðe geseceð,   ond sylf cymeð.
> Nimeð eard in þe,   swa hit ær gefyrn
> witgan wisfæste   wordum sægdon;
> cyðdon cristes gebyrd,   cwædon þe to frofre,
> burga betlicast.[30]   (Lyric III, lines 10–17a)

Section IV of *Advent* is the first to be based on a Marian antiphon: 'O uirgo uirginum, quomodo fiet istud, quia nec primam similem uisa es nec habere sequentem? Filiae Ierusalem, quid me admiramini? Diuinum est mysterium hoc quod cernitis.'[31] The *filiae Ierusalem* here come from the Song of Songs and the antiphon itself is based partly on Mary's answer to Joseph at the Annunciation, 'Quomodo fiet istud?', and partly on Caelius Sedulius's *Carmen Paschale*:

> quae uentre beato
> Gaudia matris habens cum uirginitatis honore

---

[28] Cook, 'Bemerkungen zu Cynewulfs Christ'.

[29] *Advent Lyrics*, ed. Campbell, p. 51; he translates: 'Never a touch of vileness in that region is ever seen, rather every crime is exiled far from you, every evil and struggle.'

[30] *Ibid.*, p. 51: 'Look yourself now, that through the wide creation you may broadly survey, the roof of heaven also on every side, how heaven's king seeks you widely and himself comes. He makes his home in you, as long ago wise prophets predicted; they proclaimed Christ's birth, they spoke comfort to you, brightest of cities.'

[31] Quoted in *Advent Lyrics*, ed. Campbell, p. 53: 'O virgin of virgins, how will this be, for your like was neither seen before nor will you have a follower? Daughters of Jerusalem, why do you wonder at me? What you see is a divine mystery.'

Nec primam similem uisa es nec habere sequentem:
Sola sine exemplo placuisti femina Christo.[32]

The poet expands the *uirgo uirginum* to ecstatic praise of Mary:

> Eala wifa wynn,   geond wuldres þrym
> fæmne freolicast   ofer ealne foldan sceat
> þæs þe æfre sundbuend   secgan hyrdon.[33]
>
> (Lyric IV, lines 1–3)

In the next lines Mary's reply to Gabriel seems to have influenced the poet's treatment of the 'quomodo fiet istud': her answer at the Annunciation continued 'quoniam uirum non cognosco' and this is here taken over by the daughters of Jerusalem:

> arece us þæt geryne   þæt þe of roderum cwom,
> hu þu eacnunge   æfre onfenge
> bearnes þurh gebyrde   ond þone gebedscipe
> æfter monwisan   mod ne cuðes.[34]   (Lyric IV, lines 4–7)

The poet then paraphrases the Sedulius quotation, adding the mention of Mary's *sundurgiefe,* and the *filiae Hierusalem* praise Mary's *treow* and inviolate virginity:

> Huru treow in þe
> weorðlicu wunade,   nu þu wuldres þrym
> bosme gebære,   ond no gebrosnad wearð
> mægðhad se micla.[35]   (Lyric IV, lines 12b–15a)

These lines seems to refer to the widespread idea of Mary's conception through faith (of which the common belief in her conception through her ear was an image). This conception through faith is implicitly contrasted with the generality of men, who

---

[32] *Sedulii opera omnia*, ed. Huemer, pp. 48–9, lines 66–9: 'who, having in your blessed womb the joys of a mother together with the dignity of virginity, neither was your like seen before, nor do you have a follower: you, without a model, were the only woman to please Christ'.

[33] *Advent Lyrics*, ed. Campbell, p. 53; he translates: 'O joy of women, beyond all glories noblest woman in all the earth of whom mortals have heard tell.'

[34] *Ibid.*, p. 53: 'explain to us the mystery that came to you from the skies, how you ever received a magnification by the birth of a child, and intercourse according to human notions never knew'.

[35] *Ibid.*, p. 53: 'Indeed truth in you dwelt worthy, when you the power of heaven bore in your womb, yet was not fouled your great virginity.'

185

> sorgum sawað,   swa eft ripað,
> cennað to cwealme.[36]   (Lyric IV, lines 16–17a)

This passage echoes Galatians VI.8, where 'quae enim seminauerit homo, haec et metet' is explained as meaning that he who sows in the flesh reaps corruption, whereas he who sows in the spirit reaps eternal life. Mary, then, gave birth to life rather than death because, as the last section of *Advent* declares:

> ne þurh sæd ne cwom   sigores agend
> monnes ofer moldan.[37]   (Lyric XII, lines 5–6a)

The Virgin's reply to the *filiae Hierusalem* rebuffs their curiosity, insisting, as in the antiphon, on the mystery of her conception. Her description of the 'sunu solimæ somod his dohtor' as 'geomrende gehþum mænað',[38] which Cook regards as 'inappropriate in the context',[39] was possibly prompted by texts such as the following, which are found in the *Liber responsalis* for the second Sunday of Advent:

Ierusalem, cito ueniet salus tua; quare moerore consumeris?
Ciuitas Ierusalem, noli flere, quoniam doluit Dominus super te, et auferet a te omnem tribulationem.[40]

Mary then asserts that the curse of Eve has been overthrown in her:

> ac crist onwrah
> in dauides   dyrre mægan
> þæt is euan scyld   eal forpynded,
> wærgða aworpen,   ond gewuldrad is
> se heanra had.[41]   (Lyric IV, lines 25b–9a)

The Eve–Mary relationship is of course a very ancient one and a good example of the way in which it was developed can be seen in Pseudo-Augustine *Sermo* cxx,[42] the source for the first of the Old English

---

[36] *Ibid.*, p. 53: 'sow in sorrow, so reap they again, give birth for death'.

[37] *Ibid.*, p. 77: 'nor through seed of man on earth came the ruler of victory'.

[38] *Ibid.*, p. 53: 'sorrowing lament in grief'.

[39] *The Christ of Cynewulf*, ed. Cook, p. 87.

[40] PL 78, 727: 'O Jerusalem, your salvation will come soon; why are you consumed with grief? City of Jerusalem, don't weep, seeing that the lord is sorry for you and will take away from you all your distress.'

[41] *Advent Lyrics*, ed. Campbell, p. 53; he translates: 'but Christ did reveal in the dear kinswoman of David that the sin of Eve is all nullified, the curse overthrown, and the lowlier sex is made great'.

[42] PL 39, 1984–7.

Blickling Homilies. The emphasis on Mary's bringing salvation to both sexes, with which this section of the poem ends, probably owes something to texts like the sermon by Augustine which Cook cites, where Christ's coming as a man born of a woman is seen as the result of a deliberate wish to give hope to both sexes.[43]

The next two sections of *Advent* concentrate on Christ in his eternal aspects and section VII returns to his temporal birth. A source for this passage was discovered by Hill in an antiphon from Alcuin's *De laude Dei*, composed of a question to Joseph and a statement about Mary's conception by the Holy Spirit, spoken in the voice of the church: 'O Ioseph, quomodo credidisti quod antea expauisti? Quid enim? In ea natum est de Spiritu sancto quem Gabrihel annuncians Christum esse uenturum.'[44] This antiphon certainly has the detail of Joseph's fear and Mary's conception by the Holy Spirit, but it shares none of the features peculiar to the Old English poem. It differs little from the scriptural announcement to Joseph by the angel in Matthew I.20, which we also find as an antiphon in the *Liber responsalis*: 'Ioseph, fili Dauid, noli timere accipere Mariam coniugem tuam; quod enim in ea natum est, de Spiritu sancto est.'[45] Neither text has the dialogue between Mary and Joseph and the resolution of the mystery by Mary which we find in *Advent*. Nevertheless, the poet seems to have used only antiphons beginning with 'O' as sources and Hill's discovery therefore must be considered the liturgical inspiration for this passage which the poet then developed with great freedom, drawing on other texts, notably homilies, in the process.

The theme of the doubting of Mary, whose development is outlined by Burlin, is already present in the Gospel of Matthew, I.20:

Ioseph autem uir eius cum esset iustus, et nollet eam traducere, uoluit occulte dimittere eam. Haec autem eo cogitante, ecce angelus Domini apparuit in somnis ei, dicens: Ioseph, fili Dauid, noli timere accipere Mariam coniugem tuam: quod enim in ea natum est, de Spiritu sancto est.[46]

---

43 *The Christ of Cynewulf*, ed. Cook, p. 88.
44 Constantinescu, 'Alcuin et les "libelli precum"', p. 41: 'O Joseph, how did you believe that which before you feared? Well? He whom Gabriel announced would be the Christ to come is born of her by the Holy Spirit.'
45 PL 78, 732: 'O Joseph, son of David, do not fear to take Mary your wife: that which is born of her is of the Holy Spirit.'
46 'Her husband, Joseph, as he was a just man and did not wish publicly to disgrace her, wished to send her away secretly. But as he thought about this, behold an angel of the

This brief canonical account was soon expanded in the *Proteuangelium Iacobi*, where Joseph returns after an absence to find a pregnant Mary who has, surprisingly, forgotten Gabriel's annunciation and is ignorant of the origin of the child.[47] Gabriel's visitation in a dream then solves Joseph's dilemma, as in the Gospel of Matthew. This is followed by the discovery of Mary's pregnancy and the establishing of Mary's and Joseph's innocence by the test of the drinking of the bitter waters. The *Gospel of Pseudo-Matthew*, the Latin reworking of the *Proteuangelium*, eliminates Mary's inexplicable forgetfulness and replaces it with a scene in which she is defended by the virgins who are her companions and in which she herself does not speak.[48] Again, her purity is proved by an angelic declaration in Joseph's dream. Mary's pregnancy is then rumoured ('factum est autem post haec et exiit rumor quod Maria esset grauida')[49] and the couple again prove their innocence. Of these texts, then, only the *Proteuangelium* has a direct confrontation between Mary and Joseph and in this 'she wept bitterly, saying: I am pure and I know not a man.'[50] There is, however, no evidence for knowledge of this part of the *Proteuangelium* in England, although there is a Latin translation of the earlier section of the text (on the birth and childhood of Mary) in the eleventh-century English manuscript Cambridge, Pembroke College 25. In all the apocryphal texts, it is the angel, not Mary, who reveals the mystery of the Annunciation.

It was not only in the apocrypha that this theme was developed, however, and Cook has pointed to homiletic analogues, largely Greek, but including one Latin text, Pseudo-Augustine *Sermo* cxcv.[51] These analogues contain dialogues, often very extended ones, between Joseph and Mary, and in the Greek texts Mary herself tells Joseph of her conception. The Latin homily still retains the biblical annunciation to Joseph by the angel, but the speech by Joseph is very similar to that in *Advent*.[52] The homily is an African one and it is possible that it was known to the poet, as it was

Lord appeared to him in a dream, saying: "Joseph, son of David, do not fear to take Mary your wife, that which is born of her is of the Holy Spirit." '

[47] *Evangelia Apocrypha*, ed. Tischendorf, pp. 1–48; translated by James, *The Apocryphal New Testament*, pp. 39–49.

[48] *Evangelia Apocrypha*, ed. Tischendorf, pp. 50–105; summarized by James, *The Apocryphal New Testament*, pp. 73–9.

[49] *Evangelia Apocrypha*, ed. Tischendorf, p. 73: 'but it happened after this that a report sprang up that Mary was pregnant'.

[50] James, *The Apocryphal New Testament*, p. 44.   [51] Cook, 'A Remote Analogue'.

[52] PL 39, 2107–10

widely disseminated. It occurs in many early homiliaries, where it is assigned to the Christmas period: it appears to have been one of the texts in the sixth-century homiliary of St Peter's in Rome; it is also found in the homiliary of Vienne, compiled between 650 and 750, in the eighth-century homiliary of Fleury and in the very influential eighth-century homiliary of Alan of Farfa.[53] It is one of a group of African Christmas homilies which share distinctive features (others include Pseudo-Augustine *Sermo* cxciv, cxxi and cxx, the source for the first Blickling homily) and which are remarkable for their emphasis on the Virgin and for the freedom with which they dramatize the biblical narrative and explore the feelings of the biblical characters.[54] It is not improbable that such texts influenced the Old English poet, and the impulse behind the interest in the Virgin in both homilies and poem is dominated by the same theological considerations: the wish to probe the dual nature of Christ, divine and human, which necessarily involves scrutinizing the role of Mary.

Pseudo-Augustine *Sermo* cxcv consists of an introduction in which Mary's virginity is praised and Ezechiel's prophecy of the closed gates, which Mary applies to herself, is explained, followed by Mary's account of the Annunciation, in which the scriptural dialogue between her and Gabriel is much expanded, then by a description of Joseph's reaction to Mary's pregnancy and his attempts to decide on a course of action. Although Mary does not explain her conception directly to Joseph, the homily does have a speech by Mary (in which she describes the Annunciation) and a speech by Joseph; it would not have been a large step for a poet to combine them into dialogue. Joseph's speech is remarkably similar to that in *Advent*:

Turbatur Ioseph homo iustus, quod Mariam quam de templo Domini acceperat, et nondum cognouerat, grauidam sentiebat, et quam non meruerat in coniugii honore, iam haberet in confusione; secumque diu æstuans ac disputans, dicit: Unde hoc contigit? quid euenit? Non cognoui, non tetigi; si non tetigi, non uiolaui; si non uiolaui, non grauidaui. Heu! heu! quid contigit? quid, putas, euenit? per quem Maria sic cecidit? quem sibi plus quam me adulantem inuenit? ego enim cum licentiam haberem maritalem, ante thorum nuptiarum puellarum non uexaui pudorem. Timui, multumque pertimui, quod in illo Mosaico libro Legis sententiali est uerbo præfixum: quod quæcumque uirgo paternam domum foedauerit adulterio, morienda lapidibus subiacebit: similiter et uir qui pudoris

---

[53] See Barré, 'Sermons marials inédits', p. 61.
[54] See Leclercq, 'Aux origines du cycle de Noël', pp. 10–11.

uestimentum patri non detulerit, coramque testibus replicauerit, pudorisque signaculum non demonstrauerit, moriendum et ipsi cum uirgine erit . . . Quid ergo faciam? quid agam? Anxior, gemo, doleo, curro, consilium quæro, nec plenum inuenio. Prodo, aut taceo? Quid faciam penitus nescio. Prodo adulterium, aut taceo propter opprobrium? Si prodidero, adulterium quidem non consentio, sed næuum crudelitatis incurro; quia secundum librum Moysi lapidandam esse cognosco. Si tacuero, malum consentio; et cum adulteris portionem meam pono. Quoniam ergo tacere malum est, adulterium prodere peius est; ne per me fiat homicidium, dimittam tacite coniugium.[55]

The parallels between this sermon and section VII of *Advent*, then, suggest that the poet could have developed his liturgical source by drawing upon *Sermo* CXCV (or texts like it, if more existed), which would have formed part of the Christmas services at which the 'O' antiphons were sung. He could also have been influenced by apocryphal narratives: the *Gospel of Pseudo-Matthew* was available in England in the ninth century, when it was used in the *Old English Martyrology*, and in the Benedictine reform period.[56]

The major problem with this section of *Advent* has always been the assignation of speeches. It is clear that it consists of a dialogue between

[55] PL 39, 2108–9: 'Joseph, being a just man, was troubled to find that Mary, whom he had received from the temple of the Lord and never yet had known, was big with child; and that which he had not deserved in the honour of wedlock, he should now have in disgrace. For a long time his bosom burned, and he reasoned with himself: "How hath this come to pass? what hath befallen? I have not known her, nor even touched her; if I have not touched her, I have not deflowered her; if I have not deflowered her, I have not impregnated her. Alas! alas! what hath happened? what hath come to pass? through whom hath Mary so fallen? whom hath she found to soothe her more than me? I, though I had the rights of a husband, did not trouble her maiden modesty before the nuptial couch. I feared, I greatly dreaded what is prefixed to the word of the sententious law in the book of Moses, that whatsoever virgin shall defile her father's house with adultery shall be stoned that she die. In like manner, the man who hath not taken the garment of virginity to her father, and unfolded it before witnesses, and shown the token of virginity, he shall die with the virgin . . . What therefore shall I do? What shall I under-take? I am in anxiety, I groan, I grieve, I run, I seek advice, but find none adequate. Shall I denounce her, or be silent? What to do I certainly know not. Shall I denounce the adultery, or hold my peace to avoid the shame? If I make the disclosure, I dissent from the adultery, but incur the reproach of cruelty, since I know that according to the law of Moses she is to be stoned. If I am silent, I assent to the evil, and take my portion with adulterers. Since, then, it is evil to keep silence, and worse to denounce the adultery, I will, lest I occasion manslaughter, put away the marriage privily" ' (trans. Cook, 'A Remote Analogue to the Miracle Play', pp. 446–7).

[56] See below, pp. 216, 244–5 and 248–53.

Joseph and Mary, but there are two main schools of thought on how the speeches should be distributed: all of the editors, including Thorpe, Cook, Krapp and Dobbie and Campbell favour one method of distribution, Cosijn proposed another which has since been defended by Burlin and, recently, by Harlow.[57] In the first reading of the poem, Mary addresses Joseph, saying that he must cast off her love, and Joseph answers, declaring that he has lost his reputation on her account and that he has been subjected to accusations. His speech closes with an invocation to God and an address to Mary: 'Eala, fæmne geong   mægð Maria!'[58] Mary, according to this 'fragmenting' interpretation, then asks him why he mourns and says that, as she has never found any fault in him, she does not understand why he speaks as if he were full of sins. Joseph in reply laments the unhappiness caused by Mary's pregnancy and debates on what he should do with her, before all doubts are resolved by a speech of Mary's explaining her divine conception. In the 'unifying' interpretation, on the other hand, the section begins with a much longer speech by Mary, and it is she who is bereft of *dom* and insulted. This reading necessitates an emendation of the masculine *feasceaftne* to the feminine,[59] but such a mistake in gender would be an understandable error, especially as the statement in which it occurs has the kind of general quality which might lead a scribe to expect a masculine:

> Eala ioseph min,   iacobes bearn,
> mæg dauides,   mæran cyninges,
> nu þu freode scealt   fæste gedælan,[60]
> alætan lufan mine!   Ic lungre eam
> deope gedrefed,   dome bereafod,
> forðon ic worn for þe   worda hæbbe

[57] Cosijn, 'Anglosaxonica IV'; Burlin, *Old English Advent*, pp. 119–23; Harlow, 'The Old English *Advent* VII'. The speech boundaries in this section are also discussed by S. B. Hemingway, 'Cynewulf's *Christ*, ll.173b–176a', *MLN* 22 (1907), 62–3; N. Isaacs, 'Who Says What in Advent Lyric VII? (*Christ* 11. 164–213)', *Papers in Language and Literature* 2 (1966), 162–6; J. M. Foley, 'A Structural Approach to the Speech Boundaries in "Advent Lyric VII"', *Neophilologus* 59 (1975), 114–18; E. R. Anderson, 'The Speech Boundaries in Advent Lyric VII', *Neophilologus* 63 (1979), 611–18.

[58] *Advent Lyrics*, ed. Campbell, p. 59; he translates 'O young girl, Mary the virgin'.

[59] Cosijn also proposed emending 'for þe' to 'for þy', but, as Burlin, *Old English Advent*, p. 119, n. 7, points out, this 'is both unnecessary and undesirable'.

[60] J. Pope, 'Mary to Joseph, *Christ* I, 164–67a: A Probable Scribal Error, *nu* for *na*', *Speculum* 60 (1985), 903–9, suggests that *nu* in this line should be emended to *na*, giving a reading 'you must not sever a firm affection': the suggestion deserves acceptance and is valid whichever reading of the poem one adopts.

> sidra sorga ond sarcwida,
> hearmes gehyred, ond me hosp sprecað,
> tornworda fela. Ic tearas sceal
> geotan geomormod. God eaþe mæg
> gehælan hygesorge heortan minre,
> afrefran feasceaftne.[61]   (Lyric VII, lines 1–12a)

Cosijn's reading has the major advantage of beginning Joseph's speech with 'Eala, fæmne geong': as every other *eala* in the work has an introductory function, the concluding *eala* advocated by Cook, Campbell and others appears distinctly peculiar. In an age without a highly developed system of punctuation in poetry, the quick, unsignalled interchange defended by Cook would have been almost impossible to spot. Although the boundaries between a speech by a character and the author are sometimes fluid in Old English poetry, the speeches of different characters are almost invariably introduced with unmistakable clarity. In Cosijn's reading the transitions are clearly signalled and, as in IV, the only other section with dialogue, speeches are introduced with *eala* or with a narrative introduction. In this interpretation, then, Joseph's speech consists of a question to Mary, asking her why she laments, as he has never found any fault in her, and goes on to complain of the unhappiness caused by her pregnancy.

Hill, when he proposed the antiphonal source, also suggested that it supported the traditional assignation of speeches: 'this arrangement is in accordance with the antiphon in that it is Joseph, after all, who is "expauens"' and he thinks that 'the arrangement of speeches . . . in which it is Joseph rather than Mary who is troubled, seems preferable for both aesthetic and theological reasons'.[62] He wishes, therefore, to attribute lines 3b–13a to Joseph. But the antiphon can hardly be used to prove the distribution of speeches: Joseph is shown as 'expauens' in both readings of the poem and the only difference is that, in Cosijn's and Burlin's interpretation, Mary, too, is 'expauens', and it is this feature which the 'fragmenters' have found

---

[61] *Advent Lyrics*, ed. Campbell, p. 59; he translates (omitting his punctuation, which breaks up this speech): 'O my Joseph, son of Jacob, descendant of David the great king, now must you sever a firm affection, reject my love? I suddenly am deeply disturbed, despoiled of honour, for I have for you heard many words, many great sorrows and hurtful speeches, much harm, and to me they speak insult, many hostile words. Tears I must shed, sad in mind. God easily may relieve the inner pain of my heart, comfort the wretched one.'

[62] Hill, 'A Liturgical Source', p. 14.

most difficult to accept. The unifying reading does, however, give a consistent and satisfactory text.

In both interpretations of the scene we must assume that the poet begins his account immediately after Joseph has made known his dilemma to Mary, telling her that he intends to 'occulte dimittere eam'. She reacts with sorrow, saying that she has been subjected to accusations on his account, presumably accusations that Joseph has had intercourse with her. The situation presupposed by the poet differs from that in the apocryphal narratives, where Joseph is aware of Mary's conception by the Holy Spirit before the public rumours and accusations begin: this feature of the Old English poem seems, indeed, to be unique and it heightens the dramatic impact of the scene. Opponents of Cosijn's reading tend to consider Mary's grief psychologically implausible, and Hill, for example, says that 'one can hardly imagine Mary worrying about what the neighbours would think after the Annunciation'.[63] An ample justification for her grief is contained in the first three and a half lines, however, which are invariably assigned to Mary. Although the rumours of Mary's pregnancy occur later in *Pseudo-Matthew*, the apocryphal narrative might have influenced the poet here, and in *Pseudo-Matthew* the rumours affect both Joseph and Mary. Joseph's reply begins with a question to Mary about why she is lamenting, as he has never found any fault in her, although she now speaks as if she were full of sins, and he then goes on to consider despairingly whether he should reveal or conceal Mary's crimes:

> Eala fæmne geong,
> mægð maria!   Hwæt bemurnest ðu,
> cleopast cearigende?   Ne ic culpan in þe,
> incan ænigne,   æfre onfunde,
> womma geworhtra,   ond þu þa word spricest
> swa þu sylfa sie   synna gehwylcre
> firena gefylled.   Ic to fela hæbbe
> þæs byrdscypes   bealwa onfongen.
> Hu mæg ic ladigan   laþan spræce
> oþþe ondsware   ænige findan
> wraþum towiþere?   Is þæt wide cuð
> þæt ic of þam torhtan   temple dryhtnes
> onfeng freolice   fæmnan clæne,
> womma lease,   ond nu gehwyrfed is

---

[63] *Ibid.*, p. 14.

þurh nathwylces.   Me nawþer deag,

secge ne swige.   Gif ic soð sprece,

þonne sceal dauides   dohtor sweltan,

stanum astyrfed.   Gen strengre is

þæt ic morþor hele;   scyle manswara,

laþ leoda gehwam   lifgan siþþan,

fracoð in folcum.[64]   (Lyric VII, lines 12b–32a)

What could be considered an inconsistency between lines 14b–18a and the remainder of the speech is easily explicable in terms of the contrast between Mary's past behaviour, which was faultless, and what looks like her present state of sin. In the much later *Ludus Couentriae* miracle play on the subject of Joseph's doubts, for example, he also comments on Mary's past perfection:

> I knew never with here so god me spede
> tokyn of thynge in word nor dede
> þat towchyd velany
> nevyr þe les what for thy
> þow she be meke and mylde
> With-owth mannys company
> she myght not be with childe.[65]

The inconsistency, therefore, is not in Joseph's speech, but is an apparent inconsistency in Mary's behaviour. The remainder of the dialogue is unambiguous and Mary reveals the divine mystery in which she has been made a participant, calling herself, in a very common figure, the temple of the Holy Spirit and telling Joseph to rejoice that she has become the virgin mother of the Lord and that he is called the father of Christ:

---

[64] *Advent Lyrics*, ed. Campbell, p. 59; he translates (again omitting the inverted commas): 'O young girl, Mary the virgin! What are you bewailing, crying out full of care? Never did I guilt in you, any fault ever find of accomplished wrong, yet you speak these words as if you yourself of every sin, of crimes were filled. I have too much of evil received for this pregnancy. How may I refute the hateful talk or find any answer against my enemies? It is widely known that I from the bright temple of God willingly received a pure virgin free from stain, and now she is changed by I know not what. It does me no good either speaking or keeping silent. If I tell the truth, then shall David's daughter die, killed with stones. Yet it is worse that I conceal the crime; a perjured man, hateful to all people, would live hereafter vile among the folk.'

[65] *Ludus Coventriae or the Plaie Called Corpus Christi*, ed. K. S. Block, EETS 120 (1922), 112.

þa seo fæmne onwrah
ryhtgeryno,   ond þus reordade:
'Soð ic secge   þurh sunu meotodes,
gæsta geocend,   þæt ic gen ne conn
þurh gemæcscipe   monnes ower,
ænges on eorðan,   ac me eaden wearð,
geongre in geardum,   þæt me gabrihel,
heofones heagengel,   hælo gebodade.
Sægde soðlice   þæt me swegles gæst
leoman onlyhte,   sceolde ic lifes þrym
geberan, beorhtne sunu,   bearn eacen godes,
torhtes tirfruman.   Nu ic his tempel eam
gefremed butan facne,   in me frofre gæst
geeardode,   nu þu ealle forlæt
sare sorgceare.   Saga ecne þonc
mærum meotodes sunu   þæt ic his modor gewearð,
fæmne forð seþeah,   ond þu fæder cweden
worldcund bi wene.   Sceolde witedom
in him sylfum beon   soðe gefylled.'[66]

(Lyric VII, lines 32b–50)

The reading advocated by Cosijn and Burlin does, therefore, make sense both psychologically (though it may be doubted whether that was a major interest of the poet) and in terms of Marian tradition, as well as following the structural guidelines of the poem itself in its allocation of speeches.

A different version of the 'unifying' reading has recently been proposed by Harlow: he retains the speech divisions of Cosijn and Burlin, but suggests that Mary's first speech and that of Joseph contain within them quotations from previous speeches uttered by each, which are not part of the poem.[67] Thus he translates lines 6–10a of Mary's opening speech: 'for I

---

[66] *Advent Lyrics*, ed. Campbell, pp. 59–61; he translates: 'Then the girl revealed the true mystery, and spoke thus: "The truth I utter through the son of God, Saviour of spirits, that I still do not know by copulation any man, any on earth, but to me it was granted, young in my home, that Gabriel, archangel of heaven, offered me a greeting. He said truly that the Spirit of heaven would illumine me with splendour, I should bear the glory of life, the bright son, the mighty child of God, of the glorious creator. Now that I his temple am made without spot, in me the Spirit of comfort has dwelt, so you now may completely relinquish your bitter sorrow. Say eternal thanks to the great son of God that I have become his mother, yet henceforth a virgin, and you called his father by the reckoning of the world. Prophecy had to be in himself truly fulfilled.'

[67] Harlow, 'The Old English *Advent VII*'.

have heard a multitude of great sorrows and wounding speeches, of injury, as a result of those words [of yours] (and they utter insults to me, many words of anger): "I must pour forth tears, sad in spirit".'[68] Joseph's speech, in this reading, contains two quotations from Mary: 'Why do you grieve, cry out sorrowing "I never found fault in you, any offence from defilement committed [by you upon me]?" and you utter these words as if you yourself are filled with every sin, every crime: "I have received too many evils from this childbearing. How can I refute hostile talk or find any answer to my enemies?" '[69] Harlow supports his argument by reference to a tradition of such quotations in Greek homilies on the Annunciation which contain dramatic interchanges between Mary and Gabriel and between Mary and Joseph. It may be questioned whether such a reading is plausible for *Advent*: in the first place, it is unlikely that the poet could have been acquainted with any of these Greek homilies, which do not seem to have been available in the West in translation, and in these analogues, moreover, as Harlow acknowledges, the quotations are always from speeches uttered earlier within the texts. Secondly, the supposed quotations are almost impossible to spot without a sophisticated punctuation system (which in Harlow's translation involves both brackets and quotation marks) and while the poet undoubtedly expected his readers to be familiar with the theme of the doubting of Mary, even a prior knowledge of the story would hardly allow them to recognize quotations from non-existent speeches. The two Anglo-Saxon parallels Harlow cites are unconvincing: in the case of the quotation from the Old English *Heptateuch*, the passage adduced is a faithful translation of the Latin, and *Advent* Lyric VI, lines 5–6, his second parallel, is of a very different nature and cannot be considered a quotation in the same sense.[70] His reading does not solve the problem of the worried Virgin (one of the major objections to a 'unified' reading), as she is still insulted and anxious, and it is questionable whether any devout Anglo-Saxon poet would have had the Virgin, even in a 'despondent reverie', bemoan her divine pregnancy with the words: 'Ic to fela hæbbe/þæs byrdscypes   bealwa onfongen.'[71] These lines, on the other hand, fit Joseph's stance perfectly. Harlow's proposal to allocate lines 14b–16a to Mary (as a quotation within Joseph's speech) unnecessarily suppresses the contrast Joseph sees between Mary's past and present behaviour. Such a complex version of the scene seems, then, to be

[68] *Ibid.*, pp. 111–12.   [69] *Ibid.*, pp. 111 and 110.   [70] *Ibid.*, pp. 113–14.
[71] *Ibid.*, p. 113.

unnecessarily difficult and foreign to Anglo-Saxon tradition, whereas a 'unifying' reading of this section of the work makes sense without it. The following section of the poem, VIII, returns to Christ's divine origin and his existence before the creation even of light, and the incomprehensibility of this prompts the poet to turn again to Christ's temporal birth:

> Us is eallum neod
> þæt we þin medrencynn   motan cunnan,
> ryhtgeryno,   nu we areccan ne mægon
> þæt fædrencynn   fier owihte.[72]   (Lyric VIII, lines 32b–5)

This is followed by a passage which Cook took as a reference to the virgin birth, but which Burlin wishes to interpret primarily as a reference to the gates of paradise:[73]

> Þu þisne middangeard   milde geblissa
> þurh ðinne hercyme,   hælende crist,
> ond þa gyldnan geatu,   þe in geardagum
> ful longe ær   bilocen stodan,
> heofona heahfrea,   hat ontynan;
> ond usic þonne gesece   þurh þin sylfes gong
> eaðmod to eorþan.[74]   (Lyric IX, lines 36–42a)

As the golden gates are unequivocally Mary's womb in the next section of the poem, it would appear a priori likely that they have the same meaning here, particularly as they are mentioned when the poet deliberately turns to the human generation of Christ. Burlin's objection that, as 'longevity is hardly to be thought of as one of the virtues of the womb of Mary',[75] the lines 'in geardagum / ful longe ær   bilocen' must apply to the gates of paradise, is scarcely tenable in view of lines 36b–40 and 48–51 of the next section of the work. The golden gates are a very common Marian figure and the responds of the Christmas period include texts drawing upon this

---

[72] *Advent Lyrics*, ed. Campbell, p. 63; he translates: 'For us all there is a yearning that we your maternal kin may know in truth, since we may not reckon your paternal kin one whit further.'

[73] *The Christ of Cynewulf*, ed. Cook, p. 102, n. 251 and Burlin, *Old English Advent*, p. 135.

[74] *Advent Lyrics*, ed. Campbell, p. 65; he translates: 'Mildly bless this middle world with your advent, Saviour Christ, and those golden gates, which in former days a long while ago stood locked, command to be opened, O high lord of heaven, and then seek us by your visit, humble on earth.'

[75] Burlin, *Old English Advent*, p. 135.

metaphor, e.g. 'Et ingressus est per splendidam regionem, aurem uirginis, uisitare palatium uteri; et regressus est per auream uirginis portam.'[76] The last section to be based on a Marian antiphon is IX, in this case: 'O mundi domina, regio ex semine orta: ex tuo iam Christus processit aluo, tanquam sponsus de thalamo; hic iacet in praesepio qui et sidera regit.'[77] Although this antiphon is addressed to Mary, the stress is largely on Christ, first as he goes forth from Mary's womb, then on the paradox of the Lord of the stars lying in a manger. The Old English poet alters this emphasis by stressing Mary as bride rather than Christ as bridegroom, by suppressing the last part of the antiphon and by introducing a petition to Mary, analogous to the petitions to the Lord in many of the other sections. The section begins with an expansion of the 'mundi domina' of the source, using reminiscences of liturgical texts associated with Mary (e.g. the *De laude Dei* antiphons: 'Te iusta laude praedicamus, salutis nostrae genitrix, cuius uterus intemeratus coelesti sponso thalamus est consecratus' and 'Te laudant angeli, archangeli; et clamant martyres sancti'):[78]

> Eala þu mæra   middangeardes
> seo clæneste   cwen ofer eorþan
> þara þe gewurde   to widan feore,
> hu þec mid ryhte   ealle reordberend
> hatað ond secgað,   hæleð geond foldan,
> bliþe mode,   þæt þu bryd sie
> þæs selestan   swegles bryttan!
> Swylce þa hyhstan   on heofonum eac,
> cristes þegnas,   cweþað ond singað
> þæt þu sie hlæfdige   halgum meahtum
> wuldorweorudes,   ond worldcundra
> hada under heofonum,   ond helwara.[79]   (Lyric IX, lines 1–12)

---

[76] PL 78, 731: 'He has entered through the bright region, the ear of the virgin, to visit the palace of her womb; and he has returned through the golden gate of the virgin.'

[77] Quoted in *Advent Lyrics*, ed. Campbell, p. 67: 'O lady of the world, born from a royal seed, Christ has indeed come forth from your womb like a bridegroom from his chamber; here he who rules the stars lies in a manger'.

[78] Constantinescu, 'Alcuin et les "libelli precum"', p. 50: 'We laud you with just praise, mother of our salvation, whose undefiled womb is consecrated as the bridal chamber of the heavenly bridegroom.' 'Angels and archangels praise you and holy martyrs cry out . . .'

[79] *Advent Lyrics*, ed. Campbell, p. 67; he translates: 'O great one of the world, throughout the earth the purest lady of those who have existed ever, how rightly all possessors of speech, men upon earth, name you and say with glad heart that you are the bride of the most excellent Lord of the sky. Also the highest in heaven, Christ's nobles, speak and

Mary's title as *domina* of heaven, earth and hell is a transference of Christ's designation as Lord of all three regions. The following lines then develop the Augustinian idea that Mary alone vowed her virginity to God, and this is made the basis for the Lord's choice of her as mother:

> Forþon þu þæt ana   ealra monna
> geþohtest þrymlice,   þristhycgende,
> þæt þu þinne mægðhad   meotude brohtes,
> sealdes butan synnum.   Nan swylc ne cwom
> ænig oþer   ofer ealle men,
> bryd beaghroden,   þe þa beorhtan lac
> to heofonhame   hlutre mode
> siþþan sende.   Forðon heht sigores fruma
> his heahbodan   hider gefleogan
> of his mægenþrymme   ond þe meahta sped
> snude cyðan,   þæt þu sunu dryhtnes
> þurh clæne gebyrd   cennan sceolde
> monnum to miltse,   ond þe, maria, forð
> efne unwemme   a gehealdan.[80]   (Lyric IX, lines 13–26)

In the next lines the poet replaces the antiphonal paradox of God becoming man with a figure which focuses on the paradox of the virgin mother and he describes the virginal conception in terms of the closed gate of Ezechiel XLIV.2, although he attributes it to Isaiah. Joyce Hill has convincingly suggested that the movement from the image of the bridegroom leaving his chamber to the image of the closed gates was not an arbitrary one, but was achieved by means of a common pattern of association, which she illustrates from such hymns as *Veni redemptor gentium*.[81] The closed gates as a figure for Mary's conception are, of course, a commonplace, and a good example of the way in which the passage from Ezechiel was interpreted can be found in Pseudo-Augustine *Sermo* cxcv, the closest Latin analogue for section VII:

> sing that you by holy power are the lady of the heavenly host as well as the earthly ranks under the heavens and the inhabitants of hell.'

[80] *Ibid.*, p. 67: 'You, alone among all mankind resolved splendidly, firm-minded, that you brought your virginity to God, gave it without sin. None like that came, no other from all humanity, no crowned bride who the bright gift with spotless spirit to our heaven-home has sent. For that the Lord of victory commanded his high messenger to fly hither from his glorious majesty and reveal quickly to you the fullness of power, that you the son of God might bear in a pure birth as a mercy to men, and henceforth might keep yourself, Mary, ever immaculate.'

[81] J. Hill, 'A Sequence of Associations in the Composition of *Christ* 275–347', *RES* ns 27 (1976), 296–9.

Porta facta sum coeli; ianua facta sum filio Dei. Illa porta facta sum clausa, quam in uisione diuina Ezechiel uidit propheta, de qua in me dicit prophetizans. *Vidi portam in domo Domini clausam: et dixit ad me angelus, Porta haec quam uides, non aperietur, et homo non transiet per eam; quoniam Dominus solus intrabit, et egredietur per eam, et clausa erit in aeternum.* O mirabilis prophetae uisio; sed mirabilior prophetiae adimpletio! Quid est porta in domo Domini clausa, nisi quod Maria Virgo semper erit intacta? Et quid est, *Homo non transiet per eam*; nisi, Ioseph non cognoscet eam? Et quid est, *Dominus solus intrabit et egredietur per eam*; nisi, Spiritus sanctus impraegnabit eam, et angelorum Dominus nascetur per eam? Et quid est, *Clausa erit in aeternum*, nisi quia erit Maria uirgo ante partum, uirgo in partu, uirgo post partum?[82]

This interpretation is very similar to that of the Old English poet, who first paraphrases the Ezechiel passage, then expounds it:

Nu þæt is gefylled   þæt se froda þa
mid eagum þær   on wlatade.
Þu eart þæt wealldor,   þurh þe waldend frea
æne on þas eorðan   ut siðade,
ond efne swa þec gemette,   meahtum gehrodene,
clæne ond gecorene,   crist ælmihtig.
Swa ðe æfter him   engla þeoden
eft unmæle   ælces þinges
lioþucægan bileac,   lifes brytta.[83]   (Lyric IX, lines 52–60)

The section concludes with a striking plea to Mary to intercede and to show to mankind 'þa frofre . . . þinre sylfre sunu'. In a departure from the antiphonal pleas, the poet then imagines the fulfilment of his request, as he contemplates the Child at his mother's breast:

[82] PL 39, 2017: 'I have been made the gate of heaven; I have been made the door of the son of God. I have been made that closed door which the prophet Ezechiel saw in a vision, about which he says prophesying of me: I saw the closed gate in the dwelling of the Lord; and the angel said to me, This gate which you see, it will not be opened, and no man will pass through it, because the Lord alone will enter and will go out through it and it will be closed eternally. O wonderful vision of the prophet; but even more wonderful fulfilment of the prophecy! What is the closed gate in the dwelling of the Lord, unless it be the chaste Virgin Mary? And what is, no man will pass through it, unless Joseph will not know her? And what is, the Lord alone will enter and will go out through it, unless, the Holy Spirit will impregnate her and the Lord of angels will be born of her? And what is, it will be closed eternally, unless that Mary will be a virgin before the birth, a virgin in birth and a virgin after birth?'

[83] *Advent Lyrics*, ed. Campbell, p. 69; he translates: 'Now is fulfilled that which the prophet then looked on there with his eyes. You are the gate, unique, through which the

Iowa us nu þa are   þe se engel þe,
godes spelboda,   gabriel brohte.
Huru þæs biddað   burgsittende
þæt ðu þa frofre   folcum cyðe,
þinre sylfre sunu.   Siþþan we motan
anmodlice   ealle hyhtan,
nu we on þæt bearn   foran breostum stariað.
Geþinga us nu   þristum wordum
þæt he us ne læte   leng owihte
in þisse deaðdene   gedwolan hyran,
ac þæt he usic geferge   in fæder rice,
þær we sorglease   siþþan motan
wunigan in wuldre   mid weoroda god.[84]

(Lyric IX, lines 61–73)

It is possible that this remarkable image of the congregation beholding the child at Mary's breast was influenced by artistic images: none survives from Anglo-Saxon England which shows Mary suckling the Christ Child, but the Kells Virgin and Child, which shows Mary with clearly outlined breasts, could well have been derived from such an image.[85] On the Northumbrian Dewsbury Cross of *c*. 800, the child reaches to its mother's breast.[86] The poet very possibly also knew literary treatments of the theme: the most famous is, of course, Augustine's entreaty: 'Lacte, mater . . . '[87]

Sections X and XI of *Advent* explore aspects of the eternal Deity, but the final division returns to the theme of the humanity of Christ, expanding the antiphon: 'O admirabile commercium, creator generis humani animatum corpus sumens, de uirgine nasci dignatus est, et procedens homo sine semine, largitus est nobis suam deitatem':[88]

ruling Lord into this earth journied forth and even thus Christ almighty found you, adorned with power, pure and set apart. So after him the Lord of angels, the giver of life, locked you with a mysterious key again undefiled by any thing.'

[84] *Ibid.*, pp. 69–71: 'Show us now the grace which to you the angel, God's messenger Gabriel, brought. That indeed we mortals pray, that you reveal to men that comfort, your own son. Afterward we may all single-mindedly hope, now we look on that child at your breast. Intercede for us now with vigorous words that he not leave us any longer in this valley of death to follow error, but that he transport us into his father's kingdom where we sorrowless may ever dwell in beatitude with the God of hosts.'

[85] See above, p. 148.   [86] See above, p. 156.   [87] PL 39, 1655; see above, p. 12.

[88] Quoted in *Advent Lyrics*, ed. Campbell, p. 77: 'O wondrous interchange, the creator of the human race, putting on a living body, deigned to be born of a virgin, and coming forth as a man without seed, bestowed on us his divinity.'

Eala hwæt, þæt is wræclic wrixl   in wera life
þætte moncynnes   milde scyppend
onfeng æt fæmnan   flæsc unwemme,
ond sio weres friga   wiht ne cuþe,
ne þurh sæd ne cwom   sigores agend
monnes ofer moldan;   ac þæt wæs ma cræft
þonne hit eorðbuend   ealle cuþan
þurh geryne,   hu he, rodera þrim,
heofona heahfrea,   helpe gefremede
monna cynne   þurh his modor hrif.[89]   (Lyric XII, lines 1–10)

The poem as a whole, then, demonstrates a striking emphasis upon the Virgin. Mary's importance, in the poet's view, is clearly the result of her role as *Dei genitrix*, and she is viewed largely in Christological terms. Unlike the apocryphal narratives, which deal with the extra-scriptural parts of Mary's life, her birth, childhood and death, *Advent* scarcely departs from biblical events. Mary's sojourn in the temple does come ultimately from apocryphal sources, but it had been accepted by such orthodox theologians as Ambrose. Section VII may also owe something to the apocrypha, but even this dialogue between Mary and Joseph exists to make a Christological point (that Christ was born of a human, but virgin, mother and a divine father, impossible though comprehension of this may be to human understanding), not to throw further light on Mary's life. The scriptural events, however, are seen through the Fathers and the liturgy: Mary is not simply the virgin of the bible chosen in a seemingly arbitrary fashion as the mother of God, but the unique and 'manes leas' 'byrd þæs selestan swegles bryttan', who had already vowed her virginity to God. The poet glorifies her as 'wifa wynn, 'fæmne freolicast', 'seo clæneste cwen ofer eorðan' and as lady of heaven, earth and hell. His view of her sinlessness seems to consist simply of a general notion of her complete freedom from actual sin; she is 'unmæle', 'manes leas', 'butan synnum'. Even the lines 'Nu ic his tempel eam / gefremed butan facne'[90] probably do not imply any belief that Mary had been born or conceived without sin; they convey,

[89] *Advent Lyrics*, ed. Campbell, p. 77; he translates: 'O, what a marvellous change in the life of men that mankind's mild creator received from a virgin undefiled flesh! She knew the love of man not at all nor through seed of man on earth came the ruler of victory, that was a greater feat than all earth-dwellers comprehend in its mysterious significance, how he, glory of the skies, high God of heaven, brought help to man's kind through his mother's womb.'

[90] *Ibid.*, p. 61: 'now I his temple am made without spot'.

rather, a pictorial image of her purity and were almost certainly not intended to be subjected to any kind of rigorous logical analysis. As well as clearly showing the influence of the Church Fathers' and the liturgy's interpretation of the Virgin's role in the Incarnation, the poet also makes use of their application of Old Testament figures to her: she is the antithesis of Eve, the temple of the Holy Spirit, Jerusalem and the golden gates. Mary is exalted, too, as the heavenly queen who can intercede for mankind, and the passage in which the poet pleads for her intercession is striking in its intimacy and tenderness. The poem is clearly the work of a learned, sophisticated poet, versed in liturgy and theology and with a profound devotion to the Virgin. His fascination with the double nativity must owe something to Augustinian homilies and commentaries, which return constantly to this theme. The degree of concern with Mary in *Advent* is unlike most Old English prose accounts of the Incarnation and Nativity of Christ, such as those in the Christmas homilies and in the *Old English Martyrology*. The first half and the conclusion to the text *De natale Domini* in Ælfric's *Catholic Homilies II* are the closest to *Advent* in their stress on Christ's double nativity and the way in which they deal with Old Testament prophecies of his birth involving Mary, but even this text is far from *Advent* in its Marian significance.[91]

Proposed dates for *Advent* have ranged between the ninth century, suggested mainly by those who believed in some connection with Cynewulf and by Campbell, and the monastic reform period, advocated by Woolf and Gatch. Gatch suggests that *Advent* must date from the period 940 onwards because the kind of allegorical exegesis applied to the liturgy which he sees in *Advent* would not, he argues, have been possible in England before the work of Amalarius of Metz (*ob. c.* 850) became known there: 'as the state of Anglo-Saxon monasticism was so low in the ninth century, it is difficult to imagine that *Advent* could have been composed before the time of the monastic revival of around 940, at which time a concerted effort was made to enrich the liturgy in England'.[92] Gatch's argument is not compelling, however: Amalarius may have been the first to apply exegesis – which had been confined to the bible – to the liturgy, but we find none of Amalarius's exegesis of liturgical acts in *Advent*. As most of the antiphons used in *Advent* are based on the bible, the poet need only have been indebted to biblical exegesis and homilies, which he undoubtedly

---

[91] *CH II*, pp. 3–11.   [92] Gatch, *Loyalties and Traditions*, p. 96.

knew and used. To place the beginning of the monastic reform at around 940, the year when Dunstan became abbot of Glastonbury, is probably also too early: the monastic reform did not get fully under way until the 960s and the interval between this and the writing of the Exeter Book is a very short one. *Advent* could well have been composed within this period, but Gatch's argument does not prove that it was.

Woolf also proposed a late date for *Advent*, chiefly on the basis of 'the remarkable emphasis upon the Virgin in the Lyrics', which she attributes to Eastern influences.[93] From this she concludes:

If this interpretation of the lyrics is correct, one might suppose them to belong to the period in which the Anglo-Saxon church was in touch with the colonies of Greek monks who had settled in central and southern Italy (in southern Italy there were also Syrian monks). As a result of these contacts the Eastern feast of the Conception (or the Nativity) of the Virgin was adopted at Winchester in the early eleventh century; but the partial translation of the *Gospel of Pseudo-Matthew* amongst the Vercelli Homilies shows that Anglo-Saxon interest in the apocryphal early life of the Virgin had developed before this time (Ælfric's tight-lipped brevity in his sermon for the feast of the Nativity of the Virgin is another indication of the currency of such works before the close of the tenth century). The version of the theme of Joseph's doubts in this apocryphal work does not provide the source for this lyric, but it does provide a perhaps significant analogue at about the time of the compilation of the Exeter Book. It is tempting to suppose that the compiler of this anthology of Old English poetry decided to begin his collection with a contemporary work.[94]

There are several objections to Woolf's arguments. In the first place, Anglo-Saxon knowledge of and interest in the Marian apocrypha is much earlier than the late tenth century: *Pseudo-Matthew* was used by the compiler of the *Old English Martyrology* before the end of the ninth century[95] and, if we were to consider acquaintance with this apocryphon a significant factor in dating *Advent*, then the ninth-century text is equally important. The account of the miracles on the flight into Egypt in Vercelli homily VI to which Woolf refers, was not, moreover, incorporated in the *Gospel of Pseudo-Matthew* until the eleventh century[96] and the Vercelli text cannot, therefore, be considered as evidence for knowledge of the apocryphon (although there is a translation of *Pseudo-Matthew* into Old English

---

[93] Woolf (reviewing Burlin, *Old English Advent*), *MÆ* 40 (1971), 60–1, at 61.
[94] *Ibid.*, p. 61.
[95] See below, p. 216.   [96] See Gijsel, *Die unmittelbare Textüberlieferung*, pp. 15–17.

which is probably eleventh century). A more fundamental difficulty, however, is that the kind of Marian piety which lies behind the interest in *Pseudo-Matthew* differs from the kind of Marian piety in *Advent*. Even if we were able to date the flowering of this type of devotional interest quite precisely, it would not help us to date *Advent*. The apocrypha display a fascination with the figure of Mary herself and with her life before and after the Incarnation. In *Advent*, while Woolf's observation about the prominence of Mary is undoubtedly true, the focus is on her role in the Incarnation and on the attempt to understand Christ's divine and human parentage. There are some parallels to the seventh section of *Advent* in the apocrypha, but the homiletic analogues are probably closer, so that this section of the poem can hardly be used to demonstrate direct dependence on the apocrypha. The lateness of the introduction of the feast of the Conception (not the same feast as that of the Nativity of the Virgin) prevents any attempt to connect this manifestation of Eastern influence with the composition of *Advent*, which was copied into the Exeter Book at least a generation before the Eastern feast was introduced in Winchester. Although it is possible that some kind of indirect Eastern influence lies behind the seventh section of *Advent*, in particular, it cannot, therefore, be identified with the impulse which led to the celebration of the feast of the Conception.

Rankin, in her discussion of the 'O' antiphons, has recently pointed out that the source material used by the *Advent* poet was probably available in England by the late eighth century at the latest and that 'while no exact *termini post quem* or *ante quem* for the composition of the Old English lyrics can be deduced from this evidence, it is at least likely that the poems were composed well before the mid-tenth century, when the great Benedictine revival introduced a new wave of Frankish liturgical influence'.[97] While the important role of Mary in the poem is undoubtedly consonant with the well-attested interest in the Virgin in the Benedictine reform period, the type of focus on Mary suggests, too, that it would be unwise to rule out the eighth or ninth centuries. On cultural grounds this period is perfectly possible: Kenneth Sisam has made a strong case for placing Cynewulf in the ninth century[98] and the *Old English Martyrology*, which was certainly composed by a learned man, seems to belong to this period.[99] The

[97] Rankin, 'Liturgical Background', p. 334.
[98] Sisam, 'Cynewulf and his Poetry', in his *Studies*, p. 7.
[99] Kotzor, *Das altenglische Martyrologium* II, 201–3. See below, pp. 211 and 213–17.

prayer-books copied at the beginning of the ninth century testify to a sophisticated devotional milieu.[100] The close association of the Christmas season with the Annunciation and with the Virgin in general, although never entirely supplanted by the feasts of Mary, perhaps also indicates an early date and may even have some connection with the early feast of Mary in the period before Christmas.[101] Campbell's analysis of the 'extremely inconclusive' linguistic evidence suggests a date in the eighth or ninth centuries:[102] he favours the late ninth century and a Mercian poet. This, however, does not fit the Marian evidence as well as the first half of this century does: a Mercian poet of this period would be perfectly consistent with the evidence of Mercian art and prayer in the first half of the ninth century.

OTHER OLD ENGLISH POEMS

Unlike *Advent*, which adverts to Mary with such striking frequency, the *Dream of the Rood* in the Vercelli Book contains only one reference to the Virgin (in one of the passages not contained on the Ruthwell Cross). This comes within the speech of the cross and is the climax of a series of contrasts between the present and former states of the cross:

> Hwæt, me þa geweorðode   wuldres Ealdor
> ofer holmwudu,   heofonrices Weard,
> swylce swa he his modor eac,   Marian sylfe,
> ælmihtig God,   for ealle menn
> geweorðode   ofer eall wifa cynn.[103]

Just as the cross was chosen above all other trees, so Mary was chosen above all other women to bear Christ, the lines in the poem echoing Gabriel's greeting in Luke's account of the Annunciation: 'Benedicta tu in mulieribus.' As well as this echo of the Annunciation, Ó Carragáin has suggested a more sustained set of underlying links between the Annunciation and the story of the Passion as related in the *Dream of the Rood*, supported by the coincidence of both events on 25 March, the 'historical' date of the

---

[100] See above, pp. 95–104.   [101] See above, p. 28.

[102] *Advent Lyrics*, ed. Campbell, pp. 36–42, at 41.

[103] *The Dream of the Rood*, ed. M. Swanton (Manchester, 1970), pp. 94–5, lines 90–5: 'Lo, the lord of glory, the guardian of the heavenly kingdom, then honoured me over the hill trees, just as he, almighty God, honoured his mother also, Mary herself, over all women for the sake of all mankind.'

Crucifixion. [104] The poet, he argues, imagines the Crucifixion in terms of the Annunciation and the unusual features of the narrative can be explained as a result of this. Horgan views the comparison between the cross and Mary differently, suggesting that 'it appears that the way in which He has bestowed honour on the Cross is by letting it share in His glory and His saving power, as well as by admitting it to Heaven, presumably because not only has it borne the suffering Christ but also because it shared in His suffering. The comparison set forth in lines 90–4 is a productive one if we presume the reference being made is to the doctrine of the Assumption of the Blessed Virgin Mary into Heaven.' [105] Horgan, however, overlooks the distinction between the spiritual and the corporal assumption of the Virgin. If he is referring here to the spiritual assumption, then the comparison becomes a very weak one, as many of the saints were thought to have been assumed into heaven at the moment of death. As the poet is clearly drawing a parallel that unites Mary and the cross only, then his intent can hardly have been to refer to a spiritual assumption. Peculiar to Mary was the much combated belief in her corporal assumption, but there is no question of the cross having been corporally, or materially, assumed. The cross was found and venerated, whereas Mary's body was never discovered. Horgan's suggestion, therefore, cannot be accepted.

The perhaps surprising thing about the comparison of the cross and the Virgin is the implication of ordinariness. The cross in the *Dream of the Rood* is made from a tree which is arbitrarily plucked from the forest and it emphasizes its own guilt and unworthiness; there is no hint of the apocryphal legend in which the tree is marked out for future use from the time of the Fall. If a comparison with the Virgin is pursued, it suggests that Mary, too, was chosen in an arbitrary fashion and honoured for no special reason. The poem differs in this respect from the Marian apocrypha, in which miracles attend Mary's conception and birth, and from such orthodox works as *Advent*, which follows the Church Fathers in showing Mary to have merited her role as mother of God by her faith and her vow of virginity. The *Dream of the Rood* seems to be unique in Old English literature in its disregard of Mary's special status and virtue before the Annunciation.

The unique *uirgo uirginum*, now in heaven, is, however, described in the

---

[104] See E. Ó Carragáin, 'Crucifixion as Annunciation'.
[105] A. D. Horgan, 'The Dream of the Rood and Christian Tradition', *Neuphilologische Mitteilungen* 79 (1978), 11–20, at 17.

Old English poem, *Judgement Day II*, a very close translation of Bede's Latin poem *De die iudicii*.[106] The depiction of paradise in this work includes an account of the Virgin leading the throng of virgins:

> Þær þæra hwittra   hwyrfð mædenheap,
> blostmum behangen,   beorhtost wereda,
> þe ealle læt   ænlicu godes drut,
> seo frowe þe us   frean acende,
> metod on moldan,   meowle seo clæne.
> Þæt is Maria,   mædena selast;
> heo let þurh þa scenan   scinendan ricu,
> gebletsodost ealra,   þæs breman fæder,
> betweox fæder and sunu,   freolicum werede,
> and betwyx þære ecan   uplicum sibbe
> rice rædwitan,   rodera weardas.[107]

A final text with more than a passing mention of the Virgin is a versified Creed which seems to have been composed as part of a vernacular version of the Benedictine Office and which expands the brief reference to Mary in the Creed with surprising ardour. This is very much in keeping with the emphasis on Mary at the time of the Benedictine reform:

> Ic on sunu þinne   soðne gelyfe,
> hælendne cyning,   hider asendne
> of ðam uplican   engla rice,
> þone Gabriel,   godes ærendraca,
> sanctan Marian   sylfre gebodode.
> Ides unmæne,   heo þæt ærende
> onfeng freolice,   and ðe fæder sylfne
> under breostcofan   bearn acende.
> Næs ðær gefremmed   firen æt giftum,
> ac þær halig gast   handgyft sealde,
> þære fæmnan bosm   fylde mid blisse,

---

[106] 'Judgement Day II' in *The Anglo-Saxon Minor Poems*, ed. Dobbie, pp. 58–67.

[107] *Ibid.*, lines 290–300: 'Then the band of virgins, of pure ones, moves about, hung with flowers, the brightest of hosts – the glorious beloved one of God leads them all, the lady who bore the Lord for us, the creator upon earth, the pure virgin. That is Mary, the best of maidens; she, most blessed of all, leads with a noble host through the bright shining kingdoms of the glorious Father and the Son and amid the eternal celestial peace, in the kingdom of the Counsellor, the guardian of the heavens' (see T. D. Hill, 'The Kingdom of the Father, Son and Counsellor: *Judgement Day II*, 290–300', *N&Q* ns 32 (1985), 7–8, for the details of the translation).

> and heo cuðlice cende swa mærne,
> eorðbuendum engla scyppend,
> se to frofre gewearð foldbuendum,
> and ymbe Bethleem bodedan englas
> þæt acenned wæs Crist on eorðan. [108]

Apart from this small number of works, Old English poetry contains very few references to Mary. This may be partly due to the date of the Old English poems which survive, although all questions of dating are difficult. Given the developed interest in Mary in the late Anglo-Saxon period, we might expect to find such works as versified Marian apocrypha, similar to other versified saints' lives. An Old English poem based on the *Gospel of Pseudo-Matthew* or on one of the apocryphal accounts of Mary's assumption would fit well with such works as *Andreas* or *Juliana*. Instead, we have only prose versions of these Marian works. A possible explanation is that the age of the Benedictine reform was largely an age of prose, while most of the verse saints' lives may date from an earlier period, which had less interest in Mary. In the poetic works in which she does figure, Mary's role is entirely subordinated to her son's and there is little or no trace of an apocryphal-type interest in her. In this the anonymous poetry differs greatly from the anonymous Old English prose.

[108] 'The Creed', in *Anglo-Saxon Minor Poems*, ed. Dobbie, pp. 78–80, lines 9–24: 'I believe in your true son, the saviour king, sent hither from the celestial kingdom of angels, whom Gabriel, God's messenger, announced to St Mary herself. The innocent lady readily received that message and bore under her heart the child for you, the Father himself [?]. No sin was committed in that marriage, but there the Holy Spirit gave the wedding-present, filled with happiness the virgin's bosom, and she therefore brought forth the great creator of angels for the inhabitants of earth, who became a consolation to earth-dwellers, and around Bethlehem the angels announced that Christ was born.'

8

The Virgin in Old English prose

The four feasts of the Purification, Annunciation, Assumption and Nativity of the Virgin gave rise to one of the most extensive manifestations of the cult of the Virgin. Once they were firmly established, from the eighth century onwards, they created a need for preaching and reading texts for use both within the liturgy and in paraliturgical contexts. The need was met in England partly by copying and disseminating Latin homiliaries produced on the continent, especially Carolingian ones, but an important new development was the composition of vernacular homilies and homiliaries. These Latin and English homiliaries seem to have been the main vehicle for transmitting both Marian doctrines and legends. Vernacular homilies for the feasts of the Virgin survive in English manuscripts from the late tenth century onwards, the earliest collections being the Vercelli Book[1] (second half of the tenth century), the *Blickling Homilies*[2] (*c.* 1000) and Ælfric's two series of *Catholic Homilies* (989–95).[3] The first two collections seem to have been assembled from a variety of sources and contain anonymous homilies, by different authors, whose date and place of origin are uncertain, though the language of Blickling seems to point to Mercia[4] and the Vercelli Book is a south-eastern compilation.[5] We still

---

[1] A facsimile is ed. C. Sisam, *The Vercelli Book*, and the manuscript described by Ker, *Catalogue*, no. 394.

[2] A facsimile is ed. R. Willard, *The Blickling Homilies*, EEMF 10 (Copenhagen, 1960), and the manuscript is described by Ker, *Catalogue*, no. 382.

[3] *CH I*, ed. Thorpe and *CH II*, ed. Godden. On the dates, see *CH II*, pp. xci–xciii.

[4] See R. J. Menner, 'The Anglian Vocabulary of the Blickling Homilies', in *Philologica: The Malone Anniversary Studies*, ed. T. A. Kirby and H. B. Woolf (Baltimore, 1949), pp. 56–64; H. Schabram, *Superbia: Studien zum altenglischen Wortschatz I* (Munich, 1965), p. 75.

[5] *The Vercelli Book*, ed. C. Sisam, p. 35; Scragg, 'The Compilation of the Vercelli Book'.

lack the evidence to know whether most of these works are early and date from the pre-reform period or, like the works of Ælfric, are the products of the Benedictine reform. Before this, our only substantial evidence for the cult of the Virgin in vernacular prose is that of the *Old English Martyrology*, a narrative martyrology composed some time between the second half of the eighth century and the end of the ninth and probably intended for private reading.[6] After Vercelli, Blickling and Ælfric, we have a variety of manuscripts of the eleventh and twelfth centuries, mixing works by Ælfric with those of the anonymous tradition.[7] Like the Carolingian homiliaries, these vernacular collections (which contain homilies, sermons and saints' lives) catered for different needs: although it is extremely unlikely that they could have been used for monastic reading in the Night Office, they were certainly used for preaching to the laity at mass or in a context intimately connected with the mass and they were also used for private reading.[8] The Vercelli Book, for example, is not organized according to any liturgical principle: it is 'essentially a reading book', which seems to reflect the personal interests of its compiler.[9] The *Blickling Homilies*, on the other hand, are an incomplete collection arranged according to the liturgical year, designed primarily for reading to the laity. Ælfric's first two series seem to have been intended principally for use in preaching to the laity and, to some extent, the monks, in connection with the mass: he seems to have had in mind the kind of situation which must have been relatively common after the Benedictine reform, where the laity would have attended mass in the monastic church, with the monks also present.[10]

In composing homilies for the feasts of the Virgin, the Anglo-Saxon homilists could draw on the patristic works already included in the Latin homiliaries circulating in England, as well as treatments of Mary in biblical commentaries and in apocryphal works. These Latin homiliaries offered a large variety of Marian texts. In selecting texts for his homiliary, Alan of Farfa (*c.* 750), for example, could not turn to patristic homilies deliberately composed for the feasts of the Virgin, as they had not been in

---

[6] *Das altenglische Martyrologium*, ed. Kotzor; on the function of the martyrology, see my review of Kotzor, *RES* ns 35 (1984), 347–9.

[7] See Scragg, 'The Corpus of Vernacular Homilies'.

[8] See my 'Homiliaries and Preaching'.

[9] K. Sisam, 'Marginalia in the Vercelli Book', in his *Studies*, pp. 109–18, at 118. See also Ó Carragáin, 'The Vercelli Book as an Ascetic Florilegium'.

[10] Clayton, 'Homiliaries and Preaching', pp. 230–42.

existence when the Church Fathers were writing. Like many other compilers after him, he had to resort either to patristic homilies for the Christmas period, which, particularly when they were African, stressed the role of Mary, or he had to excerpt suitable passages from biblical commentaries or other texts. Alan provided texts for the feasts of the Purification and the Assumption only: for the Purification he chose extracts from Ambrose's commentary on Luke, extracts from the letters of St Leo, a series of passages from St Augustine and a Pseudo-Augustine homily; for the Assumption, Pseudo-Ildefonsus *Sermones* vii and viii, both of which are derived from African Christmas homilies, and Pseudo-Augustine *Sermo* cxciv, another African Christmas text.[11] Bede was the first to compose a homily specifically intended for the feast of the Purification, the only feast of Mary for which he provides a text in his homiliary.[12] His Advent homilies, however, include texts commenting on the accounts of the Annunciation and the Visitation in Luke, passages which became the pericopes for the feasts of the Annunciation and the Nativity:[13] in many later homiliaries, Bede's texts are assigned to these feasts. Paul the Deacon, whose homiliary was probably the most influential of all, included the authentic part of Augustine's *Sermo* ccclxx (originally a Christmas homily), an extract from Ambrose's commentary on Luke and Bede's homily for the Purification; he has no text for the Annunciation (this feast normally falls during Lent or Easter, times when the church traditionally did not observe the feasts of saints), but his Advent homilies include Bede's homily and an extract from Ambrose's commentary on Luke, both commenting on the Annunciation pericope; originally he does not appear to have included a text for the feast of the Assumption, although he himself composed two texts for the occasion, but the gap in his homiliary was soon filled by others, very often by an adaptation of that part of Bede's commentary on Luke which deals with the Martha and Mary episode, the pericope for the day; and for the Nativity, Paul refers the user of his work to Bede's Advent homily 1.4 and an extract from Ambrose's commentary on Luke, both of which deal with the Visitation, the original pericope for the day.[14] These texts were frequently supplemented by others: often by texts from Alan of Farfa or by apocryphal narratives. The homiliary of Saint-Père-de-Chartres, a collec-

---

[11] See Grégoire, *Homéliaires liturgiques médiévaux*, pp. 36–7 and 60–1.

[12] *Opera homiletica*, ed. Hurst, pp. 128–33.

[13] *Ibid.*, pp. 14–20 and 21–31.

[14] Grégoire, *Homéliaires liturgiqes médiévaux*, pp. 86–7, 78, 103 and 104.

tion intended for preaching to the laity which was known in England, contains a homily beginning 'Conueniendum est in unum nobis . . .' for the Purification, a version of *Transitus* c for the Assumption and a translation of part of the *Proteuangelium* for the Nativity of the Virgin.[15] Paul the Deacon's homiliary was the most widely copied in England, to judge by surviving manuscripts, but Bede's homiliary, the homiliary of Saint-Père-de-Chartres and the Carolingian homiliaries of Haymo, Heiric and Smaragdus were all available also and supplied source material for vernacular texts.[16]

THE OLD ENGLISH MARTYROLOGY

Work on the *Old English Martyrology* is complicated by the fact that we do not know whether the text as we now have it is an original compilation in Old English or whether it was translated from an Anglo-Latin compilation, which could have been compiled by a different author, at a different place and time.[17] It is clear, however, that the text is in some sense a Mercian one[18] and that it is the work of a learned author, drawing on a variety of sources.[19] It contains entries for three Marian feasts, the Annunciation, Assumption and Nativity, and the Purification would doubtless also have been included, but there is a gap in the text at this point.

The entry for 25 March deals only in part with the Annunciation, as a large part of it is devoted to Christ's death which, though celebrated liturgically on Good Friday, was believed to have taken place on the same day as his conception. The beginning of the entry reads:

On ðone fif and twentegðan dæg þæs monðes com Gabrihel ærest to Sancta Marian mid Godes ærende; and on ðone dæg Sancta Maria wæs eacen geworden on Nazareth ðære ceastre þurh þæs engles word ond þurh hire earena gehyrnesse, swa

[15] Discussed and partly edited by Barré, *Les homéliaires carolingiens*, pp. 17–25; see also J. E. Cross, *Cambridge Pembroke College MS 25*, King's College London Medieval Studies 1 (London, 1987).

[16] See my 'Homiliaries and Preaching', pp. 217–20. Ælfric used Smaragdus, Haymo and Heiric as sources.

[17] *Das altenglische Martyrologium*, ed. Kotzor 1, 449–54.

[18] *An Old English Martyrology*, ed. Herzfeld, pp. xix–xxviii; C. Sisam, 'An Early Fragment of the *Old English Martyrology*', *RES* ns 4 (1953), 209–20; *Das altenglische Martyrologium*, ed. Kotzor 1, 443–8.

[19] Cross has published numerous articles on the sources. See, in particular, 'On the Library of the Old English Martyrologist' and 'The Use of Patristic Homilies'.

þas treowa ðonne hi blostmiað þurh þæs windes blæd. On ðære ylcan stowe þær hire hus ða wæs þa se engel hi ane gemette, Cristne men timbredon micle cirican.[20]

The first sentence draws on the Annunciation narrative in Luke and perhaps on a gospel commentary. The *conceptio per aurem* is a commonplace, but no direct source for the image of Mary conceiving like the trees when they blossom through the blowing of the wind has been discovered. Cross, however, has pointed to an Hiberno-Latin gospel commentary which has something similar, with the image of the trees being applied to the workings of the Holy Spirit.[21] An interesting point is the insertion of *ærest* to stress that this was the first time that Gabriel came to Mary to announce the Incarnation. The *Gospel of Pseudo-Matthew*, on which the martyrologist draws for the entry for 8 September, has two annunciations; one by a well, where Mary is greeted by Gabriel, the second on the following day, when she is told of the Incarnation. *Ærest* here suggests that the martyrologist did not agree with this tradition of two annunciations. Cross has demonstrated the martyrologist's awareness of different traditions concerning, for example, the manner of Thomas's death, and we may here have further evidence of this.[22]

This entry for 15 August is a composite one:

On þone .xv.an dæg þæs monþys biþ seo tid þæt is Sancta Marian tid. On þone dæg heo geleorde of middangearde to Criste, ond heo nu scineþ on þam heofonlican mægene betwyh þa þreatas haligra fæmnena, swa swa sunne scineþ on þisne middangeard. Englas þær blissiaþ, ond heahenglas þær wynsumiaþ, ond ealle þa halgan þær gefeoþ in Sancta Marian. Sancta Maria wæs on .lxiiii.um geara þa ða heo ferde to Criste. Sancta Maria is Godfæder snoru, and Godes suna modur, ond haligra sauwla sweger, ond seo æþele cwen þara uplica cesterwara, seo stondeþ on þa swyþran healfe ðæs Heahfæder ond ðæs Heahkyninges.[23]

---

[20] *Das altenglische Martyrologium*, ed. Kotzor II, 43–4: 'On the twenty-fifth day of the month Gabriel came first to St Mary with God's message; and on that day St Mary became pregnant in the town of Nazareth through the word of the angel and through the hearing of her ears, like the trees when they blossom through the blowing of the wind. In that same place where her house was when the angel once met her, Christian people built a large church.'

[21] 'The Use of Patristic Homilies', pp. 121–2.

[22] 'On the Library of the Old English Martyrologist', p. 236.

[23] *Das altenglische Martyrologium*, ed. Kotzor II, 181: 'On the fifteenth day of the month is the feast which is the feast of St Mary. On that day she departed from the world to Christ and she now shines in heavenly power amongst the troops of holy virgins, as the sun

The first part of this entry corresponds to parts of the responses for the feast of the Assumption in the antiphonary of Compiègne: 'O quam pulchra et speciosa est Maria Virgo Dei, quae de mundo migrauit ad Christum; inter choros uirginum fulget sicut sol in uirtute coelesti. Gaudent angeli, exsultant archangeli in Maria uirgine.'[24] These, along with some other assumption texts, occur in no other antiphonary and Capelle argues that they form a Gallican addition to the otherwise Roman antiphonary.[25] The note on Mary's age seems to derive from an addition to Eusebius's *Chronicle*, which assigns the death of Mary to the fifteenth year after the Ascension.[26] As Mary, according to the apocrypha, was fourteen at the Annunciation, and Christ lived thirty-three years, this meant that she died at the age of sixty-three, as a later Old English note on her age calculates.[27] The sixty-four of the martyrology is probably a scribal error in copying the number of years. The next part of the entry is drawn from Aldhelm's prose *De uirginitate*[28] and the conclusion, which is based on Psalm XLIV, may also have come from the *Liber responsalis*[29] or from Aldhelm, for whom, however, the queen is virginity.[30] Perhaps the most striking feature of this entry is not what it includes, but what it omits. In almost every case the martyrologist provides descriptions of the deaths of the saints and here we should expect him to draw on the apocryphal narratives of Mary's death and assumption to supply similar details. It is, of course, possible that he did

---

shines on this world. Angels rejoice there, and archangels exult, and all the saints rejoice there in St Mary. St Mary was sixth-four years old when she went to Christ. St Mary is daughter-in-law of God the Father and mother of God's son and mother-in-law of the holy souls and the noble queen of the celestial citizens, who stands on the right side of the High Father and the High King.'

[24] PL 78, 798: 'O how glorious and beautiful is Mary the virgin of God, who passed away from this world to Christ; amongst the choirs of virgins she shines like the sun in heavenly power. The angels rejoice, the archangels exult in the Virgin Mary.'

[25] B. Capelle, 'La messe gallicane de l'assomption: son rayonnement, ses sources', *Travaux liturgiques de doctrine et d'histoire* III, pp. 430–55. See also Barré, 'Antiennes et répons', pp. 219–20.

[26] See *The Prose Solomon and Saturn and Adrian and Ritheus*, ed. J. E. Cross and T. D. Hill (Toronto, 1982), pp. 79–82.

[27] See T. N. Hall, 'The Ages of Christ and Mary in the Hyde Register and in Old English Literature', *N&Q* ns 35 (1988), 4–11, on the later notes.

[28] See *Aldhelmi opera*, ed. Ehwald, p. 292. See also Cross, 'The Use of Patristic Homilies', p. 126.

[29] PL 78, 798: 'Adfuit regina a dextris tuis . . .'

[30] *Aldhelmi opera*, ed. Ehwald, p. 292.

not know them but, given his wide acquaintance with other legends, this is perhaps unlikely. He certainly knew at least one of the most important witnesses to the tradition of agnosticism on the question of Mary's death: Adamnan's *De locis sanctis*.[31] Possibly, therefore, the avoidance of any discussion of the subject was prompted by Adamnan's caution.

The third entry for a feast of Mary is that for 8 September, the feast of the Nativity of the Virgin:

On ðone .viii.an dæg þæs monþes byþ Sancta Marian acennednes. Hyre fæder wæs nemned Ioachim ond hire modor Anna, ond hi wæron .xx. geare somod ær þon hi bearn hæfdon. Þa wæron swiþe unrote; þa oþywde Godes engel hiora ægðrum onsundrum hine, ond him sæde ðæt hi sceoldon habban swylc bearn swylce næfre ær in worold come, ne ær ne eft. Da æfter .xx. gearum cende Anna dohtor, ond hieo nemde þa Maria. Ond þa hio wæs þreo geara eald, ða læddon hi fæder ond modor to Hierusalem, ond sealdon hi þer in þara fæmnena gemænnesse þe ðær on Godes huse lofsang dydon dæges ond nihtes. Þa wæs þæt cild sona snotor ond anræde, ond swa fulfremed þæt nænig æþelicor ne sang þone Godes lofsang; ond hio wæs swa beorht on ansyne ond wliti þæt mon hyre meahte uneaþe onlocyan. Ond on hyre mægdenhade hio dyde fela wundra on webgeweorce ond oþrum cræftum ðæs þe þa yldran don ne meahton.[32]

This entry draws, as Herzfeld pointed out, on the first six chapters of *Pseudo-Matthew*, summarizing the main events leading to Mary's birth and her presentation in the temple.[33]

Other entries in the *Old English Martyrology* reflect a further knowledge of legends connected with Mary. The Christmas entry, for example, concludes: 'þæt bæð þæt Sancta Maria þæt cild on baþode, þurh ðæt

[31] On the martyrologist's use of Adamnan, see Cross, 'On the Library of the Old English Martyrologist', p. 232.

[32] *Das altenglische Martyrologium*, ed. Kotzor II, 201–3: 'On the eighth day of the month is the Nativity of St Mary. Her father was called Joachim and her mother Anna, and they were twenty years together before they had a child. They were very sad; then an angel of God appeared to each of them, separately, and said to them that they were to have such a child as had never come into the world before or never would afterwards. Then after twenty years Anna gave birth to a daughter and she named her Mary. And when she was three years old, then her father and mother brought her to Jerusalem and gave her there to the community of women who performed songs of praise day and night in the house of God. Then the child was at once wise and resolute and so perfect that nobody sang God's songs of praise more excellently: and she was so bright and beautiful in her countenance that one could hardly look at her. And during her maidenhood she did many wonders in weaving and other skills which the older ones could not do.'

[33] *An Old English Martyrology*, ed. Herzfeld, p. xli.

manige untrume men þæron wurdon gehælede'.[34] Adamnan mentions the ever-full channel into which the bath-water had been poured and which was venerated, but not the healings.[35] The entries for 22 June and 28 October show a knowledge of the legend of Mary's sisters: 'On ðone tu ond twentegðan dæg þæs monðes bið þæs apostoles ond þæs Godes ærendwracan gemynd þe on gewritum is nemned Iacobus Alphei; þæt wæs Cristes modergan sune, Sancta Marian sweostorsunu, forþon he is cweden on gewritum frater Domini, Drihtnes broþor'[36] and 'On ðone .xxviii. dæg þæs monðes bið þara apostola tid Simonis ond Thaddeos. Simonis wæs Sancta Marian swystorsunu, Cristes modrian sunu, seo wæs nemned on Cristes bocum Maria Cleophe.'[37] The *Old English Martyrology*, then, testifies to a developed interest in Marian legends and to the availability of such texts in ninth-century England. That the martyrologist did not use apocryphal material for the Assumption entry suggests, however, that he regarded the apocryphal *Transitus* with a suspicion derived from one of his main sources, Adamnan.

HOMILIES FOR FEASTS OF THE VIRGIN

Altogether there are ten Anglo-Saxon homilies for feasts of Mary (who of course features in other texts as well): the Vercelli Book contains a Purification homily; Blickling has an Annunciation and an Assumption homily; there is another anonymous text for the Assumption and one for the Nativity of the Virgin; and Ælfric composed a homily each for the Purification, the Annunciation and the Nativity and two texts for the Assumption.

---

[34] *Das altenglische Martyrologium*, ed. Kotzor II, 2: 'the bath in which St Mary bathed the child, through it many infirm people were healed'.

[35] This passage is discussed by J. E. Cross, 'The Influence of Irish Texts and Traditions on the *Old English Martyrology*', *Proceedings of the Royal Irish Academy* 81C (1981), 173–92, at 185.

[36] *Das altenglische Martyrologium*, ed. Kotzor II, 125: 'On the twenty-second day of the month is the commemoration of the apostle and the messenger of God who is called James the son of Alpheus in scripture: that was Christ's maternal aunt's son, St Mary's sister's son, therefore he is called frater Domini, the brother of the Lord.'

[37] *Ibid.*, II, 240: 'On the twenty-eighth day of the month is the feast of the apostles Simon and Thaddeus. Simon was St Mary's sister's son, Christ's maternal aunt's son, who was called in the bible Mary Cleopas.'

Homilies for the feast of the Purification

The anonymous and Ælfrician Purification texts are similar insofar as neither is interested primarily in the Virgin, but instead they both concentrate on the meeting of Christ and Simeon. The Vercelli text (homily XVII) is one of a group of four in the manuscript (XV–XVIII) which appears to be of Anglian, probably Mercian, origin, with late transmission into the West-Saxon scribal tradition:[38] this group, unlike many of the other texts in the manuscript, must have been copied from a liturgically arranged homiliary.[39] Vercelli XVII appears to be freely composed, probably using a variety of sources: most of its points can be paralleled in Latin homilies or commentaries (for example, by Ambrose, Bede, Ambrosius Autpertus and Haymo), but no precise source has yet been identified.[40] No one Latin text includes all the points made by the vernacular homilist and the Latin texts are, rather, the kind of works with which the homilist would have been acquainted and from which he would have derived his interpretation of the pericope. The homily begins with a paraphrase of the biblical reading for the day, here Luke II.22-32,[41] a paraphrase which does not adapt the pericope in any way to draw attention to Mary. Indeed, despite the rubric alluding to the purification of Mary, the homilist does not even make the minimal adaptation of introducing her name, but mentions only Christ's 'aldoras'. Only the first paragraph of exegesis, with its explanation of the Judaic law of purification, is connected with the Virgin, as the homilist explains why she, though already pure, chose to subject herself to the law:

Forþan þe ealle wif þe tymende syndon hie sendon on þam bebodum, sancta Maria Cristes moder, forðan seo eadigu cwen sancta Maria, heo clæne abad þæs feowertigan dæges – nalles þæt heo þæs ænige þearfe hæfde þæt heo swylc wære on clænnesse hire lichaman, se ðe þurh æghwæt mid godcunde gestihtunge 7 mid

---

[38] Vercelli XVII is ed. Szarmach, *Vercelli Homilies*, pp. 51–5. On this group of texts, see *The Vercelli Book*, ed. C. Sisam, pp. 42–3, and Scragg, 'The Compilation of the Vercelli Book', p. 194 and 202.

[39] See my 'Homiliaries and Preaching', pp. 228–9.

[40] The homily is discussed by Szarmach, 'The Vercelli Homilies: Style and Structure', pp. 256–8.

[41] Szarmach, 'The Vercelli Homilies: Style and Structure', p. 258, says that the homilist consciously avoided traditional purification themes such as the prophecies of Simeon and the witness of Anna, but these clearly did not form part of his pericope. The pericope is the same as that in the *New Minster Missal*, ed. Turner, p. 72.

lifes geearnunge geclænsod wæs 7 þurh Haliges Gastes gife, forðan þe heo wæs unmælu 7 clæne butan eallum synnum; 7 heo in clænnesse mægðhade a ðurhwunode 7 Crist acende 7 æfter þære acennesse heo a ðurhwunode in clænnesse mægðhade. 7 heo eac forþam brohte Crist in þa tid to þam Godes tempel þæt heo wolde þæt þæt word wære gefylled þe Crist cwæð: 'Ne cwom ic to þam in worulde þæt ic Godes æ towurpe 7 tobræce; ac ic cwom to þan þæt hie gefylde 7 getrymede.'[42]

The author's exposition of Mary's obedience to the Old Law is based on an association with Matthew v.17: 'Ne cwom ic . . . .' This quotation is a common one in this connection: it is quoted or referred to by Ambrosius Autpertus[43] and Haymo,[44] for example, and all commentators, except Origen, state that Mary voluntarily and unnecessarily submitted herself to the law. Mary's purity before and after the birth is stressed by Haymo in a similar manner to the Old English:

Verum si diligentius uerba legis scrutemur, inueniemus non solum Dominum Iesum Christum a iugo legis solutum, sed etiam sanctam eius genitricem a uinculo legalis obseruantiae esse liberam . . . Illa enim sola nulla immunditia tenebatur obnoxia post partum, quam nulla immunditia praecessit ante partum. Et ideo sicut Dominus Iesus Christus nulla necessitate, sed sola uoluntate legem obseruauit, sic eius sancta genitrix, non coacta, sed spontanea iugo legis se subdidit, ut ostenderet suis temporibus legem sanctam et bonam fuisse.[45]

[42] *The Vercelli Homilies*, ed. Szarmach, pp. 51–2: 'Since all women who give birth sent themselves to the temple in accordance with the commandment, St Mary, the mother of Christ, waited in purity for the fortieth day – not at all because she had any need of that, because her body was so pure, which throughout everything was cleansed by divine dispensation and the merits of her life and through the grace of the Holy Spirit, because she was immaculate and pure without any sin; and she always persevered in the purity of virginity and gave birth to Christ and after the birth she always persevered in the purity of virginity and she, therefore, also brought Christ to God's temple at that time, because she wished that the word which Christ spoke should be fulfilled: I did not come into the world in order to destroy and overthrow God's law, but I came in order to fulfill and strengthen it'.

[43] PL 89, 1293.   [44] PL 118, 97.

[45] PL 118, 99: 'Truly if we examine more attentively the words of the law, we shall find not only the Lord Jesus Christ to have been freed of the bonds of the law, but also his holy mother to be free from the fetters of the observance of the law. Truly she alone was bound by no damaging impurity, whom no impurity touched before giving birth. And therefore just as the Lord Jesus Christ observed the law, not of necessity but only of his own accord, so his holy mother submitted herself, not by compulsion, but voluntarily, to the bonds of the law, that she might reveal the law to have been holy and good in her times.'

For Haymo, and for the Old English homilist, therefore, Mary was completely pure at Christ's nativity. The homilist details how she had achieved this state of purity: 'mid godcunde gestihtunge and mid lifes geearnunge . . . 7 þurh Haliges Gastes gife'. It is difficult to judge how precisely these three types of purification should be taken, or whether any gradation is to be inferred. The divine dispensation suggests something close to the apocryphal idea that Mary had been chosen before her birth, a notion which was given a theological basis by Paschasius Radbertus, who argued that Mary must have been freed, by God's intervention, of all original sin before her birth.[46] 'Lifes geearnunge' refers, of course, to the belief in Mary's perfect way of life before the Incarnation and, possibly, her vow of virginity, both of which are described in the apocrypha but were accepted equally by orthodox theologians. For pre-Carolingian theologians such as Augustine, Mary's way of life before the Incarnation was such that she merited to become the mother of God. The purification by the Holy Ghost perhaps implies the traditional view, expressed too by Ælfric, that Mary was also purified of all sin at the Annunciation. The three types of purification mentioned by the homilist are to some extent mutually exclusive: if Mary was purified by divine dispensation, then a further purification at the Annunciation should be unnecessary. The same lack of consistency is evident in, for example, Paschasius Radbertus's discussions of Mary's purity and the explanation is probably the same in both cases: both authors wished to convey the same notion of Mary's immaculateness, but they had not developed a wholly rigorous explanation of it.

Mary is not mentioned by name in the remainder of the homily (which deals with Jerusalem as the *visio pacis*, the offering in the temple, Simeon and Christ as light) until we reach the end, where she is briefly alluded to in the concluding prayer. With strict orthodoxy, the homilist prays to both God and Mary for God's forgiveness of sin: 'Biddan we urne Dryhten ælmihtigne 7 sancta Marian þæt he us forgife . . .'[47] The epithets used of Mary at the beginning of the homily indicate an exalted view of her ethical purity, but she is not presented as a model to be emulated, as is Simeon.

Ælfric's homily begins with an adaptation of Bede's explanation of the law of purification, then continues with a paraphrase of the pericope for the day, Luke II.22–32 (to which he adds Luke II. 32–40 at the end of the

---

[46] See above, pp. 22–3.

[47] *The Vercelli Homilies*, ed. Szarmach, p. 53: 'Let us pray to our almighty Lord and St Mary that he should grant us . . .'

text). His translation of the pericope departs from Luke in some details, notably in its treatment of the Virgin: where Luke relates the story in the plural, with Mary and Joseph as subjects, Ælfric consistently mentions Mary only, emphasizing her importance: 'Nu wæs ðeah-hwæðere þæt halige mæden MARIA, Cristes moder, Godes beboda gemyndig'[48] and 'seo halige Maria com ða to ðam temple mid þam cilde'.[49] The first of these quotations is the only hint, and that a very slight one, that Mary voluntarily submitted herself to the law, although both Bede[50] and Haymo,[51] whom Ælfric uses later in the homily, offer this traditional explanation of why Mary underwent purification. In the homily proper, Ælfric follows Bede's homily on the purification, Augustine's *Sermo* ccclxx[52] and Haymo's homilies *In circumcisione domini* and that for *Dominica infra octauam natiuitatis domini*[53] and he develops the portrayal of Simeon, the themes of pride, the offering, Simeon's prophecy, Anna, the three estates of virginity, widowhood and marriage and Christ's nature, ending with an explanation of the candlelit procession on the feast-day. Only in his treatment of Simeon's prophecy of the sword which was to pierce Mary's heart does Ælfric concentrate on the Virgin and to do this he departs from the sources he is using in this homily and turns to a text which he also used as source in the *Catholic Homilies I* Assumption homily, Paschasius Radbertus's *Cogitis me*. Paschasius here explains that Mary's martyrdom was greater than that of other saints because, while they suffered physically, she, who loved Christ more than anyone else, suffered in her soul at seeing him on the cross.[54] Ælfric combines this with Haymo's comment that, although she did not doubt his resurrection,[55] she nevertheless could not witness her son on the cross without great sorrow:

Þa cwæð se ealda Symeon to ðære eadigan Marian, 'His swurd sceal ðurhgan ðine sawle.' Þæt swurd getacnode Cristes ðrowunge. Næs seo eadige Maria na ofslegen ne gemartyrod lichomlice, ac gastlice. Ðaða heo geseh niman hyre cild, and adrifan isene næglas þurh þa handa and þurh ða fet, and syððan mid spere gewundigan on ða siðan, þa wæs Cristes ðrowung hire ðrowung; and heo wæs mare

---

[48] *CH I*, p. 134. Thorpe translates: 'Now was, nevertheless, the holy maiden, Mary, Christ's mother, mindful of God's commands.'

[49] *CH I*, p. 136. Thorpe translates: 'And the holy Mary came then to the temple with the child.'

[50] *Opera homiletica*, ed. Hurst, p. 129.   [51] PL 118, 98.   [52] PL 39, 1657–9.

[53] PL 118, 90–107; 83–90.   [54] *Der Pseudo-Hieronymus-Brief ix*, ed. Ripberger, §90.

[55] PL 118, 86.

ðonne martyr, forðon þe mare wæs hyre modes þrowung þonne wære hire lichaman, gif heo gemartyrod wære. Ne cwæð na se Symeon þæt Cristes swurd sceolde þurhgan Marian lichaman, ac hyre sawle. Cristes swurd is her gesett, swa swa we cwædon, for his ðrowunge. Þeah ðe Maria gelyfde þæt Crist arisan wolde of deaðe, þeah-hwæðere eode hyre cildes þrowung swiðe þearle into hire heortan.[56]

The role of Mary is not, then, a dominant one in this text, although it is more marked than in any of Ælfric's sources, which stress the offerings and their significance more than any other feature of the pericope. The emphasis on Mary at the beginning and the choice of Paschasius Radbertus's exegesis of the sword, which focuses on the Virgin's special position in the hierarchy of the saints, shows some desire to concentrate on her. Had Ælfric wished to compose a more emphatically Marian text, however, he could have followed the Purification homily from the homiliary of Saint-Père-de-Chartres, the first half of which is made up of praise of Mary, although without any exegesis of the pericope. He most probably knew this text, as it is found in the hagiographic collection in London, British Library, Cotton Nero E. i, a collection with which Ælfric seems to have been familiar.[57] For Ælfric, then, like the composer of the Vercelli text, the feast of the Purification was mainly Christological and he ends the homily with a reference to Christ, while his practice with feasts which he regards as Marian is to conclude with an appeal to Mary.

Homilies for the feast of the Annunciation

Strikingly different is the text for the Annunciation amongst the *Blickling Homilies*.[58] This is based largely on a late sixth- or early seventh-century African Christmas homily, Pseudo-Augustine *Sermo* cxx,

---

[56] *CH I*, p. 146. Thorpe translates: 'Then said the old Simeon to the blessed Mary, "His sword shall pierce through thy soul." The sword betokened Christ's passion. The blessed Mary was not slain nor martyred bodily, but spiritually. When she saw her child taken and iron nails driven through his hands and through his feet, and his side afterwards wounded with a spear, then was his suffering her suffering; and she was then more than a martyr, for her mind's suffering was greater than her body's would have been, had she been martyred. The old Simeon said not that Christ's sword should pierce through Mary's body, but her soul. Christ's sword is here set, as we said, for his passion. Though Mary believed that Christ would arise from death, her child's suffering went, nevertheless, very deeply into her heart.'

[57] On Ælfric's use of this collection, see Zettel, 'Saints' Lives in Old English'.

[58] *BH*, pp. 2–13.

which perhaps found its way to England via Italy.[59] Although Fiedler wished to correct Morris's attribution of the Old English text from the Annunciation to Christmas (the rubric and the beginning of the homily are missing) and although the vernacular homily retains some passages which seem to point to Christmas as the occasion of delivery, nevertheless Morris is certainly correct: the order of the manuscript supports him, as does an original passage which was clearly intended for 25 March: 'On þissum dæge astag þæt heofonlice goldhord on þysne ymbhwyrft fram þæm heahsetle ure Gescyppendes þæt wæs Crist þæs lifgendan Godes Sunu, se com to wlitignesse 7 to weorþunge his bryde, þæt syndon þonne ealle halige.'[60] In context this passage must refer to Christ's descent into Mary's womb, not his birth.

Pseudo-Augustine *Sermo* cxx is essentially a meditation on Mary based largely on Luke's account of the Annunciation.[61] It begins with rejoicing over the coming of Christ to earth, as this has brought about a reversal of the Fall, continues with a lengthy contrast between Eve and Mary and then expounds the Annunciation text, before concluding with a celebration of Christ's Incarnation and exhortations to adore him. The exposition of Gabriel's greeting and Mary's reply, which makes up most of the text, is a meditative, prayerful one: each phrase of the biblical text is made the basis of praise of, or a request to, Mary and Gabriel to help bring about the salvation of man, who is the main speaker in the homily. Blickling I is, in general, a fairly close translation, although the translator made little attempt to preserve the very stylized, antithetically structured form of the Latin. It departs radically from the source only at the end, but there are alterations and omissions throughout which show that the translator worked in a critical spirit. Occasionally he substitutes original passages for omitted sections of the source and these new passages are often as learned and esoteric as the source itself.

While the meaning of the first paragraph (§ 2) of the Latin, with its contrasts between Eve and Mary, is preserved, in the next section begins a characteristic feature of the Old English homilist's handling of his source.

[59] The source was first noted by Fiedler, 'The Source of the First Blickling Homily'; on the date see Barré, *Prières anciennes*, p. 29.

[60] *BH*, p. 11. Morris translates: 'On this day descended the heavenly treasure into this world from the throne of our creator, that was Christ, the son of the living God, who came for the adorning and honouring of his bride, that is, all who are holy.'

[61] PL 39, 1984–7.

In the Latin there is an easy, unsignalled transition between the words of the angel and Mary and the supplications of mankind: the Blickling homilist either did not perceive that mankind was also an interlocutor in the text or chose not to retain this feature. Instead all direct speech is assigned to Gabriel or Mary or it becomes explanation rather than speech. Where all of these options are impossible, passages are dropped in the Old English. Thus, for example, while the Latin quotes Gabriel's greeting at the Annunciation and then continues with an appeal by mankind to the Virgin, in the Old English this becomes an explanation rather than a prayer:

Benedicta, inquit, *tu inter mulieres*, quae uitam et uiris et mulieribus peperisti. Ede, inculpabilis femina, inuiolabilem uirum; et sic et feminam saluabis et uirum. Mater generis nostri poenam intulit mundo; genitrix Domini nostri salutem et feminae gessit et uiro . . .[62]

He cwæþ se engel to hire, 'Wes þu gebletsod betuh eall wifa cynn; forþon se wæstm þines innoþes is gebletsad.' On þæs engles wordum wæs gehyred þæt þurh hire beorþor sceolde beon gehæled eall wifa cynn 7 wera. Seo æreste modor þyses menniscan cynnes wræcwite middangearde brohte, þa heo Godes bebodu abræc; 7 on þis wræcwite aworpen wæs . . . ond nu þeos halige fæmne Sancta Maria brohte eallum geleaffullum þæs bletsunga 7 ece hælo.[63]

The change here from imperative to third person indicative alters the purport of the Latin and the translation avoids the 'saluabis' which, with perhaps dubious theological propriety, is addressed to Mary. This has the appearance of a deliberate modification, correcting the excessive enthusiasm of the source which here attributes to the Virgin that which should be ascribed to Christ alone. Similarly, where in the Latin another quotation from Gabriel is followed again by the entreaties of mankind that Mary should consent to the Incarnation and thus save the captive world, in the

[62] PL 39, 1985: 'Blessed, he said, are you amongst women, who gave birth to life for both men and women. Give birth, blameless woman, to a hallowed man; and thus you will save both woman and man. The mother of our race introduced punishment to the world; the mother of our Lord bore salvation for woman and man.'

[63] *BH*, p. 5. Morris translates: 'The angel said to her, "Blessed be thou among all women, for blessed is the fruit of thy womb." In the words of the angel was heard, that through her offspring should be healed all man and womankind. The first mother of mankind brought affliction into the world when she broke God's behests, and into this affliction was she cast . . . and now this holy virgin Mary brought to all believers these blessings and eternal salvation.'

Old English what is retained of this passage becomes part of Gabriel's speech and other parts are omitted. Thus Gabriel, rather than mankind, implores:

Eft he cwæþ, 'Openige nu þin se fægresta fæþm 7 se clæna, 7 sy þæt geteld aþened þines innoðes, 7 seo onblawnes þære heofonlican onfæþmnesse sy gewindwod on þe. Ond seo gecyndelice hætu þurh þæt mægen þas Halgan Gastes seo gestilleþ on þe, 7 sy þin þæt fæþmlice hrif mid eallum fægernessum gefrætwod. Seo readnes þære rosan lixeþ on þe, 7 seo hwitnes þære lilian scineþ on þe, 7 mid eallum missenlicum afeddum blostmum sy se Cristes brydbur gefrætwod.'[64]

The next part of the same speech seems to have troubled the translator and the most extreme statement of Mary's responsibility for the salvation of the world is omitted. In the Latin even God awaits Mary's consent: 'Deus in porta est, angelum quem moraris exspectat. O beata Maria, saeculum omne captiuum, tuum deprecatur assensum; te Domino mundus suae fidei obsidem fecit, per te parentum suorum iniurias abstergi deprecatur.'[65] The first of these sentences is omitted entirely in the Old English and the second, still assigned to Gabriel rather than man, is mistranslated, with a confusion of subject and object which does, however, stress, more than the Latin, God's direction of the course of salvation: 'Eala þu eadige Maria, eall þeos gehæft-world bideþ þinre geþafunga; forþon þe God þe hafaþ to gisle her on middangearde geseted, 7 Adames gylt þurh þe sceal beon geþingod.'[66] The following entreaty to Gabriel is again omitted, including another description of God attendant on Mary's consent: 'loquere festinus

[64] *BH*, p. 7. Morris translates: 'And again he spoke: "Open now thy fairest and pure bosom, and let the tabernacle of thy womb be expanded, and let the inspiration of the heavenly embrace be blown into thee; and the natural heat, through the might of the Holy Ghost, shall be quiescent in thee, and let thy expansive womb be decked with all adornments. The redness of the rose glitters in thee, and the whiteness of the lily shines in thee; let Christ's bride-bower be adorned with every variety of flowers that are produced."'
[65] PL 39, 1986: 'God is in the entrance, he waits for the angel whom you delay. O blessed Mary, all the captive world prays for your assent; the world has made you a hostage of its faith in the Lord, through you it prays that the wrongs of its parents may be wiped away.'
[66] *BH*, p. 9. Morris translates: 'O thou blessed Mary, all this captive world awaits thy consent; for God has appointed thee as a surety here in this world, and through thee shall intercession be made for Adam's guilt.'

ad Mariam: 'Usquequo moraris, o uirgo, nuntium festinantem? Intuere Deum in coeli me uestibulo sustinentem . . .'[67]

The Blickling homilist also showed his independence in more fundamental ways: §5 of the Latin, for example, is a complex, rather obscure passage of which the translator retains only the *Magnificat*, substituting instead an exhortation to love Mary and God: 'Lufian hie nu forþon eall wifa cynn 7 wera, 7 hie weorðian, wordum 7 dædum f[or. . .] mycel bewreah, heo onfeng on hire medmycclan bosm God Fæder Sunu, þone ne magon befon heofon and eorþe. Lufian we urne Sceppend . . .'[68] Instead of the appeal to Gabriel, the vernacular homily inserts the common explanation of Gabriel's name as 'Godes strengo', or 'fortitudo Dei', found, for example, in Bede.[69] The homilist then turns, as he himself indicates, to the gospel for the detail of Mary's fear: 'Þonne cyþeþ se godspellere þæt seo eadige fæmne Sancta Maria forhtode, 7 bifigendre stefne eaðmodlice ondswarode, 7 þus cwæþ: "Ic eom Drihtnes þeowen, geweorþe me æfter þinum wordum." Eala hwæt þær wæs fæger eaðmodnes gemeted on þære a clænan fæmnan. Se engel hire sægde þæt heo sceolde modor beon hire Scyppendes, 7 heo hie sylfe to ðeowene genemde.'[70] This emphasis on Mary's humility, which is foreign to *Sermo* cxx, is very reminiscent of Bede: 'Magnam quippe humilitatis constantiam tenet quae se ancillam sui conditoris dum mater eligitur appellat.'[71] It is significant that, although the translator rejected some of the more extreme implications of the source, his own additions nevertheless stress Mary's importance.

The final section of the Latin consists of a passage in which the bridal imagery, hitherto used of the Incarnation, is changed into an image of the

[67] PL 39, 1986. 'Say quickly to Mary: "How long, o virgin, do you delay the hastening angel? Look at God in the entrance of heaven delayed by me . . ."'

[68] BH, p. 5. Morris translates: 'Therefore, let all mankind love and honour her with word and with deed – because . . . she concealed much, she received into her humble bosom the son of God the Father, whom heaven and earth are unable to comprehend. Let us love our creator . . .'

[69] *Opera homiletica*, ed. Hurst, p. 15.

[70] BH, p. 9. Morris translates: 'Then the evangelist informs us that the blessed virgin St Mary was affrighted, and with trembling voice meekly replied and thus said, "I am the handmaiden of the Lord, be it unto me according to thy word." O what beautiful meekness was there found in the ever pure virgin! The angel said to her that she should be the mother of her creator, and she called herself a "handmaiden".'

[71] *Opera homiletica*, ed. Hurst, p. 20: 'Certainly she maintains great constancy in humility who calls herself a handmaiden when she is chosen as mother of her creator.'

union of Christ and the church, sealed by the Crucifixion, and exhortations to rejoice and to honour all those associated with the Incarnation. The Old English simplifies the beginning of this somewhat, retaining the first three Latin exhortations, but departing from the source to continue the series with an exhortation to honour Mary: 'Weorþian we Sancta Marian; forþon þe heo is us to herianne 7 to eadgienne, forþon þe heo engla þreatas eadige bodedon; swa is to lyfenne þæt englas hie georne beheoldan of þam dæge þe hie wiston þæt heo seo eadige Maria geeacnod wæs of þæm Halgan Gaste.'[72] It is significant that the author here breaks free of his source with a reference to Mary suited to the feast of the Annunciation, as if this were the point on which he particularly wished to show his independence. The passage also echoes one of the antiphons in *De laude Dei*: 'Beatam praedicant omnes angeli, cui angelorum et hominum regem procreare donatum est.'[73]

The remainder of the Old English homily has no connection with Pseudo-Augustine *Sermo* cxx and seems to have been added by the homilist. The image of the Virgin as Solomon's bed, with which it continues, is a most uncommon one, showing that the homilist must have been a man of esoteric learning:

On hire wæs gefylled þætte on Cantica Canticorum wæs gesungen, 7 þus gecweden: 'Salomones reste wæs mid weardum ymbseted, þæt wæs mid syxtigum werum, þæm strengestum þe on Israhelum wæron 7 anra gehwylc hæfde sweord ofer his hype for nihtlicum ege' – Eno nu hwæt wæs seo Salomones ræste elles buton se halga innoð þære a clænan? Þone innoþ geceas 7 gesohte se gesibsuma cyning ure Drihten Hælend Crist. Ac hwæt mænde þæt syxtig wera strongera þe þær stondende wæron ymb þa reste for nihtlicum ege? Þæt wæs þonne þæt seo halige fæmne wæs ymbseald mid þon heofonlican campweorode engla þreatas to healdenne; forþon þe hie wiston þæt on hire eardode se heofonlica cyning, swa þonne þa heofonlican englas sceldað 7 healdað ealle halige sawla on þære se gesibsuma cyning eardað.[74]

---

[72] *BH*, p. 11. Morris translates: 'Let us honour St Mary, for we ought to praise and bless her, because hosts of angels called her blessed. So must we believe that angels earnestly beheld her from the day that they knew that the blessed Mary had conceived of the Holy Ghost.'

[73] Constantinescu, 'Alcuin et les "libelli precum"', p. 50: 'All angels proclaim her blessed, to whom it was granted to beget the king of angels and men.'

[74] *BH*, p. 11. Morris translates: 'In her was fulfilled what was sung in the Song of Songs, thus saying: "Solomon's bed was surrounded by guards, that is by sixty strong men, the strongest that were in Israel, and each of them has a sword girt to his hip, on account of the terror of the night." Now then what was Solomon's bed else but the holy womb of

The image is taken from the Song of Songs III. 7–8, which was associated with the Virgin from a very early date. Jerome and Ambrose both applied epithets from the Song of Songs to Mary and Ambrose declared that what it said of the church could also be applied to her.[75] But after Ambrose this interpretation was rarely used, and Bede, for example, said that the text could not be explained in a Marian sense. The interpretation did not die out completely, however, and the Song of Songs was used for readings on Marian feasts from the ninth century, at the latest. In this way, the identification of Mary with the bride was kept alive.

No Western exegete, however, seems to have commented on this verse. The Syrian Ephrem (*ob.* 373) did explain the bed as Mary, but he considered that the sixty strong men referred to the words of scripture, not to angels.[76] Aponius, a Syrian by origin who worked in Italy at the beginning of the fifth century, is far closer to the Old English text: in his *In canticum canticorum* he interprets the verse as referring mainly to Christ and the church, but adds:

Hic ergo pacificus sibi hunc lectulum de uirga, quae egressa est de radice Iesse, fabricauit in Virgine Maria, super quam decumbens, humiliando se, hominibus loqueretur. Super quem lectulum confirmat Isaias propheta septiformem requiescere spiritum, qui proculdubio Deus est; qui etiam super animam sibi obedientem, sibique coniunctam requiescere comprobatur. In sexaginta uero fortissimis ambientibus lectulum, Angelorum erga eum ministeria demonstrauit.[77]

the ever pure virgin? The peace-loving king, our Lord Jesus Christ, chose and sought that womb. But what meant the sixty strong men who were standing about the bed for fear of nightly alarm? That was when the holy virgin was encompassed with the heavenly hosts of angels for protection, because they knew that in her abode the heavenly king. So then the heavenly angels shield and guard all holy souls in which the king of peace abides.'

[75] See Ohly, *Hohelied-Studien.*

[76] In a passage translated by Livius, *The Blessed Virgin*, pp. 95–6.

[77] PL Supplementum, ed. A. Hamman (Paris, 1958) I, 887: 'Here, therefore, the peacemaker has formed for himself in the Virgin Mary this bed of the rod which has sprung from the root of Jesse, upon which, lying down in humility, he may speak to men. On this bed the prophet Isaiah asserts that the sevenfold spirit rests, who without doubt is God, who also is proved to rest in the soul obedient to him and joined to him. Truly the sixty most strong men surrounding the bed represented the ministry of the angels towards him.'

The Old English translator could well have known Aponius: he seems to have been known by Bede[78] and an Anglo-Saxon manuscript containing his *In canticum canticorum* survives from the first half of the eighth century (Boulogne, Bibliothèque municipale, 74). If so, then the homilist would have had to have been thoroughly acquainted with the text, as it interprets the Song of Songs mainly with reference to Christ and the church. Interestingly, the immediately preceding verse of the Song of Songs, to which this verse is a reply, was used in the ninth century in Corbie as a reading on the feast of the Assumption.[79] We do not know what the readings for Marian feasts were in the ninth century in England, but it is very probable that they were similar to those in Gaul. While the homilist here emphasizes the Marian interpretation of the Song of Songs, he also alludes to the identification with the church, in his reference to angels guarding all souls in which Christ dwells and in the following sentence, where Christ comes to earth to beautify his bride, the church. The homilist's knowledge of and use of both levels of exegesis suggest a high degree of sophistication.

The conclusion of the homily is notable especially for its emphasis on Christ's and Mary's humility and purity, and she, the *regina Domini*, is presented as a model to be emulated: 'Forðon we sceolan eall ure lif on eaþmodnesse healdan, æfter þære bysne þære halgan Godes cyningan . . .'[80] The homilist recalls Mary's reply to Gabriel in a passage very similar to that which he had introduced independently earlier in the text: 'þæt wæs anrædlicu eaþmodnes þæt heo sylf hie þeowen nemde, 7 hire cyðde se engel þæt heo wæs gecoren to meder hire Scyppende; 7 he hire cyþde þæt heo wæs seo eadgeste ofer eall wifa cynn.'[81] The whole of the rather wandering section has the appearance of an addition by the Old English homilist, anxious to draw a moral at the end of the text. The theme of humility has virtually no place in the source, figuring only in the quotation from the *Magnificat*, but here it is introduced halfway through the

---

[78] Ohly, *Hohelied-Studien*, p. 52.

[79] As is clear from *Cogitis me*, in *Der Pseudo-Hieronymus Brief IX*, ed. Ripberger, §§45–7, 57, 59, 88–9, 91–2, 95 and 100.

[80] *BH*, pp. 11–13. Morris translates: 'Therefore we must lead our whole life in meekness after the example of the holy queen of God . . .'

[81] *BH*, p. 13. Morris translates: 'That was undoubted humility when she called herself "handmaiden", and the angel had announced to her that she was chosen as the mother of her creator, and had made known to her that she was the most blessed above all womankind.'

text and in this concluding section. This last passage also acts as a corrective to the enthusiastic depiction of Mary as dominant redemptress and presents a picture much closer to the humble handmaiden of the bible. The elimination of the suggestion that even God awaits Mary's permission, which could be interpreted as a limitation of his omnipotence and omniscience, also accords with these alterations.

The Blickling translator's alterations and additions suggest some unease with his source and he would probably have been far happier with the type of source chosen by Ælfric for his Annunciation homily in *Catholic Homilies I*.[82] This text comments on the pericope for the feast, Luke 1.26–38, to which is added a short commentary on the Visitation, probably because it would otherwise not have found a place in the scheme of readings covered in the *Catholic Homilies* and because Ælfric wished to comment on the main events of New Testament history within his two series, even where the readings indicated in his lectionary had to be altered for this purpose.[83] The two main sources, as Förster pointed out, are Bede's homilies 1.3 and 1.4, assigned to the Wednesday and Friday in the week before Christmas in Paul the Deacon's homiliary, Ælfric's principal source-collection in the *Catholic Homilies*.[84]

The homily opens with a summary of the background to man's need for redemption and Old Testament prophecies of Christ's birth from a virgin, Isaiah VII.14 and Ezechiel XL.1, interpreted, as was commonplace, as a prophecy of Mary's virginity *ante, in* and *post partum*. Ælfric then translates the pericope before turning to Bede, whose sentiments on the beginning of man's salvation, with the contrast between Eve and Mary, he translates closely.[85] Bede's structure of a running gloss on the reading is followed, explaining why Joseph was needed and commenting on Gabriel's greeting: here Ælfric's omissions and substitutions all result in a concentration on Mary's role as mother of God. While Bede interprets 'gratia plena' as a reference to Mary's vow of virginity, comments that she merited to behold Gabriel because she strove to imitate the angelic life and alludes to her giving birth to Christ,[86] Ælfric retains from this only the explanation of Mary's fullness of grace as being the result of her divine motherhood. For Bede's interpretation of 'Dominus tecum', Ælfric substitutes a Christo-

---

[82] *CH I*, pp. 192–205.

[83] See my thesis, 'The Cult of the Virgin Mary', pp. 330–2, on the pericope.

[84] Förster, 'Über die Quellen von Ælfric's exegetischen Homilae Catholicae', p. 20.

[85] *Opera homiletica*, ed. Hurst, p. 14.   [86] *Ibid.*, p. 16.

logical reason, the source for which seems to be the hymn *Quem terra pontus*, assigned to Marian feasts in Anglo-Saxon hymnals,[87] and he then takes over the source's gloss on 'benedicta tu in mulieribus', which again dwells on Mary's role as mother of God, thus producing a sequence of descriptions of the Virgin in relation to Christ:

Se engel grette Marian, and cwæð, þæt heo wære mid Godes gife afylled, and þæt hyre wæs God mid, and heo wæs gebletsod betwux wifum. Soðlice heo wæs mid Godes gife afylled, forðon ðe hire wæs getiðod þæt heo ðone abær þe astealde ealle gifa and ealle soðfæstnyssa. God wæs mid hire, forðan ðe he wæs on hire innoðe belocen, seðe belicð ealne middangeard on his anre handa. And heo wæs gebletsod betwux wifum, forðan ðe heo, butan wiflicre bysnunge, mid wlite hyre mægðhades, wæs modor þæs Ælmihtigan Godes.[88]

Ælfric then adopts Bede's passage on Christ's true humanity and true divinity and explains Israel and Jacob, before going on to comment on Mary's reply to Gabriel, pointing to a vow of virginity on her part even before the Annunciation. His description of the Virgin's purification by the Holy Spirit again comes from Bede and there is no trace of, for example, Paschasius Radbertus's attempt to prove Mary's sinless birth: 'Heo wæs swa ofersceadewod þæt heo wæs geclænsod and gescyld wið ealle leahtras, þurh mihte ðæs Halgan Gastes, and mid heofenlicum gifum gefylled and gehalgod.'[89] Ælfric concludes his treatment of the Annunciation pericope with an illustration of Mary's humility. Where Bede says simply: 'Magnam quippe humilitatis constantiam tenet quae se ancillam sui conditoris dum mater eligitur appellat',[90] he expands: 'Micel eadmodnys wunode on hyre mode, þaþa heo ðus cleopode. Ne cwæð heo na, Ic eom Godes modor, oððe, Ic eom cwen ealles middangeardes, ac cwæð, "Ic eom

---

[87] For the text of this hymn, see Gneuss, *Hymnar und Hymnen*, p. 347; for its use, see pp. 62 and 64.

[88] *CH I*, pp. 196–8. Thorpe translates: 'The angel greeted Mary, and said that she was filled with God's grace, and that God was with her, and she was blessed among women. Verily she was filled with God's grace, for it was permitted her to bear him who instituted all grace and all truth. God was with her, for he was shut in her womb who compasses the whole earth with one hand. And she was blessed among women, for she, without female example, with the beauty of maidenhood, was mother of the almighty God.'

[89] *CH I*, pp. 198–200. Thorpe translates: 'She was so overshadowed that she was purified from and shielded against all sins, by the power of the Holy Ghost, and with heavenly grace filled and hallowed.'

[90] *Opera homiletica*, ed. Hurst, p. 20: 'Certainly she maintains great constancy in humility who calls herself a handmaiden when she is chosen as mother of her creator.'

Godes þinen"; swa swa us mynegað þæt halige gewrit, þus cweðende, "Þonne ðu mære sy, geeadmed þe sylfne . . ." [91] For Ælfric, 'cwen ealles middangeardes' is evidently a title as self-evident as *Dei genetrix*, although Bede never designates Mary *regina*.

Ælfric then relates the visitation story and expounds the *Magnificat* very briefly, with little reference to the Virgin. Where Bede ends both his source-homilies with prayers to God, Ælfric ends his with a prayer directly to Mary, asking her to intercede for man: 'Uton biddan nu þæt eadige and gesælige mæden Marian, þæt heo us geðingige to hyre agenum Suna and to hire Scyppende, Hælende Criste, seðe gewylt ealra ðinga mid Fæder and mid þam Halgum Gaste, a on ecnysse.' [92] Bede, therefore, remains in the patristic tradition and does not address prayers directly to Mary, while Ælfric is obviously influenced by the insular and Carolingian prayers to the Virgin.

Homilies for the feast of the Assumption

While the Blickling Annunciation homilist seems to have been striving to make a possibly dubious text more conventional, the author of Blickling XIII, for the Assumption of the Virgin, strove for the opposite. This long text consists of a combination of a complete apocryphon, *Transitus* C, and part of a second, *Transitus* B2, combined in such a way as to give a very full account of the spiritual and corporal assumption of Mary. [93] *Transitus* C originally affirmed the full corporal assumption of the Virgin, ending with an account of angels putting Mary's soul back into her body when it was taken to paradise three days after her death. [94] Because it was controversial, this conclusion was often altered and the issue of a corporal assumption fudged: it is clear that the Blickling XIII homilist worked with such an altered text, in which body and soul were not reunited, and equally clear

[91] *CH I*, p. 200. Thorpe translates: 'Great humility dwelt in her mind, when she thus cried. She said not, I am the mother of God, or, I am queen of the whole world, but said, "I am God's handmaid"; as the holy writ admonishes us, thus saying, "When thou art great, humble thyself."'

[92] *CH I*, p. 204. Thorpe translates: 'Let us now pray the blessed and happy Virgin Mary, that she intercede for us to her own son and Creator, Jesus Christ, who governs all things with the Father and the Holy Ghost, ever to eternity.'

[93] See the two studies by R. Willard, 'On Blickling Homily XIII'; 'The Two Accounts of the Assumption'; and my 'Blicking Homily XIII Reconsidered'.

[94] See above, pp. 10–11.

that this did not at all suit his taste. Not only did he add to the end of his first source a second account, which offers a very detailed description of the corporal assumption, but he also introduces several other 'assumptions' as a result of the numerous mistranslations in this very deficient text, unconsciously revealing what could be said to amount to an obsession with the subject. Altogether, five assumptions, either of Mary's body or soul, can be counted in the text. While we cannot be certain that it was the author of Blickling XIII who joined the two *Transitus* texts, as some Latin versions also combine two texts, the clumsiness of the transition is very much in keeping with the numerous other faults which can be attributed to the translator, and the combination, therefore, is probably his work also.

As an account of the apocryphal events, Blickling XIII is bewildering, mainly because of the translator's poor Latinity: sentences are confused, biblical allusions are unrecognized and consequently mangled, the basic narrative is obscured and 'whenever there is a long speech and particularly if this speech contains a quotation from something said previously, the translator is sure to lose his way, to re-interpret the matter, and to make a conversation or narrative account out of direct speech'.[95] A good example of the determination to narrate the Assumption is found in a passage near the beginning of the text, where the apostles tell Mary how they were brought to her house on clouds: 'Sic omnes apostoli exposuerunt quemadmodum unusquisque de locis suis ubi praedicabant diuina praeceptione fuerunt rapti et ibidem sunt depositi.'[96] The Blickling version of this, despite the lack of any justification in the source, anticipates the assumption of the Virgin to paradise: 'swa anra gehwylc þara apostola biþ geseted to his synderlicre stowe þæt he bodige his godcundnesse 7 hire geeacnunge. 7 þa apostolas tugon hie up 7 hie gesetton on þæm fægran neorxna wange'.[97] Numerous other unedifying passages arise from the translator's incompetence, demonstrated perhaps best of all in the version of the *Magnificat* which concludes the text. As Willard has shown, this extra-

[95] R. Willard, 'The Testament of Mary: The Irish Account of the Death of the Virgin', *Recherches de théologie ancienne et médiévale* 9 (1937), 341–64, at 347.

[96] *Analecta Reginensia*, ed. Wilmart, §14: 'And all the apostles explained how every single one had been snatched by divine precept from the places where they were preaching and were set down in that place.'

[97] *BH*, p. 143. Morris translates: 'And so each of the apostles is appointed to his separate place, that he should proclaim his divinity and her conception. And the apostles drew her up and placed her in the beautiful paradise.'

ordinary rendering, 'somewhat farsed by blending with the beatitudes',[98] totally reverses the spirit of the canticle. While the Blickling I author attempted to introduce an emphasis on Mary's humility into his source, the Blickling XIII writer makes the Virgin 'appear as *dom-georn* and as *tirhwæt* as any figure in heroic tradition, so that she cries out like a prima donna hungry for publicity, demanding that the Lord extol her soul and make sure that all generations call her blessed'.[99] Somewhat incongruously, the text then ends with a meek request that Mary intercede with Christ: 'Ac utan we biddan þa fæmnan Sancta Marian þæt heo us sy milde þingere wið urne Drihten Hælendne Crist ondweardes rædes 7 eces wuldres: to þæm us gefultumige ure Drihten.'[100] Like the *Magnificat*, this is not part of *Transitus* B2, but it is possible that the version from which the translator was working had such a prayer: the version of *Transitus* C in the English manuscript, Cambridge, Pembroke College, 25, for example, adds a series of antiphons for the feast of the Assumption on to its text and finishes: 'Et ipsa intercedat pro nobis ad Dominum Iesum Christum, et mereamur uitam possidere aeternam per omnia s.s.' (117v). It is difficult to be sure from Blickling XIII what the Marian views of the translator were. Only one thing is abundantly clear: his eagerness to describe the assumption itself, which he anticipates and repeats. In doing so, he completely disregards the changes introduced in his version of *Transitus* C, which had been revised throughout to eliminate the corporal assumption, and he produces a text which even the authors of the Latin apocrypha might have refused to acknowledge as their own.

The second Old English *Transitus* text is preserved in Cambridge, Corpus Christi College 41, an eleventh-century copy of the Old English Bede given to Exeter by Leofric, into which a mid-eleventh-century hand transcribed homilies, liturgical material and other miscellaneous items.[101] The six homilies form a wild and extravagant collection, with a marked interest in apocryphal material. The adding hand may have belonged to a secular priest, who perhaps worked in the neighbourhood of Glaston-

---

[98] Willard, 'An Old English Magnificat', p. 5.   [99] *Ibid.*, p. 17.

[100] *BH*, p. 159. Morris translates: 'But let us entreat the Virgin St Mary to be a merciful advocate with our Lord Jesus Christ of present benefits and of eternal glory: and thereto may our Lord aid us.'

[101] *Three Homilies from CCCC 41*, ed. Grant, pp. 18–31.

bury,[102] and he could presumably have used the texts for preaching, although the way in which they are written, around the margins of the Bede, would not have facilitated reading aloud. The Assumption text is an abbreviated version of *Transitus* B2, which otherwise follows the source very closely and is a far superior production to Blickling XIII. The sections which have been shortened consist mainly of speeches: the angel's last speech to Mary, Mary's prayer on Mount Olivet and some of the speeches in the episode where the Jews attempt to burn her body. Such a straightforward translation of the Latin source tells us little about the translator's attitude towards the Virgin, other than the fact that he was not averse to reading an apocryphal account relating her corporal assumption in great detail.

In contrast to these two anonymous homilies, Ælfric's two texts for the Assumption deliberately avoid the apocryphal texts. His first homily for the feast is based mainly on the Pseudo-Jerome letter *Cogitis me*, to which two Mary miracles are added.[103] This letter was probably written in the first half of the ninth century and is now generally attributed to Paschasius Radbertus.[104] It is a deliberate forgery, the author professing to address Paula and Eustochium in Bethlehem, but it immediately became popular and it was included in homiliaries, amongst them Ælfric's source-collection, Paul the Deacon, and in collections of saints' lives. The structure of Paschasius Radbertus's tract is a rather rambling one. He begins by describing the circumstances which led to the composition of the tract, then deals with Mary's life after the Ascension, before breaking into praise of her. Paschasius Radbertus continues with a commentary on Gabriel's greeting at the Annunciation and on some of the antiphons for the feast of the Assumption, then describes some of the reasons for Mary's especially glorious spiritual assumption. A long digression on the Incarnation follows, then come more reasons for the Virgin's assumption and praise of her. The tract ends with exhortations to imitate Mary.

Ælfric's version of *Cogitis me* is a drastically abbreviated one and it is interesting to see what he included and omitted. Of the 117 paragraphs in Ripberger's edition of *Cogitis me*, Ælfric uses 26 and in a very different order to that of the source. He omits altogether the long digression *de fide incarnationis Christi* (§§53–81) and other passages relating more to the

---

[102] C. Hohler (reviewing Grant, *CCCC 41: The Loricas and the Missal*), *MÆ* 49 (1980), 275–8, at 275.

[103] *CH I*, pp. 436–55.   [104] *Der Pseudo-Hieronymus-Brief IX*, ed. Ripberger.

Incarnation than the assumption, the exposition of Gabriel's greeting at the Annunciation, almost all of the frequent exhortations to imitate Mary and the long description of her humility given in connection with these, the reasons why Mary was superior even to the angels and Paschasius Radbertus's humility formulas. Ælfric includes most of the other points, but more briefly, and he reorganizes them to give a more logical progression. Thus he moves from Christ's entrusting of Mary to John, to her life after the Ascension, then to her death and possible justifications for her corporal assumption, to the reasons for her especially glorious spiritual assumption and an account of this, finishing with a description of her virtues and exhortations to rejoice and praise. Ælfric's work thus presents a more coherent structure than *Cogitis me*, which is more digressive and frequently interrupted by praise and exhortation.

Ælfric begins with an introduction to the work of Jerome and to this letter in particular, then takes the famous first phrase, *Cogitis me*, turning to §7 of the Latin for the remainder of the sentence. The warning against the apocrypha also comes from here:

Witodlice ge neadiað me þæt ic eow recce hu seo eadige Maria, on ðisum dægðerlicum dæge to heofonlicere wununge genumen wæs, þæt eower mædenlica heap hæbbe þas lac Ledenre spræce, hu þes mæra freolsdæg geond æghwylces geares ymbryne beo aspend mid heofonlicum lofe, and mid gastlicere blisse gemærsode sy, þylæs þe eow on hand becume seo lease gesetnys ðe þurh gedwolmen wide tosawen is, and ge þonne þa gehiwedan leasunge for soðre race underfon. [105]

Paschasius Radbertus's caution is in the tradition of Adamnan, Bede and Ambrosius Autpertus, all of whom professed the same cautious agnosticism with regard to the fate of Mary's body. [106] Ælfric, however, seems to go beyond the source in his condemnation of the apocrypha: *gedwolmen* is the word he normally uses of heretics and *seo lease gesetnys* and *þa gehiwedan leasunga* suggest that he thought the legend completely false, rather than just dubious.

[105] *CH I*, pp. 436–8. Thorpe translates: 'Verily ye compel me to relate to you how the blessed Mary, on this present day was taken to the heavenly dwelling, that your maidenly society may have this gift in the Latin speech, how this great festival, in the course of every year, is passed with heavenly praise, and celebrated with ghostly bliss, lest the false account should come to your hand which has been widely disseminated by heretics, and ye then receive the feigned leasing for a true narrative.'

[106] See above, pp. 14, 16–19 and 20–21.

Ælfric then recounts how Mary was commended to John the Evangelist's care, comments on the particular appropriateness of a virgin being entrusted to another virgin and relates how she lived after the Ascension: 'Se heah-engel Gabriel hi ungewemmede geheold, and heo wunode on Iohannes and on ealra þæra apostola gymene, on þære heofonlican scole, embe Godes æ smeagende, oðþæt God on þysum dæge hi genam to ðam heofonlican þrymsetle, and hi ofer engla weredum geufrode.'[107] This last sentence is an excellent example of how Ælfric in this text combines short sections from different parts of the source, translating them very carefully (cf. §§ 14, 20, 38). He goes on to deal with the fate of Mary's body, drawing on *Cogitis me*, §7–12, but not including all of Paschasius Radbertus's possible justifications for a corporal assumption. Paschasius Radbertus cites the case of John the Evangelist, of whom it was said that only manna was found in his tomb, of those who rose with Christ and of David. In adducing the case of John the Evangelist, he implies that the account of his death is on the same level as the account of Mary's assumption: 'Quod et de beato Iohanne euangelista eius ministro, cui uirgini a Christi uirgo commissa est, plurimi asseuerant, quia in sepulchro eius, ut fertur, nonnisi manna inuenitur, quod et scaturrire cernitur. Verumtamen quid horum uerius censeatur, ambigimus; melius tamen Deo totum, cui nihil impossibile est, committimus, quam aliud temere definire uelimus auctoritate nostra, quod non probamus.'[108] Ælfric, however, had translated the apocryphal *Acta Iohannis* in *Catholic Homilies I*, and this was the text from which the report concerning manna was taken. He presumably, therefore, had no doubts about its authenticity and his suppression of this reference also implies this. Ælfric probably accepted the text because he was ignorant of any explicit condemnation of it. His rejections

---

[107] *CH I*, p. 440. Thorpe translates: 'The archangel Gabriel held her uncorrupted, and she continued in the care of John and of all the apostles, in the heavenly company, meditating on God's law, until God, on this day, took her to the heavenly throne, and exalted her above the hosts of angels.'

[108] *Der Pseudo-Hieronymus-Brief IX*, ed. Ripberger, §10: 'Because concerning the ministry of the blessed John the Evangelist, to whom as a virgin the virgin was entrusted by Christ, very many strongly assert that in his sepulchre, it is said, nothing but manna is found and it is perceived to be full of it. Nevertheless, we are in doubt as to which of these is to be considered more true; it is better, however, that we entrust everything to God, to whom nothing is impossible, than that we should wish rashly to define differently by our own authority that which we cannot prove.'

of, for example, the *Visio Pauli* and an episode in the *passio* of St Thomas are based, though loosely, in each case on the authority of St Augustine.[109] This suggests that his acceptance or rejection of legendary matter was based on whether or not he had any cause to doubt its authenticity rather than on any independent suspicion of its theological content. Paschasius Radbertus's second parallel, that of those resurrected at Christ's death (Matt. XXVII. 52–3) is the only one included by Ælfric. The theological controversy over the fate of the bodies of those released from hell was a long and involved one, some holding that they died again, others that they were brought to heaven.[110] Ælfric seems, to judge from other texts, to have believed that the souls and bodies of those released from hell were brought to heaven[111] and this belief in the eternal resurrection of the bodies is evident also in his treatment of this section of *Cogitis me*. There is no Old English equivalent of Paschasius Radbertus's 'certum non habemus' and 'nonnulli' is changed to the stronger 'forwel manige lareowas', so that the Old English gives a much more positive impression than the Latin, not entirely suited to the parallel with the Virgin's putative resurrection: this has then to be presented in rather more positive terms than Ælfric's introduction might lead one to expect: 'Ne wiðcweðe we be þære eadigan Marian þa ecan æriste, þeah, for wærscipe gehealdenum geleafan, us gedafenað þæt we hit wenon swiðor þonne we unrædlice hit geseþan þæt ðe is uncuð buton ælcere fræcednysse.'[112]

Ælfric then moves on to some of the reasons why Mary's spiritual assumption was particularly splendid, translating §§49–52 of *Cogitis me* closely, then summing up the importance of the feast-day with passages from §45 and §51: 'Ðes symbel-dæg oferstihð unwiðmetenlic ealra oðra halgena mæsse-dagas swa micclum swa þis halige mæden, Godes modor, is unwiðmetenlic eallum oðrum mædenum. Ðes freolsdæg is us gearlic, ac

---

[109] The *Visio Pauli* is rejected in *CH II*, p. 190, and the episode concerning St Thomas in *CH II*, p. 298. Both passages are discussed by Godden, 'Ælfric and the Vernacular Prose Tradition', pp. 101–2 and in his 'Ælfric's Saints' Lives and the Problem of Miracles', *Leeds Studies in English* 16 (1985), 83–100, at 87–90.

[110] See the discussion by H. Zeller, 'Corpora sanctorum: eine Studie zu Mt. XXVII.52-3', *Zeitschrift für katholische Theologie* 71 (1949), 385–463.

[111] See, for example, *CH I*, pp. 26–8; *Homilies of Ælfric*, ed. Pope I, 275.

[112] *CH I*, p. 440. Thorpe translates: 'Nor do we deny the eternal resurrection of the blessed Mary, though for caution, preserving our belief, it befits us that we rather hope it, than rashly assert what is unknown without any danger.'

he is heofonwarum singallic.'[113] Quotations from the Song of Songs and Paschasius Radbertus's commentary applying them to the Virgin's assumption follow in the Old English, drawing on §47 and §88ff. of the Latin. In this progression of ideas can be seen very clearly the type of organization which Ælfric imposes on the loosely structured Latin tract: he advances logically from the reasons for Mary's glorious spiritual assumption to a description of it, then translates §90 of the Latin, which argues that Mary was greater than the martyrs (a passage also used in the Purification homily).[114]

Ælfric continues with a paragraph drawing on one of the most ardent sections of *Cogitis me*, which anticipates the prayers of Anselm in its intensity: 'Quam si diligentius aspicias, nihil uirtutis est, nihil speciositatis, nihil candoris gloriae, quod ex ea non resplendeat.'[115] This, however, is only palely reflected in the Old English: 'Nis heo nanes haliges mægnes bedæled, ne nanes wlites, ne nanre beorhtnyssse; and forðy heo wæs ymbtrymed mid rosan and lilian, þæt hyre mihta wæron mid mihtum underwriðode, and hire fægernys mid clænnysse wlite wære geyht.'[116] Ælfric goes on to mention the many dwellings in the house of God (§§96 and 97), then returns to §23ff. with exhortations to rejoice, closing this paragraph with a liturgical borrowing:

Ic bidde eow, blissiað on ðyssere freols-tide: witodlice nu to-dæg þæt wuldorfulle mæden heofonas astah, þæt heo unasecgendlice mid Criste ahafen on ecnysse rixige. Seo heofenlice cwen wearð to-dæg generod fram ðyssere manfullan worulde. Eft ic cweðe, fægniað forðan ðe heo becom orsorhlice to ðam heofonlicum botle. Blissige eal middangeard, forðan ðe nu to-dæg us eallum is ðurh hire geearnunga hæl geyht. Þurh ure ealdan modor Euan us wearð heofonan rices geat belocen, and eft ðurh Marian hit is us geopenod, þurh þæt heo sylf nu to-dæg wuldorfullice inn-ferde.[117]

---

[113] *CH I*, p. 442. Thorpe translates: 'This festival excels incomparably all other saints' mass-days, as much as this holy maiden, the mother of God, is incomparable with all other maidens. This feast-day is to us yearly, but to heaven's inmates it is perpetual.'

[114] See above, pp. 221–1.

[115] *Der Pseudo-Hieronymus-Brief IX*, ed. Ripberger, §92: 'If you consider most diligently, there is nothing of excellence, nothing of beauty, nothing of the glory of brightness, which does not shine brightly from her.'

[116] *CH I*, pp. 444–6. Thorpe translates: 'She is void of no holy virtue, nor any beauty, nor any brightness; and therefore was she encircled with roses and lilies, that her virtues might be supported by virtues, and her fairness increased by the beauty of chastity.'

Ælfric ends his adaptation of *Cogitis me* with more exhortations to rejoice in the feast of the Assumption (§§24, 35 and 36), refusing to translate further because of the difficulty: this is probably a reference to the long section on the Incarnation, as the remainder of *Cogitis me* does not otherwise differ significantly from what Ælfric has already included. Much of what he omitted is, however, better suited to the convent audience for which Paschasius Radbertus wrote than the more general, mixed audience for which the Old English homily seems to have been composed.

The remainder of the Old English is composed of an account of the miracle of Theophilus and of the death of Julian, related to illustrate that the Virgin is the greatest consolation and help to Christians. In detaching the Julian narrative from the *Vita Basilii*, combining it with the Theophilus miracle and placing both in the context of a Marian homily, Ælfric was doing something quite new. The same two miracles (with, unlike Ælfric, the death of Julian narrated very briefly and the Theophilus legend more expansively) were included in a homily by Fulbert of Chartres (*ob.* 1028) for the Nativity of Mary, but this text almost certainly post-dates Ælfric's.[118] Ælfric (and Fulbert) were thus anticipating the twelfth-century collections of miracles of the Virgin which follow the same procedure on a larger scale, and they are earlier than the larger English collections which Jennings regards as innovative:

Previously, most of these stories were either incorporated into the lives of Saints to enhance the Saints' reputations or – in the eleventh century – they were put into collections compiled to emphasize the sanctity of such places as Coutances, Laon, Roc-Amador, Soissons, Pierre-sur-Dive or Chartres. Now, however, through the writings of Anselm of Bury, Dominic of Evesham and William of Malmesbury, the emphasis was placed unmistakably on the Virgin. In Dominic's collection this change can be seen quite clearly. No longer are St Basil, St

---

[117] *CH I*, p. 446. Thorpe translates: 'I pray you, rejoice in this festival: verily now to-day that glorious maiden ascended to heaven, that she, ineffably exalted with Christ, may for ever reign. The heavenly queen was to-day snatched from this wicked world. Again I say, rejoice that she, void of sorrow, is gone to the heavenly mansion. Let all the earth be glad, for now to-day, through her deserts, happiness is increased to us all. Through our old mother Eve the gate of heaven's kingdom was closed against us, through Mary it is opened to us, by which she herself has this day gloriously entered.'

[118] Canal, 'Texto crítico', pp. 60–1.

Cyriacus or St Odo of Cluny given predominance, but the Virgin's miracles have been extracted from their Lives and she has been raised to primary importance.[119]

The two miracles which Ælfric narrates resemble each other in that in both Mary's help is implored in a church dedicated to her and in both she herself appears in glory to those appealing for her intercession. As most of the monasteries of the Benedictine reform were dedicated to Mary, the care with which Ælfric notes the dedication in each miracle can hardly be accidental and the efficacy of praying to Mary in a church dedicated to her would not have gone unnoticed with his audience.

Ælfric tells the Theophilus legend very briefly, but includes all the salient points, stressing Mary's role:

Sum man wæs mid drycræfte bepæht, swa þæt he Criste wiðsoc, and wrat his hand-gewrit þam awyrgedan deofle, and him mannrædene befæste. His nama wæs Theophilus. He ða eft syððan hine beðohte, and ða hellican pinunge on his mode weolc; and ferde ða to sumere cyrcan þe wæs to lofe ðære eadigan Marian gehalgod, and ðær-binnan swa lange mid wope and fæstenum hire fultumes and ðingunge bæd, oðþæt heo sylf mid micclum wuldre him to com, and cwæð, þæt heo him geðingod hæfde wið þone Heofenlican Deman, hire agenne Sunu.[120]

The miracle of the death of Julian, brought about by the martyr Mercurius at Mary's command, is translated from 'an anonymous unabridged tenth-century Latin version'[121] of the *Vita Basilii*, a text included as a whole in Ælfric's *Lives of Saints*, with some differences in detail. The homily concludes with an exhortation to appeal to the Virgin to intercede, which follows naturally from the two miracles: 'Mine gebroðra ða leofostan, uton clypigan mid singalum benum to ðære halgan Godes meder, þæt heo us on urum nydþearfnyssum to hire Bearne geðingige. Hit is swiðe geleaflic þæt

---

[119] J. C. Jennings, 'The Origins of the "Elements Series" of Miracles of the Virgin', *Medieval and Renaissance Studies* 6 (1968), 84–93, at 90–1.

[120] *CH I*, p. 448. Thorpe translates: 'Some man was so deluded by magic that he denied Christ, and wrote his chirograph to the accursed devil, and entered into a compact with him. His name was Theophilus. He afterwards bethought himself, and revolved in his mind the torment of hell; and went then to a church that was hallowed to the praise of the blessed Mary, and therein so long with weeping and fasts prayed for her aid and intercession, till she herself with great glory came to him, and said, that she had interceded for him with the heavenly judge, her own son.'

[121] L. H. Loomis, 'The Saint Mercurius Legend in Medieval England and in Norse Saga', in *Philologica: The Malone Anniversary Studies*, ed. T. A. Kirby and H. B. Woolf (Baltimore, 1949), pp. 132–43, at 134.

he hyre miceles ðinges tiðian wylle, seðe hine sylfne gemedemode þæt he ðurh hi, for middangeardes alysednysse, to menniscum men acenned wurde . . .'[122] Ælfric's affirmation of the Virgin's powers of intercession is characteristically sober and is very similar to the ending of the Christmas text in *Catholic Homilies II*. While two of the anonymous homilies declare that Mary can ask her son for whatever she wishes, Ælfric limits this to 'þæt he hyre miceles ðinges tiðian wylle'.[123]

The Assumption is the only Marian feast for which Ælfric composed two homilies, a most unusual duplication among his texts for saints' days. Only St Stephen (presumably because his feast was regarded as part of the Christmas season) and the feast of SS Peter and Paul likewise receive a homily in each series. This can be explained either as a result of the importance of the feast in Ælfric's eyes or as the consequence of a wish to provide an exposition of the gospel pericope for the day, Luke x. 39–42. This pericope does not mention the Virgin and Ælfric therefore chose as source in the First Series a text which deals at length with her assumption, but he seems to have been unwilling to omit the pericope which, as he says, is nevertheless customarily read at her mass. Most of this Second Series homily, therefore, is a commentary on the Martha and Mary story in Luke, for which Ælfric follows two sermons by Augustine, *Sermones* ciii and civ.[124] He begins and ends, however, with references to the object of the feast-day, saying at the beginning that he has already translated Jerome's epistle on the assumption 'þurh þone he adwæscte ða dwollican gesetnysse þe samlærede men sædon be hire forðsiðe'.[125] He returns to this subject at the end with a passage very reminiscent of the First Series text: 'Hwæt wille we eow swiðor secgan be ðisum symbeldæge. buton þæt maria cristes modor wearð on ðisum dæge of ðisum geswincfullum middanearde genumen up to heofenan rice. to hire leofan suna. ðe heo on life abær. mid ðam heo blissað on ecere myrhðe. a to worulde.'[126] He goes on to refer to the authorities who have cautioned

---

[122] *CH I*, pp. 452–4. Thorpe translates: 'My dearest brothers, let us call with constant prayers to the holy mother of God, that she may intercede for us in our necessities with her son. It is very credible that he will grant much to her, who vouchsafed through her to be born a human being for the redemption of the world . . .'

[123] See above, p. 119.   [124] *CH II*, pp. 255–9.

[125] *Ibid.*, p. 255: 'through which he suppressed the heretical compositions which half-learned people related about her death'.

[126] *Ibid.*, p. 259: 'What more shall we say to you about this feastday except that Mary, Christ's mother, was on this day taken from this toilsome world up to the kingdom of

against the apocryphal accounts of the assumption and his attitude is the same as found in these sources, one of discreet agnosticism:

Genoh is geleaffullum mannum to rædenne and to secgenne þæt þæt soð is. and feawa is ðæra manna ðe mage ealle ða halgan bec. ðe þurh godes muð. oððe ðurh godes gast gedihte wæron fulfremedlice þurhsmeagan; Læte gehwa aweg ða dwollican leasunga ðe ða unwæran to forwyrde lædað. and ræde gehwa oððe hlyste þære halgan lare ðe us to heofenan rice gewissað. gif we hi gehyran wyllað. [127]

The authorities Ælfric mentions are Augustine, Jerome and Gregory, who have, he says, rejected the works of the heretics who 'be heora agenum dihte oððe be swefnum fela lease gesetnyssa awriton'[128] but which are, nevertheless, available in Latin and in English. As Barré suggests, Augustine here is probably to be identified with Ambrosius Autpertus, whose sermon for the Assumption circulated under the name of Augustine (*Sermo* ccviii): in this text Ambrosius Autpertus objected to the apocrypha in terms very similar to Ælfric's.[129] The Jerome is almost certainly Paschasius Radbertus's *Cogitis me* and Gregory is probably also Paschasius, who is credited with three Pseudo-Ildefonsian sermons on the Assumption.[130] In the manuscripts these are attributed variously to Gregory, Isidore, Leo, Maximus of Turin and others. They show the same distrust of the apocrypha as *Cogitis me*. Ælfric, therefore, seems to have known quite a range of texts for this feast which opposed the apocrypha and it is clear, especially from the reference to English apocrypha, that he was also acquainted with the apocryphal sources themselves: he was not simply imitating authorities he respected in alluding to these texts, but had personal knowledge of what he repudiated. The homily concludes with a prayer which seems to be based on a respond for the feast of the Assumption ('Ecce exaltata es super choros angelorum, intercede pro nobis ad Dominum Deum nostrum'):[131]

heaven, to her beloved son, whom she had borne in life, with whom she rejoices in eternal joy, for ever and ever.'

[127] *Ibid.*, p. 259: 'It is enough for believers to read and to say what is true and there are few people who can completely comprehend all the holy books which were dictated by God's mouth or through God's spirit. Let everyone put away the heretical lies which lead the unwary to destruction and let everyone read or listen to the holy teaching which will guide us to the kingdom of heaven, if we wish to hear it.'

[128] *Ibid.*: 'according to their own dictation or according to dreams wrote many false compositions'.

[129] Barré, 'La croyance à l'assomption corporelle', p. 76, n. 58.   [130] *Ibid.*

[131] PL 78, 798: 'Behold you are exalted above the choirs of angels; intercede for us to the Lord our God.'

'Uton nu geornlice biddan. þa eadigan marian. þe nu todæg wæs ahafen. and geuferod. bufon engla ðrymme. þæt heo us ðingige. to ðam ælmihtigan gode. se ðe leofað and rixað. on ealra worulda woruld.'[132] The beginning and end of this text, therefore, effectively turn it into a Marian text, unlike its main sources.

Homilies for the feast of the Nativity of the Virgin

Like the legends concerning the death and assumption of the Virgin, the apocryphal texts on the birth and childhood of Mary were explicitly rejected by Ælfric. In *Catholic Homilies II* he bluntly refused to compose a homily for the feast of the Nativity of the Virgin, stating in a note appended to the homily for the sixteenth Sunday after Pentecost that he did not wish to relate the apocryphal story and that the gospel (the genealogy of Joseph at the beginning of Matthew) for the day was too difficult to expound:

Hwæt wylle we secgan ymbe Marian gebyrdtide. buton þæt heo wæs gestryned þurh fæder. and ðurh moder. swa swa oðre men. and wæs on ðam dæge acenned þe we cweðað Sexta Idus Septembris; Hire fæder hatte Ioachim. and hire moder Anna. eawfæste men on ðære ealdan æ. ac we nellað be ðam na swiðor awritan þy læs ðe we on ænigum gedwylde befeallon; Eac þæs dæges godspel is swiðe earfoðe læwedum mannum to understandenne. hit is eal mæst mid haligra manna naman geset. and hi habbað swiðe langsume trahtnunge. æfter ðam gastlican andgite. ði we hit lætað unsæd.[133]

This refusal is most unusual as Ælfric had set out to include in the *Catholic Homilies* texts for the feasts kept by the English people, of which the Nativity of the Virgin was one. His objection here is phrased in vague

---

[132] *CH II*, p. 259: 'Let us now eagerly entreat the blessed Mary, who today was raised up and elevated above the host of angels, that she intercede for us to almighty God, who lives and reigns for ever and ever.'

[133] *CH II*, p. 271; 'What shall we say about the time that Mary was born except that she was begotten by a father and a mother, just like other people, and was born on the day which we call the eighth of September? Her father was called Joachim and her mother Anna, righteous people according to the old law, but we do not wish to write any more about that lest we should fall into any heresy. This day's gospel is also very difficult for lay people to understand: it is for the most part fully composed of the names of holy men and they require a very long exposition according to the spiritual sense; therefore we leave it unexplained.' See my discussion of this note in 'Ælfric and the Nativity of the Blessed Virgin Mary', pp. 286–94.

terms and he clearly accepted the legends to some extent, as he takes from them the names of Mary's parents and the detail of their righteousness: he seems, in fact, to have been unsure about what precisely was wrong with these texts, knowing only that he should avoid them. Ælfric himself would almost certainly have been acquainted with the apocrypha as all of the different Latin versions available seem to have been circulating in England in the late Anglo-Saxon period: a Latin translation of the first part of the Greek *Proteuangelium* is included in the Bury St Edmunds homiliary, Cambridge, Pembroke College 25; the *Gospel of Pseudo-Matthew* forms part of the collection of saints' lives in BL, Cotton Nero E. i., a manuscript which contains Ælfric's chief source-collection for his saints' lives; and the *De natiuitate Mariae* is included in the versions of Paul the Deacon in Durham, Cathedral Library, A. III. 29 (a manuscript which must be in some way connected with Winchester, as it has texts for the two feasts of Swithun, one for Birinus and one for Æthelthryth) and Salisbury, Cathedral Library 179. These manuscripts are all monastic homiliaries and legendaries and it would seem, therefore, that Ælfric was here setting his face against texts which were part of the pious reading-matter of his monastic confrères. He himself seems to have been uneasy about the legends because they were forbidden by authorities which he respected: of these, he knew at least one, the Gelasian decree, contained in a manuscript associated with Ælfric, Boulogne-sur-Mer, Bibliothèque municipale, 63.[134] They were not reckoned as part of the canon; Ælfric, therefore, was unwilling to run the danger of heresy and chose to avoid all but the briefest mention, as he appears to have been unclear about the exact reason for their exclusion. He also regarded the pericope expositions available to him as unsuitable because of their difficulty and therefore omitted any text for the feast from the *Catholic Homilies*.

The *Catholic Homilies* were written during the years 989–95 and about ten years later Ælfric changed his mind on the question of providing a text for the feast of the Nativity of Mary. We do not know whether this happened in response to a request or was the result of Ælfric's own anxiety about the circulation of apocryphal texts: whatever the reason, he composed a long text for the feast, probably *c.* 1015–16, and inserted it in his revised edition of *Catholic Homilies I*, cancelling his earlier note in his

---

[134] On Ælfric and this manuscript, see E. N. Raynes, 'MS Boulogne-sur-Mer 63 and Ælfric', *MÆ* 26 (1957), 65–73.

revision of *Catholic Homilies II*.[135] This later text is most illuminating on
Ælfric's Marian views as he chooses as his main source a text which had no
prior connection with a feast of the Virgin and which is neither homily nor
biblical commentary, but an Augustinian tract written for female virgins,
De sancta uirginitate.[136] Only the first section of the Anglo-Saxon text,
entitled in the manuscripts *Natiuitas Sanctae Mariae Virginis*, deals with
Mary and the rest, entitled *De sancta uirginitate*, treats of virginity.

The first section of the text is very reminiscent of the note in *Catholic
Homilies II*, rehearsing Ælfric's fear of falling into some heresy if he were to
relate the story of Mary's birth:

> Men ða leofostan,   we synd gemyngode
> þurh ðyses dæges wurðmynt,   þe we wurðiað
> to lofe þære eadigan Marian,   eow nu to secgenne
> sum ðing be hyre,   beþam ðe us to onhagað.
> Ac we nellað secgan   be þære gesetnysse
> of ðam gedwylde,   þe gedwolmen setton
> be hyre acennednysse,   forðan þe hyt tocwædon
> þa wisan lareowas,   and be hyre forðsiðe,
> þe ða halgan boceras   forbudon to secgenne.[137]

As with the assumption apocrypha, Ælfric here declares that his objection
to the nativity apocrypha stems from authorities, 'wise teachers', who
forbade these legends. He then names the Virgin's parents once again,
again emphasizing their righteousness, declares that Mary gave birth to the
human and the divine Christ, and says that on this feast celebrating her
great merits, men appeal for her intercession with her son. He goes on to
explain that, while other saints are commemorated on the day of their birth
into eternal life (their death-day), only Christ, John the Baptist and the

---

135 *Angelsächsische Homilien und Heiligenleben*, ed. Assmann, pp. 24–48. On the date, see
Die Hirtenbriefe Ælfrics in altenglischer und lateinischer Fassung, ed. B. Fehr, Bibliothek der
angelsächsischen Prosa 9, reprinted with a supplementary introduction by P. A. M.
Clemoes (Darmstadt, 1966), pp. xlvi–liii, and on the homily's place in the revised *CH
I* see Clemoes, 'The Chronology of Ælfric's Works', p. 234.

136 PL 40, 395–428.

137 *Angelsächsische Homilien und Heiligenleben*, ed. Assmann, p. 24, lines 1–9: 'Beloved
people, we are reminded by the dignity of this day, which we honour in praise of blessed
Mary, to tell you now something about her, as it befits us. But we do not wish to recite
the narrative of the heresy which heretics composed about her birth, because wise
teachers have forbidden it, and about her death, which the holy scholars have forbidden
us to relate.'

Virgin are remembered on their human birth-days also: this, Ælfric says, is 'for ðam micclum mærðum   mancynnes alysednysse'.[138] He thus avoids any connection based on the miracles attending all three births, presumably as those associated with the Virgin's birth were known only from the apocrypha, and avoids too the kind of connection Paschasius Radbertus draws between the sinlessness of all three at birth.[139]

The remainder of the homily is entitled *De sancta uirginitate* after Augustine's tract, but like much of Ælfric's later work in particular, it is a very free adaptation of its source, drawing on many other works for details and additions.[140] The first hundred lines, for example, are almost unparalleled in *De sancta uirginitate*, although their themes, Christ's double nativity, the church as bride of Christ and the church as virgin and mother, are common Augustinian ones. Ælfric's text was clearly written principally for a celibate monastic audience and it deals with the virgin faith and motherhood of the church; Mary as mother and virgin and the parallels between her and the church; freely offered vows of virginity; offerings in general; the differences between virgins, the married and the widowed; the danger of pride in virgins; the rewards of virginity; and the Beatitudes. Much of the text has nothing to do with the Virgin, but in dealing with her, Ælfric concentrates on the parallels between Mary and the church, both virgins and mothers, Mary physically and the church spiritually, and on Mary's freely offered vow of virginity, which makes her a model for all the celibate. Ælfric retains Augustine's treatment of the episode where Christ rejects his mother and brother, explaining it as an indication that Mary was more blessed in her faith than in her physical maternity: this faith was manifested in her vow of virginity, which is evident from her reply to Gabriel:

> God mihte hi hatan,   þæt heo heolde hyre mægþhad
> to swilcere acennednysse,   ac wæs swa þeah
> hyre willa mærlicor,   þæt heo wolde hyre sylf
> hyre mægðhad behatan   þam heofonlican gode,
> ærðan þe heo wiste,   hwæne heo acennan sceolde,
> and wæs gode gehalgod   be hyre agenum cyre,
> na swylce geneadod   mid nanre hæse,

[138] *Ibid.*, p. 26, line 48: 'for the great glory of mankind's redemption'.
[139] See above, p. 22.
[140] For a detailed discussion, see my 'Ælfric and the Nativity of the Blessed Virgin Mary'.

eallum mædenum to bysne,   þe on mode geceosað,
þæt hi for Cristes lufon   on clænnysse þurhwunion. [141]

While Mary alone is physically mother and virgin, other virgins can spiritually share in her experience if they do the will of God, as the entire church is mother of Christ's members through baptism. In his text for the Nativity of the Virgin, therefore, Ælfric avoids all mention of Mary's life but for two incidents from the bible and concentrates on the most fundamental Marian belief, her virginal motherhood, and on the analogies between Mary and the church in this respect. This stress on Mary's virginity undoubtedly owes much to Ælfric's views on the necessity of celibacy for priests and monks, a theme to which he returns frequently throughout his work, and is connected with Mary's role in the reformed monasticism of which Ælfric was a primary exponent.

Despite Ælfric's strictures, part of the apocryphal *Gospel of Pseudo-Matthew* was translated into Old English and is extant in three manuscripts, all of which are largely composed of Ælfrician texts. [142] The apocryphon has been adapted to form a reading for the feast of the Nativity of the Virgin and it is assigned to the feast in all three manuscripts. [143] Although the textual affiliations are with the Latin type which Gijsel terms PI, a type already circulating by the year 800, [144] the Old English text is probably eleventh-century. Of the manuscripts one is from the third quarter of the eleventh century and the other two are twelfth-century. While Ælfric refers to vernacular Assumption apocrypha, he does not appear to know of a vernacular version of the Nativity apocrypha, and the text is also missing from some earlier manuscripts where we might expect

---

[141] *Angelsächsische Homilien und Heiligenleben*, ed. Assmann, p. 32, lines 198–206: 'God could have commanded her that she should preserve her virginity for such a birth, but her desire, however, was more glorious, in that she herself wished to vow her virginity to the heavenly God, before she knew to whom she would have to give birth, and she was consecrated to God by her own choice, not compelled thus by any command, as an example to all virgins who choose in their minds that they will persevere in purity for love of Christ.'

[142] *Ibid.*, pp. 117–37.

[143] Oxford, Bodleian Library, Hatton 114; Cambridge, Corpus Christi College 367, pt. I; and Oxford, Bodleian Library, Bodley 343.

[144] Gijsel, *Die unmittelbare Textüberlieferung des sogenannten Pseudo-Matthäus*, pp. 18–20.

it, had it been available (CCCC 198, for example).[145] While it is notoriously difficult to attempt to date a type of piety, the additional prologue and epilogue seem relatively advanced and, therefore, rather late. The prologue consists of an exhortation to honour Mary's nativity, three explanations of her name and explications of these:

Men ða leofestan! Weorþian we nu on andweardnysse þa gebyrdtide þære eadigan fæmnan Sancta Marian. Seo wæs cennystre ures drihtnes hælendes Cristes. Nu is hyre nama gereht hlæfdige oððe cwen oððe sæsteorra. Heo is hlæfdige gecweden, forðan þe heo cende þone hlaford heofonas and eorðan. And heo is cwen gecweden, forðan þe heo com of ðam æðelan cynne and of ðam cynelican sæde Dauides cynnes. Sæsteorra heo is gecweden, forðan þe se steorra on niht gecyþeð scypliðendum mannum, hwyder bið east and west, hwyder suð and norð. Swa þonne wearð þurh ða halgan fæmnan Sancta Marian gecyþed se rihte siðfæt to ðam ecan life þam ðe lange ær sæton on þeostrum and on deaþes scuan and on þam unstillum yðum þære sæ þises middaneardes. And a syððan wyston ealle halige þone fruman mid-daneardes and ende and heofona rices wuldor and helle wite. Nu wille we eow secgan be ðære gebyrde þære eadigan fæmnan Sancta Marian, hu seo geworden wæs and acenned.[146]

Domina, *regina* and *stella maris* are all Marian titles which are found from an early date. One of the first occurrences of *regina* is, in fact, in the *Gospel of Pseudo-Matthew* itself, in the scene in which the other virgins in jest call Mary their queen and are rebuked by the angel, who declares that prophets long ago proclaimed that she would be queen of the earth. *Domina* and *stella maris* can be found in Jerome, who seems to have been the originator of the etymology of Mary as *stella maris*:

---

[145] The CCCC 198 compiler chose Blickling XIII for the feast of the Assumption and it is natural to assume that he would have included an apocryphal narrative for the Nativity, had one been available to him.

[146] *Angelsächsische Homilien und Heiligenleben*, ed. Assmann, pp. 117–8: 'Beloved people! Let us now at this present time honour the nativity of the blessed virgin St Mary. She was the mother of our lord, Christ the Saviour. Now her name is interpreted *lady* or *queen* or *star of the sea*. She is called lady, because she gave birth to the lord of heaven and earth. And she is called queen, because she came from the noble race and the royal seed of the race of David. She is called star of the sea, because the star at night shows forth to seafarers where east and west, south and north are. Likewise then, through the holy virgin St Mary was the right way to eternal life made known to those who for a long time had sat in darkness and in the shadow of death and in the restless waves of the sea of this world. And ever since all the saints knew the origin and the end of the earth and the glory of the kingdom of heaven and the punishment of hell. Now we wish to tell you about the birth of the blessed virgin St Mary, how she came to be and was born.'

Mariam plerique aestimant interpretari, illuminant me isti, uel illuminatrix, uel smyrna maris, sed mihi nequaquam uidetur. Melius autem est, ut dicamus sonare eam stellam maris, siue amarum mare: sciendumque quod Maria, sermone Syro domina nuncepatur. [147]

Bede also takes over both meanings: 'Maria autem Hebraice stella maris Syriace uero domina uocatur et merito quia et totius mundi dominum et lucem saeculis meruit generare perennem'[148] and 'Nec praetereundem quod beata Dei genetrix meritis praecipuis etiam nomine testimonium reddit. Interpretatur enim *stella maris*. Et ipsa quasi sidus eximium inter fluctus saeculi labentis gratia priuilegii specialis refulsit'.[149] As is evident from these quotations, these early treatments of the *stella maris* image place the emphasis more on Christ than on Mary: she is a star because she bore the light of the world or because she reflects back his light. The same is true of the use of the image in Pseudo-Ildefonsus *Sermo I* (probably by Paschasius Radbertus):

Ipsa igitur stella maris, quam hodie coelum suis recepit sedibus, appellatur, quia secundum uerbum Hebraicum Maria ita interpretatur. Hinc agite, dilectissimae, ut lucifer ille qui nescit occasum, oriatur in cordibus uestris, dum in hoc saeculo estis. Nam mare praesens saeculum est, stella autem beata uirgo Maria, de qua ortus est ille per quem illuminatur omnis mundus. Hinc securius accedite ad laudem Virginis, et illuminamini, quoniam ipsa est per quam uera lux in mare huius saeculi refulsit. [150]

[147] PL 23, 842: 'And very many consider that the name Mary is to be explained *these enlighten me* or *illuminator* or *myrrh of the sea*, but I do not consider this right at all. But it is better that we should say she signifies *star of the sea* or *bitter sea*: and that it should be known that Mary is called lady in the Syrian language.'

[148] *In Lucae euangelium expositio*, ed. Hurst, p. 31: 'But Mary in Hebrew is called *star of the sea*, and, indeed, in Syriac *lady* and deservedly, because she deserved to give birth to the Lord of all the world and the perpetual light for the ages.'

[149] *Opera homiletica*, ed. Hurst, p. 15: 'We must not pass over the fact that the blessed mother of God bears witness by her special merits and even by her name. For it is interpreted *star of the sea*. And she, like an excellent star amidst the waves of the passing time, shone forth by grace of her special privilege.'

[150] PL 96, 241: 'She herself therefore is called the *star of the sea*, whom today heaven received into its abodes, because according to the Hebrew word Mary is thus interpreted. Henceforth act, most beloved ones, that the morning-star which knows no setting may rise in your hearts, while you are in this world. For the sea is the present world, the star on the other hand is the blessed Virgin Mary, from whom was born him through whom the whole world is illuminated. Henceforth approach more fearlessly the praise of the Virgin and be enlightened, since it is through her that the true light has shone brightly upon the sea of this world.'

However, even towards the end of the ninth century, the emphasis can be seen to be moving towards Mary, as in the hymn *Aue maris stella*:

> Aue maris stella,
> dei mater alma.
> atque semper uirgo.
> felix celi porta.
>
> Solue uincla reis.
> profer lumen cecis.
> mala nostra pelle.
> bona cuncta posce. [151]

By the eleventh century, we get a mini-allegory worked out from the image of the star, with a firm stress on Mary herself as the guiding light, as, for example, in the following passage from a sermon by Fulbert of Chartres for the Nativity of Mary:

Haec itaque electa et insignis inter filias, non fortuito quidem aut solo parentum placito ut plerique, sed diuina dispensatione nomen accepit, ita ut ipsa quoque uocabuli sui figura magnum quiddam innueret: interpretatur enim maris stella. Quid ergo mysticum haec interpretatio gerat, per similitudinem ostendamus. Nautis quippe mare transeuntibus, notare opus est stellam, haud longe a supremo celi cardine choruscantem, et ex respectu illius aestimare atque dirigere cursum suum, ut portum destinatum aprehendere possint. Simili modo, fratres, oportet uniuersos xpisticolas, inter fluctus huius saeculi remigantes, adtendere maris stellam hanc, id est Mariam, quae supremo rerum cardini deo proxima est, et respectu exempli eius cursum uitae dirigere. Quod qui fecerit non iactabitur uanae gloriae uento nec frangetur scopulis aduersorum, nec abssorbetur scyllaea uoragine uoluptatem, sed prospere ueniet ad portum quietis aeternae. [152]

[151] Quoted from *Facsimiles of Horae de Beata Virgine Maria*, ed. Dewick, col. 15: 'Hail star of the sea / Kindly mother of God / And ever-virgin / Happy gate of heaven. Loose the bonds of the guilty / Extend light to the blind / Expel our evils / Demand all blessings.'

[152] J. M. Canal, 'Texto crítico', pp. 58–9: 'She, therefore, chosen and distinguished amongst women, not by chance, it is true, or only at the pleasure of her parents, as is general, but by divine dispensation, received a name such that she might indicate also by the form of her name something great, for it is interpreted *star of the sea*. Therefore the mystery that this interpretation holds, we shall show by a simile. Certainly when sailors are crossing the sea, it is necessary to observe the star, shining not at all far from the highest pole of the sky, and in respect of that to estimate and direct their course, that they may be able to reach the harbour they have decided upon. Similarly, brothers, it is necessary for all Christians, rowing amidst the flood of this world, to turn towards this star of the sea, that is Mary, who is near to the pole of the highest God of the world,

The Old English represents a stage of development similar to that in Fulbert's sermon. It uses scriptural–liturgical reminiscences in expanding the image, but here it is Mary, not God, who directs those 'sedentibus in tenebris et umbra mortis' (Psalm CVII. 10).

The epilogue consists of a longer list of epithets and a prayer to Mary:

Wæs seo halige fæmne, swa we ær cwædon, of Iesses wyrtruman and of Dauides cynne, and heo wæs drihtnes modor, ures hælendes, and heo is hordfæt þæs halgan gastes and heo is cwen þæs heofonlican cyninges gecweden and heo is engla hiht and ealra manna frofor and fultum, forðan þe ealles middaneardes hælo þurh hi becom on þas woruld. And forðan hi nu englas eadigað and ealle þeoda and ealle cneorissa, gehwylc mancynnes geleafulra. And mid þisra bletsunga and herenyssa heo becom beforan þæt þrymsetl þæs heofonlican deman and beforan gesyhðe ealra haligra, þær heo nu dæghwamlice þingað for eall þis mennisce cynn. Ac uton we nu hi eadmodlice biddan, þæt heo us si milde mundbora and bliðe þingere to ðam heofonlican mægnþrymme. Nu we geare witan, þæt heo mæg æt hire þam deoran sunu biddan, swa hwæt swa heo wile, and beon ðingere to urum drihtne, þæt he us forgyfe gesibsum lif and ece eadignysse a butan ende. God us to ðam gefultumige![153]

Latin equivalents of the epithets applied to Mary here would be approximately the following: *Dei genetrix, sacrarium spiritus sancti, regina regis coelorum, spes angelorum, consolatio et adiumentum cunctorum, clemens protectrix/ interpellatrix, felix interuentrix.* Most of these can be found very early: *sacrarium spiritus sancti* can be found in the sermon *Legimus in ecclesiasticis*

and direct the course of their lives with regard to her example. Because whoever will have done so will not be tossed by the wind of vainglory nor broken by the rocks of the enemies, nor devoured by pleasure in the scyllean abyss, but will come successfully to the harbour of eternal rest.'

[153] *Angelsächsische Homilien und Heiligenleben*, ed. Assmann, pp. 136–7: 'The holy virgin, as we said before, came from the root of Jesse and the race of David, and she was mother of the Lord, our Saviour, and she is the treasure-chest of the Holy Spirit and she is called queen of the heavenly king and she is the hope of angels and the consolation and help of all men, because the salvation of all the earth entered the world through her. And therefore angels and all peoples and all generations, all the faithful of mankind, now call her blessed. And with this blessing and praise she came before the throne of the heavenly judge and into the sight of all the saints, where she now daily intercedes for all this human race. But let us now humbly ask her that she be a merciful advocate for us and gracious intercessor to the heavenly power. Now we know well that she can ask her beloved son for whatever she may wish, and be an intercessor to our Lord, that he may give us a peaceful life and eternal happiness for ever and ever. May God help us to attain that!'

historiis (ninth century);[154] *regina* from the sixth century onwards; *spes angelorum* itself is very uncommon, but already Alcuin uses, for example, *uitae spes maxime nostrae*;[155] *adiutrix* and *interpellatrix* are found in the Book of Cerne.[156] 'And forðan hi nu englas eadigað' obviously echoes the liturgy: 'Te laudant angeli . . .'[157] The power of asking her son for whatever she wants also seems to be an echo of one of the prayers to the Virgin in Cerne.[158] Despite the early parallels, the cumulative effect of this passage is more akin to, for example, the eleventh-century Winchester prayers than to the ninth-century Anglo-Latin texts. In particular, the description of Mary pleading before the throne of the judge seems later. The striking features of this passage are the overwhelming emphasis on Mary's powers of intercession and the total confidence in these powers. Except for the interesting and important prologue and epilogue, the Old English is almost entirely a faithful translation from the Latin. These additions, however, demonstrate a fervent devotion to and profound belief in Mary and are comparable to the eleventh-century prayers from Winchester. The Old English text, then, most probably comes from the eleventh century, and from one of the centres where devotion to the Virgin was flourishing.

Other texts

As well as objecting to the circulation of assumption and nativity apocrypha, Ælfric also took issue with another Marian belief, that Mary could save the souls of those condemned by Christ on the Last Day:

Sume gedwolmen cwædon þæt seo halige Maria cristes modor. and sume oðre halgan sceolon hergian æfter ðam dome ða synfullan of ðam deofle. ælc his dæl. Ac þis gedwyld asprang of ðam mannum. þe on heora flæsclicum lustum symle licgan woldon. and noldon mid earfoðnyssum þæt ece lif geearnian; Ne hopige nan man to ðyssere leasunge. Nele seo eadige Marian ne nan oðer halga lædan ða fulan. and þa manfullan. and ða arleasan. þe æfre on synnum þurhwunodon. and on synnum geendodon. into ðam clænan huse heofenan rices myrhðe. Ac hi beoð deoflum gelice. and on ecnysse mid deoflum on helle fyre cwylmiað; Ne mæg eal middaneard anum ðæra geðingian. þe crist þus to cweð; Discedite. . .[159]

---

[154] J. E. Cross, 'Legimus in ecclesiasticis historiis', p. 117.

[155] *Alcuini carmina*, ed. Dümmler, p. 325 (no. XII, line 2).

[156] See above, pp. 99 and 101.   [157] PL 78, 735.   [158] See above, p. 119.

[159] *CH II*, p. 333: 'Certain heretics said that the holy Mary, Christ's mother, and certain other saints will pluck the sinful from the devil after the judgement, each [taking] a

What Ælfric is here referring to is a belief, unique in this form to Anglo-Saxon England, which finds a place in several anonymous Old English texts: in Vercelli xv, a Last Judgement text, in an Easter homily found in CCCC 41 and CCCC 303 and, in a different form, in a Last Judgement homily in Oxford, Bodleian Library, Hatton 114.[160] In Vercelli, the souls are assembled for judgement and Mary, Michael and Peter in turn fall to Christ's feet and plead, Mary on the basis of her divine maternity, Michael on his lordship over heaven and Peter on his possession of the keys of heaven and hell: each is granted a third of the assembled souls and the remainder is then consigned to hell. The scene with the Virgin reads:

Þonne gesyhð ure leofe Hlæfdie sancta Maria, Cristes moder, þone earman heap 7 þone sarigan 7 þone dreorigan, 7 þonne ariseð heo mid wependre stefne 7 gefealleð to Cristes cneowum 7 to his fotum 7 heo swa cweð: 'Min Drihten Hælenda Crist, ðu þe gemedomadest þæt ðu wære on minum innoðe eardiende; ne forlæt ðu næfre þa deofla geweald agan ðus myclan heapes þines handgeworces.' Donne forgifeð ure Dryhten þryddan dæl þæs synfullan heapes þære halgan sancta Marian.[161]

The CCCC text is similar, but the scene here takes place after Christ has uttered his judgement, and each intercessor transfers his or her third of the sinners from Christ's left to his right side.[162] The Hatton text is rather confused, but it describes the judgement of an individual soul, with Mary pleading for it after it has been condemned: 'Þonne clypað Sancta Maria to hyre suna urum Drihtne Hælende Criste, þæt is se Nazarenisca Hælend, and heo cweð to him: "Min Drihten, hwæt, þu wast þæt þu to þinum

---

share. But this heresy originated with those people who wished to remain always in the grip of their corporal desires and did not wish to earn eternal life with hardships. Let no man have confidence in this lie. Neither the blessed Mary nor any other saint will wish to lead the impure and the wicked and the impious, who always persevered in sins and died in sins, into the pure dwelling of the joy of the kingdom of heaven. But they will be like devils and will suffer eternally in hell-fire with the devils. All the world cannot intercede for one of those to whom Christ will say thus: Discedite . . .'

160 See my discussion in 'Delivering the Damned'.

161 *The Vercelli Homilies*, ed. Szarmach, pp. 37–8: 'Then our beloved lady St Mary, Christ's mother, will see the wretched and sorrowful and sad troop and she will arise with a weeping voice and will fall to Christ's knees and to his feet and will say thus: "My Lord, the Saviour Christ, you humbled yourself in order to dwell in my womb; never allow the devils to have power over such a great company of your handiwork." Then our Lord will give the holy St Mary a third part of the sinful company.'

162 Hulme, 'The Old English Gospel of Nicodemus', p. 613.

gingrum gecwæde þeah hwylce eorðlice menn fram ðe gewiten hæfdon, gyf hi eft gecyrran woldon to þe, þæt hi wurdon englum gelice." '[163] This theme seems to derive ultimately from the *Apocalypse of Mary*, which describes how Mary and the apostles, directly after her assumption, were brought to what is called hell, so that they could view the torments of those in punishment. There, they and Michael plead for those in suffering, and the souls are granted a respite.[164] In the Old English this scene seems to have been transferred to a Last Judgement context, a transfer which we also find with other scenes in Anglo-Saxon, and this results in the theological unorthodoxy of the saints pleading for the damned. In its original context, the scene had no such implications and it is clear that the sinners for whom a respite is gained are not those doomed to eternal torment, but those suffering in purgatory, although it is not so named. This is why the Anglo-Saxon version of the theme also has to have a total release for the souls, not the temporary relief of the Latin, Greek and other versions: a respite has no meaning on Doomsday, when the eternal fate of the souls is being decided. This theme was not only influential in Old English prose, but it also exerted an influence over Anglo-Saxon artists, as can be seen from the depiction of Mary and Peter as intercessors at the Last Judgement in the Cambridge ivory and the use of these figures to point to a Last Judgement context in the New Minster Charter and the Winchester *Liber uitae*.[165]

Two versions of the 'Sunday Letter' similarly make use of Mary and other saints as intercessors, but here they avert the imminent destruction of the entire world.[166] It is possible that this theme, which is not restricted to Anglo-Saxon England, is also connected in some way with the *Apocalypse of Mary*.

In Blickling VII[167] and in a homily in Oxford, Bodleian Library, Junius 121,[168] both Easter texts, we find another aspect of Mary as intercessor.

---

[163] *Nuove omelie anglosassoni*, ed. Fadda, p. 49: 'Then St Mary will call to her son, our Lord, Christ the Saviour, that is the Nazarene Saviour, and she will say to him: "My Lord, lo, you know that you said to your disciples that, even if all men on earth had gone from you, if they wished to return to you, they would be like angels."'

[164] See my 'Delivering the Damned', p. 97, for the Latin version.

[165] See above, pp. 159 and 175–6.

[166] *Wulfstan: Sammlung der ihm zugeschriebenen Homilien*, ed. Napier, pp. 226–32 and R. Priebsch, 'The Chief Sources of Some Anglo-Saxon Homilies', *Otia Merseiana* I (London, 1899), 129–38.

[167] *BH*, pp. 82-97.   [168] See Fadda, 'De descensu Christi ad inferos'.

Both texts describe the Harrowing of Hell and in each of them Eve pleads with Christ for release from punishment, basing her appeal on her motherhood of Mary: 'Ic þe halsige nu, Drihten, for þinre þeowene, Sancta Marian, þa þu mid heofonlicum wuldre geweorþodest; hire innoþ þu gefyldest nigon monaþ mid ealles middangeardes weorþe; þu wast þæt þu of minre dehter, Drihten, onwoce; 7 þæt hire flæsc is of minum flæsce, 7 hire ban of minum banum. Ara me nu, min Drihten, for hire wuldres weorþmyndum . . .'[169] Each of these texts seems to have been translated independently from similar Latin material[170] and another Latin source of the same type seems to lie behind the entry for 26 March in the *Old English Martyrology*, where Eve again appeals to Christ in similar terms, though much abbreviated: 'Da ða hie gesawon his þæt beorhte leoht æfter þære langan worolde, þær Eua hine halsode for Sancta Marian mægsibbe ðæt he hire miltsade. Heo cweþ to him "Gemyne, min Drihten, þæt sèo wæs ban of minum banum, and flæsc of flæsce. Help min forþon."'[171] The poem *Christ and Satan*, too, although its treatment of the descent into hell is otherwise very different to that of the homilies, also includes an appeal by Eve,[172] and Campbell suggests that the poet may here be drawing from memory on a text close to the Blickling–Junius texts. The only Anglo-Latin witness to this theme is an *oratio* in the Book of Cerne which, however, seems to be incomplete.[173] It describes the descent into hell and ends with a speech by Eve, which, it is thought, must have extended beyond the point at which it now ends: it probably continued with a reference to Mary, as does the almost identical appeal in Blickling VII. All

---

[169] *BH*, p. 89. Morris translates: 'I entreat thee now, Lord, for the sake of thy servant St Mary, whom thou hast honoured with heavenly glory. Thou didst fill her womb for nine months with the prize of all the world. Thou knowest that thou, o Lord, didst spring from my daughter, and that her flesh is of my flesh, and her bone of my bones. Have mercy now upon me, Lord, for the honour of her glory.'

[170] See the discussion by Campbell, 'To Hell and Back'.

[171] *Das altenglische Martyrologium*, ed. Kotzor II, 46–7: 'When they saw his bright light after that dark age, Eve entreated him to have mercy on her because of her kinship with St Mary. She said to him: "Remember, my Lord, that she was bone of my bones and flesh of my flesh. Help me because of that."' See also Cross, 'The Use of Patristic Homilies', p. 117–20.

[172] *Christ and Satan*, ed. M. D. Clubb, Yale Studies in English 70 (New Haven, 1925), 26, lines 437–42.

[173] *The Book of Cerne*, ed. Kuypers, pp. 196–8; see also the discussion and edition of this text by Dumville, 'Liturgical Drama', pp. 375–88.

of these texts, then, bear witness to an interest in the Eve–Mary opposition, widespread in patristic texts.

Another text which, while not a Marian homily as such, was of importance in the history of the cult of the Virgin, is the life of Mary of Egypt, a translation of which is found in three eleventh-century Anglo-Saxon manuscripts.[174] This text was translated from Greek into Latin in the ninth century by Paul, a deacon of Naples, who also translated the legend of Theophilus. Both stories, as Barré points out, 'montraient, par un example saisissant, l'efficace et compatissante intervention de la mère du Sauveur dans la conversion des pécheurs les plus endurcis'.[175] The life of Mary of Egypt was of importance because, as well as illustrating God's mercy even to hardened sinners, it also provided examples of prayer to the Virgin. Mary, a prostitute who makes her way to Jerusalem and attempts to enter the temple there, is prevented by a divine force from gaining entrance and realizes that this is because of her sinfulness. She repents and prays to a statue of the Virgin.

Eala þu wuldorfæste hlæfdige þe þone soðan god æfter flæsces gebyrde acendest. geara ic wat þæt hit nis na gedafenlic. ne þæslic. þæt ic swa grimlice forworht eom. þæt ic þine anlicnysse sceawige. and gebidde mid swa mænigfealdum besmitenum gesihþum. þu wære symle fæmne oncnawan. and þinne lichaman hæbbende clæne. and unwemmed. forþon witodlice genoh rihtlic is me swa besmitenre fram þinre clænan ungewemmednysse beon ascirod. and fram aworpen. ac swa þeah-hwæðere forþan ðe ic gehyrde þæt god wære mann forðy gefremod þe þu sylf acendest. to þon þæt he þa synfullan to hreowsunge gecygede. gefultuma me nu ænegre ælces fylstes bedæled.[176]

She is then emboldened by 'þære arfæstan godes cennestran mildheortnysse' and enters the temple.[177] Mary of Egypt prays twice more to the

---

[174] *Ælfric's Lives of Saints*, ed. Skeat II, 2–53.   [175] Barré, *Prières anciennes*, p. 91.

[176] *Ælfric's Lives of Saints*, ed. Skeat II, 30. Skeat translates: 'Oh! thou glorious lady, who according to the birth of the flesh didst bear the true God, well I wot that it is not fitting nor meet that I, who am so grievous a sinner, should behold thy form, and should pray with looks that have been so repeatedly polluted. Thou wast ever known as a virgin, keeping thy body pure and undefiled; wherefore indeed it is very right that I who am so foul should be separated and cast out from thy pure virginity. Nevertheless, inasmuch as I have heard that the God whom thyself barest was made man for that very reason, that he might call sinners to repentance, assist me now, who am desolate and deprived of any help.'

[177] *Ælfric's Lives of Saints*, ed. Skeat II, 30. Skeat translates: 'the pity of the worthy mother of God.'

Virgin, before going to the Jordan and crossing the desert, as the Virgin directs her. As models, these prayers were enormously influential and, although the main point of the homily is to celebrate Mary of Egypt, the text also obviously glorifies the Virgin.

Ælfric's most interesting comments on Mary outside of the Marian homilies come in his Christmas text in *Catholic Homilies II*. Although it is a Christmas homily it is, as Ælfric says in the title, 'excerptus de testimoniis prophetarum' and many of the prophecies of Christ's birth naturally involve Mary. Ælfric again develops the parallel with the church: both are virgin mothers and Mary's physical maternity parallels the church's spiritual motherhood of all Christians. Mary's virginity is emphasized both because of its exemplary quality and because of its importance as a touchstone of orthodoxy. A correct understanding of Christ's double nature is impossible without an understanding of Mary's role and Ælfric cites the prophecy of the dry rod of Aaron to explain the virginal conception and quotes the supposedly virginal bees as a figure of Mary:

Nis nan wifhades mann hire gelica. for ði naðer ne ær ne siððan næs nan mæden þæt bearn gebære. and syððan mæden þurhwunode buton hire anre; Sindon þeahhwæðere sume gesceafta þe tymað buton hæmede. and bið ægðer ge seo moder mæden. ge seo dohtor þæt sind beon; Hi tymað heora team mid clænnysse; Of ðam hunige hi bredað heora brod. and beoð acennede þa geongan mid mægðhade. and ða yldran wuniað on mægðhade;[178]

This may have been derived, as Cross suggests, from Rufinus or Augustine,[179] but it could also have come from the liturgy. The text for the blessing of the candle on Easter Saturday in the Leofric Missal, for example, compares the Virgin and the bees: 'O uere beata et mirabilis apes, cuius nec sexum masculi uiolant, fetus non quassant, nec filii destruunt castitatem. Sicut sancta concepit uirgo maria, uirgo peperit, et

---

[178] *Ibid.*, p. 5: 'There is no woman like her; for neither before nor since was there a virgin who bore a child and afterwards remained a virgin, save her alone. Nevertheless, there are some creatures who propagate without intercourse and both mothers and daughters are virgins: these are bees. They bring forth their offspring in purity. From the honey they nourish their brood and the young are brought forth in virginity and the older ones remain virgins.'

[179] J. E. Cross, 'Ælfric and the Medieval Homiliary – Objection and Contribution', *Scripta Minora Regiae Societatis Humaniorum Litterarum Lundensis* 4 (Lund, 1963), 17.

uirgo permansit.'[180] The homily ends with a prayer to Mary, as is Ælfric's practice in Marian texts:

Uton beon eac gemyndige hu micelre geðincðe sy þæt halige mæden Maria cristes moder; Heo is gebletsod ofer eallum wifhades mannum. heo is seo heofenlice cwen. and ealra cristenra manna frofer and fultum; Ure ealde moder Eua us beleac heofenan rices geat. and seo halige Maria hit eft us geopenode. gif we hit sylfe nu mid yfelum weorcum us ne belucað; Micel mæg heo æt hire bearne abiddan. gif heo bið geornlice to gemynegod; Uton for ði mid micelre geornfulnysse hi gebiddan. þæt heo us ðingige to hire agenum bearne. se ðe is ægðer ge hire scyppend. ge hire sunu. soð god and soð mann an crist. se ðe leofað and rixað mid fæder. and mid halgum gaste. hi ðry an god a. on ecnysse; amen:-[181]

In another Christmas homily (Pope 1), Ælfric uses a passage from Quoduultdeus, who is not one of the main sources for this text, to show that Mary's virginity can be used to counter the Manichean heresy.[182]

Paschasius Radbertus's *Cogitis me*, Ælfric's source for his first Assumption text, is also used in his *Catholic Homilies I* text for the feast of All Saints, the main source for which is the sermon *Legimus in ecclesiasticis historiis*, where the section on Mary reads: 'Beata Dei genetrix et semper uirgo Maria, templum domini, sacrarium spiritus sancti, uirgo ante partum, uirgo in partu, uirgo post partum, presentis solemnitate diei, cum suis uirginibus, expers nullo modo credenda est.'[183] This is augmented in the Anglo-Saxon with several passages from *Cogitis me* (§§38–9), lending the whole a far more ardent air:

---

[180] *The Leofric Missal*, ed. Warren, p. 97: 'O truly blessed and miraculous bee, whose virginity neither males violate nor offspring shatter nor does motherhood impair your chastity. So the holy Mary conceived as a virgin, as a virgin she gave birth and remained a virgin.'

[181] *CH II*, p. 11: 'Let us be mindful of how great the dignity of the holy virgin Mary, Christ's mother, is. She is blessed above all women. She is the heavenly queen and the consolation and help of all Christian people. Our first mother Eve locked the gate of the heavenly kingdom against us and the holy Mary opened it again to us, if we ourselves do not lock it against ourselves by evil deeds. She can obtain much from her child, if she is eagerly reminded of it. Let us therefore pray to her with great eagerness that she may intercede for us to her own son, who is both her creator and her son, true God and true man, one Christ, who lives and reigns with the Father and the Holy Spirit, those three one God, for ever and ever.'

[182] *The Homilies of Ælfric*, ed. Pope 1, 213–14.

[183] Cross, 'Legimus in ecclesiasticis historiis', p. 117: 'Blessed mother of God and ever-virgin Mary, temple of the Lord, shrine of the Holy Spirit, virgin before birth, virgin in birth, virgin after the birth. It is not to be believed that she, with her virgins, would have no part in the solemnity of the present day.'

Eala ðu, eadige Godes cennestre, symle mæden Maria, tempel ðæs Halgan Gastes, mæden ær geeacnunge, mæden on geeacnunge, mæden æfter geeacnunge, micel is ðin mærð on ðisum freols-dæge betwux þam foresædum halgum; forðan ðe ðurh þine clænan cenninge him eallum becom halignyss and ða heofonlican geðincðu. We sprecað be ðære heofonlican cwene endebyrdlice æfter wifhade, þeah-hwæðere eal seo geleaffulle gelaðung getreowfullice be hire singð, þæt heo is geuferod and ahafen ofer engla werod to þam wuldorfullan heahsetle. Nis be nanum oðrum halgan gecweden, þæt heora ænig ofer engla werod ahafen sy, buton be Marian anre. Heo æteowde mid hire gebysnungum þæt heofonlice lif on eorðan, forðan þe mægðhad is ealra mægna cwen and gefera heofonlicra engla. Ðyses mædenes gebysnungum and fotswaðum fyligde ungerim heap mægðhades manna on clænnysse þurhwunigende, forlætenum giftum, to ðam heofonlicum brydguman Criste geþeodende mid anrædum mode, and haligre drohtnunge, and sidefullum gyrlan, to þan swiðe, þæt heora for wel menige for mæigðhade martyrdom geðrowodon, and swa mid twyfealdum sige to heofonlicum eardungstowum wuldorfulle becomon.[184]

Ælfric and the anonymous homilists

Ælfric's orthodoxy is evident throughout his work. In his treatment of the Annunciation and the Purification, he dwells on the Virgin's role in relation to Christ and, although emphasizing her importance in redemption history, shows only a limited interest in Mary herself. The most advanced of his Marian sources is *Cogitis me* and this appears to have greatly influenced his views. Not only is it the main source for the *Catholic Homilies*

---

[184] *CH I*, p. 546. Thorpe translates: 'O thou, blessed parent of God, ever maiden Mary, temple of the Holy Ghost, maiden before conception, maiden in conception, maiden after conception, great is thy glory on this festival among the aforesaid saints; because through thy pure childbirth holiness and heavenly honours came to them all. We speak of the heavenly queen, as is usual, according to her womanhood, yet all the faithful church confidently sing of her, that she is exalted and raised above the hosts of angels to the glorious throne. Of no other saint is it said, that any of them is raised above the hosts of angels, but of Mary alone. She manifested by her example the heavenly life on earth, for maidenhood is of all virtues queen, and the associate of the heavenly angels. The example and the footsteps of this maiden were followed by an innumerable body of persons in maidenhood, living in purity, renouncing marriage, attaching themselves to the heavenly bridegroom Christ with steadfast mind and holy converse, and with wide garments, to that degree, that many of them suffered martyrdom for maidenhood, and so with twofold victory went glorious to the heavenly dwelling-place.'

I Assumption text, but a passage from it forms the most fervent paragraph in his Purification homily and he also draws on it in the All Saints text, where it is used to underline Mary's superiority to other saints. In treating of the Virgin's life on earth, Ælfric almost always deliberately confines himself to the bible or biblical exegesis; even *Cogitis me* uses as much biblical material as possible and, although its description of Mary's spiritual assumption is obviously not based on the New Testament, it follows the liturgy for the feast in interpreting suitable passages from the Song of Songs as a description of her assumption. The only uncharacteristic feature is Ælfric's belief that Mary, the mother of James and John, was the sister of the Virgin: this occurs frequently in Ælfric without any prompting from the main Latin source.[185] Even this notion could be termed in some sense a scriptural one, as it is based on a series of inferences from the New Testament Crucifixion narratives. Ælfric's most respected authorities, Jerome, Augustine, Gregory and Bede, had all interpreted the biblical evidence differently, however, and Ælfric's departure from their example is rather unusual. Apart from this, Ælfric's avoidance of unscriptural Marian sources is striking: in both Assumption and Nativity homilies he explicitly takes issue with the proscribed apocryphal texts and in the homily for the *Natale sanctarum uirginum* he combats the idea that Mary could save the souls of the damned at Doomsday. In general, he is very conscious of the difference between his work and that of many other Anglo-Saxon homilists, declaring in the preface to *Catholic Homilies I* that he had seen and heard much *gedwyld* in English books and that the unlearned mistakenly took this as wisdom.[186] This rejection of the apocrypha is atypical of Old English homiletic prose: no non-Ælfrician homily issues a warning against any kind of Marian heresy. Blickling XIII translates the apocryphal *Transitus*, another *Transitus* is found in CCCC 41; Vercelli XV and another homily in CCCC 41 include the notion that Mary could save the souls of the damned and the *Gospel of Pseudo-Matthew* was translated into Old English.

With such an evident discrepancy between the anonymous homilies and Ælfric, it has been argued that Ælfric was reacting against the anonymous works. Godden, for example, has suggested that Ælfric consciously reacted against the kind of fictitious, sensational narrative typical of the anonymous homilies: 'What Ælfric objected to in these earlier homilies was not

---

[185] Discussed by Pope, *Homilies of Ælfric* I, 217–20.   [186] *CH I*, p. 2.

primarily their theological ideas or their views on religious practices, but rather their use of sensational narratives which were clearly fictitious and in some cases of dubious morality.'[187] Source-studies suggest, however, that this picture may be somewhat distorted. Ælfric's objection to the view that Mary could save the souls of the damned seems, indeed, to be an independent reaction as this belief does not appear to have any counterpart in Latin. His objection here is a moral one: those who believe in the saving powers of the Virgin persist 'on heora flæsclicum lustum'[188] rather than repenting and amending their ways. His warnings against the assumption and nativity apocrypha, however, are taken over directly from his sources, and Ælfric appears to have been in some doubt about what precisely was wrong with these texts. It is unlikely to have been their sensational narratives: equally sensational narratives were incorporated with no alterations in the *Catholic Homilies*. The homily on the assumption of John the Evangelist in the First Series of *Catholic Homilies* is especially indicative in this respect. This text is almost identical in import to the Marian assumption texts which Ælfric rejected, but, presumably because he knew of no authoritative warning against it, Ælfric appears to have had no compunction about translating it. Furthermore, he suppressed the references to it in *Cogitis me*, where Paschasius Radbertus implied that it and the *Transitus Mariae* had the same, rather doubtful, standing. In his eschatological homilies, too, Ælfric translates texts similar in their moral and theological implications to the *Visio Pauli* which he had rejected – the story of Fursey (*CH II*.xx), for example. Ælfric's acceptance or rejection of these texts seems, therefore, to have been guided more by his knowledge or ignorance of authorities which called a text into question than by individual discrimination. He never accuses any of the Marian apocrypha of a specific doctrinal error, but says only that *dwolmen* composed them 'be hire agenum dihte oððe be swefnum'.[189] It was because his authorities rejected these texts as uncanonical that Ælfric also repudiated them. 'Rejection' suggests more individual judgement than Ælfric seems, in general, to have exercised in this respect: where an authoritative source condemned a text or an incident in a text, he generally conformed; where an equally outrageous text was not directly challenged, he was often happy to accept it. His Carolingian sources, which appear not to have been accessible to the majority of the anonymous homilists, are the distinguishing factor in the case of the Marian homilies.

[187] Godden, 'Ælfric and the Vernacular Prose Tradition', p. 102.   [188] *CH II*, p. 333.

[189] *CH II*, p. 259: 'according to their own dictation or according to dreams'.

The differences between Ælfric and the anonymous homilists have also given rise to the view that there were two traditions of thought within the vernacular homiletic prose: an early pre-reform tradition which drew freely on heterodox and proscribed sources and, with the monastic revival, a new school, anxious to reform preaching along orthodox lines. Ælfric, in this view, is seen as a flag-bearer of the reform, expressing attitudes typical of the whole movement. Gatch, for example, sees Ælfric's eschatological works as possessing 'consistency, clarity and strict orthodoxy',[190] unlike the 'picturesque, confused and disorderly'[191] anonymous works, and regards the monastic revival as 'the theological watershed' which lies between the two schools.[192] Greenfield and Calder, too, say that the Blickling and Vercelli collections 'represent the synthetic tradition of vernacular preaching before the watershed of the monastic revival'.[193] There are difficulties with this, however: in the first place, it involves making Ælfric into a school, whereas he was unique in his condemnations. While it is clear that Ælfric was attempting to reform Anglo-Saxon preaching on the Virgin, his stance is not at all self-evidently a reflection of reform thinking. Wulfstan, the other principal preacher associated with the Benedictine reform, has almost no interest in the Virgin, mentioning her only in her role as *Dei genitrix*. Secondly, we have no unambiguous proof that the anonymous works do belong to the pre-reform period, rather than to a date closer to the dates of compilation of the manuscripts in which they are found. Perhaps simply because they seem so different to the works of Ælfric, we feel that the anonymous homilies must belong to a different milieu and the monastic reform appears to provide us with a convenient divide. Before we can date them with any confidence, however, we need more detailed analysis of these collections and we also need to examine the homilies against the background of other types of evidence from the period, such as that of the art, liturgy and the Latin manuscripts. Much of the evidence from these realms can be more precisely dated and localized than the vernacular prose and there is a better chance of our being able to 'place' the anonymous works in terms of milieu if we advert to testimonies of this nature.

Witnesses other than the literary ones suggest that the thought-world of

---

[190] Gatch, *Preaching and Theology*, p. 103.   [191] *Ibid.*, p. 102.

[192] *Ibid.*, p. 8.

[193] S. B. Greenfield and D. G. Calder, *A New Critical History of Old English Literature* (New York and London, 1986), p. 71.

the anonymous works is in many ways closer to other types of evidence from the monastic revival than is that of Ælfric. The evidence of the presence of apocrypha in the monastic homiliaries and legendaries of Anglo-Saxon England suggests that the reformed monks read, in the Night Office, from precisely those texts to which Ælfric so strenuously objected: even in Ælfric's immediate circle, therefore, apocryphal works in Latin were accepted.[194] The artistic evidence, too, indicates a similar willingness to admit the apocryphal narratives, with an illustration dependent on a *Transitus* text finding a place even in Æthelwold's own benedictional.[195] The Cambridge ivory and the presence of Mary and Peter in the New Minster Charter and the Winchester *Liber uitae* point to a tradition of depicting these two saints as intercessors at the Last Judgement:[196] while this does not necessarily mean that the artists who portrayed them thus believed in their ability to rescue the souls of the damned from hell, it nevertheless indicates a strong belief in their powers of intercession on the Last Day. In the generation after Ælfric, feasts whose narrative basis is purely apocryphal found a place in the liturgy of Winchester and the apocryphal narratives also influenced the liturgical texts composed for these feasts.[197] It would seem, then, that the picture is not as simple as the theory of two schools, pre- and post-reform, might lead us to believe. There can be no doubt that the reformed monks, in general, read and approved of the Marian apocrypha. If we were to take Ælfric's efforts to achieve strict orthodoxy as typical of the reform then we should be forced to restrict that reform to Ælfric alone. The climate of opinion even in Winchester, the city at the heart of the monastic revival, where Ælfric was educated, was plainly favourable to extra-biblical Marian texts, both in the generations before and after Ælfric, as well as in his own time. His rejection of the apocrypha would seem, then, to have been an isolated phenomenon, resulting from his use of Carolingian sources. Instead of aiming his condemnations at a pre-reform tradition, therefore, he seems to have been attacking his fellow-monks. The cult of the Virgin in late Anglo-Saxon England was undoubtedly, to judge from the evidence of the preceding chapters, a monastic one, and it makes sense that Ælfric should have been protesting at the excesses of this cult in the monasteries. While this does not, of course, prove that the anonymous texts were the products of the monastic reform, it should make us cautious about assigning them to the pre-reform

[194] See above, p. 23–4.   [195] See above, pp. 161–5.

[196] See above, pp. 159 and 167.   [197] See above, pp. 82–7.

period solely on the basis of the contrast between them and the works of Ælfric: in this respect, he is a lone voice, a maverick rather than a representative, protesting in a world where such niceties meant little. We can see where he comes from in terms of the Carolingian traditions behind him, but it is difficult to know why he alone adopted this particular stance.

In addition, it should be pointed out that the contrast between Ælfric and the anonymous works can be overemphasized: the two cannot be divided simply on an apocryphal/anti-apocryphal basis and a concentration on this distorts the issue. Vercelli XVII, for example, is of impeccable orthodoxy and its view of Mary is more muted than that of Ælfric. The source of Blickling I is a vivid and colourful text, but hardly unorthodox, and the Old English translator seems to have deliberately omitted some of the more *outré* passages and introduced instead an independent emphasis on Mary's humility, very reminiscent of Bede. These texts hamper any effort to see a stark contrast between the works of Ælfric and those of the anonymous homilists and cast doubt, too, on any impression that Ælfric monopolized theological orthodoxy in Anglo-Saxon England. The intellectual picture is not such a simple one and, although there are undoubtedly important differences between the works of Ælfric and those of the anonymous homilists, these differences should not be exaggerated.

Subsequent transmission

Ælfric's works proved enormously popular with scribes after his death. None of the manuscripts written after him which has texts for feasts of Mary fails to include works by Ælfric, except for CCCC 41, and his far outnumber the anonymous texts.[198] We have only one eleventh-century copy of Blickling XIII and no other copy of Blickling I, Vercelli XVII or the CCCC *Transitus*. Of the anonymous works, it is only the apocryphal ones that were at all attractive to scribes, and the theologically more acceptable ones were neglected, as far as we can tell. Of Ælfric's works, those in the original version of *Catholic Homilies I* were the most favoured: there are nine copies of the Purification homily, twelve of the Annunciation homily and ten of the Assumption homily, while there are only five of the Second Series Assumption homily and three of the later Nativity text. The second

---

[198] For an analysis of the transmission of the Marian texts, see my 'The Cult of the Virgin Mary', pp. 420–32.

Assumption homily is never preferred to the first and all five manuscripts also contain the First Series text.

Despite the undoubted popularity of Ælfric's texts, however, the scribes did not always respect his wishes. In Oxford, Bodleian Library, Bodley 342, an early eleventh-century manuscript, Ælfric's note in the First Series on his reasons for not composing a homily for the feast of Mary's Nativity prompted the scornful scribal comment: 'Ne geberaþ ðys naht þærto. buton for ydelnysse.'[199] Ælfric's denunciation of the assumption and nativity apocrypha did not suffice to keep his own texts from being mixed with the apocrypha and, even in manuscripts which contain chiefly works by Ælfric, the apocryphal texts found a place. CCCC 198 mixes a *Transitus* text with Ælfric's homilies and all three collections containing *Pseudo-Matthew* are composed largely of Ælfrician material. Even though the number of copies of Ælfric's homilies far outweighs that of the anonymous texts, his works were not preserved in a pure state. The collections he himself had issued or to which he had given his authorization were all composed of his own texts only, but they were almost immediately added to, or individual works were extracted to form other types of collection, in which the anonymous texts also found a place. These combinations of Ælfric's homilies and the anonymous ones suggest that the scribes failed to take Ælfric's condemnations seriously.

[199] *CH II*, p. 271: 'this has no bearing on the matter, except for idleness'.

9
Conclusions

The evidence of this book shows that the cult of the Virgin is an unexpectedly important aspect of Anglo-Saxon spirituality. It flourished particularly at two different periods: a substantial body of evidence, from the late seventh through to the early ninth centuries, shows that the Anglo-Saxons eagerly read Marian texts, had begun to celebrate her feasts, prayed to her and depicted her in their art; an intense and lively interest in Mary developed in the second half of the tenth and in the eleventh centuries. The earlier cult is chiefly an Anglian one, Northumbrian and Mercian, whereas the later is a product of the monastic reform and is, therefore, concentrated in the south of the country.

In the early period, the Roman feasts of Mary – the Purification, Annunciation, Assumption and Nativity of the Virgin – were introduced, at first slowly and sporadically, into England and in the course of the eighth century full liturgical celebrations of all four feasts became established. We know little about the liturgy for these feasts, but the selection of antiphons made by Alcuin for his devotional florilegium *De laude Dei* proves that fervent Marian texts were available to the Anglo-Saxons. Images of Mary were imported too, and one seventh-century Anglo-Saxon wood-carving of the Virgin still survives. It is based on Mediterranean models and shows the Virgin with the Child across her knee, a 'complementary profiles' arrangement which is much more informal than the strictly frontal group common in this period. Sculpture in stone survives from the first half of the eighth century onwards in Northumbria, where Mary features in several scenes on the most famous Northumbrian cross, that at Ruthwell. There is also a number of Virgin and Child images, including the affectionate Dewsbury Cross, with its portrayal of the Child reaching to its mother's breast. The sculptural tradition then spread to Mercia at the beginning of the ninth century and the group working in Barnack stone *c*. 800–850 produced a number of Marian works, most notably the Breedon Virgin. This seems to be a cult-image and was probably intended for a church dedicated to Mary.

Doctrinal works which treat Mary also found their way to England and, as with the artistic images, they paved the way for a native tradition. This begins with Aldhelm and Bede: Aldhelm prays to and praises Mary, while Bede wrote the first Western homily for the feast of the Purification, composed a hymn for the Assumption and celebrated Mary's humility and virtue. In addition to such orthodox treatments, apocryphal narratives dealing with the Virgin began to circulate in this period. Adamnan alludes to the fate of Mary's body as a subject which one cannot 'pro certo scire',[1] but in a manner which suggests that he knew of uncanonical *Transitus* narratives, and Bede knew and quoted from *Transitus* B, pointing out that, as its chronology did not agree with that of the Acts of the Apostles, the apocryphon was suspect. An account similar to that in this *Transitus*, but confused in some details, is later included in Hygeburg's *uita* of St Willibald (*c*. 780) and no suspicion of the text is evident here. The carved stone slab at Wirksworth (*c*. 800), in addition to other Marian scenes, features the earliest surviving depiction of Mary's assumption, with an iconography obviously drawn from the apocrypha. In the *Old English Martyrology* from the same period, there seems, on the other hand, to be a conscious avoidance of the assumption apocrypha, even though the *Gospel of Pseudo-Matthew* is drawn on for the entry for the feast of the Nativity of Mary. The Marian apocrypha appear, therefore, to have been widely known in the seventh and eighth centuries, though treated by some with caution and distrust.

A tradition which seems to be insular in origin is that of collections of private prayers: although prayer was always a feature of Christian life, the early texts are all included in works of a different genre and it is only at the end of the eighth century and the beginning of the ninth that we begin to find texts explicitly composed for private devotion and collected into prayer-books. The earliest of these are English and manuscripts of *c*. 800 contain three prayers to Mary, which seem to be either Northumbrian or Mercian: one of these, Cerne 56, is of a fervour unique among early English testimonies to the cult of the Virgin, showing a profound belief in Mary's

---

[1] See p. 14.

powers of intercession. Mary is 'sancta Dei genetrix semper uirgo, beata, benedicta, gloriosa et generosa, intacta et intemerata, casta et incontaminata Maria, immaculata, electa et a Deo dilecta, singulari sanctitate praedita atque omni laudi digna'[2] and, according to the prayer, she can obtain from her son everything she wishes.

The only vernacular poem which deals extensively with Mary, *Advent*, may also date from the eighth or ninth century. Its view of the Virgin is largely that of the Church Fathers and the liturgy: the poem's stress is Christological and Mary's role as *Dei genetrix* is emphasized. She is seen as having been chosen as mother of God because of her freely offered vow of virginity, as completely free of sin and as the fulfilment of Old Testament prophecy. In contrast to the apocrypha, which supply the gaps in the bible by offering descriptions of her life before the Incarnation and after the Ascension, *Advent* expands the biblical narrative with a dialogue between Mary and Joseph which expresses human bewilderment in the face of the divine miracle of the conception of Christ.

All of these texts probably belong to a learned, largely monastic, context. There can be no doubt about the provenance of the Anglo-Latin texts, and the vernacular ones, too, seem to issue from a similar milieu. The *Old English Martyrology* appears to have been a reference book by a relatively learned man, and *Advent*, with its sophisticated meditations on liturgical texts, is again hardly intended for a lay audience.

The evidence from the early Anglo-Saxon period points to a fairly extensive knowledge of the narrative and doctrinal aspects of the cult of the Virgin as developed on the continent and to a considerable degree of interest in her as a historical figure and as a focus of devotion, but also to an awareness of the need for caution. The cult seems to have reached England largely from Rome: the early dedications to Mary are in imitation of Roman dedications, the feasts came from there, Mediterranean images provided models for English ones and liturgical texts were imported into England from Italy. While Rome was not, in general, notable in the early Middle Ages for Marian zeal, there was a period at the end of the seventh and at the beginning of the eighth centuries when Eastern popes brought with them the more enthusiastic oriental devotion to Mary (all the popes from Sergius (687–701) to Zachary (741–52) were either Syrian or Greek,

---

[2] Barré, *Prières anciennes*, p. 67: 'holy mother of God and ever-virgin, holy and blessed, glorious and excellent, untouched and undefiled, Mary chaste and pure, chosen and beloved by God, endowed with unique sanctity and worthy of all praise'.

except one). At this period the Anglo-Saxon church was in close contact with Rome [3] and could probably have absorbed this Marian ardour from there, an ardour which was then nourished by apocrypha and the liturgy.

As with many other aspects of Anglo-Saxon history, we have little evidence of attitudes to Mary from much of the ninth and the first half of the tenth centuries. The main vernacular remains from this rather blank period are the works of the Alfredian circle, which show no noticeable interest in the Virgin. From the beginning of the Benedictine reform, however, we have an abundance of evidence for an eager interest in Mary. The almost universal practice of dedicating, or even rededicating, monasteries to her must have been deeply influential in causing those who worshipped in them to regard the Virgin as their personal *protectrix*. The prayer prefixed to the Royal Office of Mary, for example, demonstrates that she is seen as a local saint and identified in terms of her patronage of the Nunnaminster. The *Regularis concordia* decreed that all reformed monasteries should celebrate a votive mass in honour of Mary on Saturdays, as well as a daily suffrage. From this first generation of the reform comes the earliest mention of an Office of Mary in England, if the note concerning Æthelwold's recitation of such an Office can be trusted. Dunstan's prayer to the Virgin, singling her out above all the other saints, who are addressed only in groups, is the first of a considerable number of prayers to Mary which were written in the reformed centres up to, and of course after, the Conquest.

The art of Winchester, too, evinces a heightened interest in the Virgin. The dormition and coronation of the Virgin are depicted in the Benedictional of Æthelwold, in what seems to be an independent composition based on literary models: this shows an acceptance of the *Transitus* texts, as well as a desire to portray Mary in her exalted role as *regina*. In the Harley Psalter we find the earliest example of the Virgin weeping into her mantle at the Crucifixion.

The dedications, monastic devotions and illuminations show, then, that the Virgin was of great importance from the beginnings of the reform movement, and Winchester appears already to have been at the centre of her cult in Æthelwold's time. This intensity of devotion seems to have been a product of the reform: the abundant expressions of interest in the Virgin do not appear to be merely the result of evidence, lacking for the previous

---

[3] See Levison, *England and the Continent*, pp. 15–44.

hundred years, now becoming available again. The rise in Marian dedications is dramatic, and the fact that so many rededications are attested points to the newness of this increased attention to Mary.

In the eleventh century, too, we find a marked interest in new liturgical celebrations associated with the Virgin, while new monasteries continued to be dedicated to her. The two Eastern feasts of the Conception and the Presentation of Mary in the Temple, which were not celebrated anywhere else in Western Europe in this period, were introduced in Winchester *c.* 1030 and spread from there to Canterbury and Exeter. The masses and episcopal benedictions for the feasts show clearly that they were regarded as commemorations of the events described in the Marian nativity apocrypha. Texts for a daily Office of Mary, first as a private devotion, then as a communal one, are found in English manuscripts from *c.* 1030 onwards and, at the very end of the Anglo-Saxon period, there is a text for the Saturday Office of Mary. The texts for these Offices appear to have been composed in England, almost certainly in Winchester and in Canterbury. Although we have earlier evidence for the existence of such Offices on the continent, the English texts are among the very earliest texts we possess. The eleventh-century Winchester prayers, too, are of an advanced nature, demonstrating the type of devotional impulse commonly associated with the twelfth century, not the Anglo-Saxons.

In the art, Mary is now shown with symbols of power, a crown or a sceptre, in addition to (or even instead of) the Child. In Canterbury images of the Incarnation, the artists appear consciously to have stressed her active participation in the redemption. There is an artistic, as well as a literary, tradition of Mary as intercessor on the Last Day and she is seen standing on the right-hand side of the enthroned Christ in Judgement. In the Crucifixion scenes Mary is depicted either as an impassive witness or, in more affective portrayals, as a sobbing grief-stricken mother; in the Judith of Flanders Gospels Mary's emotional participation is such that she reaches up to wipe the wound in Christ's side. At the end of the Anglo-Saxon period, the *Gospel of Pseudo-Matthew* provides the basis for two illustrations (the earliest surviving in Western manuscripts), in which the hand of God is shown blessing the infant Mary.

In England, as on the continent, the main vehicle for Marian narrative and doctrinal discussion was the homiliary. The Latin homiliaries and legendaries from late tenth- and eleventh-century England show that the Anglo-Saxon monks, in addition to reading the Marian works of the

Church Fathers, were reading the apocryphal *Transitus Mariae* and various apocrypha describing Mary's birth and early life, as well as such texts as the Theophilus story and the story of Mary of Egypt, in which the Virgin plays an important part. The Anglo-Saxon homiliaries of the same period carried the monastic cult of the Virgin into the lives of the laity, and the provision these collections make for Marian feasts shows the degree of importance attached to these feasts in preaching to the laity. The Anglo-Saxon homiliaries, like the Latin ones, show that a range of apocrypha, as well as patristic texts on the Virgin, circulated in England: Blickling I uses a Pseudo-Augustine sermon and perhaps Aponius; the author of Vercelli XVII seems to have composed his homily by freely drawing on different authors; Ælfric used Bede, Augustine, Haymo and Paschasius Radbertus, and it appears from comments at the end of his *Catholic Homilies II* Assumption text that he knew of a Marian homily by Ambrosius Autpertus and other Marian texts by Paschasius Radbertus. There is a clear difference between Ælfric and some of the anonymous homilies with regard to the apocrypha, with Ælfric following Carolingian sources in his rejection of both assumption and nativity apocrypha, but in this he seems to have been a lone voice protesting to an unheeding multitude. The caution which is so characteristic of all aspects of Ælfric's Marian thinking (not only of his rejection of the apocrypha, but also of the way in which he curtails Paschasius Radbertus's fervour and of the very restrained prayers to the Virgin with which he concludes his Marian homilies) does not seem to have been a feature of the reform. The thought-world manifested in, for example, the *Blickling Homilies* is closer to the art and devotions of Winchester than is Ælfric's work. Ælfric's condemnations and censure seem to have been directed against his fellow-monks in the reform movement, not an anterior tradition which was foreign to his own circle.

All of the evidence suggests that Ælfric's fellow-monks would have been more in need of his warnings than the laity. The cult of the Virgin in late Anglo-Saxon England seems to have been principally a monastic one, rooted in the centres of power and learning. There is nothing peripheral or provincial about it, and in their homilies the monks actively encouraged the laity to venerate the Virgin.

Most of the evidence for this monastic cult comes from two centres, Winchester and Canterbury. The new feasts and Offices, the new liturgical texts and the majority of eleventh-century prayers to the Virgin are associated with these two centres. This may be due partly to the paucity of manuscripts from other centres, but such witnesses that we have from, for example, Exeter and Worcester, seem to draw entirely on Winchester models. The Exeter texts for the Presentation and Conception of Mary come from Winchester, and the Worcester Portiforium of St Wulfstan, which contains the first Saturday Office of the Virgin, seems to have been copied from a Winchester exemplar. The extant texts suggest that Winchester and Canterbury were the only innovative centres of spiritual life in late Anglo-Saxon England.

The cult of the Virgin in these centres seems to be new to England, at least in this degree of intensity, and it does not appear to be attributable to the main roots of the reform movement in Fleury and Ghent. The sudden wave of dedications to Mary is not found in these centres, and, although all of the new Marian devotions, except the feasts of the Conception and the Presentation of the Virgin in the Temple, can be paralleled in different places on the continent, the English monks cannot have derived them from any one continental centre. It is difficult to explain why it captured the imagination of the reformers to such a marked degree, unless it be that they wished to adopt as patron saint of the new celibate monasticism a saint who was known above all for her virginity and to whom the first leaders of the movement, Dunstan and Æthelwold, already had a personal devotion. The explanation does not seem to lie, at the beginning of the monastic revival at any rate, with the connections between Mary as *regina caeli* and the position of the English queen: the royal overtones of English monasticism do not become prominent until the 970s, when many of the reformed monasteries were already under the patronage of the Virgin.[4] The literature does not place a greater emphasis on *Maria regina* than elsewhere at this period, although Anglo-Saxon art does stress this aspect of her cult. The cult of Mary was undoubtedly fostered by the power of eschatological thinking in late Anglo-Saxon England: because of its dominance, intercessors were of vital importance, and devotion to the Virgin was certainly nurtured by the belief that she would be an effective intercessor on the Last Day.

It is clear, therefore, that there was a developed cult of Mary in pre-Conquest England, a point made over sixty years ago by Edmund Bishop, who commented on the 'spread of devotion to the Blessed Virgin which was so marked a feature of the English church from the close of the tenth century to the Conquest'.[5] This cult was principally a monastic one

---

[4] See Deshman, 'The Iconography', pp. 232.   [5] Bishop, *Liturgica Historica*, p. 227.

and does not seem to have been responsible for any major innovations in Marian devotion, but is remarkable chiefly for the way in which it embraced Marian material of all kinds and for the way in which features of devotion to the Virgin, such as church dedications, were developed to a hitherto unknown degree. Once new practices were introduced, like the feasts and Offices, texts were then composed in England. This cult is not associated with any conscious development of new theories related to Mary or any explicit theological discussion, except in Ælfric. Ælfric's references to doctrinal issues lack any independent speculation, however; we do not find this in England until Eadmer. The pre-Conquest cult was a purely devotional one, originating in the piety of the monks, who showed little interest in Marian doctrine.

Bibliography

Alexander, J. J. G., 'The Benedictional of St Æthelwold and Anglo-Saxon Illumination of the Reform Period', in *Tenth-Century Studies*, ed. Parsons, pp. 169–83.

Insular Manuscripts: 6th to 9th Century (London, 1978)

Amann, E., ed., *Le Protévangile de Jacques et ses remaniements latins* (Paris, 1910)

Anderson, E. R., 'The Speech Boundaries in *Advent Lyric VII*', *Neophilologus* 63 (1979), 611–18

Assmann, B., ed., *Angelsächsische Homilien und Heiligenleben*, Bibliothek der angelsächsischen Prosa, 3, repr. with a supplementary introduction by P. A. M. Clemoes (Darmstadt, 1964)

Backhouse, J., D. H. Turner and L. Webster, ed., *The Golden Age of Anglo-Saxon Art* (London, 1984)

Barlow, F., *The English Church 1000–1066: A History of the Later Anglo-Saxon Church*, 2nd ed. (London and New York, 1979)

Barré, H., 'La croyance à l'assomption corporelle en Occident de 750 à 1150 environ', *Etudes Mariales* 7 (1949), 63–123

'Deux sermons du xiiᵉ siècle pour la fête de la Conception', *Sciences ecclesiastiques* 10 (1958), 314–59

'L'homiliaire carolingien de Mondsee', *RB* 71 (1961), 71–107

'L'apport Marial de l'Orient à l'Occident de Saint Ambrose à Saint Anselm', *Etudes Mariales* 19 (1962), 27–89

Les homéliaires carolingiens de l'école d'Auxerre, Studi e Testi 225 (Rome, 1962)

Prières anciennes de l'Occident à la mère du Sauveur (Paris, 1963)

'Sermons Marials inédits "in natali Domini"', *Marianum* 25 (1963), 39–93

'Antiennes et répons de la Vierge', *Marianum* 29 (1967), 153–254

'Un plaidoyer monastique pour le samedi marial', *RB* 77 (1967), 375–99

Barré, H. and J. Deshusses, 'A la recherche du Missel d'Alcuin', *EL* 82 (1968), 1–44

Batiffol, P., *A History of the Roman Breviary*, trans. A. M. Y. Baylay from the 3rd French ed. (London, 1912)

Battiscombe, C. F., ed., *The Relics of St Cuthbert* (Oxford, 1956)

Becker, A., *Franks Casket: Zu den Bildern und Inschriften des Runenkästchens von Auzon*, Sprache und Literatur, Regensburger Arbeiten zur Anglistik und Amerikanistik 5 (Regensburg, 1972)

Beckwith, J., *Ivory Carvings in Early Medieval England* (London, 1972)

Best, R. I. and H. J. Lawlor, ed., *The Martyrology of Tallaght*, HBS 68 (1931)

Bestul, T. H., 'St Anselm and the Continuity of Anglo-Saxon Devotional Traditions', *Annuale Mediaevale* 18 (1977), 20–41

'Continental Sources of Anglo-Saxon Devotional Writing', in *Sources of Anglo-Saxon Culture*, ed. Szarmach and Oggins, pp. 103–26

Beumer, J., 'Die marianische Deutung des Hohen Liedes in der Frühscholastik', *Zeitschrift für katholische Theologie* 76 (1954), 411–39

Beyers, R., ed., *De natiuitate Mariae: Kritische Voorstudie en Tekstuitgave*, Proefschrift voor het doctoraat in de Wijsbegeerte en Letteren, groep Klassieke Filologie, aan de Katholieke Universiteit Leuven (Antwerp, 1980)

Billet, B., 'Culte et dévotion à la Vierge dans l'ordre monastique aux viiie–ixe siècles', *De cultu Mariano saeculis vi–xi: Acta Congressus Mariologici-Mariani internationalis in Croatia anno 1971 celebrati*, 4 vols. (Rome, 1972), IV, 203–16

Birch, W. de G., ed., *Cartularium Saxonicum*, 3 vols. (London, 1885–93)

An Ancient Manuscript of the Eighth or Ninth Century Formerly Belonging to St Mary's Abbey or Nunnaminster, Winchester, Hampshire Record Society (London and Winchester, 1889)

Liber Vitae, Register and Martyrology of New Minster and Hyde Abbey, Winchester, Hampshire Record Society (London and Winchester, 1892)

Bishop, E., 'Liturgical Note' in *The Book of Cerne*, ed. Kuypers, pp. 234–83

Liturgica Historica: Papers on the Liturgy and Religious Life of the Western Church (Oxford, 1918)

Botte, B., *Les origines de la Nöel et de l'Epiphanie*, Textes et études liturgiques 1 (Louvain, 1932)

'La première fête mariale de la liturgie romaine', *EL* 47 (1933), 425–30

Brotanek, R., ed., *Texte und Untersuchungen zur altenglischen Literatur und Kirchengeschichte* (Halle, 1913)

Brou, L., 'Restes de l'homélie sur la Dormition de l'Archevêque Jean de Thessalonique dans le plus ancien antiphonaire connu, et le dernier *Magnificat* de la Vierge', *Archiv für Liturgiewissenschaft* 2 (1952), 84–93

Bullough, D. A., 'Alcuin and the Kingdom of Heaven: Liturgy, Theology, and the Carolingian Age', in *Carolingian Essays: Andrew W. Mellon Lectures in Early Christian Studies*, ed. U.-R. Blumenthal (Washington, D.C., 1983), pp. 1–69

Burgert, E., *The Dependence of Part I of Cynewulf's Christ upon the Antiphonary* (Washington D.C., 1921)

Burlin, R. B., *The Old English Advent: A Typological Commentary*, Yale Studies in English 168 (New Haven, 1968)

Campbell, A., Review of Vleeskruyer, *The Life of St Chad*, *MÆ* 24 (1955), 52–6

Campbell, A., ed., *Æthelwulf De abbatibus* (Oxford, 1967)

Campbell, J. J., 'To Hell and Back: Latin Tradition and Literary Use of the "Descensus ad inferos" in Old English', *Viator* 13 (1982), 107–58

Campbell, J. J., ed., *The Advent Lyrics of the Exeter Book* (Princeton, 1959)

Canal, J. M., 'Oficio parvo de la Virgen: Formas viejas y formas nuevas', *Ephemerides Mariologicae* 11 (1961), 497–525

'Texto crítico de algunos sermones Marianos de San Fulberto de Chartres o a él atribuibles', *Recherches de théologie ancienne et médiévale* 30 (1963), 55–87

'El Oficio parvo de la Virgen de 1000 a 1250', *Ephemerides Mariologicae* 15 (1965), 464–75

Capelle, B., 'La fête de la Vierge à Jérusalem au vᵉ siècle', *Le Muséon* 56 (1943), 1–33

'Vestiges grecs et latins d'un antique "Transitus de la Vierge"', *AB* 67 (1949), 21–48

Travaux liturgiques de doctrine et d'histoire III (Louvain, 1967)

Carroll, M. T. A., *The Venerable Bede: His Spiritual Teachings*, Catholic University of America Studies in Medieval History, ns 9 (Washington, D.C., 1946)

Chase, C., 'God's Presence through Grace as the Theme of Cynewulf's *Christ* II and the Relationship of this Theme to *Christ* I and *Christ* III', *ASE* 3 (1974), 87–101

Chavasse, A., 'Les plus anciens types du lectionnaire et de l'antiphonaire romains de la messe', *RB* 62 (1952), 3–94

Le sacramentaire gélasien (Vaticanus Reginensis 316), Bibliothèque de Théologie 4. 1 (1958)

Clayton, M., 'The Cult of the Virgin Mary in Anglo-Saxon England with Special Reference to the Vernacular Texts' (unpubl. DPhil dissertation, Oxford Univ., 1983)

'Homiliaries and Preaching in Anglo-Saxon England', *Peritia* 4 (1985), 207–42

'Ælfric and the Nativity of the Blessed Virgin Mary', *Anglia* 104 (1986), 286–315

'Assumptio Mariae: An Eleventh-Century Anglo-Latin Poem from Abingdon', *AB* 104 (1986), 419–26

'Delivering the Damned: A Motif in Old English Homiletic Prose', *MÆ* 55 (1986), 92–102

'Blickling Homily XIII Reconsidered', *Leeds Studies in English* 17 (1986), 25–40

Clemoes, P. A. M., 'The Chronology of Ælfric's Work', in *The Anglo-Saxons: Studies in Some Aspects of their History and Culture presented to Bruce Dickins*, ed. P. A. M. Clemoes (London, 1959), pp. 212–47

Review of Willard, *The Blickling Homilies*, MÆ 31 (1962), 60–3

'Ælfric', in *Continuations and Beginnings*, ed. E. G. Stanley (London, 1966), pp. 176–209

Cockerton, R. W. P., 'The Wirksworth Slab', *Derbyshire Archeological Journal* 82 (1962), 1–20

Colgrave, B., ed., *The Life of Bishop Wilfrid by Eddius Stephanus* (Cambridge, 1927)

Collingwood, W. G., 'Anglian and Anglo-Danish Sculpture in the North Riding of Yorkshire', *Yorkshire Archaeological Journal* 19 (1907), 266–413

'Anglian and Anglo-Danish Sculpture in the West Riding', *Yorkshire Archaeological Journal* 23 (1914), 129–299

Constantinescu, R., 'Alcuin et les "libelli precum" de l'époque carolingienne', *Révue d'histoire de la spiritualité* 50 (1974), 17–56

Cook, A. S., 'Bemerkungen zu Cynewulfs Christ', in *Philologische Studien: Festgabe für Eduard Sievers* (Halle, 1896), pp. 21–9

'A Remote Analogue to the Miracle Play', *Journal of English and Germanic Philology* 4 (1902–3), 421–51

Cook, A. S., ed., *The Christ of Cynewulf* (Boston, 1900)

Cosijn, P. J. 'Anglosaxonica IV', *Beiträge zur Geschichte der deutschen Sprache und Literatur* 23 (1898), 109–30

Cothenet, E., 'Marie dans les apocryphes', in *Maria*, ed. du Manoir, VI, 71–156

Cramp, R., 'Schools of Mercian Sculpture', in *Mercian Studies*, ed. A. Dornier (Leicester, 1977), pp. 191–233

Cramp, R. and J. T. Lang, *A Century of Anglo-Saxon Sculpture* (Newcastle-upon-Tyne, 1977)

Crawford, S. J., ed., *The Old English Version of the Heptateuch, Ælfric's Treatise on the Old and New Testament and his Preface to Genesis*, EETS os 160 (London, 1922)

Cross, J. E., 'Legimus in ecclesiasticis historiis: A Sermon for All Saints and its Use in Old English Prose', *Traditio* 33 (1977), 101–35

'On the Library of the Old English Martyrologist', in *Learning and Literature*, ed. Lapidge and Gneuss, pp. 227–49

'The Use of Patristic Homilies in the *Old English Martyrology*', ASE 14 (1985), 107–28

Davis, H. F., 'The Origins of Devotion to Our Lady's Immaculate Conception', *Dublin Review* 228 (1954), 375-92

Delehaye, H., *Commentarius perpetuus in Martyrologium Hieronymianum*, Acta Sanctorum, Nov. II. ii (Brussels, 1931)

Deshman, R., 'The Iconography of the Full-Page Miniatures in the Benedictional of St Æthelwold' (unpubl. PhD dissertation, Princeton Univ., 1970)

'Anglo-Saxon Art after Alfred', *Art Bulletin* 56 (1974), 176–200

'Benedictus monarcha et monachus: Early Medieval Ruler Theology and the Anglo-Saxon Reform', *Frühmittelalterliche Studien* 22 (1988), 204–40

'Servants of the Mother of God in Byzantine and Medieval Art', *Word and Image* 5 (1989), 33–70

Deshusses, J., ed., *Le sacramentaire grégorien. Ses principales formes d'après les plus anciens manuscrits*, Spicilegium Friburgense 16 (Fribourg, 1971)

See also under Barré, H.

Dewick, E. S., ed., *Facsimiles of Horae de Beata Maria Virgine from English Manuscripts of the Eleventh Century*, HBS 21 (London, 1902)

The Leofric Collectar (Harley MS 2961), I, HBS 45 (London, 1914)

Dewick, E. S., and W. H. Frere, ed., *The Leofric Collectar Compared with the Collectar of St Wulstan*, HBS 56 (London, 1921)

Dickinson, J. C., *The Shrine of Our Lady at Walsingham* (Cambridge, 1956)

Dobbie, E. V. K., ed., *The Anglo-Saxon Minor Poems*, ASPR 6 (New York, 1942)

See also under Krapp, G. P.

Dodwell, C. R., *Anglo-Saxon Art: A New Perspective*, Manchester Studies in the History of Art 5.3 (Manchester, 1982)

Drage, E., 'Bishop Leofric and the Exeter Cathedral Chapter (1050–72): A Re-Assessment of the Manuscript Evidence' (unpubl. DPhil dissertation, Oxford University, 1978)

Dubois, J., *Les martyrologes du moyen âge latin*, Typologie des sources du moyen âge occidental 26 (Turnhout, 1978)

Dümmler, E., ed., *Alcuini carmina*, MGH, Poetae Aevi Carolini Latini I (Berlin, 1881), 160–351

Dumville, D. N., 'Liturgical Drama and Panegyric Responsory from the Eighth Century. A Re-Examination of the Origin and Contents of the Ninth-Century Section of the Book of Cerne', *Journal of Theological Studies*, ns 23 (1972), 374–406

Ehwald, R., ed., *Aldhelmi opera*, MGH, Auct. Antiq. 15 (Berlin, 1919)

Fadda, A. M. L., '"De descensu Christi ad inferos", una inedita omelia anglo-sassone', *Studi medievali* 13 (1972), 989–1011

Fadda, A. M. L., ed., *Nuove omelie anglosassoni della rinascenza benedettina*, Filologia germanica testi e studi I (Florence, 1977)

Farrell, R. T., 'Reflections on the Iconography of the Ruthwell and Bewcastle Crosses', in *Sources of Anglo-Saxon Culture*, ed. Szarmach and Oggins, pp. 357–76

Farrell, R. T., ed., *Bede and Anglo-Saxon England*, British Archaeological Reports 2, British Series 46 (Oxford, 1978)

Feuillet, A., 'La Vierge Marie dans le Nouveau Testament', in *Maria*, ed. du Manoir VI, 15–69

Bibliography

Fiedler, H. G., 'The Sources of the First Blickling Homily', *MLQ* 6 (1903), 122–4

Fillitz, H., Review of Beckwith, *Ivory Carvings*, *Kunstchronik* 27 (1974), 429–34

Förster, M., 'Über die Quellen von Ælfrics exegetischen Homiliae Catholicae', *Anglia* 16 (1894), 1–61

'Die Vercelli-Codex CXVII nebst Abdruck einiger altenglischer Homilien der Handschrift in *Festschrift für Lorenz Morsbach*, ed. F. Holtausen and H. Spies, Studien zur englischen Philologie 50 (1913), 20–179

Zur Geschichte des Reliquienkultes in Altengland, Sitzungsberichte der Bayerischen Akademie der Wissenschaften, Phil.-hist. Abteilung, Heft 8 (1943)

Fournée, J., 'L'abbaye de Fécamp et les origines du culte de l'Immaculée Conception en Normandie', in *L'Abbaye Bénédictine de Fécamp, ouvrage scientifique du xiiie centenaire*, 4 vols. (Fécamp, 1959–63) II, 164–70

Fraipont, J., ed., *Bedae Venerabilis opera: Pars IV, opera rhythmica*, CCSL 122 (Turnhout, 1955)

Freeman, E. A., *The Norman Conquest: The History of the Norman Conquest of England, its Causes and its Results*, 6 vols. (Oxford, 1867–79)

Frénaud, G., 'Le culte de Notre-Dame dans l'ancienne liturgie latine', in *Maria*, ed. du Manoir VI, 157–211

Gamber, K., *Codices liturgici latini antiquiores*, 2nd ed., Spicilegii Friburgensis subsidia 1 (Freiburg, 1968)

Garcia, V. B., ed., *San Ildefonso. De uirginitate beatae Mariae*, Textos latinos de la edad medina espanola 3 (Madrid, 1937)

Gatch, M. McC., *Loyalties and Traditions: Man and his World in Old English Literature* (New York, 1971)

Preaching and Theology in Anglo-Saxon England: Ælfric and Wulfstan (Toronto, 1977)

Gem, R., 'Towards an Iconography of Anglo-Saxon Architecture', *Journal of the Warburg and Courtauld Institutes* 46 (1983), 1–18

Gijsel, J., 'Zu welcher Textfamilie des Pseudo-Matthäus gehört die Quelle von Hrotsvits Maria?', *Classica et Mediaevalia* 32 (1980), 279–88

Die unmittelbare Textüberlieferung des sogenannten Pseudo-Matthäus, Verhandelingen van de koninklijke Academie voor Wetenschappen, Letteren en schone Kunsten van België, Klasse der Letteren 43 (1981)

Gneuss, H., ed., *Hymnar und Hymnen im englischen Mittelalter, mit einer Textausgabe der lateinisch-altenglischen Expositio hymnorum (nach den Handschriften Cotton Julius A. vi und Cotton Vespasian D. xii)*, Buchreihe der Anglia 12 (Tübingen, 1968)

'A Preliminary List of Manuscripts Written or Owned in England up to 1100', *ASE* 9 (1981), 1–60

'Liturgical Books in Anglo-Saxon England and their Old English Terminology', in *Learning and Literature*, ed. Lapidge and Gneuss, pp. 91–141

Godden, M. R., 'Ælfric and the Vernacular Prose Tradition', in *The Old English Homily and its Backgrounds*, ed. Szarmach and Huppé, pp. 99–118

Godden, M. R., ed., *Ælfric's Catholic Homilies. The Second Series: Text*, EETS ss 5 (Oxford, 1979)

Grabar, A., *Christian Iconography: A Study of its Origins*, Bollingen Art Series 35.10 (Princeton, 1968)

Graef, H., *Mary: A History of Doctrine and Devotion*, 2 vols. (London, 1963)

Grant, R. J. S., ed., *Three Homilies from Cambridge, Corpus Christi College, 41* (Ottawa, 1982)

Grégoire, R., *Homéliaires liturgiques médiévaux: analyse de manuscrits*, Biblioteca degli Studi Medievali 12 (Spoleto, 1980)

Haibach-Reinisch, M., ed., *Ein neuer 'Transitus Mariae' des Pseudo-Melito* (Rome, 1962)

Hall, D. J., *English Mediaeval Pilgrimage* (London, 1965)

Hamilton, N. E. S. A., ed., *Willelmi Malmesbiriensis monachi de gestis pontificum Anglorum*, Rolls Series 52 (London, 1870)

Harlow, C. G., 'The Old English *Advent* VII and the "Doubting of Mary" Tradition', *Leeds Studies in English* ns 16 (1985), 101–17

Hart, C. R., *The Early Charters of Eastern England*, Studies in Early English History 5 (Leicester, 1966)

Hennecke, E. and W. Schneemelcher, eds., *New Testament Apocrypha*, trans. and ed. R. M. Wilson, 2 vols. (London, 1963–5)

Herzfeld, G., ed., *An Old English Martyrology*, EETS, os 116 (London, 1900)

Hill, T. D., 'Notes on the Imagery and Structure of the Old English *Christ I*', *N & Q* 217 (1972), 84–9

'A Liturgical Source for *Christ I*, 164–213 (*Advent Lyric* VII)', *MÆ* 46 (1977), 12–15

Hohler, C., 'The Type of Sacramentary Used by St Boniface', in *Sankt Bonifatius: Gedenkgabe zum zwölfhundertsten Todestag* (Fulda, 1954), pp. 89–93

'Les saints insulaires dans le Missel de l'Archevêque Robert', in *Jumièges: Congrès scientifique du xiiie centenaire. Rouen 10–12 juin, 1954*, 2 vols. (Rouen, 1955), I, 293–303

'Some Service Books of the later Saxon Church', in *Tenth-Century Studies*, ed. D. Parsons, pp. 60–83

Holder-Egger, O., ed., *Vita Willibaldi episcopi Eichstetensis*, MGH Scriptores 15.1 (1887)

Holthausen, F., 'Altenglische Interlinearversionen lateinischer Gebete und Beichten', *Anglia* 65 (1941), 230–54

Huemer, J., ed., *Sedulii opera omnia*, CSEL 10 (Vienna, 1885)

Hughes, A., ed., *The Portiforium of St Wulstan*, HBS 89 and 90 (London, 1958–60)

Hughes, K., 'Some Aspects of Irish Influence on Early English Private Prayer', *Studia Celtica* 5 (1970), 48–61

Hulme, W. H., 'The Old English Gospel of Nicodemus', *Modern Philology* 1 (1903–4), 579–614

Hunt, W., ed., *Two Chartularies of the Priory of St Peter at Bath*, Somerset Record Society 7 (1893)

Hurst, D., ed., *Bedae Venerabilis opera homiletica*, CCSL 122 (Turnhout, 1955)
In Lucae Euangelium exposito, CCSL 120 (Turnhout, 1960)

James, M. R., ed., *The Apocryphal New Testament* (Oxford, 1924)

Jewell, R. H. I., 'The Pre-Conquest Sculpture at Breedon-on-the-Hill, Leicestershire' (unpubl. PhD dissertation, Courtauld Institute, London, 1982)

John, E., *Orbis Britanniae and Other Studies*, Studies in Early English History 4 (Leicester, 1966)

Joussard, G., 'Marie à travers la patristique: maternité divine, virginité, sainteté', in *Maria*, ed. du Manoir, I, 69–157
'La nouvelle Eve chez les pères anténicéens', *Etudes Mariales* 12 (1954), 35–54
'The Fathers of the Church and the Immaculate Conception', in *The Dogma of the Immaculate Conception*, ed. E. D. O'Connor (Notre Dame, 1958), pp. 51–85

Jugie, M., 'La première fête mariale en Orient et en Occident, l'Avent primitif', *Echos d'Orient* 22 (1923), 129–52
'Homélies mariales byzantines II', PO 19 (1926), 287–526
Le mort et l'assomption de la Sainte Vierge: Etude historico-doctrinale, Studi e Testi 114 (Rome, 1944)
L'Immaculée Conception dans l'écriture sainte et dans la tradition orientale (Rome, 1952)

Ker, N. R, *Catalogue of Manuscripts Containing Anglo-Saxon* (Oxford, 1957)

Keynes, S., 'King Athelstan's Books', in *Learning and Literature*, ed. Lapidge and Gneuss, pp. 143–201

Kitzinger, E., 'The Coffin-Reliquary', in *The Relics of St Cuthbert*, ed. Battiscombe, pp. 202–304

Klauser, T., *Das römische Capitulare Euangeliorum, 1: Typen*, Liturgiegeschichtliche Quellen und Forschungen 28, 2nd ed. (Münster in Westfalen, 1971)

Knowles, D., and R. N. Hadcock, *Medieval Religious Houses: England and Wales*, 2nd ed. (London, 1971)

Kotzor, G., ed., *Das altenglische Martyrologium*, 2 vols, Bayerische Akademie der Wissenschaften, Phil.-hist. Klasse, Neue Folge, 88.1 (Munich, 1981)

Krapp, G. P., and E. V. K. Dobbie, ed., *The Exeter Book*, ASPR 3 (New York, 1936)

Kurth, B., 'The Iconography of the Wirksworth Slab', *The Burlington Magazine* 86 (1945), 114–21

Kuypers, A. B., ed., *The Prayer Book of Aedeluald the Bishop, Commonly called the Book of Cerne, with a Liturgical Note by E. Bishop* (Cambridge, 1902)

Lafontaine, J., *Peintures médiévales dans la temple dit de la Fortune Virile à Rome* (Brussels and Rome, 1959)

Lafontaine-Dosogne, J., *Iconographie de l'enfance de la Vierge dans l'empire byzantin et en Occident*, 2 vols. (Brussels, 1964–5)

Laistner, M. L. W., ed., *Bedae Venerabilis expositio actuum Apostolorum et retractatio* (Cambridge, Mass., 1939); rptd CCSL 121 (Turnhout, 1983)

Lambot, C., 'L'homélie du Pseudo-Jérôme sur l'assomption et l'évangile de la nativité de Marie d'après une lettre inédite d'Hincmar', *RB* 46 (1934), 265–82

Lapidge, M., 'The Hermeneutic Style in Tenth-Century Anglo-Latin Literature', *ASE* 4 (1975), 67–111

'Byrhtferth and the *Vita S. Ecgwini*', *MS* 41 (1979), 331–53

Lapidge, M. and J. L. Rosier, trans., *Aldhelm: The Poetic Works* (Cambridge, 1985)

Lapidge, M. and Gneuss, H., ed., *Learning and Literature in Anglo-Saxon England: Studies Presented to Peter Clemoes on the Occasion of his Sixty-Fifth Birthday* (Cambridge, 1985)

Leclercq, J., 'Aux origines du cycle de Noël', *EL* 60 (1946), 7–26

'Formes successives de l'Office votif de la Vierge', *EL* 72 (1958), 294–301

'Formes anciennes de l'Office marial', *EL* 74 (1960), 89–102

Levison, W., *England and the Continent in the Eighth Century* (Oxford, 1946)

Livius, T., *The Blessed Virgin in the Fathers of the First Six Centuries* (London, 1893)

Lowe, E. A., *Codices Latini Antiquiores*, 11 vols. and supp. (Oxford, 1934–72)

Manoir, H. du, ed., *Maria*, 8 vols. (Paris, 1949–71)

Mayr-Harting, H., *The Coming of Christianity to Anglo-Saxon England* (London, 1972)

Meerssemann, G. G., *Kritische Glossen op de Griekse Theophilus-Legende (7ᵉ eeuw) en haar latijnse Vertaling (9ᵉ eeuw)* Mededelingen van de Koninklijke vlaamse Academie voor Wetenschappen, Letteren en schone Kunsten van België, Klasse der Letteren 25 (1963)

Meyvaert, P., 'Bede and the Church-Paintings at Wearmouth-Jarrow', *ASE* 8 (1979), 63–77

Mildner, F. M., 'The Immaculate Conception in England up to the Time of John Duns Scotus', *Marianum* 1 (1939), 86–99

Moeller, E. E., ed., *Corpus benedictionum pontificalium*, 4 vols., CCSL 162, 162A–C (Turnhout, 1971–9)

Corpus praefationum, 5 vols., CCSL 161 (Turnhout, 1980–1)

Morris, R., ed., *The Blickling Homilies of the Tenth Century*, EETS os 58, 63 and 73 (1874–88, repr. as one vol., 1967)

Napier, A. S., ed., *Wulfstan: Sammlung der ihm zugeschriebenen Homilien* (Berlin, 1883)

Ó Carragáin, É., 'The Vercelli Book as an Ascetic Florilegium' (unpubl. PhD dissertation, Queen's University, Belfast, 1975)

'How Did the Vercelli Collector Interpret "The Dream of the Rood"?', in *Studies in English Language and Early Literature in Honour of Paul Christophersen*, ed. P. M. Tilling, Occasional Papers in Linguistics and Language Teaching 8 (Coleraine, 1981), pp. 63–104

'Crucifixion as Annunciation: The Relation of "The Dream of the Rood" to the Liturgy Reconsidered', *English Studies* 63 (1982), 487–505

'The Ruthwell Crucifixion Poem in its Iconographic and Liturgical Contexts', *Peritia* 6–7, forthcoming

Ohlgren, T. H., ed., *Insular and Anglo-Saxon Illuminated Manuscripts: An Iconographic Catalogue c. A. D. 625 to 1100* (New York and London, 1986)

Ohly, F., *Hohelied–Studien* (Wiesbaden, 1958)

Otero, A. de S., ed., *Los evangelios apocrifos* (Madrid, 1963)

Parsons, D., ed., *Tenth-Century Studies: Essays in Commemoration of the Millennium of the Council of Winchester and the Regularis Concordia* (Chichester, 1975)

Pattison, I. R., 'The Nunburnholme Cross and Anglo-Danish Sculpture in York', *Archaeologia* 104 (1973), 209–34

Plummer, C., ed., *Venerabilis Baedae opera historica*, 2 vols. (Oxford, 1896)

Pope, J., ed., *Homilies of Ælfric: A Supplementary Collection*, EETS os 259 and 260 (London, 1967–8)

Prescott, A., 'The Structure of English Pre-Conquest Benedictionals', *British Library Journal* 13 (1987), 118–58

Quentin, H., *Les martyrologes historiques du moyen âge* (Paris, 1908)

Rademacher, F., *Die Regina Angelorum in der Kunst des frühen Mittelalters*, Die Kunstdenkmäler des Rheinlandes 17 (Düsseldorf, 1972)

Rankin, S., 'The Liturgical Background of the Old English Advent Lyrics: A Reappraisal', in *Learning and Literature*, ed. Lapidge and Gneuss, pp. 317–40

Raw, B. C., 'The Inglesham Virgin and Child', *Wiltshire Archaeological and Natural History Magazine* 61 (1966), 43–6

Rice, D. T., *English Art 871–1100* (Oxford, 1952)

Ripberger, A., ed., *Der Pseudo-Hieronymus-Brief IX 'Cogitis me': Ein erster marianischer Traktat des Mittelalters von Paschasius Radbert*, Spicilegium Friburgense 9 (Fribourg, 1962)

Robinson, J. A., *St Oswald and the Church at Worcester*, British Academy Supplemental Papers 5 (London, 1919)

The Times of St Dunstan (Oxford, 1923)

Rosenthal, J. E., 'The Historiated Canon Tables of the Arenberg Gospels' (unpubl. PhD dissertation, Columbia Univ., 1974)

Sawyer, P. H., *Anglo-Saxon Charters: An Annotated List and Bibliography*, Royal Historical Society Guides and Handbooks 8 (London, 1968)

Scheffczyk, L., *Das Mariengeheimnis in Frömmigkeit und Lehre der Karolingerzeit*, Erfurter Theologische Studien 5 (Leipzig, 1959)

Schiller, G., *Iconography of Christian Art*, I, trans. from the 2nd German ed. (1969) by J. Seligman (London, 1971)

Die Ikonographie der christlichen Kunst IV.2 (Gütersloh, 1980)

Scragg, D. G., 'The Compilation of the Vercelli Book', *ASE* 2 (1973), 189–207

'The Corpus of Vernacular Homilies and Prose Saints' Lives before Ælfric', *ASE* 8 (1979), 223–77

Shepherd, D., 'An Icon of the Virgin: A Sixth-Century Panel from Egypt', *Bulletin of the Cleveland Museum of Art* 56 (1969), 90–120

Siffrin, P., 'Das Walderdorffer Kalendarfragment saec. viii und die Berliner Blätter eines Sakramentars aus Regensburg', *EL* 47 (1933), 201–24

Sims-Williams, P., 'Thought, Word and Deed: An Irish Triad', *Ériu* 29 (1978), 78–111

'Thoughts on Ephrem the Syrian in Anglo-Saxon England', in *Learning and Literature*, ed. Lapidge and Gneuss, pp. 205–26

Sisam, C., *The Vercelli Book*, EEMF 19 (Copenhagen, 1976)

Sisam, K., *Studies in the History of Old English Literature* (Oxford, 1953)

Skeat, W. W., ed., *Ælfric's Lives of Saints*, 2 vols., EETS os 76, 82, 94 and 114 (1881–1900, repr. in 2 vols., 1966)

Smid, H. R., *Protevangelium Jacobi: A Commentary*, trans. G. E. Van Baaren-Pape (Assen, 1965)

Söll, G., *Mariologie: Handbuch der Dogmengeschichte* 3.4 (Freiburg, Basel and Vienna, 1978)

Southern, R. W., 'The English Origins of the "Miracles of the Virgin"', *Medieval and Renaissance Studies* 4 (1958), 176–216

Stenton, F. M., *Anglo-Saxon England*, 3rd ed. (Oxford, 1971)

Stokes, W., *Félire Oengusso céli dé: The Martyrology of Oengus, the Culdee*, HBS 29 (London, 1905)

Strycker, E. de, ed., *La forme la plus ancienne du Protévangile de Jacques* (Brussels, 1961)

Symons, T., ed., *Regularis concordia Anglicae nationis monachorum sanctimonialiumque* (London and New York, 1953)

Szarmach, P. E., 'The Vercelli Homilies: Style and Structure', in *The Old English Homily and its Backgrounds*, ed. P. E. Szarmach and B. F. Huppé (Albany, 1978), pp. 241–67

Szarmach, P. E., ed., *The Vercelli Homilies ix–xxiii*, Toronto Old English Series 5 (Toronto, 1981)

Szarmach, P. E., and V. D. Oggins, ed., *Sources of Anglo-Saxon Culture*, Studies in Medieval Culture 20 (Kalamazoo, 1986)

Talbot, C. H., trans., *The Anglo-Saxon Missionaries in Germany* (London, 1954)

Temple, E., *Anglo-Saxon Manuscripts 900–1066* (London, 1976)

Thorpe, B., ed., *The Homilies of the Anglo-Saxon Church. The First Part, Containing the Sermones Catholici, or Homilies of Ælfric*, 2 vols. (London, 1843–4)

Tischendorf, C., ed., *Apocalypses Apocryphae* (Leipzig, 1866)

Evangelia Apocrypha, 2nd ed. (Leipzig, 1876)

Tolhurst, J. B. L., ed., *The Monastic Breviary of Hyde Abbey, Winchester*, 6 vols., HBS 69, 70, 71, 76, 78 and 80 (London, 1932–42)

Tristram, H. L. C., *Vier altenglische Predigten aus der heterodoxen Tradition* (Freiburg, 1970)

Turner, D. H., ed., *The Missal of the New Minster, Winchester*, HBS 93 (London, 1962)

Van Dijk, S. J. D., 'The Origin of the Latin Feast of the Conception of the Blessed Virgin Mary', *Dublin Review* 228 (1954), 251–67 and 428–42

Waitz, G., ed., *Vita Leobae abbatissae Biscofesheimensis auct. Rudolfo Fuldensi*, MGH Scriptores 15.1 (Berlin, 1887), 118–31

Warner, G. F. and H. A. Wilson, ed., *The Benedictional of St Æthelwold*, Roxburghe Club (Oxford, 1910)

Warren, F. E., ed., *The Leofric Missal* (Oxford, 1883)

The Antiphonary of Bangor, 2 vols., HBS 4 and 10 (London, 1893–5)

Webster, L., 'Stylistic Aspects of the Franks Casket', in *The Vikings*, ed. R. T. Farrell (London and Chichester, 1982), pp. 20–31

Wenger, A., *L'assomption de la très Sainte Vierge dans la tradition byzantine du vi^e au xe siècle*, Archives de l'Orient chrétien 5 (Paris, 1955)

'Foi et piété mariales à Byzance', in *Maria*, ed. du Manoir V, 923–81

Willard, R., 'On Blickling Homily XIII: The Assumption of the Virgin', *RES* 12 (1936), 1–17

'The Testament of Mary: The Irish Account of the Death of the Virgin', *Recherches de théologie ancienne et médiévale* 9 (1937), 341–64

'The Two Accounts of the Assumption in Blickling Homily XIII', *RES* 14 (1938), 1–19

'An Old English Magnificat', *Studies in English* (University of Texas, 1940), 5–28

Wilmart, A., *Auteurs spirituels et textes dévots du moyen âge latin* (Paris, 1932)

Wilmart, A., ed., *Analecta reginensia*, Studi e Testi 59 (1933)

Wilson, H. A., ed., *The Calendar of St Willibrord*, HBS 55 (1918)

Woolf, R., Review of Burlin, *The Old English Advent*, *MÆ* 40 (1971), 60–1

Woolley, R. M., ed., *The Canterbury Benedictional*, HBS 51 (London, 1917)

Wormald, F., ed., *English Kalendars before* A. D. 1100, HBS 72 (London, 1934)

Collected Writings 1: Studies in Medieval Art from the Sixth to the Twelfth Centuries, ed. J. J. G. Alexander, T. J. Brown and J. Gibbs (London, 1984)

Wrenn, C. L., 'Some Aspects of Anglo-Saxon Theology', in *Studies in Language, Literature and Culture of the Middle Ages and Later*, ed. E. B. Atwood and A. A. Hill (Austin, 1969), pp. 182–9

Wright, D. H., Review of Battiscombe, *The Relics of St Cuthbert*, *Art Bulletin* 43 (1961), 141–60

Zettel, P., 'Saints Lives in Old English: Latin Manuscripts and Vernacular Accounts: Ælfric', *Peritia* 1 (1982), 17–37

Index